The Mutinous Regiment

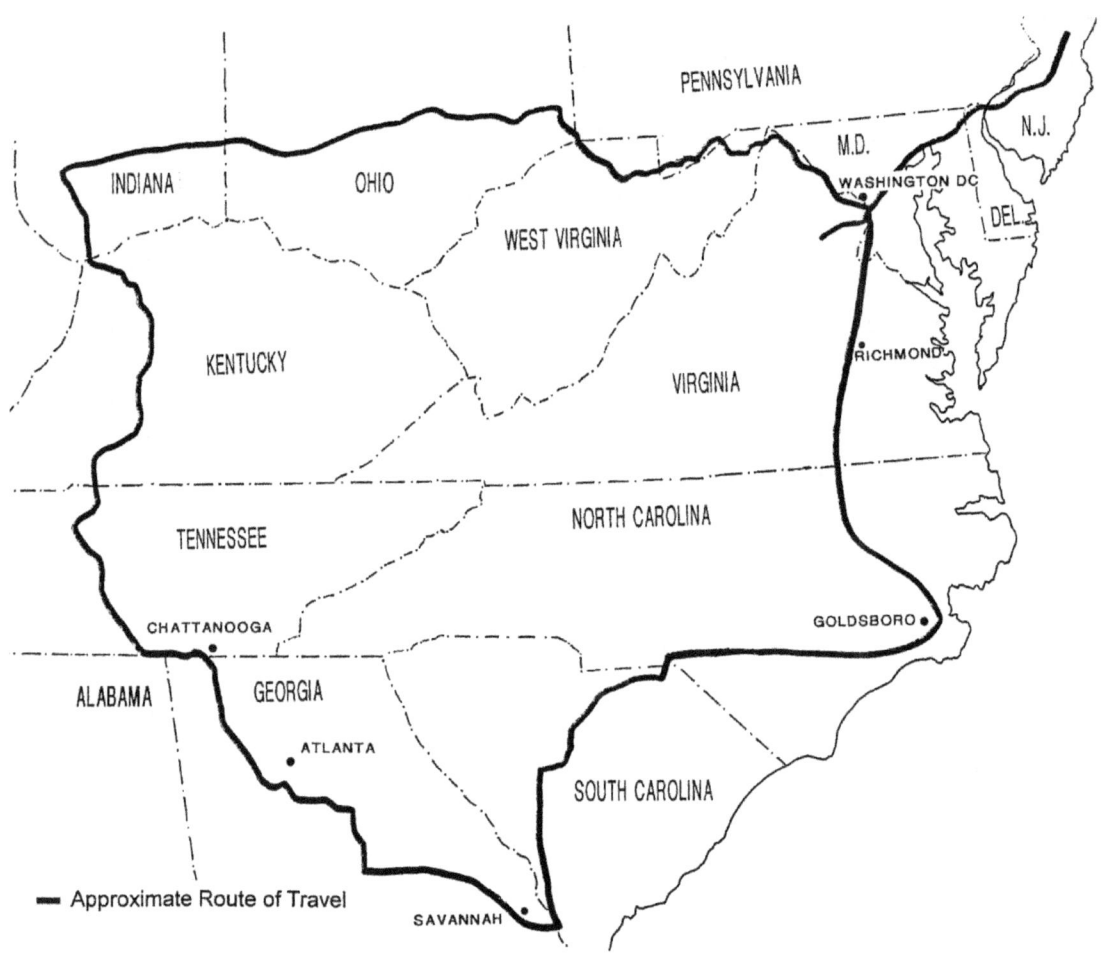

Travels of the 33rd New Jersey, 1863–1865. *Andrea LaConte Magno.*

The Mutinous Regiment

The Thirty-Third New Jersey in the Civil War

JOHN G. ZINN

McFarland & Company, Inc., Publishers
Jefferson, North Carolina, and London

The present work is a reprint of the illustrated case bound edition of The Mutinous Regiment: The Thirty-third New Jersey in the Civil War *first published in 2005 by McFarland.*

LIBRARY OF CONGRESS CATALOGUING-IN-PUBLICATION DATA

Zinn, John G., 1946–
The mutinous regiment : the Thirty-third New Jersey in the Civil War / John G. Zinn.
p.   cm.
Includes bibliographical references and index.

ISBN 978-0-7864-6635-1
softcover : 50# alkaline paper

1. United States. Army. New Jersey Infantry Regiment, 33rd (1863–1865).
2. New Jersey—History—Civil War, 1861–1865—Regimental histories.
3. United States—History—Civil War, 1861–1865—Regimental histories.
4. New Jersey—History—Civil War, 1861–1865—Registers.
5. United States—History—Civil War, 1861–1865—Registers.   I. Title.
E521.533rd .Z56 2011   973.7'449—dc22   2005014056

BRITISH LIBRARY CATALOGUING DATA ARE AVAILABLE

© 2005 John G. Zinn. All rights reserved

No part of this book may be reproduced or transmitted in any form or by any means, electronic or mechanical, including photocopying or recording, or by any information storage and retrieval system, without permission in writing from the publisher.

Cover images © 2011 Clipart.com

Manufactured in the United States of America

*McFarland & Company, Inc., Publishers
Box 611, Jefferson, North Carolina 28640
www.mcfarlandpub.com*

To Carol and Paul, beloved wife and son,

and to New Jersey's Civil War veterans

Table of Contents

Preface and Acknowledgments   1

I. "I have had uphill work here"   5
II. "You will no doubt be surprised to know that I am out here"   20
III. "A victory almost over nature herself"   37
IV. "I thought I could bear it without a tear"   59
V. "Bullets began to rain about me"   76
VI. "More like hell than God's beautiful earth"   90
VII. "A very hard day"   112
VIII. "The old flag floats over Atlanta"   132
IX. "A hard campaign and we expect nothing else"   150
X. "The destroying flame scarcely attracted our attention"   167
XI. "There will be no rest"   183
XII. "Haul up, stuck in the mud"   198
XIII. "Cries of joyful recognition"   214

Appendix. Regimental Roster, by Company   233
Chapter Notes   251
Bibliography   269
Index   273

Preface and Acknowledgments

For as long as I can remember I have been interested both in the writing of history and in writing a book of my own. More than ten years ago I was looking for a possible topic related to the Civil War and my native state of New Jersey, and I found something interesting in John Cunningham's history of Newark. In the section about the Civil War there were a few paragraphs about the 33rd New Jersey Regiment. Among other things, Cunningham wrote that the 33rd was "a storied regiment" and that it followed "a trail of glory and savagery" through the Confederacy.[1] However, when I looked for more information I found that no matter how "storied" the regiment might have been, no one had ever taken the time to write that story. I did some research at that time, but reality quickly set in. My son, Paul, was about to start high school and the combination of my responsibilities at work and home precluded my taking on a project of this magnitude.

Then in 1994 Paul took a course on the Civil War at St. Benedict's Prep in Newark, New Jersey. His instructor, Thomas McCabe, had also read Cunningham's book and one of the possible term paper options he assigned was the 33rd New Jersey. Paul chose that topic on his own and then came home and asked me to get him a book about the regiment! I had to tell him that there was no such book, but he was able to make use of my initial research for his assignment. That experience made me think that I was apparently destined to write such a book. I contacted Dr. David Martin of Longstreet House, a publisher of Civil War books, and with his encouragement set out to research the 33rd New Jersey.

John Richards Boyle served in the 111th Pennsylvania during the war and later became an ordained minister. Around the beginning of the twentieth century, he wrote a history of that regiment called *Soldiers True*. In the introduction to his book, Boyle wrote, "The actual story of the great war can never be really known until the service of each participating regiment and battery and ship is narrated."[2] The purpose of this book is to close one specific gap in the story of what Boyle called "the great war." I hope that doing so will open a window on the experience of those

New Jersey men who chose to join the 33rd during the summer of 1863. The commonly held knowledge about the regiment is that it was plagued with desertion at its formation and that, unlike most New Jersey regiments, it served in what was then called the west. Both of these facts are true, but only by looking at the regiment's story in detail can we understand and appreciate its long journey through the Confederacy.

Any work of history requires research, and research requires the help of others. I received significant help that has improved this book considerably. Some of the research was done at or through the United States Military History Institute in Carlisle, Pennsylvania, the Jersey City Public Library, the Newark Public Library, the Sussex County Library, the Camden County Historical Society, the National Archives, and the Library of Congress. I would like to thank the staffs of those institutions for their help. Our local library in Verona, New Jersey, was a helpful source of materials through interlibrary loan. An especially important source of information was the Western Reserve Historical Society in Cleveland, Ohio. Through that institution's William P. Palmer collection of Civil War manuscripts, I was able to obtain copies of the correspondence of William H. Lloyd of Company H of the 33rd. Lloyd was a prolific writer to his long suffering wife back in New Jersey, and his letters give an inside picture of the experiences and feelings of a Civil War soldier.

In March 1998, my wife, Carol, and I made a trip to Tennessee and Georgia to follow the path of the 33rd. While there we visited the library at the Chickamauga National Historical Park and were assisted by James Ogden III. While the library did not have much material on the 33rd, Mr. Ogden made every effort to help us, which we greatly appreciated. Back home, the New Jersey State Archives is the holder of the 33rd's regimental records, and I made numerous visits to go through their holdings. Bette M. Epstein of that facility was very helpful and directed me to other important sources at other institutions.

As part of my son's research assignment in 1994, he and his class went to the New Jersey Historical Society in Newark, which holds among other things the Civil War diary of Colonel George Mindil, the commander of the 33rd. Paul's experience led me to the Society, which was then located in the north ward of Newark. Since then much has changed; the Society has moved to a modern facility in downtown Newark, and I have the distinct privilege of being the chairman of the board of that institution. Under the leadership of Sally Yerkovich, president; Janet Rassweiler, director for programs and collections; and Chad Leinaweaver, director of the library, the New Jersey Historical Society is a wonderful resource about New Jersey and its history. My hope and dream is that more and more people will visit NJHS and come to understand this. I especially want to thank Chad Leinaweaver and James Lewis, reference librarian, for their assistance in including some of the pictures in this book, especially the photo of Georg Muller.

When I first began my research at the New Jersey Historical Society I was excited to find a series of letters from Georg Muller, a member of the 33rd. Some of that excitement lessened when I found that the letters were written in German. I turned to my longtime friend, Richard Lloyd, who was then director of alumni relations at my alma mater, Rutgers University. He introduced me to Gisela Ristau of the German

Department at Rutgers, who translated the letters for me. I have since provided a copy of those translations to the New Jersey Historical Society so that this source of information about the 33rd will be more widely available.

A great deal of the research for this book was done at the Alexander Library at Rutgers University. I am embarrassed to say that I spent far more time there researching this book than I did during my four years as an undergraduate, but I am making up for lost time. The Special Collections Department of the Library holds the letters of John J. Toffey along with the diary of David Peloubet. However, most of my time at Alexander Library was spent in the Periodical Department reading old newspapers on microfilm, especially those from Newark and Paterson. These newspapers give detailed accounts about the troubled formation of the regiment and provide eyewitness accounts of the officers and men of the 33rd. For more than 40 years, Rutgers has been an important part of my life, and that has continued with this book.

New Jersey has an active Civil War community, which provided both information and guidance. Although Longstreet House did not ultimately publish this book, I do want to thank David Martin for his comments and encouragement. Certainly his review of earlier versions of the manuscript has made this a better book than it otherwise would have been. One of the first people that David Martin had me contact was Joseph Bilby who, generously shared with me a list of the sources that he was using for a comprehensive history of New Jersey's Civil War regiments. It was from him that I learned of the William Lloyd letters. John Kuhl provided a number of the pictures of officers and men of the 33rd as well as Nathaniel Bray's diary, which is one of the few eyewitness accounts of the Carolina campaign. John is a true gentleman and it has been a pleasure to work with him.

Although they are not directly part of the New Jersey Civil War community, I was also assisted by Fred Stickel and his son, Steve, who provided me with the story of their ancestor, James McSorley, as well as his photograph. Steve came all the way from Maryland to hear a relatively brief talk that I gave on the 33rd at the North Jersey Civil War Roundtable. Their interest in this project has been important to me as the book has moved towards publication. Robert Jones, who helps keep the 33rd alive through re-enacting, provided a picture of Theodore Johnson of Company H.

Family and friends also played an important part in this book. Our longtime neighbor, Trish Verrone, read the initial drafts of the first two chapters and helped me to believe that I could actually write an entire book. Judith Seelbach helped me with the illustrations and, as always, was there when I needed her to listen to me. Barbara Lescota helped wherever she was needed as she has for more than 20 years. My cousins, Peggy and Paul Shubnell and Jim Walsh, all read the first draft of the manuscript and began the effort to get my punctuation somewhere near the realm of literacy. As the manuscript moved to final submission, my nephew, Greg LaConte, read the final draft with the critical eye of a recently graduated history major. His sister, Andrea LaConte Magno, provided the maps at the same time that she was adjusting to life as a wife and homeowner.

As I noted earlier, Paul Zinn's request for a book about the 33rd helped motivate me to resume this project. It is fair to say that Paul reinvigorated my interest in the Civil War (as he has with other things as well) and led me to become much more knowledgeable than I was before. I will always remember and treasure our trips to Civil War sites along the East Coast, especially a week's vacation in Virginia. A sophomore in high school when the real research began, Paul has now graduated college and begun his own career. During a lull in finishing this book, we began working together on a book about the 1916 baseball season, which I hope we can now move to completion. Both Paul and his fiancée, Sarah Kaufman, are a joy to Carol and myself.

Finally, one thing that is clear above all else to me is that this book would never have been written without the ongoing support of Carol Zinn. It has been my privilege and great good fortune to be her husband for the past 30 years. Although the Civil War was not one of her greatest interests, Carol has helped in many ways to make this book a reality. As noted earlier, she accompanied me on a week-long trip through Georgia looking for obscure sites related to the 33rd New Jersey. In addition, she has spent countless hours in libraries throughout New Jersey either helping me find materials or just providing moral support. During the final hectic weeks of preparing the manuscript for submission she took time from her own teaching schedule to help proofread the text; she made many important corrections. In this project, as in our lives together, her support has made all the difference in the world to me.

In spite of all this help, I want to acknowledge that the responsibility for the book is mine and mine alone. I hope that the book does justice to the regiment's story and is worthy of their sacrifices. A reporter for the local Verona newspaper once commented to me about the scarcity of Civil War monuments in New Jersey. Perhaps in a small way this book can be such a monument to the 33rd New Jersey and to our state's contribution to this important part of American history.

John G. Zinn
Fall 2005

I

"I have had uphill work here"

Early in July 1863 a young man stepped off the train in Newark, New Jersey. Although George Washington Mindil was not quite 20, he was a colonel in the Union army. That rank had been earned as the commanding officer of the 27th New Jersey Infantry. When the 27th returned to Newark, their service completed, Mindil went in search of a new command.[1] While his initial experience of regimental command had been brief, Mindil was anxious both to continue to serve the Union cause and to advance his military career. Since the Union demand for manpower was high, it did not take Mindil long to get what he wanted. Now he was back in Newark with federal and state authorization for a new regiment, the 33rd New Jersey Veteran Volunteers.[2]

When Mindil returned to Newark, he entered a city that had become "one of America's great industrial centers"[3] even before the war began. With a population of almost 72,000, Newark was the twelfth largest city in the United States.[4] Included in the population were over 20,000 factory workers, primarily of Irish and German descent. From their labor, the city's factories produced goods worth almost $28 million, seventh highest in the nation. For his labor, the average working man earned just over $300 per year. Somewhere between 65 and 75 percent of Newark's production was sold in Southern states with major markets in Virginia, the Carolinas, and Georgia. As members of the 33rd New Jersey, some of the city's sons would visit the latter three states on a very different kind of business trip.[5]

Although Mindil was committed to the Union cause, feelings in Newark and the rest of the state in 1863 were not as clear cut. Even though there was great excitement about recent Union victories, the cost of the war had become very real to the people of New Jersey. Furthermore, negative feeling was building about the imminent imposition of conscription. All of these tensions were superimposed on divisions that had existed in the state since the war began. Factors such as Newark's dependence on Southern trade have fueled theories of New Jersey's alleged sympathy or neutrality towards the Confederacy. However, the most recent academic analysis concludes that "New Jerseyans and their state government supported the war from

beginning to end."⁶ At the same time there was some vocal opposition to the war, and one Newark newspaper, the *Daily Journal,* was stridently antiwar.⁷

Mindil had had no reason to worry about obtaining authorization to form a new regiment. By the middle of 1863 the term of service for a number of nine-month and two-year regiments had ended. Simultaneously, mounting casualty lists and the expansion of the scope of the war had increased Union manpower needs. The new regiment was to be a veteran volunteer regiment to serve until the end of the war or for at least three years, and was to have a minimum of 400 members with at least nine months of prior service. The primary focus on recruiting was to be Newark and the surrounding counties.

A number of factors affected the recruiting of the 33rd New Jersey. On the positive side was the progress of the Union war effort. On July 4, a Union meeting in Newark was interrupted by news of the triumph at Gettysburg, which set off jubilant celebrations. When this was followed by word of Grant's conquest of Vicksburg, false expectations arose about the end of the war⁸ that permitted a favorable prediction of the new regiment's role. The prowar Newark *Mercury* encouraged enlistment, claiming, "It is now received as a positive fact that the hard fighting of the war is over."⁹ However, by far the most important influence on recruiting was the Conscription Act of 1863. By 1863 volunteers no longer met the demands of the Union war machine. While those motivated by emotional and ideological appeals had already volunteered, the wartime economy provided plenty of jobs for those who did not wish to serve. In short, the supply of soldiers had declined while the demand was expanding. Although the obvious solution was mandatory military service, prior to the Civil War there had never been a draft or conscription in the U.S. Since the nation needed soldiers, but hated the idea of a draft, Congress came up with a "semidraft," or, in other words, "a threat to spur volunteers."¹⁰

The Conscription Act of 1863 applied to single and married men ages 20–45, both citizens and immigrants who intended to become citizens. As a national law, the act introduced federal control of recruiting, which had previously been a state task. Under the act's administrative structure, a draft board was established for each Congressional district. Each draft board's first task was to count, or enroll, all those who met the eligibility criteria. From those eligible, the number of men drafted would be determined by quotas based upon population. Since Newark was a major population center, the city would have a very high quota.

Two of the act's most controversial provisions permitted the payment of a commutation fee of $300 or the hiring of a substitute. While the commutation fee set off immediate complaints of "rich man's war, poor man's fight," the provision at least set a ceiling on the price of a substitute. Without such a provision, the price could have escalated well beyond the capacity of all but the very wealthy. Quickly the whole idea of a draft became an extremely controversial issue. Due to the combination of coercion and escape hatches for those with money, the draft was especially

Opposite: The corner of Broad and Market streets in Newark during the 1860s, showing the offices of the **Daily Journal** and the **Daily Advertiser**. *From the collections of the New Jersey Historical Society.*

Colonel George W. Mindil and officers. Mindil is seated on the left, standing in the center is Captain James Sandford, standing on the right is Major David Peloubet, and the others are unidentified. *John W. Kuhl Collection.*

unpopular in urban areas with large immigrant populations.[11] In June of 1863, women in working class neighborhoods of Newark threw stones at officials seeking to register eligible men.[12]

While Colonel Mindil organized recruiting efforts, resistance to the draft exploded in New York and spread throughout the North, including New Jersey. Although the actual drawing of the names of draftees began in New York City on July 11, the violence did not begin until the morning of Monday, July 13. At the outset the mob's anger was directed against the draft, but the violence quickly spread against businesses, wealthy Republicans, and especially blacks. As the rioting became widespread, chaos reigned as angry mobs took control of the city. Since its authority to enforce a draft was at stake, the Federal government sent in troops from Pennsylvania. Ultimately some 20,000 soldiers were required before order was restored to the city. Gradually the troops restored the peace, but at least 105 people, primarily rioters, were killed.[13]

Back in New Jersey, unrest followed the news from New York City. Those motivated by the news from New York received further encouragement from a scathing editorial in the antiwar Newark *Daily Journal*. Titled "Conscription — The Press Gang," the editorial predicted that white men would be dragged away from their loved ones in chains to fight for the freedom of blacks. As a reward for their services, the white men would then have to compete for jobs with the former slaves.[14] Fueled by these and other antidraft sentiments, a crowd formed in front of the offices of the prowar Newark *Daily Mercury* about 9 P.M. on July 13. Some in the crowd urged an attack on the paper's offices and after about an hour, bricks were thrown and the doors to the building were broken. Defensive measures by the paper's staff and the police prevented further damage. Then the attention of the crowd shifted to the home of Provost Marshall Elias Miller on Fulton Street. But friends got Miller and his family out of the house before the mob arrived, and there was only minor damage. When a heavy rain began at 11 P.M., the crowd gradually dispersed and there were no further incidents that night.[15]

The next night the mayor of Newark, Moses Bigelow, addressed a crowd of "some thousands" that gathered outside the *Mercury*'s offices.[16] Both Bigelow and General Theodore Runyon, who spoke after him, expressed opposition to the draft and doubts about its legality. This, along with a request for time to allow the legal process to work, seemed to satisfy the crowd.[17] Antidraft crowds also gathered in Orange, Jersey City, Hackettstown, and Morristown, but as in Newark there was little damage and no loss of life. While events in New York may have stimulated the reaction in New Jersey, opposition to the draft was real in 1863. Faced with this opposition, state and local officials tried to avoid the draft at almost all costs. Finally Joel Parker, the Democratic governor of New Jersey, obtained a postponement to try to meet the state's quota through voluntary enlistment.[18] Some localities, such as New York City, resolved the draft crisis by paying the commutation fee of anyone drafted.[19] But New Jersey communities would instead provide liberal cash incentives called bounties.[20] Such bounties would wreak havoc with the formation of the 33rd New Jersey.

Mindil began recruiting the regiment in the midst of all this turmoil. One of his first steps was to meet on July 14 with officers and men from the returning nine-month regiments.[21] Although Mindil had commanded a regiment, he had little or no experience in recruiting one. The 27th New Jersey had been formed in Newark in the fall of 1862. Since it and other nine-month regiments were technically state militia units, the officers elected the regimental commander; however, the officers of the 27th were unable to agree upon a commanding officer. Cortland Parker, a prominent Newark businessman, knew of Mindil through Mindil's service on the staff of General Phillip Kearny. When Parker recommended Mindil to the regiment's officers, he was elected unanimously.[22] Mindil would be joined in the 33rd by several members of his old regiment including William Lambert, James Titman, J. Henry Stiger, Chaplain John Faull, Nathaniel Bray, and Stephen Pierson. There would not, however, be a significant number of men from the old 27th in the new regiment. Even the most generous comparison of the two rosters indicates that no more than 35 officers and men from the 27th joined the 33rd.[23] In the 27th, Mindil had a reputation for discipline and training,[24] which may or may not have had something to do with the reluctance of its members to serve under Mindil a second time.

George Washington Mindil, colonel and general. *John W. Kuhl Collection.*

Mindil's task was to recruit a Civil War infantry regiment, which was formed by recruiting ten companies. A company's strength could range between 83 and 101 and each company was to have a captain in command, two lieutenants, five sergeants and eight corporals. This leadership commanded between 64 and 82 privates who did the bulk of the work and the fighting. The ten companies then formed a regiment, which had a minimum strength of 845 men and a maximum of 1,025. Overseeing all of this was a colonel, who had a staff of 14.[25] Given the environment, the problem was not exceeding the regiment's maximum strength, but achieving the minimum necessary to avoid the draft. The original plan was to recruit four companies from Newark, one each from Paterson, Hoboken, Jersey City and Camden, with the other two to come from Essex, Morris, and Hudson counties. However, the major issue became meeting each municipality's assigned quota, with the result that little attention was paid to the original plan. With the largest population, Newark had the largest quota, and 75 percent of the regiment's men were credited against Newark's quota regardless of where they came from.[26]

Why did men join the 33rd New Jersey? Unfortunately, the surviving letters and diaries shed very little light on their motivations. But clearly economics was a driving force in the recruitment of the enlisted men. While wartime inflation had raised prices, immigration had actually increased Newark's population; this kept wages down. These conditions further magnified another provision of the Conscription Act of 1863: cash bonuses, or bounties, paid to those who volunteered.[27] Such cash bounties became a major incentive for enlistment, especially given the risk of being drafted anyway. Combined federal and state bounties ranged from $174 for a single man without experience to $618 for married veterans. These amounts were in addition to the soldier's regular pay of $13 per month, while draftees would receive only the regular monthly pay. When compared to average annual wages of just over $300 the incentives were very appealing, especially since one might have to serve anyway.[28] Beyond these incentives were local bounties specifically aimed at avoiding the draft. However, there were two major problems with the municipal and county bounties. While the federal bounties were paid gradually over three years, the local bounties were fully paid in advance. Furthermore, although the federal bounties were uniform, the local bounties were not.[29] Large up-front cash payments created the temptation of bounty jumping: enlistment, receipt of bounty payment, followed by desertion. The lack of uniformity in bounties drove up the cost and further encouraged bounty jumping. The city of Newark paid out almost $80,000 in such bounties.[30]

Newspaper accounts of the recruiting process that summer described it as "brisk" or "quite brisk." Simultaneously, however, these accounts expressed the fear that the quota would not be met in time to avoid the draft. On August 4, it was reported that 200 men had enlisted. This more than doubled on August 12 when a total of 500 men was mentioned.[31] When Mindil wrote to State Adjutant Stockton on August 15, he reported that 550 had enlisted. But Mindil also wrote, "I have had uphill work here" due to the absence of uniforms and tents. With uniforms, Mindil believed he could hold parades and create some patriotic excitement.[32] By August 17, the Newark *Daily Advertiser* reported total enlistment of 700,[33] while the next day, the *Mercury* stated that 40-50 men were enlisting a day. Four days later Mindil confirmed that 711 had now enlisted; more than half were from Newark with the next largest group from Jersey City.[34] But on August 22, the *Advertiser* still worried that the city quota would be missed by several hundred.[35] However, on September 1 the paper reported that the 33rd had 900 men at Newark's Camp Frelinghuysen.[36] The problem now became keeping them there.

Among the enlisted men were William Lloyd and Robert Harriot. Lloyd, who was from Hoboken, had apparently jumped the bounty with a New York regiment and planned to do so again. Robert Harriot was an Irish immigrant more popularly known as Mickey Free. In February of 1861, Free had climbed onto the platform in Jersey City to shake hands with President-elect Lincoln. After doing so, he was promptly knocked off the platform by a policeman. Apparently still full of patriotic spirit, Free subsequently enlisted in the Fifth New Jersey and was wounded at Williamsburg, where he lost two fingers. Then Free, who listed his profession as "pedestrian", walked home to Jersey City from a Philadelphia hospital. Attracting characters like Lloyd and Free was perhaps an omen that the regiment's experience would differ from the norm.[37]

Lloyd, Free, and the rest of the new regiment gathered at the unit's initial home, Camp Frelinghuysen in Newark. Officially known as Rendezvous Number Four, the camp was actually a large field in the Roseville section of Newark. The site was bordered by Roseville Avenue, Orange Street, Bloomfield Turnpike and the Morris Canal. While the canal was seldom needed for transportation, it was used for bathing and one can only imagine what else. Surrounding fields served as training areas, with wooden barracks and tents providing accommodations for "several thousand soldiers."[38] Beyond the business of getting the regiment organized, there was apparently some time for fun. On August 21, the *Advertiser* reported that Colonel Mindil had approved an "afternoon of sport" for August 24. Scheduled activities were to consist of races, games, and a performance by none other than Mickey Free. During his performance, Free was to "jump hurdles, pickup 50 stones and pickup eggs with his mouth."[39] When reporting the results, the *Advertiser* noted that John Riley of Company B won the one-mile race, William Herbert of Company C (this article was in error; Herbert was a member of Company I and Johns was a member of Company B), the sack race, and Charles Johns of Company C the one-half mile race. Johns put his speed to good use shortly thereafter on September 8 when he literally ran away from the regiment. Considering what lay just ahead, Mindil may have come to regret giving the men any practice at running. No doubt satisfying his many fans, Mickey Free did some hurdle jumping and was the beneficiary of a collection from which he "realized quite a sum."[40]

By this time all ten barracks at Camp Frelinghuysen were used to house troops, while the officers lived in tents. Not entirely satisfied with their accommodations, some men cut down tree branches to provide shade. But this was stopped by the owner of the woods, who was unwilling to contribute to the Union cause in this way.[41] Another incident of note was reported in the Newark *Daily Journal* under the headline, "Martial Law Proclaimed." The paper reported that one or two "big whiskered privates" had, on their own, established a blockade on the canal bridge near Roseville Avenue. When cars of the "Orange horse railroad" tried to pass over this bridge, they were stopped at bayonet point with demands for all kinds of documentation. According to the paper, when one train tried to run the blockade, its horse was almost killed by a bayonet. Apparently, once the blockade was brought to the attention of the authorities it was stopped.[42] White males of the Civil War era and discipline were like oil and water, and the men of the 33rd were no exception.[43]

While at Camp Frelinghuysen, the regiment was gradually provided with uniforms and weapons. The 33rd was established as a Zouave unit, which was supposed to assist with recruiting because of the colorful uniforms.[44] However, the special nature of these uniforms caused delays in equipping the men.[45] Although different from standard issue, the regiment's uniforms did not include the bright red pants of some Zouave units. Enlisted men wore dark blue pants and short blue jackets trimmed in red. The jackets were worn over a vest with brass buttons, which was also trimmed in red. The overall effect was topped off by a crimson sash. Officers wore essentially the same uniform, with red braid rank and unit insignia. The 33rd was also issued the standard uniform, which was probably worn when function was more important than style. The unit's weapons were almost equally divided between Enfield and Springfield rifled muskets.[46] The regiment maintained their Zouave uniforms until after the Atlanta campaign, when they reverted to standard Union issue.[47]

At the same time it was being equipped, the regiment's command structure was also being finalized. In spite of his relative youth, Colonel Mindil did not lack for real military experience. Mindil and some other young men in Philadelphia had formed a volunteer military company even prior to the firing on Fort Sumter. After the Union defeat at the first battle of Manassas, Mindil and the rest of the company were mustered into the Union army as part of the 23rd Pennsylvannia.[48] As a young and inexperienced officer, Mindil went on to serve with distinction in the Peninsula campaign, where his performance was repeatedly praised in Union dispatches.[49] Long after the war, he was awarded the Medal of Honor for his leadership of a charge at the battle of Williamsburg on May 5, 1862.[50] Meanwhile, his record caught the eye of General Phillip Kearny from New Jersey, who named Mindil to his staff. When Kearny was killed at second battle of Manassas, this connection and Mindil's reputation led him to the command of the 27th New Jersey in the fall of 1862.[51]

In addition to Mindil, ten officers of the 27th joined the 33rd.[52] Service with the 27th did not provide much combat experience, since like most of New Jersey's nine-month regiments, the 27th saw little fighting. Foreshadowing the 33rd's experience, the 27th first served in Virginia and was then ordered west. Again, foreshadowing what would happen to the 33rd, the regiment suffered a tragic accident during a river crossing.[53] While the regiment was on their way home in June of 1863, Mindil received word of Lee's invasion of the north. Mindil wired President Lincoln to offer to extend the regiment's service during the emergency, and the offer was accepted.[54] This also earned Mindil a Medal of Honor.[55] William Lambert, who would also serve in the 33rd, also earned a Medal of Honor for this "action."[56] Both medals were awarded due to inconsistencies in the implementation of the Medal of Honor legislation and were rescinded in 1916. Mercifully, both Mindil and Lambert were dead before this happened.[57]

Lieutenant Colonel Enos Fouratt, Headquarters. *John W. Kuhl Collection.*

The 33rd's second in command, Lieutenant Colonel Enos Fouratt of New Brunswick, was also a veteran officer. Prior to joining the regiment, Fouratt had been a senior officer in two other New Jersey regiments, the First and Fourth. Fouratt had been on active duty since First Manassas and was wounded at Crampton's Pass in the Maryland campaign of 1862. His prior experience was important, as Fouratt would frequently take Mindil's place as regimental commander.[58] Andrew Rogers of Paterson was to have been the major, but he resigned in a letter to Adjutant Lambert, saying it was due to "the peculiar positions I have been placed in by Colonel Mindil and the line officers of this regiment."[59] With Rogers' resignation, David Peloubet of Newark, who had served with the First New Jersey, became major.[60] In total, 19 of the regiment's officers had prior experience, but almost half had served with the nine-month regiments; not much experience for a regiment that would leave for the front with very little training.

The seeds sown by the up-front payment of large municipal bounties were to bear a bitter fruit near the end of the regiment's time in New Jersey. When about 70 men from Jersey City reported to Camp Frelinghuysen on August 19 and received their bounty money, the first danger signs appeared. With the money in hand about 20 of them changed into civilian clothes, left their uniforms in a cornfield and "skedaddled." Although some were caught, most escaped. Further payment of bounties was delayed until security could be improved, but improved security was not enough.[61]

The next large scale desertion took place on August 30 when 59 men from Company A deserted. Another 20 men, this time from Company I, followed suit on September 1.[62] With the arrival of 300 men from the U.S. 14th Infantry on September 2 to provide better security, desertion slowed down temporarily.[63] But as the regiment's departure loomed closer, the situation escalated. An additional 165 men deserted for a total of 244 out of an original muster of 902 enlisted men. The desertions were spread throughout the regiment, with every company having at least ten deserters. Altogether the regiment lost more than 25 percent of its men even before leaving the state, much less before coming within range of Confederate guns.[64] This was in spite of everything Mindil and the local authorities did to try to prevent desertion. After the regiment left Newark, the *Daily Journal* even claimed that Mindil had ordered all civilian clothing burned to prevent men from discarding their uniforms and deserting.[65] This claim, however, was vehemently denied by Capt. Charles Courtois in a letter to the Newark *Daily Mercury*.[66]

When the contingent from the U.S. 14th Regiment arrived on September 2, inmates of the guardhouse tried to burn it down in an unsuccessful attempt to escape. Three days later on September 5, a portion of the Third Vermont Volunteers arrived to replace the 14th Regiment as camp guards.[67] With the 33rd's departure imminent, there was considerable speculation in the Newark newspapers about their destination. Rumored possibilities ranged from Washington, D.C., to South Carolina and even Texas.[68]

While the loss of manpower was serious enough, on the evening of Monday, September 7, desertion had tragic consequences. Anticipating the regiment's departure, a crowd of 200 men tried to desert on the east side of the camp near the Morris

Canal. Some accounts claimed that the men had weapons. The danger was sufficient enough for Major Thomas Nelson, commander of the Third Vermont, to call out his entire regiment. However, before all the Vermont men got into position, the guard fired into the crowd. John Everly, a 50-year-old soldier, was shot through the heart and died instantly; Oscar Schawager was shot through the left calf. Schawager had the misfortune to have his wound dressed by some of the men as no surgeons were present. He died from his wound, probably from infection, on September 17. Once the Third Vermont was formed in line, they were able to keep all but 15 men from escaping. With some semblance of order restored, the rest of the regiment was sent back to their barracks and there were no further problems that night.[69]

Although some of the men claimed that Everly just wanted to see his family one more time, the officers seemed certain that he intended to desert.[70] In reporting the incident, the Hudson County *Democrat* stated that the men from Hudson County had expected a final furlough, official or otherwise, prior to departure.[71] There was also some precedence for such furloughs. Both the 13th and 26th New Jersey had large members of men leave camp without permission for one last fling or trip home. In some of these cases, the guard even left, and the commanders had no alternative but to grant a retroactive furlough. In most cases, however, those men did return.[72] Given the mass prior desertions, it is reasonable to believe that in this case desertion was the real motive. In any event, the prior desertions had brought in a camp guard that did not "know anything about blank cartridges or firing in the air."[73] Such precautions eliminated the possibility of complicity by friendly guards.

The desertion of a quarter of a regiment was without question disgraceful and hurt the reputations of both the regiment and the state. In retrospect, however, it should not have been a surprise. A study of Civil War desertion concluded that "in general, those States which gave the most liberal local bounties were marked by the largest population of deserters."[74] Although "intended as inducement to enlistment," the bounties instead "became in truth an inducement to desertion."[75] However, the regiment's final reputation should rest with the record of those who did serve, not with those who never intended to do so.

Tragically, the problems did not end with the mass skedaddle on September 7. Early the next morning there was a great deal of activity at the camp with men "running to and fro, packing valises, boxes and etc."[76] By 10:00 A.M., several thousand spectators had arrived and the horse railroad could not accommodate all those who wanted to come. When the regiment left camp at 11:00 A.M., they were guarded front and rear by the Third Vermont, with other guards posted along the route. In spite of these precautions, some soldiers still got out of ranks, changed into civilian clothes and left uniforms, weapons, and the army behind. Being marched through the streets of Newark under an armed guard must have been a bitter pill for every officer and man trying to do his patriotic duty. From Camp Frelinghuysen, the regiment and its escort marched down Orange and Broad Streets and turned left on to Market Street. They proceeded to Mulberry Street and then to the Hospital dock, arriving there about noon. Upon arrival at the dock, the regiment stacked arms and waited for the boats that would take them to transport ships in New York Harbor.[77]

But for some reason, the boats did not arrive. The troops waited and waited.

J. Henry Stiger, assistant surgeon. *John W. Kuhl Collection.*

Nicholas Aspen, 1st sgt., Company A; 1st lt., Company K. *U.S. Army Military History Institute.*

Although the Third Vermont was still on guard, wives and other women smuggled in liquor. Some men already had it in their canteens. Before long the combination of heavy drinking and a long frustrating wait boiled over into disorder and fighting that required the "most stringent measures."[78] One particularly disgusting incident occurred while Alvan Bell of Company H of the Third Vermont was standing guard.

Bell had his hand over the muzzle of his musket when John Peck, of Company F of the 33rd, "deliberately stooped and pulled the trigger."[79] Bell's hand had to be amputated. Some accounts claimed that Peck was drunk and was trying to get back at members of the Third Vermont for incidents at Camp Frelinghuysen. While Peck was reported as being under arrest, he did go on to serve with the regiment for the rest of the war. In another incident, Lieutenant Somerville received a slight bayonet wound while trying to break up a fight.[80]

Things got even uglier in the hospital dining room, which was being guarded by Sergeant White of the Third Vermont. At about 5 P.M., White was ordered to clear the dining room. As he did so, about a dozen members of the 33rd tried to force their way inside. They grabbed White's musket, but with the help of Captain O'Connor of the 33rd, he got it back. When the troublemakers tried a second time, the gun accidentally went off. A minie ball hit Sergeant John Clark of the Veterans Reserve Corps, who fell against policeman John Gott saying, "I'm shot." As Gott laid Clark down, he tried to tell him that he had not been hit, but Clark said, "Yes, I am." Those were Clark's last words. After passing through Clark, the bullet hit Sergeant John Shay of Company H of the 33rd, a resident of Sussex County. The bullet hit Shay on the right side, fracturing his ribs and pelvis. From the dining room, Shay was taken into the hospital and operated on that night, but he died the next day. While an inquiry ultimately cleared White of any wrongdoing, there was some suggestion that he had pointed and aimed his weapon. Finally things quieted down and an uneasy night was passed on the dock.[81]

The next day, the regiment continued to wait for transportation, which by noon still had not appeared. By now the regiment had been waiting a full day. Fortunately, the men were generally quiet, mostly talking, sleeping or playing cards. Some diehards, however, were caught trying to escape in civilian clothes. Finally, at 2 P.M., two small steamers and a barge arrived at the dock to take the regiment "below the bar." Probably feeling at this point that anything would be an improvement, the men cheered the arrival of the boats. Although the barge took the first group off at 3:30 and the other two boats sailed at 4:00, there were still 200 men left on the dock. Then the steamer *Catlin*, which was to return for the remaining men, got stuck on a sand bar. This was attributed to the heavy load and alleged inexperience of its pilot. There was no alternative but to wait for the tide to come in, so the last 200 men did not get off the dock until 3:00 A.M. on September 10. This unfortunate remnant had been there almost two full days. Lieutenant Sherwood and two men from each company were left behind to look for stragglers and deserters. All the missing were given until 8:00 A.M. on September 14 to report without repercussions.[82]

The officers of the regiment, the Third Vermont, and the citizens of Newark must have breathed a huge collective sigh of relief that the unit was finally off to war. When the citizens of Newark read the account of the unit's departure in the Newark *Daily Advertiser*, they probably did not connect the regiment's future with a headline that appeared the same day.

CHATTANOOGA OURS

THE REBELS IN RAPID RETREAT[83]

II

"You will no doubt be surprised to know that I am out here"

The first order of business for a new Union regiment was to travel to the "seat of war." While eastern regiments typically went to Washington and then on to Virginia, western regiments usually traveled to some point on the edge of the Confederacy. Although from the east, the 33rd New Jersey effectively made both trips during the regiment's first 30 days of existence. In fact, during the 33rd's first 60 days, a permanent assignment was anything that lasted two weeks. When the regiment arrived in Lookout Valley, Tennessee, in November, they had traveled at least 1,500 miles across six states from Virginia to Alabama. With good reason, the 33rd's adjutant, William Lambert, claimed that probably no other regiment "in so short a time has seen so much."[1]

Unlike most New Jersey regiments, the 33rd began their travels by boat rather than train due to an order from General Henry Halleck. Halleck wanted the regiment in Virginia and ordered the local authorities to "send by water."[2] While this may have seemed preferable to several days on the train, the trip from New York Harbor aboard the *DeMolay* and *Dudley Buck* was no pleasure cruise. The latter ship was described by a soldier from Company H as "an excellent cattle boat," since the "accommodations for this description of passenger are probably unsurpassed."[3] William Lloyd, another member of Company H, expressed similar feelings when he complained of rough seas, little food, and sleeping "in tobacco juice on deck."[4] Although the accommodations were, no doubt, rough, the complaints of the men were probably magnified by their feelings about leaving home. In civilian life, the men of the 33rd, for the most part, did hard physical labor for low pay. Even though they worked long hours in shops, factories, and on farms, there was also a predictable routine along with some level of independence in their private lives. Now they had

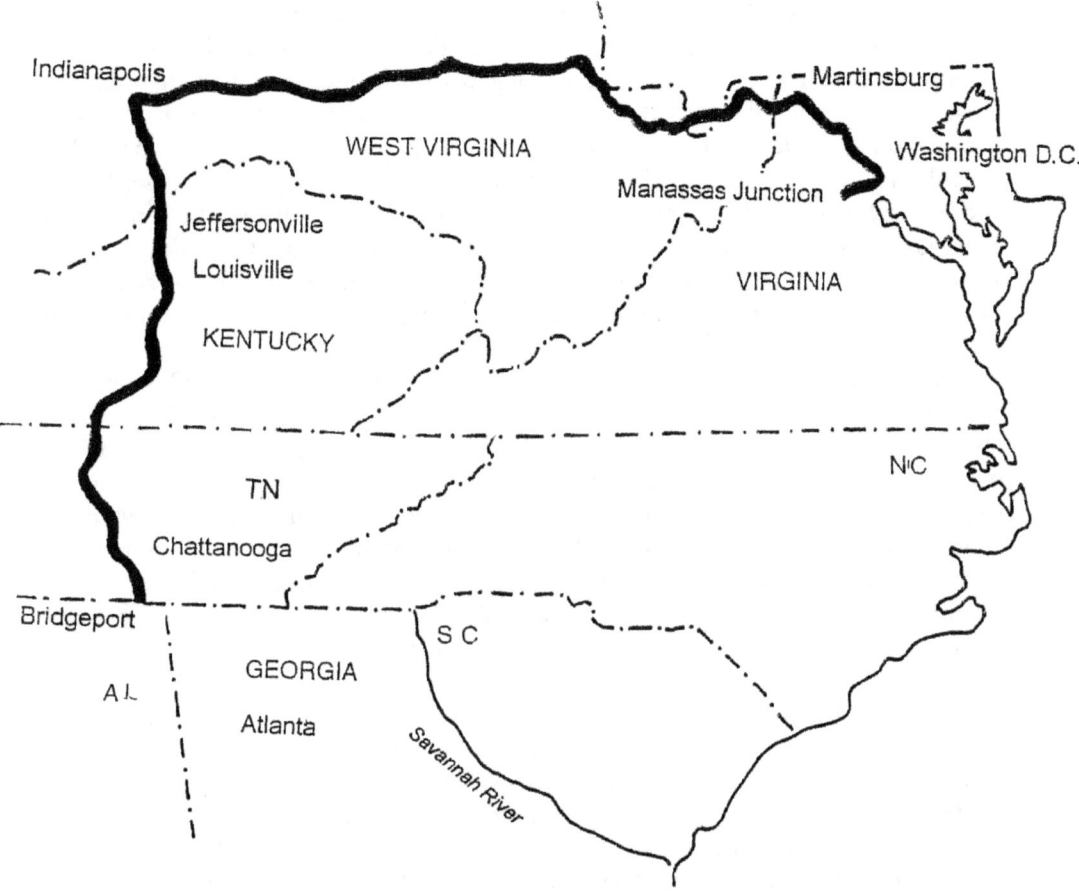

The 33rd's route west. *Andrea LaConte Magno.*

exchanged this for the equally demanding but far more dangerous and uncertain life of a soldier. Most, if not all, of them must have wondered about the wisdom of their decision. Some wondered because they had no idea of what lay ahead; others wondered because they did know.

Thus far in the 33rd's brief history, the regiment had been plagued by death and desertion. While the ocean voyage prevented desertion, death was not so easily inhibited: Private Henry Ford of Newark died on the *DeMolay* on September 10. At first, the Newark *Daily Advertiser* reported that Ford died from wounds suffered on the Hospital dock that were not properly treated by the regiment's surgeon. However, a day later, the paper had a new report that Ford had died of dissipation and was given "every attention" by the surgeons. Adjutant Lambert denied any neglect, stating that Ford died of "delirium tremens."[5] The regimental records simply attribute the death to "fits."[6]

When the boats reached Alexandria, Virginia, on Saturday, September 12, William Lambert noted that the journey had been marked by "the incidents peculiar to sea transportation of four days."[7] Most likely, this was Lambert's way of avoiding a more detailed description of the cattle-boat–like quarters and other unpleasant details. After this brief experience on water, it is unlikely that any of the men had illusions that the navy was easier duty than the army. At about 11:00 the next morning, the boats took the regiment on the brief voyage to Washington, where they disembarked. When the 33rd left the boats, they marched across the Long Bridge and arrived at Fort Albany after dark.[8] Since proximity to dry land offered more options for escape, desertion resumed. During the regiment's brief stay at Alexandria, four members of Company H managed to desert.[9] Later the same day, three members of Company A saw their chance near the Long Bridge and promptly "skedaddled."[10]

Since the 33rd had been on boats since leaving Newark, arrival at Fort Albany marked the first time the men had made camp. Although they did so after dark, there must have been some level of military discipline to the regiment's efforts. When morning came, a member of the regiment reported, with some pride, "Our camp of wedge tents spread out their white sides to the glare of the sun." That day, Monday, September 14, was a day of rest for the regiment. Having made camp, the men had nothing to do but "loaf round" and "speculate about our future locations." While the officers and men hoped the regiment would stay at Fort Albany to get organized, all sensed "it could not last."[11] Such perceptions proved to be correct as orders were received to join the Army of the Potomac at Warrenton, about 50 miles from Washington.[12] By 4 P.M. on September 15, the 33rd "was winding its sinuous length along the Warrenton Road."[13] As they began the first of many days of marching, the regiment was untrained and untried, marching through territory not fully under Union control. Fortunately, the first march was uneventful and the regiment spent their first night in the field at Frazier's Run.[14]

Almost every regiment underwent a baptism of marching and the 33rd was no exception. However, the regiment would not only do a lot of marching, but would often do so under adverse conditions. The march to Warrenton was a sampling of things to come. A member of Company H reported that the march was made in "almost continuous rain" which caused mud a foot deep. However, the soldier noted, the terrain was not all mud. For variety, the mud was interspersed with pools of water, two to three feet deep. When the march ended, the soldier felt the men had no complaints other than "saturated clothes, unwashed persons, long marches, aching limbs and short rations."[15] If the soldier had had any inkling that these conditions and worse would be the regiment's standard fare, he probably would have deserted on the spot. Sharing these sentiments was William Lloyd, who complained that he had not had his shoes off or slept under cover since leaving Newark.[16]

While enduring these conditions, the regiment passed through Fairfax on September 16 and camped near Centreville. The following day the regiment moved through Centreville, crossed Bull Run, and camped for the night.[17] Adjutant Lambert described the countryside as "desolate and almost entirely deserted." Since the area was subject to attacks by Mosby and other Confederate raiders, Colonel Mindil put out skirmishers, but there was only minor contact.[18] However, the risk was real, as there were frequent reports of sightings of Confederate raiding parties.[19] Upon reaching New Baltimore, about ten miles from Warrenton, Mindil learned that the Army of the Potomac was no longer there.[20]

Faced with an even longer march, Mindil was concerned about his unsupported, "comparatively green regiment," especially in the face of reports of the presence of Confederate guerrillas.[21] As a precaution, Mindil sent Lambert ahead to reconnoiter. When Lambert reached Warrenton, he found a squad of 50 Confederate cavalry. Since he was a rational man, Lambert "concluded he alone was unable to capture the place" and returned to the regiment. After he came back with Captain O'Connor and Company F, the Confederates retreated. While Company F occupied the town, the rest of the regiment came up within an hour and camped for the night on the outskirts of Warrenton.[22] Having come in contact with the enemy, Mindil put out a heavy picket line and had the men sleep ready "to spring to arms" at the first shot.

Alfred W. Bergen, sgt., Company C; 1st sgt., HQ; 2nd lt., Company A. *U.S. Army Military History Institute.*

Tired from their exertions, most of the men were soon asleep. Suddenly the silence of the misty night was shattered by a single musket shot, and the regiment responded "with less order than alacrity." The men poured out of their tents, grabbed their weapons, formed what had to be a very irregular line, and waited anxiously. Although those on guard claimed an enemy attack was "handsomely repulsed," there was some skepticism that this could have been done with one shot. But those on guard were adamant and all wanted to get back to sleep, which they did. The truth was learned the next day when a wounded mule was found near the regiment's position.[23]

Even though somewhat embarrassed, the regiment had survived their first night in enemy territory. Mindil and his men were, however, still in a difficult situation, almost out of rations and isolated. Since there were no other options, the 33rd had to move towards the closest Federal position at Warrenton Junction.[24] As an added precaution, Mindil divided the regiment into two wings for the march with the wagon train in between the wings. When the 33rd moved forward at 8:00 A.M. on September 19, Mindil commanded the right wing with Major David Peloubet in command of the left wing. The regiment made the 11-mile march in about three hours, with

Captain Charles Courtois, Company D, sometime correspondent to the Paterson newspapers. *U.S. Army Military History Institute.*

very little straggling, and camped near Catlett's Station.[25] Arrival at the new campsite was something of a homecoming for William Lloyd. He wrote to Mary that he was now sleeping on the same ground that he had left last June to see her. Loosely translated, Lloyd meant that this was the place where he had deserted from his prior unit. Lloyd confirmed this, noting he had passed through the same woods "that I threw my clothes away in." Present circumstances, however, did not augur well for a repeat performance as Lloyd told Mary that he "wouldn't undertake it now under no consideration." According to Lloyd, 18 of the regiment's deserters had been caught in Washington and the talk was that they would be shot. While this talk may have intimidated Lloyd, there is no record of any shooting of the few deserters who were caught.[26]

As part of this most recent movement, Mindil reported to General George Meade by telegraph and also wrote to Major General Oliver Howard to ask for assignment to Howard's XI Corps. While Mindil admitted that the regiment was "without instructions, undisciplined and totally unready for a campaign," he believed a few weeks of drill and instruction would remedy the situation.[27] Since there was probably no Union commander who would turn down reinforcements, no matter how unready, Howard gladly accepted the offer. Howard promised to supply the regiment, as "he would be glad to have it."[28] Regardless of the regiment's combat readiness, the men were certainly tired. Lloyd wrote to his wife of a cold and sore feet due to the "God damned march of five days over the cursed hills of Virginia."[29] Before the war ended, Lloyd would have plenty of opportunity for equally graphic comments about other geographic features of the South. In any event, the regiment now had a military home, the XI Corps. In the Army of the Potomac, each corps consisted of two or three divisions, a force of as many as 36,000 men. Each division, in turn, consisted of two to three brigades, which were typically made up of three to six regiments.[30] Within the XI Corps, the 33rd was assigned to the First Brigade of the Second Division.[31]

When Mindil described his regiment as undisciplined, he was not just referring to the enlisted men. On September 21, he wrote twice to higher headquarters about problems with his officers. The first concerned Captain Henry Bartlett, the commander of Company G. While the Captain had "general and specific orders" to travel with the regiment from Newark, Mindil reported that Bartlett had been absent. Although Mindil asked that Bartlett be dismissed for this offense, without pay or benefits,[32] he must ultimately have had a change of heart. Shortly thereafter Bartlett rejoined the regiment and was allowed by Mindil to make the trip west.[33]

While Mindil was not pleased about Bartlett, he was even more concerned about an event that occurred the day the regiment arrived at Catlett's Station. That night Captain John Sandford, commander of Company E, and Captain Samuel Waldron, commander of Company I, went off on what was apparently a drunken binge. Somehow the officers had illicitly obtained the password and left camp without Mindil's permission. Along with a private from the 27th Pennsylvania, they then passed the picket line and went to a house in the vicinity. The men on picket duty informed the commander of the guard, who went to the house and found the private sleeping on the ground floor with the officers sleeping on the floor above. The officer arrested the private, but left the two officers alone, returning the next morning to demand their names. When the incident was reported to General Adolph von Steinwehr, the division commander, he passed the information on to Mindil for action.

Upon being confronted with these accusations, Waldron defended himself, claiming he could not have left Sandford because of his condition. According to Mindil this meant Sandford was drunk. However, Sandford claimed that he was hungry so he went to a sutler's to buy food and then fell asleep. Regardless of the validity of these explanations, there was no explanation for failing to ask permission, which violated a standing order, or for obtaining the password "clandestinely." In considering appropriate punishments, Mindil noted that this was Waldron's first offense. In addition, Mindil believed Waldron's previous conduct had been "splendid" and felt a private reprimand was sufficient. However, with regard to Sandford, Mindil's patience had run out. Either at Newark or on the trip to Washington, Sandford had been placed under arrest for "grave offenses" but had been let off with a private reprimand. Apparently not having learned anything, Sandford had violated direct orders from Mindil on the road to Warrenton, which resulted in a second admonition. When this was followed by Sandford's going AWOL almost as soon as the regiment was in camp, Mindil had had more than enough.[34] He recommended that Sandford be given a dishonorable discharge, which took effect on October 2.[35]

In reporting these incidents, Mindil claimed that he was not like other field officers who overlooked this kind of behavior; he would "punish the guilty."[36] Some rumors of these incidents appeared in the Newark newspapers without any names being mentioned.[37] In a letter to the *Daily Mercury*, Major David Peloubet acknowledged the unpleasantness of such actions, but emphasized their necessity if the 33rd was to be an effective regiment. This kind of discipline served two significant purposes. The enlisted men could see that officers would also be held accountable for their behavior and, perhaps more importantly, officers who could put everyone's lives in danger in a combat situation would be weeded out.[38]

As Mindil dealt with these discipline problems, other events were underway that would drastically affect the regiment. The Army of the Cumberland under General William S. Rosecrans suffered a major defeat at Chickamauga on the Tennessee-Georgia border. As bad as the actual defeat was Rosecrans' response to it, a retreat from a favorable defensive line. When this was followed by his decision to abandon all the natural defenses around Chattanooga, the situation got even worse. The Confederate Army under General Braxton Bragg gradually moved forward and effectively surrounded Chattanooga. Rosecrans' army was left with only one supply line, a long difficult journey of 60 miles.

Magnifying Rosecrans' actions were a series of panic-stricken telegrams he sent to the War Department in Washington. A furious secretary of war, Edwin Stanton, called for an emergency council of war, where he argued that reinforcements were needed as soon as possible. Stanton claimed the quickest solution was to send 30,000 men from the Army of the Potomac, who could reach Chattanooga in five days. But President Lincoln, probably becoming more realistic every day of the war, thought it would take that long just to get the men to Washington. When the proposal was finally approved, an order was issued at 2:30 A.M. on September 24 to send the XI and XII Corps under General Joseph Hooker to Tennessee. To save time, Hooker was told to leave his horses and wagons behind and replace them at Nashville. However, sufficient replacements did not exist at Nashville and Hooker would not have adequate transportation for almost a month.[39] This would ultimately have tragic implications for the 33rd New Jersey.

The journey was imposing, covering 1,200 "circuitous miles" across the Allegheny Mountains and requiring four changes of railroads.[40] At least Mindil and some of his officers had experience with such a journey, having made a similar move with the 27th New Jersey. Before daybreak on September 25, the regiment left Catlett's Station and marched to Manassas Junction,[41] arriving about noon. Upon arrival they boarded railroad cars for Washington and reached the capital about 6 P.M. After a delay of several hours, the regiment was on another train heading west.[42] Desertion, which had declined after the movement to Warrenton, picked up as five men disappeared between Catlett's Station and Washington.[43]

Having seen the downside of an ocean voyage, the 33rd would now experience the disadvantages of railroad travel. Since time was crucial, the trains put together for the trip included "cattle cars, box cars, hog cars, flat bottom cars or anything that would run on wheels and keep on the tracks."[44] While some cars were equipped with rough seats, the men tore these out and knocked huge holes in the car walls. When the trains arrived at their destination, a number of the cars consisted of little more than "frame and roof."[45] Although the norm was 50–60 men per car, some of the 33rd's cars were so crowded that half of the men had to ride on the roof.[46]

The regiment left Washington the night of September 25–26 on the Baltimore and Ohio Railroad and traveled through what is now West Virginia to the end of the line at the Ohio River.[47] Once west of Martinsburg, Virginia, the railroad passed over a steep mountain range. Since the slope was very severe, the cars carrying the troops were divided into sections of two to three cars each and the sections were moved up the mountain by two engines, one pulling and one pushing. At various points, the riders could see miles of "unbroken autumnal foliage." Nor was the drama over once the train reached the summit. The trains then passed on trestles over "yawning abysses" and through tunnels until the descent began, an equally exciting and hair raising ride down.[48] Once they reached the Ohio River, the regiment marched over a pontoon bridge to Bellaire, Ohio. When they arrived, Adjutant Lambert remarked with some sarcasm that they enjoyed a "substantial supper of coffee and hardtack." Before leaving Bellaire, the regiment was divided. The bulk of the men left immediately with Colonel Mindil while a smaller group remained behind with Lieutenant Colonel Fouratt. After this group waited several hours, they were given the "pleasant duty" of bringing up the corps' stragglers.[49]

The first group proceeded across Ohio and Indiana arriving in Indianapolis about 9 P.M. on September 28.[50] Since eastern Ohio was also mountainous, the railroad went through numerous tunnels and over many bridges, a circuitous route with scenic views of the countryside.[51] Throughout this part of the trip, the men received friendly pro–Union receptions with large crowds, free food, and cheering women at all stops. During a ten-hour delay in Indianapolis, the regiment had supper at the Soldier's Home. Then it was back on the train to Jeffersonville, Indiana, where they arrived on September 29.[52] The connection to the next railroad junction was made by a five-mile march and a ferry ride across the Ohio River into Louisville, Kentucky.[53] Once the regiment crossed into Kentucky there was a change in the political climate, which became decidedly "cool." Becoming accustomed to military travel, Lambert reported that "after the inevitable delay accompanying military transportation," the regiment was back riding the rails. After spending September 30 traveling through Kentucky and Tennessee, the 33rd finally arrived at the end of the line in Bridgeport, Alabama, either late at night on the 30th or early the next morning in a "heavy rain."[54] The move took less than a week and was probably complete before friends and family in New Jersey knew what was going on. When Lieutenant John Toffey wrote to his parents on October 5, he noted, "You will no doubt be surprised to know that I am out here." Toffey commented that the journey had taken him through six states he had never visited before, which was probably typical for the regiment.[55] Little did they know how much more of the South they would see, most of it from this point on foot.

The overall movement was completed on schedule, the "swiftest of all the mass movements of troops in history." Some 20,000 troops, 10 artillery batteries, and 100 railroad cars carrying baggage had moved from Virginia to Tennessee.[56] While duty in the west would not be easy, the significance of the regiment's transfer should not be underestimated. Fate or randomness had a great deal to do with the fortunes of both regiments and individuals.[57] Had the 33rd remained in the east, the regiment would have been part of Grant's overland campaign in 1864 and shared in the terrible losses. Although the members of the regiment were not clairvoyant, there was a clear sense that duty in the west was preferable to service with the Army of the Potomac.[58] During this period no journey of the 33rd would be complete without desertion. Since leaving New Jersey, the regiment had suffered almost 30 more desertions, reducing its strength to between 670 and 700. All of these losses were before the regiment had fired a shot in anger, with the exception of the wounded mule in Virginia.[59]

Arrival in Bridgeport, Alabama, must have resulted in culture shock for the

Joseph Couse, 2nd lt., Company H; 1st lt., Company A; Captain, Company I. *U.S. Army Military History Institute.*

regiment. Even those from Sussex County could not have been prepared for the rural South. Adjutant Lambert said that Bridgeport "was a town, it is now a military station without a single house."[60] Located five miles from the Tennessee state line, the area was described as wild and primitive. Georg Muller from Newark found the area a "complete wilderness" with the closest home 20 miles away.[61] Seeking to help readers back home get a mental picture, one soldier from the Paterson area told the local paper that the mountains were comparable to "Garret Rock in Paterson."[62] While the regiment was in strange surroundings, all of the correspondents agreed that the men were in good health and good spirits. Even though this may have been true in general, the regiment would not be spared the scourge of all Civil War regiments, disease. When Joseph Ribble of Company A died of typhoid fever on October 21, he became the first, but not the last, such casualty.[63]

Beyond the problems of adapting to new surroundings, there were other difficulties. While the officers were without tents, baggage, and horses,[64] much more serious was the fact that as in Chattanooga, rations were inadequate. With some irony, a Paterson man noted "we are living quite sparingly on the government since coming here."[65] Since there were few if any government rations available, the men were forced to buy food in the local economy. Several men complained of paying 25 cents for a loaf of bread of dubious quality, five to six times what it would cost in Paterson or Newark.[66] William Lloyd complained to his wife that they were on one-quarter to one-half rations; forced to buy food, he now had only 35 cents left.[67] A further difficulty was adjusting to the weather, which ranged from hot days to cold nights.[68]

As this was one of the longest periods the regiment had spent in one place, there was finally time for badly needed drill and training.[69] To be an effective fighting force, Civil War regiments had to move efficiently from one formation to another. Such teamwork and coordination of movements could only be developed through training, something for which the 33rd had had precious little time.[70]

The establishment of a semipermanent base made at least one major contribution to morale: the regiment could now receive mail. A number of historians have written about the differences between Civil War soldiers and those of the twentieth century, especially post–World War II.[71] But one thing that the Civil War soldier shared with his military descendants was a need — almost an obsession — for mail from home. Both sides recognized the impact of mail on morale, and more important, they did something about it. The Federal government worked hard to move mail quickly. The sheer volume of mail was impressive with 90,000 pieces of mail passing through Louisville each day.[72] But even more impressive was the efficiency. Letters from the North to both Virginia and Tennessee traveled at about the same speed as today.[73]

Such efficiency was important as the men wanted mail regularly, did not hesitate to say so, and complained to those who they felt were not writing frequently enough.[74] While still on the *Dudley Buck* on September 11, William Lloyd began telling his wife to write, a refrain he kept up through September and October.[75] At various times, Lloyd even wondered if she was deceiving him and said he never expected to see her again. Finally on October 29, he noted, with joy, the receipt of her welcome letter.[76] Other members of the regiment simply expressed their gratitude and stressed the importance of mail. Sergeant John Fenner of Company E wrote his sister that mail "affords us more pleasure than anything in the world."[77] Captain Charles Courtois of Company D informed the Paterson *Daily Register* that "a letter from home is far better than a cup of coffee on a cold morning."[78] Given the importance that coffee had for the Civil War soldiers, this was a powerful expression of the value of mail.

In addition to communicating with family and friends, several officers wrote to the local newspapers about the regiment. Their purpose was to claim that in spite of the 33rd's embarrassing beginnings, the regiment would still make the state proud. The 33rd's performance at drill and the "regularity and cleanliness" of the camp were cited as evidence of the regiment's potential.[79] Major David Peloubet was especially moved by the sight of the men at worship in the Alabama woods, "bowed and uncovered."[80]

With communications now open, Colonel Mindil was able to deal with some assignments for officers. Once Captain Sandford had been discharged, Mindil recommended to the state adjutant general that 1st Lieutenant Charles Field be promoted to captain and commander of Company E. Field's place would be taken by Joseph Miller with a promotion.[81] While Mindil also wanted to promote the regiment's sergeant major, Stephen Pierson, to 2nd lieutenant of Company F, the company had fewer than 80 men and was not authorized to have a 2nd lieutenant. Therefore, Mindil sent Pierson back to New Jersey to recruit ten additional men, which would "ensure his muster." Having made the trip from Virginia to Tennessee, Pierson, less than one month later, had to go all the way back. Besides ensuring "his muster," the trip also meant that Pierson would miss the Chattanooga campaign.[82] During this period, Mindil also apparently changed his mind about Captain Bartlett. Although Bartlett had been mustered out of the 33rd due to his two-week absence, he had rejoined the regiment in time for the trip west and had been performing his duty. Since Mindil believed that Bartlett was a "good officer," he asked for his reinstatement, which was granted, as were his other requests.[83]

While the personnel issues were important, Mindil was also concerned about uniforms and wrote to Washington seeking some 300 additional Zouave uniforms. Unless more could be obtained, there was no alternative but standard issue. This was important to Mindil as he and the rest of regiment preferred "their peculiar uniforms," or at least that was Mindil's opinion.[84] Although desertion was down somewhat, three men deserted during the regiment's time at Bridgeport,[85] which could only be an act of desperation considering the remote location. William Lloyd recognized that desertion was no longer an option, so he was now trying to find another way out of the army. Lloyd asked his wife to send him certain medicines that would allow him to fake illness, but she did not do so.[86]

The 33rd moved again after two and one-half weeks in Bridgeport. Along with two other regiments, the 33rd was ordered to move six miles up the Tennessee River to a junction with Battle Creek.[87] The movement was part of the larger effort to keep open the sole supply line to Chattanooga.[88] When the movement began on October 19, the three regiments marched for four hours and halted for the night at the foot of a spur of the Cumberland Mountains. After a night in the Tennessee wilderness, the regiment moved the next day, one-quarter of a mile to their new camp.[89] Their assignment was to guard a pontoon bridge and to help wagons along the "muddy and worn out roads."[90] At least one member of the regiment found the assignment as an advance guard for Bridgeport an honor for the 33rd.[91]

A major advantage of the regiment's new assignment was moving into the camp of the 34th Illinois. That regiment thought, and perhaps hoped, they would be there all winter, so they had constructed small board huts with brick chimneys. These huts were built with materials allegedly taken from the ruins and remains, of houses, barns and sheds. No one in the 33rd could know whether the residents had first abandoned their property or if destruction of property forced their evacuation. Regardless of the history of the structures, the officers and men of the 33rd were quite happy with the "small village of one story buildings." One member of the regiment wrote to the Newark *Daily Mercury* that if the Bridgeport camp was "regular and clean," this was "beautifully regular and exact." While William Lambert admired the log huts, he also praised the campsite for well graded streets with excellent drainage and found the smoke ascending from the many chimneys "almost homelike." Not only were the cabins functional, but many were furnished with tables, chairs, carved mantelpieces and even clocks, all of which seemed like "relics of a bygone civilization."[92]

This homelike position fronted on the Chattanooga road with the regiment's right ending at Battle Creek. The Tennessee River was at the regiment's rear, while the left was in the mountains and plains of Tennessee. While the accommodations were better, the roads were not. Although Lambert had considered the roads in Virginia bad, he felt that in Tennessee and Alabama they were worse. Tennessee roads, he claimed, consisted almost entirely of "mud, corduroy, water, and gullies." By the end of the war members of the regiment would be experts on the many shortcomings of Southern roads. The roads at Battle Creek may not have been good to begin with, but the situation was not helped by the weather, which was "very wet and disagreeable."[93] Neither the bad weather nor the roads helped the supply shortages, with butter, cheese, bread, and fruit unavailable at any price,[94] William Lloyd had to survive on hardtack and coffee.[95] In addition to all these problems, the atmosphere was not helped by a countryside almost deserted except for Union troops.[96]

Meanwhile, the risk of starvation of the Union forces in Chattanooga was becoming greater and greater. Clearly something had to be done to open a more effective supply line. As preparations got underway for this effort, the other regiments at Battle Creek were recalled to Bridgeport on October 24. Now on their own, the 33rd had to cover an area formerly guarded by a brigade. To carry out this larger responsibility, Colonel Mindil sent two companies of 120 men under Captain Boggs to Jasper, a small town five miles away. In addition, a squad of one officer and 20 men was sent to guard a bridge over the Sequatchie River.[97] Although Jasper was described as once being "quite a large shire town," it was now "now quite deserted."[98] At Jasper, Lieutenant John Toffey took a detachment to repair a bridge. When he asked a local commander for rations, he was told to forage, so he and Lieutenant Harrison took a squad of men went to do just that. First, they took 30 loaves of bread from a sutler in exchange for a receipt and then went to a bakery where the proprietor claimed that he had no flour. Skeptical, Toffey ordered a search that turned up two barrels. Toffey had one barrel ground in exchange for a receipt. Finally they took one steer from a

William H. Lambert, adjutant; Captain, Company C; and Major, HQ, sometime correspondent to the Newark *Daily Advertiser. U.S. Army Military History Institute.*

"rank secessionist" and again gave a receipt.[99] This diligence in giving receipts would probably provide ironic memories for the members of this squad who would take part in the Savannah and Carolina campaigns.

Even though the wood huts provided comfortable accommodations, the time at Battle Creek began to wear thin with the men. Gradually the combination of a lack of food, poor weather, and the remote location had a negative impact on morale. Lloyd described the area to his wife on October 29 as "miserable looking country, nothing, but mountains." While there were no reports of encounters with the Confederates, the duty was not without stress. Lloyd wrote that going a mile through the woods in the dark to relieve someone on guard gave him chills all over, a good way "to take a leaden pill." Both Lloyd and Georg Muller found the combination of hot days and cold nights unpleasant. Muller wrote his parents on October 30, "I would give anything to be out of this wilderness." Although dissatisfied with conditions at Battle Creek, both men knew that the "conditions" in battle would be much worse and would have been willing to remain at Battle Creek all winter.[100] But even as these letters were being written, an action had taken place that would bring the 33rd out of the wilderness to rejoin the rest of the army and the war.

While the men of the 33rd suffered to some degree from a lack of rations, the situation was far worse in Chattanooga, which had become a "starvation camp." One soldier at Chattanooga felt the only worse experience for a Union soldier was as a Confederate prisoner of war. When Rosecrans abandoned all the natural defenses around Chattanooga, he left the Union army stuck between the Tennessee River and a series of mountains and ridges. Now the only supply route open to the city was 60 miles in length over Walden's Ridge to the north, consisting of poor roads that were worse in bad weather. The 33rd had been guarding part of that route at Battle Creek. Unavailable as supply routes were the railroad, the parallel wagon road, and the river, all of which were controlled by the Confederate forces around Chattanooga.

When he took command of the Union forces, General Ulysses S. Grant's first priority was to open better supply lines. To do so, he approved a plan prepared by General William Smith for an amphibious night assault by pontoon boats on Brown's Ferry, five miles down the river from Chattanooga. At the same time, General Hooker was to move the XI and XII Corps from Bridgeport through Lookout Valley to make a connection at Brown's Ferry. The other regiments at Battle Creek had been recalled to be part of this force. The amphibious assault was made during the early morning of October 27 and the attack succeeded with very little opposition. Once the area was secure, the pontoon boats were used to construct a bridge that was in use by 4:30 that afternoon. While this was going on, Hooker advanced 15 miles in Lookout Valley. The next night, October 28, the Confederates launched an unsuccessful night attack on Hooker, and Hooker's command then made the connection to Brown's Ferry. As a new regiment, the 33rd was fortunate not to have its baptism of fire during a night attack, a rarity during the Civil War. Since the joint effort was successful, the Federal forces regained control of Lookout Valley, Brown's Ferry and Raccoon Mountain, which opened up two good supply lines. The success of the operation was crucial since Grant claimed the existing supply line could not have supported Chattanooga for more than another week. Although Union forces were still short of supplies, at least the threat of starvation had ended. The success of this operation was the turning point in the Chattanooga campaign because Federal forces could now go on the offensive.[101] Such an offensive would ultimately bring the 33rd New Jersey into combat for the first time.

Since the new supply lines were open, the 33rd was no longer needed at Battle

Georg Muller, private and corporal, Company B, wrote frequently to his parents in Newark. *From the Collections of the New Jersey Historical Society.*

Creek. On November 4, the regiment left Battle Creek, gathering up their detachments at Jasper and the Sequatchie. On the first day the regiment made 13 miles, good progress over bad roads. When they reached Kelley's Ford just past noon on November 5, Lambert noted, "the usual rain attended us."[102] The rain only added to an arduous march over high rocky mountains through mud up to the hips in some places.[103] After a night's rest or what passed for it, the regiment crossed the river the next morning in pontoon boats with the horses swimming alongside. Once the crossing was complete about 2 P.M., the regiment, for some reason, halted until dark. Even more strangely, the 33rd then moved forward in the dark, two miles of "staggering over stones, and into ruts and through sloughs," before they finally stopped for the night. At last on November 7, the regiment moved three miles into the brigade camp in Lookout Valley.[104]

As was noted earlier, the 33rd and all of Hooker's command had come west without their wagon trains. When the 33rd moved to Lookout Valley, the regiment did not have sufficient wagons for the sick, not to mention all the baggage and stores, so the sick and the supplies were to be moved by boat.[105] Among the sick was William Lloyd, who had been ill with fever for six days. Lloyd was now feeling better and thought that he had finally gotten lucky. While the regiment would have a hard march to Kelley's Ford, he was anticipating "a nice sail down the river."[106] But boats were also scarce and no boat arrived until about 7 P.M. on Saturday, November 7.[107] The men and baggage were loaded on a steamboat and a flatboat, "facetiously denominated a barge," which was to be towed behind the steamboat.[108] When the sick men were placed on the flatboat, they first had to pump it free of water from numerous leaks; then Lloyd and the others fell asleep.[109]

However, the journey was not to be "a nice sail," as Lloyd awoke to find sick men screaming and boxes and water running over him. Fearing the flatboat was sinking, he got his coat off as he jumped into the river. Near him was another sick man, pleading to be saved, but Lloyd had all he could do to save himself and saw the man go down for the last time. The night was so dark that it was almost impossible to see. Since Lloyd's clothes were weighing him down, he decided he had "to adopt another plan." First, he got his shoes off, and then he got both arms around boxes containing tea and hardtack, which were buoyant enough to enable him to get to the steamboat. Once he regained his composure, Lloyd informed his wife that he would send her some of the tea that helped save his life. Lloyd also noted, "I haven't been warm since."[110]

In addition to Lloyd's eyewitness account, reports were made to two Newark newspapers. "Miles Alienus" wrote to the *Daily Journal* that he had heard that the flatboat was overloaded with the private property of a speculator due to an "official favor," which weighed the flatboat down to within six to eight inches of the waterline. When one of the ropes snapped, the front of the flatboat swung with the strong current while the rear end went under "the guard of the steamboat." The flatboat was then forced underwater, which washed off men and baggage. Lieutenant Somerville, who was sick himself, jumped in twice and pulled some of the men to safety.[111] William Lambert, writing to the *Daily Advertiser,* stated that the accident occurred about six miles from Kelley's Ferry. Without mentioning the speculator, Lambert wrote that the fireman on the steamboat had been mixing dry and green wood up to that point, but then had nothing but dry wood left. When only the dry wood was used, the boat picked up speed, the bow of the flatboat went under the water and the current washed off the men and heavy objects. Once the flatboat was lighter, it righted itself. According to Lambert, all of the 10–12 men on the flatboat were swept off into the water. Along with Somerville, Lambert reported that Lieutenant Titman, the quartermaster and others jumped on to the flatboat and tried to pull the men aboard. As they were saving some, others like Lloyd were able to save themselves. Not so fortunate were Theodore Drake and Oscar Lathrop of Company C, Patrick Delaney of Company B and Louis Witte of Company I, all of whom drowned. Lambert mourned them, writing, "It is hard for the soldier to die — away from homes and friends — but to die thus is harder still."[112]

When the flatboat was finally cut loose, the steamboat proceeded to its destination. The next day Titman and three others went back in a pontoon boat to see if any of the baggage could be found. Unfortunately what they found was "in proportion to the whole relatively small."[113] To make matters worse, the officers had worn their least desirable uniforms on the march.[114] According to Lambert, the officers could no longer wear their Zouave uniforms, "the envy and admiration of our fellow officers."[115] "Alienus" reported that although some were blaming the quartermaster, he, "Alienus," was not sure who was to blame, but knew someone was, probably alluding to the official favor.[116] Ultimately no charges were filed.[117] Colonel Mindil, who had seen his previous regiment suffer a similar tragedy with even greater loss of life, probably wondered what other calamities lay ahead.

As they mourned their lost comrades, the regiment occupied their new camp in Lookout Valley. On November 10, "Miles Alienus" wrote to the *Daily Journal* that the weather had turned very cold with a severe frost the night before. The last three nights had been difficult, the men "shivering in our wretched dog tents" from a "severe northwind." The conditions probably made some nostalgic for the huts at Battle Creek. Although "Alienus" said things were quiet, he was sure that this was the lull before the storm. "Certain it is," he wrote, "one hundred and twenty thousand men are not massed here for nothing."[118]

III

"A victory almost over nature herself"

As "Miles Alienus" had foreseen, there were very tangible reasons why so many men had gathered around Chattanooga. The combined Confederate and Union forces were almost 50 times the city's population of 2,500, clear evidence of Chattanooga's strategic importance. Although described as "more of an idea than a place," Chattanooga was a crucial transportation hub. Two important railroads, the Chattanooga and Cleveland and the Western and Atlantic, passed through the area. While the former was the primary communications and supply link to Virginia, the latter served a similar purpose for Atlanta and the coast. For the Confederacy, these railroads were vital supply lines. For the Union, the area was the essential supply base for any invasion of the deep South. Chattanooga was, thus, of immense importance to both sides, a place well worth a battle.

Chattanooga was also a place of impressive physical features, especially towering Lookout Mountain. When Rosecrans made his disastrous retreat after Chickamauga, the Union Army had abandoned all of the natural defenses to the Confederates. However, the amphibious landing at Brown's Ferry and Hooker's advance into Lookout Valley had retaken the essential supply routes. While this had improved the Union situation, both Lookout Mountain and Missionary Ridge were still controlled by the Confederacy. Lookout Mountain dominated Chattanooga much the same way that, back in New Jersey, Garrett Mountain dominated Paterson. Some four miles from Lookout Mountain, across Chattanooga Valley, was Missionary Ridge, which began two and one-half miles northeast of Chattanooga and extended 15 miles south by southeast. Although nowhere near the height of Lookout Mountain, Missionary Ridge was covered with trees, fallen timber, and outcroppings of rock, making for a difficult climb even without the threat of Confederate bullets.[1]

The Union forces around Chattanooga that would have to attack these positions consisted of three very different elements. In Chattanooga, the largest was the Army

Captain William Boggs, Company A, died of wounds received at Chattanooga, November 23, 1863. *U.S. Army Military History Institute.*

of the Cumberland, now commanded by Major General George Thomas. Primarily from the Midwest, these units had retreated from Chickamauga and had suffered the most in the "starvation camp" at Chattanooga. More recent arrivals were the XI and XII Corps under Major General Joseph Hooker, sent west from Virginia after the Chickamauga debacle. Still on their way to Chattanooga from Mississippi was Grant's Army of the Tennessee, now commanded by William Tecumseh Sherman. Although they were all part of the same army, there was real tension among the three groups. When Hooker's eastern troops made the connection at Brown's Ferry, the men from the Army of the Cumberland cheered them. However, after a few good meals, taunting began in earnest, which would only intensify with the arrival of Sherman's men at the end of November.[2]

While the primary importance of the fighting over Lookout Valley was the reopening of supply lines, the Union victory had an important by-product that affected the rest of the campaign. During the fighting, a night attack by Confederate general James Longstreet had failed; this was the final break in his already poor relationship with Confederate commander Braxton Bragg. Afterwards, largely out of spite, Bragg seized upon a suggestion of Jefferson Davis and sent Longstreet with his two divisions of approximately of 15,000 men to eastern Tennessee. After they arrived there, Longstreet and his men were to operate against Union general Ambrose Burnside's Army of the Ohio. This decision had been described as the "most egregious error of his [Bragg's] checkered career" since it further weakened an already outnumbered Confederate force.[3] Although Longstreet and his men were gone from Chattanooga, their operations in eastern Tennessee would have implications for the 33rd New Jersey.

With Union supply lines now reopened, Grant's attention turned to an offensive to drive the Confederates out of Chattanooga. As with Brown's Ferry, Grant relied on the planning skills of General William Smith. After Smith made an extensive reconnaissance of the area, he learned that the Confederate right on the northern end of Missionary Ridge was relatively weak. Based on this information, Smith developed a plan that called for Sherman's men, once they had arrived, to cross the Tennessee River at Brown's Ferry and then make a second crossing north of Chattanooga. Once this movement was completed, the Union force would be in position to outflank the Confederate right. Since Sherman's men would be out of sight of the Confederates as they crossed the river, the movement would also confuse Bragg about Union intentions. As the attack was being made, Thomas was to attack the Confederate center on Missionary Ridge and Hooker their left on Lookout Mountain. Although favoring the attack on the Confederate right, Sherman and Grant modified the plan by canceling the attack on Lookout Mountain and dividing Hooker's force. While the XII Corps would remain in Lookout Valley, the XI Corps, including the 33rd New Jersey, would move north of Chattanooga under the command of General Howard. This move dramatically changed the 33rd's role at Chattanooga, both during and after the impending battle.[4]

While the offensive was being planned, the 33rd occupied their new home in Lookout Valley. According to Lieutenant John Toffey, they were located in a "very pleasant camp."[5] Trying to be hopeful, William Lambert found the new moon, "smiling upon the tents that dot the valley," a good omen.[6] While the officers meditated about the scene, Georg Muller and the men were assigned picket duty, where Muller found he could converse with Confederate pickets only 30 feet away. Although the camp was largely out of range of Confederate artillery, Muller reported that a shell landed 20 feet from his tent, but fortunately it did not explode.[7] Even though it was now November, the weather was still warm with overcoats needed only at night. Another incident suggested that the regiment was still in a learning mode. When some of the officers gathered in Toffey's tent to demand an inquiry into their lost luggage, they suddenly heard the "long roll," a drum roll signaling an attack. After the regiment fell in (one hopes more efficiently than back in Virginia), all were "much chagrined to find out that it was the Seventy-third Pennsylvania beating tattoo." Although tattoo was a routine signal of camp life, Toffey claimed that the Pennsylvanians beat it like the long roll.[8] Even so, the confusion was just as likely to have been due to the 33rd's lack of experience in camp life as well as battle. While there were no combat casualties during this period, death from disease hit the regiment in earnest. Six men, Charles Matonia, Henry Steer, Lawrence Van Nostrand, James P. Jones, Joel Jones, and William Roain, died of disease during the first three weeks of November.[9]

The plan of attack had been decided, but the offensive was continually delayed as Sherman had extensive problems getting his army to Chattanooga because of both bad roads and bad weather. When Sherman's men finally passed through Lookout Valley, the rivalry among the Union armies erupted. While the western army always had a rough and ready appearance, this was magnified even more by their difficult march to Chattanooga. Such a lack of military formality came as a shock to the more formal eastern troops and insults flew between the two groups. Unfortunately, some members of the 33rd were involved. A member of the 5th Iowa wrote that, "the worst of this class was the 33rd New Jersey." Apparently some of the Jersey men described Sherman's men as Grant's "Vicksburg gophers" and as being so "dirty and ragged" that "they aint fit to be seen."[10] Although tired from their march, Sherman's men were at no loss for insults. Some said that the easterners would make "elegant corpses" and hoped that "they might not be compelled to eat their hardtack without butter."[11] Such verbal fisticuffs were probably natural, but members of an untested unit like the 33rd would have been better advised not to get involved, especially since their distinctive uniforms made them easy to remember.

The interlude in Lookout Valley ended on the afternoon of November 22, when the 33rd was ordered to move with the XI Corps into Chattanooga. First, the regiment crossed the Tennessee River on the pontoons at Brown's Ferry. They then recrossed the river on another pontoon bridge into Chattanooga. Once across, the 33rd moved through Chattanooga with "bayonets fixed, colors flying and drums beating."[12] Along with the rest of the XI Corps, the regiment camped on a plain about 200 yards to the right of Fort Wood.[13] When darkness fell, the men lit campfires both to cook the evening meal and for warmth. Others did the same up and down the Union line as did their Confederate counterparts. While observing this scene, William Lambert found the view to be one of great beauty with "the camp fires of our army extending right and left as far as the eye could reach." At the same time, opposite and above them, Missionary Ridge and Lookout Mountain were "dotted — like a clear winter sky — with the lights of the fires of our enemy."[14] Although Major Peloubet also admired the splendid view, he was also realistic. "Everything," he noted in his diary, "seemed to betoken now the arrival of a great battle in which our regiment was for the first time to face the enemy."[15]

Although the night may have been beautiful, the beauty was gone the next morning, which began "murky and gloomy." While it was quiet, except for the occasional "challenges" of Union artillery, the time must have been one of anxious waiting.[16] Given the close proximity of the Confederate lines, all must have known that a battle was imminent. Despite this much being clear to all, the overall situation was much less clear to the Union high command. As hoped, the crossing at Brown's Ferry had confused Confederate commander Bragg, who eventually came to the erroneous conclusion that Sherman was going after Longstreet in east Tennessee. Late on the afternoon of the 22nd, Bragg responded by ordering General Patrick Cleburne to take two divisions to aid Longstreet. This movement, in turn, confused Union officers who wondered if the whole Confederate army was retreating. On the 23rd, Grant ordered Thomas to make a reconnaissance in force against the Confederate picket line to determine if the Confederates were still there. The immediate objective was Orchard Knob, a "steep, craggy knoll some two thousand yards east of Fort Wood," about 100 feet high. To the left of Fort Wood, a long line of Confederate rifle pits extended all the way to the Tennessee River. After the reconnaissance was complete, the Federal units returned to their original position.[17]

The relative quiet ended about noon with the sound of bugles blowing and drums beating coming from regiment's right. While the day had begun overcast, Thomas' men fell in to formation under "chill, but crystal blue autumn skies."[18] About one hour later the 33rd was ordered to fall in and stack their knapsacks.[19] Although the men had retained their overcoats, the knapsacks held the men's blankets and shelter halves. While they probably expected to recover their knapsacks before nightfall, they would not see them again for almost a month. As the regiment fell in, the surgeon spotted Lieutenant John Toffey, who had been sick with a fever for a week and off duty. Toffey made it clear that he intended to go with his company, but the surgeon said to him, "You know you are not able, so come and go with me to the hospital." Toffey was not about to miss the regiment's first fight so he declined.[20] To the right, Thomas' units under the command of General Wood moved forward at about 1:30 P.M. The awe inspiring sight of the ranks of blue clad soldiers impressed even the Confederate pickets, who mistakenly thought they were watching some kind of dress parade. Wood's men quickly disabused them of that notion by moving forward and easily capturing Orchard Knob. When Grant and Thomas recognized the importance of this success to the Army of the Cumberland's morale, they quickly countermanded the order to withdraw and directed Wood's men to dig in.[21]

The 33rd was too far to the left to see what was happening, but the sounds made it clear that the "the Battle of Chattanooga had commenced."[22] Shortly thereafter, the arrival of an officer with orders signaled that the regiment's participation also was about to commence.[23] Since Wood's new position was some 2,000 yards to the front of the existing Union lines, Howard and the XI Corps were ordered to "close up on Wood's flank."[24] When the First Brigade formed in two lines, the 33rd New Jersey was on the left of the first line with the 134th New York to the regiment's right. Behind the first line was a second line of five regiments formed in column. About one-half mile from the first line was Citico Creek, which was surrounded by woods.[25] Some 150 yards in front of the 33rd's main line were Captain Boggs and Company A serving as skirmishers.[26] The regiment was now about to go into a real battle, not handsomely repulsing assaulting mules or guarding against guerrilla raids that never came. At last the 33rd was going to "see the elephant," experience Civil War combat first hand.

When the regiment advanced at about 3:30 P.M., they went no more than ten yards before coming under musket fire from the woods around the creek, a railroad bridge, and several buildings. Besides being well protected, the Confederates were there in force, firing at close range. Almost immediately, Captain Boggs was shot through the arm, a wound he would die from in early December.[27] As a replacement, Colonel Mindil ordered Lieutenant Toffey forward to take his place, apparently unaware of Toffey's condition. Although Toffey had already had a hard time keeping up during the movement, he went forward to take charge of the skirmish line. Just reaching the skirmish line was dangerous work. Toffey said that "the bullets flew like hailstones," the hottest skirmish line that he had ever experienced. After he got there, Toffey had barely begun to give orders when he was hit with a musket ball in his thigh. Down Toffey went, he stayed there for about an hour before being taken to the hospital.[28] Even though the wound was not fatal, Toffey's active military service was over. At the urging of Colonel Mindil, Toffey would be awarded the Congressional Medal of Honor for distinguished gallantry some 34 years later in 1897.[29]

It was clear that the skirmishers needed assistance, so Captain O'Connor and Company F were ordered forward as reinforcements. This additional firepower drove the Confederates across Citico Creek. After the skirmishers reached the near side of the creek, they exchanged heavy fire with the Confederates at a distance of only ten yards. However, both sides were firing from well protected positions so there were few losses. Although Colonel Mindil had no further orders, he believed the goal was to drive the Confederates out of their positions. To accomplish this, he sent Captain Field and Company E forward to further strengthen the advance party. With a force of about 160 men, Captain O'Connor was to advance to the far side of the creek. When the advance party moved forward, Mindil and the rest of the regiment advanced under heavy fire to within 50 yards of the bridge.[30] While correcting his company's alignment during the advance, Captain Waldron was killed instantly by a bullet through the heart.[31] As the regiment moved forward, Major Peloubet was sent back to the brigade commander for further orders. Peloubet returned with instructions just to hold the railroad bridge and the near side of the creek, but the skirmishers had already crossed the waist-deep water under heavy fire.[32] When Adjutant Lambert tried to get word to Captain O'Connor, his horse was killed. However, Lambert persevered and the men held the far side of the creek until darkness ended the fighting.[33] At about 8 P.M., the regiment was relieved by the 27th Pennsylvania and withdrew to a bivouac position some 300 yards to the rear.[34]

While the 33rd underwent their baptism of fire, the regiment was observed by Private George Metcalf of the 136th New York. According to Metcalf, the 33rd was marching in column until the center of the regiment hit a barn. After this happened, Metcalf claimed that the men took cover behind the barn and refused to move in spite of the efforts of the officers. Then, Metcalf said, "the whole of that regiment doubled up and packed themselves behind it like a flock of frightened sheep," opening a gap in the Union line. Singularly unimpressed, Metcalf stated that the regiment consisted of "all new men and a cowardly set too."[35] If true, this incident reflected poorly on the regiment especially in light of their taunting of Sherman's men. Fortunately or unfortunately, Metcalf was the only one to report this incident, which did not appear in any officer's after-action reports (of the 33rd or otherwise) or in any accounts by members of the 33rd. While this is not necessarily surprising, as no one would want to call attention to such an embarrassing incident, it is not clear, even if true, how much real damage was done. Certainly, it was not unusual for a regiment in the attack to be slowed down by a barrier, man-made or otherwise.[36] When General Howard mentioned the regiment in his report, he wrote that the 33rd was "here for the first time engaged, and with credit."[37]

Being engaged also meant combat casualties. Along with Captain Waldron's death came the revelation that he had been "Miles Alienus," the correspondent of the Newark *Daily Journal*.[38] Considering the problems Waldron had had in Virginia, he had probably been wise to adopt a pen name. Although most Civil War dead were buried in the immediate area, both Waldron's and Captain Boggs' bodies were returned to Newark for burial. This was the only recorded incident of the regiment's dead being returned to New Jersey. During the Chattanooga and Atlanta campaigns, most of the 33rd's dead would be buried at Chattanooga or Marietta. Besides Waldron, the other immediate fatality was Private Thomas Marsh of Company H, who had been shot in the head. Leading the list of the regiment's wounded was Lieutenant John Toffey, followed by 12 enlisted men. William Post of Company D had been shot through both thighs and died two days later. The rest of the wounded would recover.[39]

Even though the successful attack on Orchard Knob may have boosted the confidence of the Army of the Cumberland, the action also woke up Braxton Bragg to the real danger on the Confederate right. Fortunately for Bragg, this happened just in time to recall Cleburne and his troops, who were about to board trains at Chickamauga Station. While the Confederates began moving back towards Missionary Ridge, Sherman's men moved into staging areas to cross the Tennessee River. Once across, they would be in position for the long delayed attack on the Confederate right. As at Brown's Ferry in October, the strategy was for an amphibious assault in pontoon boats. Also as at Brown's Ferry, when the riverbank was secure, the pontoon boats would be used to erect a bridge. The landing took the Confederates completely by surprise and Sherman's three divisions crossed the river as planned.[40]

While this movement was underway, the 33rd New Jersey was starting the new day some one and one-half miles to the south.[41] Unlike the bugle calls of camp, on the morning of November 24 the regiment "awoke to the reveille of firing in the front." Although the 33rd formed in column to defend against an attack, the firing

Private Elsi B. Dawson, musician, Company C. *U.S. Army Military History Institute.*

soon stopped. Then about 10 A.M., under the personal direction of General Howard, the First Brigade moved to the left, crossed the railroad and then Citico Creek itself. Once Sherman's forces were across the river, Howard took Bushbeck's brigade to connect with Sherman's right flank.[42] Since the brigade was moving around the Confederate right wing, they followed a circuitous route.[43] When the 33rd moved through a large cornfield, a heavy skirmish line under the command of Major Peloubet was established. Then the march halted, while a reconnaissance party went out to determine their position in relationship to the Tennessee River. While waiting, they came under a "brisk fire" from the railroad on the right. Captain Bartlett and Company I moved out on the flank, but there were no casualties. As the movement resumed, the 33rd was in the lead moving parallel to the river, with the 27th and 73rd Pennsylvania to the rear.[44] At about noon, Howard's column connected with Sherman's troops at the pontoon bridge just below the mouth of South Chickamauga Creek. In order to further strengthen his force, Sherman asked Howard to leave Bushbeck's brigade with him, to which Howard agreed.[45] With this latest march completed, the regiment had moved all the way from the Union right in Lookout Valley to the left at the northern edge of Missionary Ridge.[46]

After Sherman's newly augmented command was in position, the movement towards Missionary Ridge began at about 1:30 P.M. in a light cold drizzle. At the far right on Sherman's force was Ewing's division, with the 33rd New Jersey and the rest of Bushbeck's brigade to Ewing's right and rear. Between them and Missionary Ridge were one and one-half miles of swamp, fields, and forests. Even though there were very few Confederates in the area, Sherman had his units proceed very carefully.

Unfortunately for Sherman and his men, at the same time Cleburne and his division were being rushed towards Tunnel Hill. Tunnel Hill was the highest point on Missionary Ridge, about 250 yards north of the actual railroad tunnel. When the first contact was made between Union and Confederate units about 3 P.M., it became clear that Sherman's entire advance was very disorganized. Although Sherman's objective was Tunnel Hill, the lead units mistakenly ended up on some detached hills to the north of Missionary Ridge. While the Union troops operated in confusion, the Confederates used the time to get their defenses organized. Even though Sherman had a huge numerical advantage, which probably could have driven the Confederates off of Missionary Ridge, he, ordered his men to dig in.[47] In their position to the right and rear of the advance, the 33rd saw no action. Although the disorganized march in the rain through swamps and forests must have been tedious to most, Major Peloubet had not lost his sense of romance. To Peloubet, "Marching through the woods, concealed from the enemy, the heights of Missionary Ridge towering above us, the troops in two columns making the ascent, and getting into position, the effect was very grand."[48] Grand or not, the men finished the march at the bottom of Missionary Ridge, where they set up a breastwork of fence rails and logs and made camp for the night.[49]

After a day of mist and rain, the weather cleared at night with a full moon. By the moon's light, the men of the 33rd and all of the troops along Missionary Ridge caught glimpses of the fighting on Lookout Mountain. Earlier that day, Grant had agreed to Thomas' request for some kind of "simple diversion" against Lookout

Mountain, which was in no way to be a full scale attack. However, Union generals Joseph Hooker and John Geary had other ideas and launched such an attack anyway. Throughout the day and into the evening, the Union troops struggled up the slopes of Lookout Mountain. The physical exertion of the climb was more of an obstacle than Confederate opposition, which retreated during the night. After the morning mist cleared to reveal the Stars and Stripes flying atop Lookout Mountain, there was cheering all along the Union line.[50]

Dawn also finally brought the implementation of the much delayed plan to drive the Confederates out of Chattanooga. The intent continued to be for Sherman to make the main attack on the Confederate right with support on the left and center. However, the fact that Sherman was not in the right place only became clear when the mist cleared that morning. This error was further magnified when Sherman once again moved very slowly and failed to take advantage of his almost four-to-one numerical superiority. When Sherman finally ordered an attack from the north and northwest only two of his nine brigades were involved. Both the first attack at 10:30 A.M. and the second an hour later failed to make any headway.[51]

While the prior day had begun for the 33rd with a reveille of musket fire, November 25 began with "sharp cannonading along the line." The noise was accompanied by artillery shells flying around "in uncomfortable proximity." After a day in the rain, the regiment had spent a second night without tents or blankets. Uncomfortable at best, the men must have faced the day's events with some level of anxiety. Artillery fire probably did nothing for their morale and the waiting probably did not help either. Finally at about 11:00 A.M., the 33rd and the two Pennsylvania regiments moved to the right through some woods and crossed an open space into another wooded area at the bottom of Tunnel Hill. At this point, the 73rd Pennsylvania was to the front as skirmishers with the 33rd in support; to the 33rd's right was the 27th Pennsylvania. Considering what was about to happen, the 33rd was extremely lucky to be in a reserve position when the movement halted at the edge of the woods.[52] The purpose of the maneuver was for the brigade to be in position to support Loomis' brigade when they made Sherman's second assault on Tunnel Hill.

Loomis' men moved forward to cross one-half mile of flat, open ground immediately in front of Tunnel Hill. As they came out of the protection of the trees, they were hit by heavy Confederate artillery fire that halted the attack halfway across the open ground. Although Loomis got a second order to attack and tried again, little progress was made because of the heavy fire. When Loomis asked Bushbeck to close a gap that had opened on Loomis' left, Bushbeck ordered forward the two Pennsylvania regiments. The two regiments moved toward the Glass farm, but their advance was stopped by two Georgia regiments. The Pennsylvanians eventually outflanked the Georgians and the Confederates withdrew. At first the Pennsylvania regiments continued to advance, but in the confusion of the attack, half of the force stopped at the bottom of the hill. However, the other half kept going up the 600-foot slope and got to within 30 yards of the top. Since Sherman's attacks from the north had stopped, the Pennsylvania men got the full force of the Confederate artillery fire.

Over the next few hours, two more Union brigades tried to climb Tunnel Hill, only to come under increased Confederate artillery fire including some from Cor-

Major David Peloubet, HQ, maintained a diary of the Chattanooga campaign. *New Jersey State Archives, Department of State.*

put's battery. This would not be the last time the 33rd was involved with this battery. Although each of the assaults was eventually stopped, gradually the Union troops started to build up some significant numbers, putting the Confederate position at risk. When Cleburne and his commanders recognized the danger, they ordered a counterattack at about 4 P.M. The Confederate charge was the final blow for Sherman's assault, with many of the Union attackers themselves being taken prisoner. Once at the bottom of the hill, the Union troops dug in and stopped the Confederate charge. Both Pennsylvania units suffered severe casualties and had men taken prisoner.[53]

While this debacle was underway, the 33rd was in reserve, concealed from the Confederate artillery by a fence, "observers of all that took place."[54] Why was the 33rd not ordered into battle when the Pennsylvanians ran into so much trouble? Although one reason may be that the need was for brigade-size units rather than regiments, another real possibility is that no one thought of using the regiment. From the beginning, the whole situation was very confused, with the use of Union units "improvised from below rather than orchestrated from above."[55] Whatever the reason, the 33rd was doubtless spared serious losses. When the Union forces fell back, however, the regiment's luck ran out. Some of the stragglers came across the 33rd's front, drawing heavy Confederate artillery fire on their position. In response, Mindil ordered the left wing to move by the left flank, both to let stragglers through and to move away from the artillery fire. Unfortunately, the order was misunderstood by the men on the right, who simply fell back, getting the stragglers mixed up with the regiment. During this confusion, the Confederate artillery was "firing most rapidly and with good effect." After what must have seemed like an eternity, the 33rd finally got out of range of the artillery fire and returned to their camp of the prior night.[56]

When this artillery barrage hit the 33rd, seven members of the regiment were wounded.[57] Although five men were only slightly injured, Samuel Seering of Company E and Lewis Mangold of Company G were less fortunate. Seering was hit in the leg by a shell; his leg was amputated, but he died from his wound on December 4.[58] Mangold was hit in the arm by a shell and had the dubious distinction of having his treatment, such as it was, described in the *Official Records*. When Mangold arrived at the hospital, his arm was numb and useless. After a few days there was a great deal of swelling, discoloration, and "much constitutional distress," i.e., pain. These symptoms were treated by making deep and long incisions in the arm and then placing warm fomentations and tinctures of iodine above the incision. Since this did not help, Mangold's arm was amputated above the elbow on December 22; the surgeon found two fractures. Although the surgeon's report ended with the comment that Mangold had been sent to a field hospital on December 29 with "termination unknown," Mangold died three days later.[59] Given this treatment for what was in fact a broken arm, it is no surprise that Civil War soldiers avoided the hospital at all costs.

As the 33rd cared for their wounded and made camp, they could hear musket and artillery fire to their right. Since darkness was not far off and Sherman's advance was stopped, Grant had only one option left: a frontal assault on Missionary Ridge. Although this was thought to be the strongest part of the Confederate position, the defenses were actually poorly put together. Grant ordered a demonstration by Thomas' men against the rifle pits at the bottom of Missionary Ridge, which was a somewhat risky maneuver. Even if successful, the attacking force would then be vulnerable to heavy Confederate artillery and musket fire from the top of Missionary Ridge. The attack began at 3:30 P.M. and by 4:00 P.M. the rifle pits were taken. After the attackers realized the danger of stopping, the attack, almost spontaneously, continued right up Missionary Ridge. Even though the climb was difficult, sufficient numbers got to the top to tear big gaps in the Confederate line. As the assault was being made, Hooker's force arrived from Lookout Mountain and the combined Union forces ultimately controlled four and one-half miles of Missionary Ridge. Since this created a major threat for the remaining Confederate units, Bragg had no alternative but to withdraw from Missionary Ridge. Nothing had gone according to plan, but the Union had won the battle of Chattanooga.[60]

Even while events were building to a climax at Chattanooga, Grant had been under continued pressure from Washington to relieve Burnside at Knoxville since Burnside had mistakenly been reported to be in danger from Longstreet. After the Confederates retreated from Missionary Ridge, the pressure only escalated, which made Grant uncertain as to how to best follow up on the success of November 25. At first, he ordered one of Thomas' divisions under Granger to relieve Burnside, with the rest of Sherman and Thomas' forces to pursue the Confederates. At the head of the pursuit was Davis' division, which was not engaged at Tunnel Hill, followed by Howard's corps and the rest of Sherman's army. Although the pursuit continued until 4:00 A.M., a heavy fog made further efforts too difficult. Davis' division halted and was joined by Howard's corps at 7:00 A.M. Finally, an hour later, the fog lifted enough for them to proceed and the head of the pursuing column reached Chickamauga Station at noon.[61]

Although reveille was more conventional for the 33rd on November 26, it came well before daybreak, and by 4:00 A.M. the regiment was on the move, joining the pursuit. In spite of the early hour, morale was good due to the word of the Confederate retreat.[62] After a somewhat "tedious march" through the woods, the regiment rejoined the XI Corps.[63] The weather was clear and fine and morale continued to improve since for the first time the 33rd experienced the role of the pursuer.[64] Once across Chickamauga Creek, they moved towards Chickamauga Station.[65] When the regiment arrived there, they found the Confederate supply depots on fire and joined other units in recovering flour, grain, molasses, and other supplies.[66] During the day there was no fighting, but about dark, there was heavy firing to the front and the Confederates fell back. After a long day of marching, the regiment camped within four miles of Graysville.[67] Up ahead, the Confederate retreat reached Ringold where they waited for a Union attack early the next morning.[68]

While the pursuit continued on the morning of November 27, Sherman detached Howard's corps from the pursuit and sent them to Red Clay to cut the East Tennessee and Georgia Railroad.[69] Since Colonel Mindil was now temporarily in command of the brigade, Major Peloubet was in command of the regiment.[70] Along with the rest of the corps, the regiment marched rapidly through a "well wooded and mountainous district" to Red Clay where they destroyed three miles of railroad track. By the end of the war, the regiment would be as experienced at railroad destruction as at fighting. After their initial work of such destruction was complete, they camped for the night in a heavy drenching rain.[71] If the men had not yet missed their blankets and tents, they did now, and this was only the beginning. At the same time that Howard's corps was on this mission, the Union retreat was stopped at Ringold Gap where Cleburne handily stopped Hooker's pursuit. Wisely deciding not to push their luck, Grant, Hooker, and Sherman met at Ringold and formally called off the pursuit. Since Granger had not yet left for Knoxville, Grant decided to put Sherman in charge of the relief effort. Unfortunately for the 33rd, Grant also added Howard's corps to the force ordered towards Knoxville.[72]

After several days of fighting and the subsequent pursuit, the original plan was to make November 28 a day of rest for the XI Corps before returning to Chattanooga. Although the men did get some rest from marching that day, they were no longer on their way back to Chattanooga. Instead, they would join the long march towards Knoxville. And even though the XI Corps did not move that day, there were a lot of preparations to make for the march; this was not easy as supply wagons were all over the area with many stuck in the mud.[73] The 33rd remained at their campsite amidst a heavy rain that did not clear off until about 4 P.M., but the regiment did receive two days' worth of rations.[74] When the rations had been distributed, all wagons except for those carrying ammunition were sent back to Chattanooga.[75] Although winter was coming on, the march would begin with little food and no tents, blankets or extra clothing.

The 33rd began their march towards Knoxville at 6:00 A.M. the next day, moving towards Cleveland, Tennessee.[76] Perhaps the only good thing about the missing knapsacks was that the men's burdens were lighter than usual. Fortunately, the road was good, the weather clear, and the men relatively fresh.[77] With all these things in their favor, the regiment covered the 22 miles to Cleveland, which was described as "a pretty town." When the advance Union forces arrived about 5 P.M., the Confederate cavalry was withdrawing.[78] While the weather was clear, the march took place in a "bitter piercing cold" which continued throughout the night.[79] At least the regiment had plenty of firewood for their camp in a cornfield about one-half mile east of the town.[80] Although no one in the relief column could know, the march to Knoxville already was no longer necessary. Earlier that day, Longstreet's troops had been soundly defeated in a frontal assault on Burnside's position.[81]

Since Union commanders still believed that they were needed in Knoxville as soon as possible, the regiment moved again at 6:00 A.M. on November 30.[82] The goal of the day's march was Charleston on the Hiwassee River. Once again, the Union columns reached their destination just as Confederate cavalry, artillery, and about 300 infantry left. Although the Confederates were driven off, they did have time to destroy the pontoon bridge over the river, but not some railroad cars filled with rations. From this unexpected source of supply, the Union troops were able to get two days' worth of flour and a week's worth of salt. Repairs to the pontoon bridge took the balance of the day and evening, so the troops also got a rest,[83] although the conditions were unpleasant as the weather continued to be very cold with ice forming in puddles that could bear a man's weight. Since the men had no change of clothes or the opportunity to boil them, as they would have in camp, infestation with vermin became a problem.[84]

Thus fortified with a day's rest, the march got off to an early start on the first day of December with the regiment on the move by 5:00 A.M. Since the weather was so cold, the men were probably just as happy to be marching to generate some warmth.[85] After crossing the Hiwassee on the pontoon bridge, they passed through the villages of Calhoun, Riceville and Athens.[86] When the regiment camped for the night about two miles past Athens at 4 P.M., they had covered 18 miles in weather that was described as "fine."[87] Morale probably improved somewhat when word was received of the defeat of Longstreet's assault on November 29.[88]

The news of Longstreet's defeat did not, however, stop the march. On the morning of December 2, the regiment got off to a relatively late start, moving at 7:00 A.M.[89] Although the weather had improved, the roads had deteriorated, making for rough going.[90] After a stop for dinner at Sweetwater, the regiment continued on towards Philadelphia.[91] William Lambert warned the readers of the *Daily Advertiser* not to judge these villages by their impressive sounding names. According to Lambert, Philadelphia was "a weak, poor looking spot, whose riches are in its name." Lambert also noted that the regiment was in the same part of Tennessee where Andrew Jackson had fought the Indians. Perhaps wishfully thinking back to a simpler time, he commented that this was "when treason had not yet even in South Carolina dared to raise its hideous head."[92] The day was one of hard marching over bad roads by troops who were "much fatigued." After covering 17 miles, the tired men did not get into camp until 6 P.M. when it was quite dark.[93]

Having marched 35 miles in two days, the men had to be tired, but in spite of their late arrival, the regiment was off again well before daylight at 5:00 A.M. On this day, however, the march came to an abrupt halt at 8:00 A.M. after covering only 6 miles.[94] When the Union force reached Loudon, they found that all the river crossings had been destroyed, including the railroad bridge of which nothing was left but the stone pillars. Before retreating, the Confederates had also destroyed three locomotives, up to 75 railroad cars filled with commissary supplies, and a pontoon bridge. What was left of the railroad equipment and the cars' contents had been pushed into the main channel of the Tennessee River. In spite of all this destruction, there were still sufficient supplies left in the warehouses to resupply the XI Corps even after providing for the Confederate wounded.[95] The 33rd themselves received two days' worth of half rations from this source.[96] Like Lambert, Major Peloubet was singularly unimpressed with the towns they were passing through. Loudon, he wrote, was like the others, "stores, etc. deserted and closed, people, quiet and suspicious."[97]

While the bridge repairs were underway, the men got a well deserved day of rest. The weather continued to be mild, giving an additional boost to the men's morale.[98] Although the Confederate destruction of the crossings had been thorough, a crossing was established through a feat of "Yankee ingenuity." Howard's men found 30 Confederate wagons that were only partially damaged and repaired them sufficiently to drive them to Davis' Ford some six miles away. Once there, the wagons were driven into the river to create the base for a makeshift infantry bridge,

1st Lt. John J. Toffey, Company G, wounded at Chattanooga, November 23, 1863; awarded Congressional Medal of Honor. *U.S. Army Military History Institute.*

which was completed with movable trestles. Such ingenuity was also a sign of things to come. Throughout their campaigns in Georgia and the Carolinas, Sherman's army would find their way over and through water barriers that would have stopped less enterprising men. Gaps in the bridge were filled by planks taken from wooden building, as the local residents cheerfully helped in this effort.[99] Even though Major Peloubet had commented about "suspicious people," eastern Tennessee had a large pro-Union population. Their loyalty was the primary reason that Lincoln had put so much pressure on Grant to help Burnside.[100]

While there was no movement during the day, the regiment's respite from marching did not extend into the evening, as orders were received to be ready to move at midnight. By 1:00 A.M. on December 5 in "cold and frosty" conditions, the regiment was on the move towards Davis' Ford. After they arrived there, they waited until there was enough light to cross on the wagon bridge.[101] Many of the men probably wondered why they could not have done all their waiting in camp rather than move and then wait. But "Hurry up and wait" is a time honored military tradition. The crossing did not take place until 6:00 A.M., with horses and wagons fording the river. Even worse, the day's march did not end until 8:00 P.M. at Louisville, Tennessee, some 21 miles and 19 hours later.[102] Although this was no doubt an attempt to make up for lost time, no more such marches would be necessary. During the day, word was received that Longstreet had retreated from Knoxville and there was no need to complete the march.[103]

The forced march into eastern Tennessee had added to the regiment's ever expanding experience of the rural South, which would continue throughout the war. While Lambert preferred the area to some of the "barren desert plains" of Virginia, he was not thrilled with some of the local customs. Although Lambert did not want to believe that every woman in the area used tobacco, he lamented, "I saw no female who was not addicted to the use of tobacco in one form or another." Generalizing even further, he went on to observe, "Neither custom, nor the language and appearance of the people is prepossessing." But even Lambert's relatively brief experience in the war had taught him what was really important, and he praised the population's loyalty to the Union. While passing through Louisville, Lambert was particularly impressed with one young woman who cried out, "They said our town would never be blue with the Yankees again; but I knew better, and I said they would and now they've come. Hurrah for New Jersey." Sentiments such as these made up for a lot of tobacco chewing as well as long marches and bad weather.[104]

After the exertions of the prior day and the news from Knoxville, December 6 was a badly needed day of rest. Since it was also the Sabbath, the regiment's chaplain, John Faull, led worship in the local church. William Lambert was especially moved by hymns that created images of "peace and quiet in the years when wars shall be no more forever."[105] Major Peloubet reported that the men were in good spirits despite the lack of rations and the arduous marching.[106] During the day, Colonel Mindil accompanied Howard and Sherman into Knoxville to meet with Burnside.[107] Over a sumptuous dinner, Sherman became furious when he learned the true situation at Knoxville. In reality, Burnside had never been completely surrounded and was well supplied by the loyal citizens of east Tennessee. It can be hoped that the men never learned that their hard march over bad roads in some bad weather was essentially unnecessary.[108]

When the return march began on December 7, the men at least knew the destination and had some sense of the journey's length. In preparation for the march, corps commander General Howard sent his commissary officers ahead to seize local mills and grind grain purchased from local farmers. Since these mills operated day and night, there was at least bread for the return march.[109] Once the 33rd moved at 8:00 A.M., they were on their way "home or at least campward."[110] In another long day's march, they covered 17 1/2 miles and camped one mile south of Davis' Ford which they had earlier crossed on the wagon bridge.[111] Meat as well as flour was distributed during the day. Although rations were available, Major Peloubet reported seeing ambulances full of "barefooted and sore footed men unable to march."[112] A lack of shoes would be a chronic problem for the 33rd, but by the end of the war they would march on with or without them.

Things deteriorated the next day. The weather ceased cooperating and a 17-mile march was made in rainy and stormy weather.[113] Even so, the regiment passed through Philadelphia and camped one mile from Sweetwater on the Chattanooga side. Although Major Peloubet claimed that the men's spirits were good, there had to be an element of wishful thinking in the claim, as he also reported, "Rations are scarce and the great portion of the men are suffering much from the want of food and shoes." At least the weather improved on the next day's march, which ended about dark at Athens.[114] Once at Athens, the regiment would remain there until December 12 allowing for some badly needed rest. While the rest was important, stopping for two days was a calculated risk. As unpleasant as conditions had been, thus far there had been no snow or consistently subfreezing temperatures. Since the regiment was without blankets, tents, and now shoes, and had only limited rations, real winter weather would be a major disaster. During the next two days, the men rested, got some rations and even repaired some shoes as the 33rd got a supply of leather for essential shoe repairs.[115]

When the 33rd resumed the march on Saturday, December 12, they did so in a drizzle, which turned into heavy rain. In spite of the rain, however, the regiment covered 18 miles before they made camp two miles past Charleston.[116] After a long wet march, the men struggled to start fires in the pouring rain.[117] Even with the shoe repairs of the prior day, Major Peloubet reported, "Barefooted men are extremely numerous."[118] The next day's march began at 7:00 A.M. under cloudy skies and ended at Cleveland, the site of their camp on the first night of the march. When the regiment made camp, one-half mile out of town on the Charleston and Cleveland road,[119] they did so in heavy rain that had made the roads almost impassable. Since they were now within two days' march of Lookout Valley, it was considered prudent to stop again for a few days. The break would give the troops some rest and, with luck, allow the roads to improve. In addition, the proximity of Chattanooga allowed a supply train to bring in some rations. Without exaggeration, Major Peloubet noted that "the sight of a cracker was a great thing for the men."[120] Morale must have been at low ebb. Although still a relatively inexperienced regiment, their first combat had been followed by three weeks of some of the hardest duty imaginable.

James Titman, quartermaster. *U.S. Army Military History Institute.*

The morning of December 16 brought fine weather, and the regiment moved on good roads towards McDonald's Gap.[121] While the regiment's records recorded only one desertion on the march, that of Jeremiah Dodge, he had not, in fact, deserted and another member of the regiment would meet him again. That meeting would occur in a place that meant nothing in December of 1863, but would become synonymous with the worst suffering possible for Union soldiers—Andersonville

Captain Samuel F. Waldron, Company I, killed in action at Chattanooga, November 23, 1863; correspondent to the Newark *Daily Journal* as "Miles Alienus." *U.S. Army Military History Institute.*

prison.[122] At the beginning of the day, it appeared that those in command had picked the correct time to resume the march, but the worst was yet to come as the rain returned in the mountains. There, Lambert wrote, "in a storm which exceeds all that have gone before it, we make McDonald's Gap, where we sleep in mud, which nearly engulfs us."[123] According to Major Peloubet, the night was "the most miserable of the whole march."[124] Such weather could not help but affect the roads for the next day's march, which General Howard described in one word: "execrable."[125]

Finally, on December 17, the 33rd New Jersey returned to their camp in Lookout Valley. Although they marched in soaked clothing, at least there was no additional rain. They continued on the road for a short distance, but then went up the railroad past Tunnel Hill and Citico Creek, the site of their first combat[126] — the place, Lambert wrote, where Waldron and others "fell martyrs to the good cause of right and freedom." From there they marched through Chattanooga into their former camp in Lookout Valley.[127] Although the regiment had seen no combat on the march, they had won "a victory almost over nature herself."[128] Even though there had been no combat since Missionary Ridge, death was not absent. Andrew Hildebrand and James Bligh both died of disease in Chattanooga during this period. On the march itself, James Stoll of Company H was accidentally killed at Cleveland on December 14. Francis Mulvey and George Waters also died of disease, possibly contracted during the march.[129]

When Sherman's command returned to Lookout Valley, the struggle for Tennessee was over, a decisive triumph for the Union. As a result the Confederates had lost Tennessee forever and would now be on the defensive in the west. Instead of being a "starvation camp," Chattanooga would become a vast Union supply depot that would make possible the Atlanta campaign.[130] For the 33rd, the campaign marked, in Lambert's words the regiment's "baptism of blood." Lambert believed that the long march towards Knoxville and back had been more trying than combat itself.[131] Both Lambert and the rest of the regiment would have plenty of opportunity to compare both alternatives in the remaining 15 months of the war. But above all, Lambert praised the spirit of the men of the regiment, in the face of all their hardships. Like many young men of his generation, Lambert was quite mindful of the legacy of the American Revolution and wondered about the experience of earlier patriots at Valley Forge and Morristown. Surely, he thought, the suffering of those early patriots could not have been worse than the sufferings of the 33rd. Wet, cold, muddy, without blankets or tents, shoes worn out, and no regular rations, "yet the men pressed on with scarce a murmur."[132] One company commander wrote, "To chronicle the sufferings of the men and the patience with which they submitted to the various hardships is impossible."[133]

Sergeant John Fenner of Camden offered a similar perspective when he wrote his mother back in New Jersey. His description of the march was like the others,' but he went on to say that there was consolation for their suffering. Fenner felt that he was suffering not just for his country, but also "for my loved ones at home." Such experiences made him long for the day when he could step into his home and see his family living in peace. A day when the war "shall no longer torture the bodies of the poor soldiers and the hearts of their families." Unfortunately, Fenner would not live to see that day. Perhaps concerned that these sentiments were too heavy, Fenner closed on a lighter note, reporting, "I am as lousy as a hog."[134]

It would be improper to make too much of the 33rd's experiences at Chattanooga since the regiment's real combat service would come in the Atlanta campaign. But things had changed a great deal since the regiment left Newark in September. The ultimate sacrifices of Boggs, Waldron, Post, Seering, Mangold and others had at least wiped out the stigma of the "mutinous regiment." It is nice to know that in 1896, in honor of their sacrifices, New Jersey was the first state to erect a monument at Chattanooga in memory of her sons who fought there.[135]

IV

"I thought I could bear it without a tear"

While the officers and men of the 33rd took part in the battles at Chattanooga and the Knoxville relief expedition, the anxiety of family and friends in New Jersey was magnified by the nature of communications in 1863. Although news of the battles reached New Jersey relatively quickly by telegraph, any news of the fate of individuals had to wait, in most cases, for casualty lists to arrive at local newspapers. When the Newark *Daily Journal* finally published regimental casualty lists a week after the battle, misspellings still left doubts as to who had actually been killed or wounded. Lieutenant John Toffey, for example, was listed twice, once as Lieutenant Taffey and once as Lieutenant John J. Toppey.[1] The Paterson *Daily Press* received more efficient and happier news, when Captain Courtois of Company D wrote that no one from Paterson had been hurt. Stating the obvious, the paper observed that the news was "gratifying intelligence to many a mother and lover."[2]

Even with the misspellings and other confusion, there was no doubt that Captain Samuel Waldron had been killed. Throughout the next week, articles in the Newark newspapers disclosed both Waldron's role as "Miles Alienus," special correspondent for the *Daily Journal*, and that he had had a premonition about his death.[3] A veteran of service with the 27th New Jersey, Waldron had been a schoolteacher and amateur actor in civilian life. Most deeply affected by his death were his wife and two young children, for whom funds were now being raised.[4] In addition to the newspaper accounts of Waldron's death, Major Peloubet took time to write about Waldron to the War Department. According to Peloubet, Waldron had been under charges at the time of the battle. Since a battle was clearly imminent, Waldron asked "to be assigned to some honorable post." When he rejoined the regiment for the battle, the charges were withdrawn and Waldron died while giving his men "an example of determined steadiness rarely if ever equaled." Although Waldron had been in trouble for the drunken spree in Virginia, he had reportedly gotten off with a verbal

Francis Childs, 2nd lt., Company I; 1st lt., Company B. *U.S. Army Military History Institute.*

Charles Downs, 1st sgt. and 2nd lt., Company D. *U.S. Army Military History Institute.*

reprimand. Major Peloubet may have been talking about a new incident or perhaps using dramatic license with the prior one.[5]

A third casualty among the officers was Captain William Boggs, who died shortly after the 33rd's return to Lookout Valley. After being wounded at Citico Creek on November 23, Boggs' arm was amputated. Since his death came almost four weeks later, infection, all too common with Civil War wounds, seems the most likely cause of death. When William Lambert wrote to the *Daily Advertiser* of Boggs' death in early January, he did so as a newly promoted captain, Boggs' successor as commander of Company A. Like Waldron, Boggs was from Newark and he left a wife and three children.[6] While most of the dead at Chattanooga were buried in the new military cemetery there, the regiment paid to send both men's bodies home to Newark for burial. As a further gesture of their support, the regiment adopted resolutions that were sent to the Newark newspapers, praising both men and mourning their deaths.[7]

The bodies of both men were shipped by train from Chattanooga and arrived in Newark on January 15.[8] When Boggs' funeral took place on January 17 at the Methodist Episcopal Church on Halsey Street, there was "a very large concourse of friends" in attendance. The procession escorted the body from the deceased man's home on South Prospect to the church and then to Fairmount Cemetery for burial.[9] While Waldron's funeral came second, his ceremony was apparently a grander military affair. Some four days later, on January 21, the procession left Waldron's home at the corner of Wickliffe and Bank Streets and proceeded to Trinity Church on Military Park. At the head of the procession was a military escort and Rubsam's Brass Band, followed by the hearse. After the hearse came the male teachers of the public grammar schools with black crepe on their left arms. Also marching, with crepe on their left arms, were the children of the Second Ward School with the added touch

Chaplain John Faull, sometime correspondent to the Sussex *Register*. *U.S. Army Military History Institute.*

of a sprig of evergreen in the buttonhole. Since Waldron had been a teacher at the Second Ward School, all of the city's schools closed for the afternoon in his memory. After the Episcopal burial service for the dead was read at the church, the cortege proceeded to Fairmount Cemetery for the burial.[10] By 1863, Newark families had lost many of their sons in Civil War battles. However, the mourning for Boggs and Waldron demonstrated that the people of the city still cared about those who had made the ultimate sacrifice.

While these final farewells were underway, back in Lookout Valley the rest of the 33rd settled down to their first and only winter quarters of the war. Although the recent campaign had lasted well into December, this was fairly unusual. Since most roads were not paved, military movements were almost impossible in the winter months. Even though the norm was to suspend operations until spring, the 33rd seldom followed the norm. The winter of 1864 was the only time the regiment would enjoy such a respite from campaigning. Their first priorities were rest, eating and, no doubt, drying out. Among their hardships, the regiment had been unable either to send or receive mail during the march to and from Knoxville. Now back in a permanent camp, officers and men had the opportunity to get caught up on correspondence both personal and professional.

Alexander Eason, 2nd and 1st lt., Company F; Captain, Company B. *U.S. Army Military History Institute.*

Colonel Mindil used the time to deal with both regimental matters and self-promotion. When he wrote to State Adjutant General Stockton on December 20, Mindil actually did both at the same time. In a letter signed "your friend," Mindil reported on the campaign and asked Stockton and Governor Parker for help in being promoted to brigadier general.[11] Nine days later, Mindil apparently decided to eliminate intermediaries and applied directly to Abraham Lincoln. Although generals Howard and Hooker endorsed this application, no promotion was forthcoming.[12] Lincoln may have wondered why there was such a rush to promote someone who was not yet 20 years old. While pursuing his own interests, Mindil did not ignore regimental business, writing to the quartermaster in Washington to ask for 200–300 Zouave uniforms. Obtaining these uniforms would allow the 33rd to keep their distinctive outfits for at least one more year.[13] In a more practical effort to help some of the men, Mindil asked permission to pay 30 of the regiment's best soldiers as veteran volunteers in spite of some problems with their records. Apparently these men had received disability discharges, which raised questions as to whether they had performed the prior service necessary to receive the substantial Federal bounty.[14] Although there is no record of how this was finally resolved, one can only hope the men got their money, since they would certainly earn it by war's end.

Captain Barent Frazer, Company H; William Lloyd's commanding officer. *U.S. Army Military History Institute.*

Unconcerned with promotion or regimental issues, William Lloyd resumed his tense correspondence with his wife, Mary. Although her letters have not survived, if they were anything like his, then one must wonder what life was like when they were together. Not surprisingly, Lloyd was suffering from a bad cold due to the long march without blankets, tents or adequate food. But then he went on to respond to a request from her last letter. Not mincing any words, Lloyd told Mary that if she went out with any man other than two whom Lloyd apparently trusted, then he would "discard you forever, I may as well as speak plain." When Lloyd had gotten these feelings out of his system, he claimed he was too sick to write any more.[15] While Mary presumably did not want her husband to be sick, she was probably glad that this letter was fairly brief.

Although Lloyd had suffered on the march, he was still better off than the badly wounded John Toffey. However, in spite of his slow convalescence, Toffey, who was learning to walk with crutches, wrote letters of a gentler nature. While lying in bed on Christmas morning, Toffey had thought about his family, especially the children. Since he did not wish to be overly solemn, he assured his parents that he would be happy to celebrate a belated Christmas with them when he returned home and closed by wishing everyone a happy new year.[16] Toffey must have left Chattanooga fairly soon after that as he wrote to his parents on January 13 from Lincoln Army Hospital in Washington.[17] After further recuperation in Washington, Toffey returned home to New Jersey. When he wrote to his grandmother on March 11, he reported that one wound had completely healed. Unfortunately, the other had not changed much since the day it occurred, and Toffey noted fatalistically, "I presume there is more pieces of bone to come out."[18] This prediction proved accurate

2nd Lt. William Harrison, Company G. *John W. Kuhl Collection.*

by the end of April when Toffey informed "Friend Billy" that a one-inch piece of bone had come out of the wound, the fifth piece to do so. While Toffey would never return to active duty, he did recover sufficiently to join the Veteran Reserve Corps in Washington.[19] The Veteran Reserve Corps consisted primarily of wounded soldiers, unable to return to active duty, who could perform other duties, that freed other soldiers for duty in the field. Still in Washington in 1865, Toffey would be an eyewitness to history.

Perhaps the worst storm of the winter hit on the night of December 31. Rain was accompanied by gale force winds that ripped tent pegs out of the ground. Later the weather became so bitterly cold that the wet tent canvas froze and soldiers were forced to sleep by the fire to avoid freezing to death. However, the wind was so strong that the men got no heat on one side of their bodies and smoke and sparks as well as heat on the other.[20] As bad as the weather was around Chattanooga, things were worse at Nashville, where ten inches of snow fell.[21] Clearly, the army needed more than tents to get through the winter, so the men set about building log cabins. A typical cabin was eleven feet long, eight feet wide and six feet high.[22] Even though the cabins limited exposure to the elements, they did not provide adequate protection against the cold. Frequently, men would have to get up during the night and warm themselves by the fire before going back to sleep.[23]

The camp itself became a source of something far more lethal than the weather: disease. Hygiene was severely lacking in Civil War camps, where eating utensils were "cleaned" by scraping them and then not after every meal. Knives and forks would turn almost black before being "cleaned" by sticking them in the dirt.[24] Even worse than the condition of eating utensils was the inadequate disposition of human waste, which contaminated the water supply. The quality of the water used by the men was horrible, only mitigated by the fact that coffee (made with boiled water) was the beverage of choice. Almost without exception, Civil War armies suffered the most from disease when they stayed in one place for a long period of time. Remaining stationary contaminated the entire environment which, in turn, became a breeding ground for disease. While long marches in bad weather, like the Knoxville relief expedition, were difficult, they were nowhere near as dangerous as simply living in one place for an extended period of time.[25]

Since basic living conditions were so unhealthy it is no surprise that disease was a greater killer than battle. Of the 300,000 Union men who died during the war, two-thirds died of disease. By the end of the war there were 6 million cases of sickness, with the average soldier being sick more than twice a year. The most common illnesses were intestinal diseases, especially typhoid fever and diarrhea. Diarrhea was an almost "universal ailment," which would typically affect over 70 percent of all soldiers at one time during the year. Sometimes known as the "Tennessee quickstep," its prevalence led to the belief that "bowels are of more consequence than brains . . . in the army." While diarrhea was the most common illness, typhoid fever was the leading killer, spread either from person to person or through contaminated food and water.[26] Living in such conditions, there was little chance that the men of the 33rd could come through unscathed, and they did not. During the winter of 1864 typhoid fever claimed the lives of Nicholas Rheinheimer, William Barry, Thomas Henderson, Charles Greiner, William Townley, Andrew Folt and Edmund Leaver. Other forms of disease, including pneumonia and diarrhea, caused the deaths of Hiram Babcock, Charles Brehm, John Ford and Martin Krom. Seven of the eleven deaths occurred in either January or early February. The fact that the men were in weakened physical condition from the Knoxville relief expedition made them even more susceptible to the dangers of the unsanitary living conditions. During this period, there was only one death that was at all combat related, that of John Sortsman, who died of wounds.[27] The mere listing of the names does not make real the cost of these deaths. Charles Greiner left behind a widow and six children in Newark.[28]

After the deprivations the regiment had been through, the men must have been frustrated or worse to find that supplies around Chattanooga were still not adequate. Although not starving, the army was not yet on full rations, because the worsening weather made the use of the dirt wagon roads from Bridgeport difficult at best. This was a problem for the short term, but it was even more important for the future since Chattanooga could only support a spring offensive if the city was adequately supplied. When Colonel David McCallum was put in charge of all railroad operations, the problem was finally solved. Since there were plenty of supplies at Nashville, the first priority was to reopen the railroad to Lookout Valley. This was accomplished on January 14, when the connection from Bridgeport was reopened; this in turn connected Chattanooga to Nashville.[29] Only a week later, Lambert noted that in addition to badly needed rest, the regiment was getting sufficient rations and supplies, especially shoes.[30] Equally important to morale was improvement in mail delivery when a "station" was established near the camp so the mail did not first have to go through Chattanooga.[31] After the supply lines got sorted out, the standard issue of rations consisted of fresh bread daily, fresh meat two days in five, plus various forms of vegetables to prevent scurvy.[32]

Shortly after the railroad reopened, Stephen Pierson, who now became the adjutant, returned from New Jersey with 18 new recruits.[33] Among this group were what appear to be two sets of brothers, Charles and John Anys and John and Martin Braan. Only one of the four would ever return to New Jersey.[34] Just before the arrival of the new recruits, a special ceremony was held where General Howard presented the regiment with a "beautiful silk flag on behalf of the State."[35] According to one witness, Howard gave a "lengthy, animated and patriotic speech."[36] Howard emphasized that the new state flag was "in its proper place side by side with the stars and stripes" and told the men that their duty was to see that the two flags were never separated.[37] After Howard finished speaking, "cheer after cheer was given for him."[38] In responding for the regiment, Major Peloubet claimed that this was "the proudest day of my soldier's life" and pledged that, "no traitor hand shall every tarnish this beautiful banner, it shall never be dishonored."[39] When he wrote to the *Daily Advertiser* about the ceremony, William Lambert was no less eloquent. Lambert was confident the flag would be returned to Trenton "with no mark, with no association, which shall cause the State to regret having inscribed upon its silken folds the name of Her 33rd regiment."[40] Almost six months later these words would have a bitter taste, words more easily spoken on the parade ground than the battlefield.

A few days later on January 25 there was another ceremony, this one to present Chaplain John Faull with a new horse. When the regiment left Virginia in September they brought seven horses with them, six of which had now died, including Faull's.[41] Besides providing spiritual support for the regiment, Faull had been praised by Mindil for his bravery in helping to remove the wounded at Citico Creek.[42] In reporting on the ceremony, William Lambert claimed that no officer was more respected by the men on account of both his bravery and his commitment to the regiment. Even if Lambert exaggerated to some degree, there must have been truth in this, since the money to purchase the horse had been raised by the men in just a few hours.[43] In response for the gift, Faull named the horse "the maid of New Jersey" and thanked the regiment in a "neat, forcible and humorous way."[44] In addition to being popular, the chaplain certainly worked hard at his calling. The diary of a soldier from the 136th New York recorded his attendance at nine different prayer meetings held that winter in the 33rd New Jersey's camp.[45]

Although these ceremonies might not seem to be out of the ordinary, they stood out against the monotony of camp life. Another writer to the *Daily Advertiser*, "Nemo," complained that there was little going on except the "dull regularity of camp."[46] Shortly after this, life may still have been boring, but there was certainly a lot more activity. When the regiment first returned to Lookout Valley, the men were given a month to rest and recuperate. After the men had recovered from the prior campaign, the regiment resumed a full military routine of drill twice a day, dress parades as well as fatigue and picket duty. The weather improved from the harsher conditions that existed through the middle of January. "SH" wrote that as soon as the men had built log cabins and gotten appropriate clothing, the weather had turned springlike.[47] The relatively mild weather would continue for the rest of the winter. Men from other regiments described weather conditions as "pleasant" more than 50 percent of the time.[48]

Although welcome, the springlike weather was a harbinger of things to come, things that would not be so pleasant. William Lloyd wrote to his wife that the weather "makes me feel lazy," but more significantly, he noted that the sick had been sent to Murfreesboro, typically a sign of an impending move. Lloyd hoped any such move would be short "as the warm weather will kill me as fat as I am at present"; this was probably to some degree in jest. Lloyd soon turned to his real concern, another battle. He wrote, "What I dread is going into another battle, I saw enough when I was in the other one to satisfy my curiosity." Although Lloyd claimed he was not afraid, he did have "a dread," as anyone who had seen a battle "never need want to see another."[49] Since Lloyd had this much anxiety, it was probably just as well that he did not know that what lay ahead would show that Citico Creek was a skirmish, not a battle. Like Lloyd, Georg Muller praised the weather and the camp and wanted no part of a move.[50]

Despite the removal of the sick, no move was imminent. Actually at about this time, a number of men in the Army of the Cumberland went home on furlough. Most of these did so on the 30-day leave granted to units that had re-enlisted. As "SH" noted, these furloughs were not meant for the 33rd. "Nothing, he said, "but good, plausible and strong reasons could obtain one, as we had been in the field and away from home but a short time."[51] Whether for "good, plausible, strong reasons" or not, probably no one was surprised when the *Daily Advertiser* reported that the irrepressible Mickey Free was home on a brief leave. While Free claimed that the regiment was in good health and good spirits, Free himself was, no doubt, in better spirits.[52] Also on his way home was Colonel Mindil, who left Chattanooga on February 1 on sick leave. According to William Lambert, Mindil had been suffering from a heavy cold at the time of the battles around Chattanooga. Obviously the Knoxville relief expedition had done nothing to improve his condition.[53] Not sick but also on his way home was William Lloyd, who no doubt had an interesting reunion with Mary.

While this group was on their way home, some other men got to travel, but not to their homes. Patrick Slattery of Company K was certified as being insane and Corporal Jackson of Company A was detailed to take him to the hospital in Washington. When the train stopped in Wheeling, Virginia, Slattery was put off the train without Jackson's knowledge. As soon as Jackson discovered that Slattery was missing, he had the train stopped and searched, but to no avail. Finally, Jackson reported to the provost marshal, where he found that Slattery had been arrested as a deserter. Fortunately for both of them, Jackson had all the necessary paperwork. Once the confusion was cleared up, Jackson finished his assignment and delivered the unfortunate Slattery to the hospital in Washington.[54] Although the mental hospital was certainly not a pleasant place to be, it was preferable to being shot as a deserter.

At the same time that these members of the 33rd were traveling, the balance of the regiment spent the rest of the winter in Lookout Valley. During this period, the men found that a new form of duty had been added. The reopening of the railroad necessitated additional security, and as a result, the 33rd provided details of 100 men at a time to guard a section of the railroad between Bridgeport and Chattanooga. Such assignments lasted for two days before another group of 100 took over. Some of the men preferred this to other duty as "their time is then devoted exclusively to that, and they can easily make themselves comfortable."[55] According to Georg Muller, the regiment performed this duty fairly frequently. Although the reopening of the railroad required additional duty, Muller was especially grateful for the improvement in rations. Since the supply situation had improved, he had regained the 16 pounds that he had lost during the Knoxville expedition. Muller was also hopeful about the rumor that had the regiment guarding the railroad all summer, which he believed to be a universal sentiment as, "we really don't like the sound of the awful whistling of bullets."[56] The fact that both Muller and Lloyd put such sentiments in writing suggests that by 1864 soldiers no longer felt compelled to conceal their apprehensions about combat.

When Lieutenant Colonel Enos Fouratt returned at the end of February, he took over command of the 33rd from Major Peloubet. Fouratt had gone to Nashville on sick leave and then was detached for temporary duty there, thus missing the Chattanooga campaign.[57] After Fouratt assumed command at a dress parade on Saturday, February 20, there was a reunion of the officers that night in Fouratt's honor. In describing the event to his friend, John Toffey, William Cochrane wrote that the "Major laid aside *all his dignity* so we were quite fun and sociable,"[58] which might give some insight into the major's character. William Lambert described the event as one of "good feeling," but "in keeping with the strict requirements of discipline." However, Lambert did note that the meeting "adjourned before the Sabbath dawned," suggesting that the long winter's night was put to good use.[59]

At the same time that the officers were being "sociable," the enlisted men took advantage of opportunities to let off steam. John Fenner wrote to his mother about a boisterous party that took place on February 22. After some soldiers managed to forge sufficient paperwork, they were able to obtain whisky from a sutler. Thus fortified, what followed was "a good old fashioned drunk" including some fighting. When some officers tried to get involved, they received punches for their trouble, since "shoulder straps are of no consequence in a drunken crowd." Although one lieutenant literally had his shoulder straps torn off, Fenner claimed this was because the officer, like the men, was drunk. While Fenner did not want to see anyone get hurt, he felt that "a good healthy rough and tumble drunken spree was fun to

Quartermaster John Miller, HQ. *U.S. Army Military History Institute.*

watch."[60] One wonders how Fenner's mother responded to his behavior as a sergeant and especially as a son.

Going on furlough was wonderful, but ultimately the furlough came to an end. When he reached Nashville on March 11, William Lloyd was in the process of finding this out.[61] Besides the period of his furlough, Lloyd's return had been delayed due to some type of health problem.[62] The long trip back to Lookout Valley took a physical and emotional toll on Lloyd, who was tired, but more upset about leaving home again. Being back with the regiment drove home the obvious point that "this is not like home." But it was not just a matter of homesickness, as Lloyd told Mary how

John W. Jackson, corporal, Company A; 2nd lt., Company I. *U.S. Army Military History Institute.*

hard it was to leave her again: "I thought I could bear it without a tear, but I could not." Clearly, he also felt guilty about some of his behavior while he was home, so much so that he asked for forgiveness, admitting, "I was wrong sometimes, but you made me mad and I couldn't help it." Seldom sparing his wife's feelings, Lloyd closed by telling her to take care of young Harry, as "it may be the only thing you have to remember me by."[63]

A few days later Lloyd wrote again to tell Mary of his return to the regiment, which he found camped in the same place. Even though the men were glad to see him, they were also surprised, so that Lloyd now felt he "was a damned fool for returning at all." Although he was apparently not in trouble for returning late, he felt that the company commander, Captain Barent Frazer, was angry about something. There had apparently been discipline problems during Lloyd's absence. Frazer had had John Burke tied to a tree for two days for swearing. Since Lloyd claimed that Frazer swore at the men all the time, he found this punishment inconsistent at best. In addition, Lloyd also reported that Sergeant Miller of Company H was under arrest and was to be court-martialed. Clearly the boredom and loneliness of winter camp was taking its toll.[64]

While getting caught up on life in Company H, Lloyd also heard rumors that the regiment was going to rejoin the Army of the Potomac, which he did not believe. As March dragged on, William Lambert reported that rumors of all kind were rampant. Such rumors included the one that Muller had heard about guarding the railroad, and talk of movements to either western Virginia or to rejoin the Army of the Potomac as Lloyd had heard. The end of March saw the first significant snowfall, with almost a foot of snow on the ground. Lambert reported that the "camp is uproarious with the excitement of a snowball fight."[66]

In addition to the men returning from furlough, some new recruits joined the 33rd. Seeing these new volunteers led Lambert to hope that there would be enough new enlistments to avoid the draft, thus making all the regiments of New Jersey volunteer regiments.[67] After William Lloyd saw some new recruits, he had slightly different advice for anyone back home who was thinking of enlisting. He told Mary that any such person was better off in New Jersey. More importantly, the prospective volunteer would think so too, "if he ever got into a fight or stood picket on a dark cold stormy night." Then, "he would cry for his feather bed at home and wish for something to eat."[68]

Even though there was no major combat activity over the winter, 100 men from the regiment got a change of pace at the end of March, serving in a force under the overall command of Colonel Adolphus Bushbeck. Under the leadership of Captain Bray, assisted by Lieutenants Miller and Couse, the group from the 33rd along with three other regiments made a reconnaissance into Georgia. The mission lasted three days, but they had no contact with the Confederates. As the weather continued to improve in April, Lambert began to admit to a degree of boredom.[69] The winter camp of 1864 would be the regiment's longest time in one place. "SH" noted that they had been in Lookout Valley more than one-half of their time in the service.[70] Although Georg Muller was becoming increasingly tired of picket duty, he was not tired or bored enough to desire a return to the front, which he knew "is not a desir-

2nd Lt. William L. Shaw, Company A. *U.S. Army Military History Institute.*

able place to be." Perhaps knowing their stay near Chattanooga was not permanent, Muller as well as Lloyd took the opportunity to climb to the top of Lookout Mountain.[71] William Lambert wondered how much longer it would be before they would hear the almost forgotten words, "three days rations and sixty rounds." Lambert was appreciative of the mild winter, but he was also smart enough to recognize that there would be a price to pay for the warmer climate. He could see that "summer marches under a southern sky may not be quite as pleasant as a summer camp."[72]

William Lloyd also noted the arrival of spring, but the nicer weather did not seem to help his disposition. Lloyd now felt that everyone had forgotten him, and he had decided that if he survived the war, he would leave the country. Such expressions of feelings of sadness and loneliness apparently prompted Mary to respond in kind. Perhaps recognizing the impact of his letters, Lloyd hoped he was not making his wife sad. Although he promised not to write any more discouraging letters, it remained to be seen how long he could keep that promise. On a more hopeful note, Lloyd mentioned that he had applied for a commission with a colored regiment, which would mean more pay and another leave.[73] While this might have made Lloyd happy at least briefly, it was probably fortunate for all, especially the enlisted men in the colored regiment, that this never occurred.

All of these observers were accurate in recognizing that the winter hiatus was coming to an end. When General John Geary wrote to his wife in early April, he noted that the roads were still bad, but should be able to support troop movements by May 1.[74] At the end of April, Colonel Mindil left home to rejoin the regiment.[75] Upon his arrival Mindil found some changes in both the organization of the army and the officers of the regiment. Although General Hooker was still in command of the troops that had come west from Virginia, the XI and XII Corps had been merged to form the XX Corps. As part of this change, the 33rd would become part of the Second Brigade of the Second Division commanded by General Geary, more commonly known as the White Star Division.[76]

Changes in the regiment's officers had come about through both death and resignation. As was noted earlier, the death of Captain Boggs had resulted in the promotion of William Lambert to captain and commander of Company A. Lambert's promotion opened up the adjutant's position, which was filled by Stephen Pierson, who was promoted to 2nd lieutenant. The death of Captain Waldron led to Nathaniel Bray taking over as commander of Company I. After the regiment's quartermaster, James Titman, resigned in January, he was replaced by John Miller. Company B saw the promotion of Alexander Eason to 1st Lieutenant (he had joined with Company F as a 2nd lieutenant) to replace James Somerville who had resigned. Three other officers resigned during the winter: William Miller of Company D, George Begbie of Company F and William Harrison of Company G. Unlike William Lloyd, Harrison's application for a command of colored troops was successful. Taking their places were Charles Downs, Patrick Daily (a member of Company F before his promotion) and Charles Hemlee (also on Company F roster prior to being promoted) respectively.[77]

By the beginning of May, the 33rd had enjoyed an almost five-month respite from combat. William Lloyd and Georg Muller were wiser than they knew in dreading a return to the front. Gone forever were the days of a single battle followed by a long period of inactivity. The 33rd would not enjoy a significant period of rest for almost four months since it would take them and the rest of Sherman's army that long to travel the relatively short distance to Atlanta. But between them and Atlanta was the Confederate Army of Tennessee, defending the Confederate heartland and the last hopes of the Confederate cause.

V

"Bullets began to rain about me"

Throughout the winter of 1864, while the officers and men of the 33rd New Jersey enjoyed the relative security of winter quarters and endured its daily tedium, plans were being made for the spring and summer campaigns of 1864, which would set the regiment's future course. Although 1863 had ended well for the Union cause, 1864 was a presidential election year that had special risks. The election would be a national referendum on the war. Even the perception of not winning on the battlefield could lose the election and, thereby, the war. This reality was not lost on President Lincoln so he acted in March to strengthen and unify the Union high command. Ulysses S. Grant was summoned to Washington for promotion to lieutenant general and to take command of all Union ground forces. When Grant decided that his place should be in the east with the Army of the Potomac, he had no doubts about his replacement. As a result, William Tecumseh Sherman became commander of the Military Division of the Mississippi on March 18.

Before any plans for the spring offensive could be implemented, there was another major issue that had to be resolved. Although the opening of the railroad to Chattanooga had solved the day-to-day supply problems, the system could not yet support the logistical demands of an offensive deep into the Confederacy. For a spring and summer campaign, Sherman wanted to have at Chattanooga 70 days of supplies for 100,000 men and 35,000 horses and mules. Sufficient supplies were available at Nashville, but a lack of railroad cars plus the poor quality of the track severely limited the railroad's ability to provide ongoing support for an army in the field. With the approval of the secretary of war, Stanton, Sherman seized all of the railroads in the state, which almost doubled the supply of rolling stock. Steps were also taken to upgrade the railroad itself. By the spring the only major logistical concern was the danger of Confederate cavalry raids on the railroad.

When they planned the western portion of the overall Union strategy, Grant and

Map of the Atlanta campaign. *Andrea LaConte Magno.*

Sherman agreed the goal of the offensive should be Atlanta. Similar to Chattanooga, Atlanta was a railroad hub of great strategic importance. Four separate railroad lines passed through Atlanta, connecting almost all that was left of the Confederacy. As the center of this railroad network, Atlanta also attracted arsenals, supply bases, and the manufacturing of weapons and ordinance. While the destruction of these sources of military supplies was important by itself, the capture of railroad lines would deny Lee's army in Virginia a major source of their food supply. Furthermore, by taking Atlanta, the Union forces would be in an excellent position to drive further into the deep South. Finally, the conquest of Atlanta would wreak havoc on the Confederate strategy of winning by not losing while hoping for a favorable outcome of the presidential election. Sherman's emphasis on taking Atlanta as opposed to destroying the Confederate Army would benefit the soldiers, including the members of the 33rd New Jersey. Focusing on the city itself enabled Sherman to rely more on flanking movements than direct assaults with correspondingly lower casualty rates.

To execute these plans, Sherman had three armies that totaled in excess of 100,000 men. By far the largest of these armies was the Army of the Cumberland with 73,000 soldiers, larger than the entire Confederate army at Dalton, Georgia. Included in this vast force, commanded by General George Thomas, was the new XX Corps, the result of the merger of the old XI and XII Corps. Since their arrival from Virginia in the fall of 1863, these units had acted in a semiautonomous manner under General Hooker. The primary purpose of the merger was to end this status and to place Hooker (whom both Grant and Sherman disliked) under the direction of Thomas. As noted earlier, the 33rd New Jersey would now be part of the newly formed XX Corps. Although they were also designated as armies, the balance of Sherman's command consisted of the smaller 24,500 man Army of the Tennessee, under the leadership of General James McPherson, and the even smaller 11,400 man Army of the Ohio, commanded by General John Schofield.

Opposing this mammoth force was the Army of Tennessee, now commanded by General Joseph Johnston. When Confederate president Jefferson Davis replaced Braxton Bragg after the debacle on Missionary Ridge, he reluctantly appointed Johnston to take his place. Although Davis and Johnston disliked each other intensely, Davis simply had no other alternative. Throughout the campaign there would be constant friction between the two men, especially about the Army of Tennessee going on the offensive. Davis would consistently urge such action and Johnston would just as consistently contend that the army was not capable of doing so against a larger foe. When Johnston took command in December, there were 40,000 men in the army, with only two-thirds of them available for duty. While he awaited Sherman's opening move, Johnston's primary task was to improve the morale, equipment, and the training of his command.[1]

After the logistical issues were resolved, Sherman's next concerns were the natural barriers between his forces and Atlanta. Of special significance was the mountainous terrain of northern Georgia, its dense forests filled with undergrowth. Since these obstacles limited supply wagons to the existing roads, which were few, Sherman was further tied to the railroad.[2] The first natural barrier in northern Georgia was the aptly named Rocky Face Ridge, a 700-foot high ridge running north and south for miles. On the Atlanta side of the ridge, Johnston's army was in winter quarters at Dalton, Georgia. Since going around the ridge was not feasible, as it would detach Sherman's command from the railroad, they had to find a way over it.[3]

During February, General Thomas had led a reconnaissance expedition in and around Rocky Face Ridge. While there he found two routes over the mountain. One was Mill Creek Gap or Buzzard's Roost, northwest of Atlanta, the route of the railroad. Since this was the obvious approach, the gap was heavily guarded by the Confederates. Less heavily guarded was Dug Gap, some five miles south of Mill Creek Gap. As the name implies, Dug Gap was little more than a rough road cut or dug out of the ridge. When he returned from this expedition, Thomas was convinced that there were other openings over Rocky Face Ridge. A review of the very limited existing maps revealed Snake Creek Gap, about 11 or 12 miles south of Dug Gap. In a proposal with life and death implications for the 33rd New Jersey, Thomas recommended demonstrations against Mill Creek Gap and Dug Gap. While these actions were underway, the Army of the Cumberland would outflank the Confederates by going through Snake Creek Gap.[4] Further modifications of the proposal by Sherman would have even more severe implications for the 33rd.

The winter had given Sherman ample time to reflect on the disaster at Tunnel Hill in November, and he had apparently learned from the experience. That attack had been delayed for days due to the time that it took to move not only Sherman's army but its supply trains.[5] "Supply train" was a Civil War term for a large number of horse- or mule-drawn wagons, that carried supplies in addition to those carried by the men. These wagons moved slowly at all times, but especially over bad roads in bad weather; this could be a major problem in northern Georgia, which had little but bad roads. As a preventative measure for increased mobility, Sherman ordered that all excess baggage be left behind. Each regiment would be limited to one wagon and ambulance with a company pack mule for the needs of the officers. Division and brigade wagons would carry only "food, forage, ammunition and clothing."[6]

According to Stephen Pierson, adjutant of the 33rd, these instructions were followed by the men of the regiment, who carried almost everything they needed. Each man carried most of his own housing, which consisted of a shelter half, along with both a woolen and a rubber blanket. The eating and drinking utensils were usually limited to a canteen and tin plate. The men also carried the coffee, sugar, and hardtack portions of their rations. The balance of the infantryman's burden was his musket and 60 rounds of ammunition, 40 in a cartridge box and 20 in a haversack.[7] Since the men always carried the haversack with them, they used it to carry the basic essential items, rations and bullets. Blankets and the shelter half were carried in the knapsack, which was normally left behind for greater mobility when the unit went into combat. When the 33rd had followed this standard procedure at Citico Creek, the result was their going on the Knoxville relief march with no more protection than their overcoats.

When Colonel Mindil returned from sick leave on May 1, even the most wishful thinker must have known that departure from Lookout Valley and a new campaign was imminent. On the next day the 33rd had a final skirmish drill, a last tune-up for the campaign. Then on May 3 Mindil received the orders that many had been dreading, but all had been expecting. The regiment was to move the following day.[8] When the 550 officers and men of the 33rd left Lookout Valley at 4 P.M., they began the march with the physically demanding climb up and over Lookout Mountain.[9] Once over the mountain, they proceeded across the old Chickamauga battlefield where some of the shallow graves were wearing away.[10] Both the arduous climb and

The Union assault at Dug Gap. *Harper's Weekly.*

the reminder of the ultimate risk of combat were signs that the forthcoming campaign was going to be hard and dangerous. Since most of the day's march had been vertical, the regiment covered only four miles before making camp one mile from Rossville, Georgia.[11]

After breaking camp at 8:00 A.M. on May 5, the regiment and the rest of the Second Brigade joined the balance of the Second Division of the XX Corps. Since they were now moving over easier terrain, the 33rd covered 12 miles including passing through Rossville Gap.[12] At the end of the day they camped at the intersection of the Ringold and Rossville roads near Harrison's Farm, some four miles outside of Ringold.[13] Although the campaign had just begun, some soldiers like Martin Denniston were already having difficulties. Denniston was a new recruit who had only experienced the easy life of winter camp. Now that the regiment was on the move, he complained that the regiment had "marched all the week early and late," giving him sore feet. Reacting in the time-honored pattern of new recruits on the march, Denniston left along the way his "overcoat, woolen blanket, Zouave jacket and everything I did not need."[14] While this may have made Denniston's load somewhat lighter, disposing of his Zouave jacket did nothing for Colonel Mindil's efforts to maintain the regiment's distinctive uniform.

When the regiment broke camp at 5:00 A.M. the next day, May 6, the combination of avoiding the heat of the day and some lighter loads probably made the day's march somewhat easier. The 33rd moved past Ringold and made camp early near Pea Vine Church. Although the next day also began early with the regiment again on the march at 5:00 A.M., this time they did not stop until dusk. During the day's march, they crossed over Taylor's Ridge and camped on the Rome Road. Since the 33rd was now in the vicinity of the enemy, the regiment put out their first pickets of the campaign while the rest slept in a line of battle.[15] After four days of marching, the regiment was now within a day's march of the Confederate headquarters at Dalton. However, between the two armies was not just a day's march but also the imposing obstacle of Rocky Face Ridge. Looming high above the 33rd's camp, it was almost twice as high as Missionary Ridge, and it was steeper and consisted of solid rock and large boulders, all of which favored the Confederate defenders.[16]

On the other side of Rocky Face Ridge, Confederate commander Joseph Johnston knew of the approach of the Union Army. Johnston hoped Sherman would attack the heavily defended Mill Creek Gap, but he believed a flanking movement at the south end of the ridge was more likely. Before the campaign began, General Thomas' proposal to Sherman had been for the huge Army of the Cumberland to do just that. Thomas' idea was for his command to move through Snake Creek Gap while the two smaller armies kept the Confederates busy by demonstrating against Mill Creek Gap and Dug Gap. Although Sherman approved the basic proposal, he changed the specific assignments. The Army of the Cumberland and the Army of the Ohio would do the demonstrating and McPherson's Army of the Tennessee would move through Snake Creek Gap.[17]

These changes made the 33rd unlucky not once, but twice. If Thomas' original proposal had been accepted, the regiment would have been part of the force marching through Snake Creek Gap, thus avoiding any contact with the Confederates. Once Sherman changed the roles of the participants, the 33rd became part of the force that would do the demonstrating. Since the regiment was to move against the more lightly defended of the two gaps, this would appear to have been less dangerous. However, the stronger position at Mill Creek Gap was so well defended that no direct assault was made. The regiment had two chances to avoid combat at Rocky Face Ridge, by being part of the original flanking movement or by being part of the force assaulting Mill Creek Gap. Neither happened, so the 33rd would now take part in the main assault at Dug Gap.[18]

Dug Gap might not have been as impregnable as Mill Creek Gap, but the difference was academic. The position was not heavily defended only because the Confederates did not believe that the Union army would be foolish enough to attack there. This part of Rocky Face Ridge was described as "an almost inaccessible mountain, steep, thickly wooded, and crested with a rocky palisade." The gap itself was little more than a "slight depression in the palisades," into which a road had been dug. The natural palisade of rock allowed access to the top at only a few sporadic breaks.[19] On May 8, Dug Gap was defended by only 1,000 Confederate troops, but some of defenders believed the position offset a ten-to-one manpower disadvantage.[20] To "demonstrate" against this position, Thomas sent the Second Division of the XX

Corps under General John Geary. Geary's orders were to take Dug Gap, if possible, but he was at least to keep the Confederates busy during the movement through Snake Creek Gap. Geary was a politician who hoped to use military victories to political advantage,[21] so he intended to use every opportunity to the fullest as he had at Lookout Mountain.

The Second Division consisted of three brigades, but one of these had been detached on the prior day. At about 11:00 A.M., the remaining two brigades and two artillery batteries moved towards Dug Gap, but without the 33rd New Jersey. The 33rd had been left behind on picket duty, but this good luck was only temporary. Although it was only the first week in May, the weather was "hot and stifling." Geary had no map of the area, so he took a local citizen along as a guide as they marched five miles into Mill Creek Valley. When they entered the valley, Geary's command encountered their first opposition from some Confederate cavalry pickets. Once contact was made, the Confederates promptly retreated across Mill Creek and up the road to the crest, where the main Confederate force was in plain view. Before advancing any further, Geary deployed his artillery so that their fire could reach the ridge. After the artillery was in place, the two brigades formed in two lines of battle and at about 3:00 P.M. they crossed Mill Creek preparatory to assaulting the ridge. Crossing the creek was itself difficult as there were marshy thickets on both sides and the bottom of the creek was treacherous.[22]

Captain Henry Bartlett, Company G, killed in action at Dug Gap, May 8, 1864. *U. S. Army Military History Institute.*

Colonel Bushbeck's arrangements for the Second Brigade's portion of the assault had the 134th New York on the right flank and the 73rd Pennsylvania on the left. In between these two regiments were the 27th Pennsylvania and the 154th New York on the right and left center respectively. Out in front of the line of battle were the 119th New York as skirmishers. When the Second Brigade units began to climb the mountain, the ascent was so steep that the men had to take frequent rests. Once the attackers reached a point within 300–400 yards of the palisades of solid rock at the top, they came under steady Confederate fire. Although some of the Union troops got through breaks in the rock to reach the top and even plant their regimental flags, they were soon driven back. Two separate assaults were made without success, and finally the Union forces had to fall back. Since the ground was so steep near the top, the regiments from left to right center had to fall back some distance to reform. On the far right the 134th New York was more fortunate and only had to withdraw about 100 paces.[23]

As the two unsuccessful assaults were being made, the 33rd was relieved from picket duty and ordered to rejoin the brigade and, therefore, the battle. When troops first approached a battle, their view was very limited due to the combination of smoke and terrain. Although at Dug Gap smoke was less of a problem, the elevated nature of the battlefield obscured the view even more than normal. The regiment had watched a similar kind of assault at Tunnel Hill, but there most of the fighting took place closer to the bottom. At Dug Gap the opposite was true. The 33rd moved towards the base of the ridge along a narrow road clogged with both artillery and ambulances. Casualties, in this case in ambulances, were normally the first thing that a regiment could actually see of a battle.[24] Obviously this never helped morale, especially if the men knew any of the victims. Since the attacking force was from the same brigade there was some chance of this being the case.

Although both of the prior assaults had failed, the Union forces still greatly outnumbered the Confederate defenders, probably by almost to five to one.[25] Since Geary was aware that Confederate reinforcements had to be on the way, any chance of success required prompt action. In preparation for another assault, Geary ordered one of his batteries to open fire on the summit to cover an attempt from the right.[26] Once the 33rd arrived, they were just in time to have "the honor to try to get up there."[27] This time, the attempt would take place about one-half mile to the right of the original assault, since no Confederates had been seen in that area. The rest of the brigade was to keep the Confederate defenders busy while the 33rd would try to outflank them. When and if they got to top of the ridge, cheers from the regiment would be the signal for an assault by the rest of the brigade.[28]

As the men left their knapsacks at the foot of the ridge, some of them may have wondered when they would see them again, even if they survived the attack.[29] Things went poorly right from the beginning of the assault, as the climb alone was incredibly difficult.[30] Even today the road through Dug Gap is a difficult climb by car, much less on foot with a rifle and other equipment. The footing consisted primarily of slippery and loose stones that provided little or no traction. The men had to grab onto bushes just to avoid falling back down the mountain.[31] While climbing, the regiment drew "moderately heavy" fire from the Confederate skirmishers. When the regiment got part way up the ridge, they hit the first palisade of perpendicular rock. The assigned route of attack was blocked by "steep, perpendicular rocks and inaccessible cliffs" that could not be scaled, so the men were forced to move to the left. Although they were not able to proceed as directed, the regiment was at least able to connect with the 134th New York on their left.[32] Since the men would not have been in prime campaign condition yet, the climb up a slippery, steep slope in hot weather must have left them exhausted as they reformed. All along the line men would have been draining their canteens or gasping for air.

The original flanking maneuver was no longer viable so the last chance was for a joint force of the two regiments to storm the crest.[33] Two large companies of the 33rd would go first as skirmishers, one out in front and one on the flank. Four other companies from the regiment would be positioned on the left of the New York regiment. This "storming" party, under the command of Colonel Mindil, would charge the summit.[34] While the attack proceeded, the balance of the 33rd, 200 lucky men, would stay in reserve either to follow up a successful attack or to resist a counterattack should the assault fail.[35] Martin Denniston, one of the greenest members of the regiment, was one of the skirmishers. His experience of combat began with his seeing Captain Sandford shot through the right knee; the leg would be amputated, ending the captain's war. Although there was apparently no shortage of bullets coming at the attackers, Denniston did not actually see a Confederate until he was almost at the top of the ridge. Half bent over, carrying his musket at his side, Denniston saw a man step from behind a tree and raise his weapon. Denniston dropped to the ground and the bullet hit about six inches from his side. Reflecting on this near miss, the new recruit could only say, "I cannot express my feelings at that moment." In spite of this experience, Denniston kept going, spending the next 20 minutes moving from tree to tree, firing as he moved. Finally the skirmishers could go no further and took cover as best they could.[36]

Behind the skirmishers, the main force also had little success as they tried to advance towards the crest. Captain Henry Bartlett of Company G was killed leading the charge of his company. First Lieutenant Joseph Miller of Company E was ordered to take Bartlett's place, but he was wounded almost as soon as he arrived. As he lay on the ground urging the men on, he was killed by a second shot.[37] Second Lieutenant Sidney Smith was next, but his right arm was shattered by a minie ball. Adjutant Stephen Pierson said Smith's screams sounded "as if some great animal was in mortal agony and terror." While Smith was half running and rolling down the side of the mountain, his suffering provoked a strange reaction. According to Pierson, "in spite of the tragedy of it all and the tragedy that was going on all around us, we couldn't help laughing, though we knew it might be our turn next."[38] Although this took gallows humor or denial to a new low, Smith was probably in too much pain to be aware of the lack of support from his comrades.

The climb got even harder as the men neared the top. They had to climb around large boulders while dodging others that the Confederates were rolling down on them. The combination of moving "over treacherous rolling boulders and under heavy constant volleys of musketry" was as deadly as it could be.[39] The 33rd was now at the heart of the lethal chaos of the battlefield. The terrain and smoke severely limited visibility, while the smoke as well as the brutal ascent made it hard to breathe, much less fight. At the same time, the air was full of "lethal projectiles" with sounds ranging from crackling and screeching to high pitched whines. An added sound and danger was that of bullets ricocheting off trees, boulders, and rocks. Less frequent but far more sickening was the sound of bullets hitting flesh.[40]

The combined force reached a second set of palisades, even steeper and more inaccessible. Here, Lambert reported, probably with some hyperbole, "Undaunted by the rocky walls, with cheers and yells, men gallantly endeavored to gain the summit and despite the terrible obstacles many reached the crest only to fall beneath the murderous bullet or to be pushed headlong to the rocks beneath."[41] While not in any way discounting the regiment's courage, what probably carried the men to the top was the physiological reaction to stress that sustained many Civil War charges. In such situations, adrenalin and norepinephrine are secreted into the bloodstream by the adrenal glands, creating a "flight or fight" reaction. Although the first impulse is to flee, if this is resisted, the individual becomes oblivious to danger and fear with "almost superhuman strength and agility."[42] All accounts agreed that some members of the regiment moved through gaps in the rocks to reach the top. However, the gaps were so small that only a few men could get through at a time and there were never enough to maintain a position on the crest.[43]

James Deegan, 1st sgt., Company F; sgt. major, HQ; 1st lt., Company H. *U. S. Army Military History Institute.*

Finally, all of the attackers withdrew at least 30–50 yards from the summit of the ridge.[44] They held on there while the Confederate fire eventually died down, which gave Adjutant Pierson, in his first battle, the opportunity to pick up a Confederate musket. When he began firing at some Confederates, this foolhardy move revealed the position of Pierson and an old veteran. Not surprisingly, the result was that "bullets began to rain about me and the old veteran." Unconcerned about rank at a time like this, the old veteran said, "Adjutant, you fool, stop that nonsense." Fortunately both of them survived Pierson's ill-timed offensive.[45] Although this may

Stephen Pierson, sgt. major, adjutant, captain, and major, HQ; author of "From Chattanooga to Atlanta in 1864." *U.S. Army Military History Institute.*

have offered some comic relief, the regiment now had to listen to the suffering of their wounded comrades. For the wounded the first sensation was normally not pain, but numbness around the wounded area such as when hit with a club or a hammer. However, before long this would be followed by the combination of pain and thirst.[46] Dug Gap was not the last time, that the regiment had to listen to the cries of their fallen comrades; cries for help, cries for water, cries of pain, and ultimately cries of despair, cries that had no answer.

The 33rd remained in this physically and emotionally uncomfortable position until 7:00 P.M., when Geary learned that McPherson's army was safely through Snake Creek Gap. Since there was no longer any reason to hold the position, the entire division withdrew to the foot of the mountain. As the 33rd moved into the woods and made camp, they were exhausted, hungry, mindful of their losses, and painfully aware that the campaign had begun in earnest. Concerned about the possibility of a Confederate counterattack, Geary ordered the troops to build breastworks,[47] which would become a way of life in the Atlanta campaign. As a further deterrent, Union artillery opened fire on the Confederate positions so that "by the light flashes of the division artillery actively playing upon the crest, the troops went into bivouac."[48]

After the Second Division of the XX Corps withdrew from Dug Gap, the first battle of the Atlanta campaign was over. Since the Union forces lost 357 men, killed, wounded or missing compared to less than 20 for the Confederates, the battle has been described as "a one sided Confederate victory."[49] However, success in the Atlanta campaign can and should be measured in a number of different ways. The successful movement through Snake Creek Gap made Rocky Face Ridge untenable as a Confederate defensive position. Even with these losses, Sherman had gotten past one of the most difficult physical barriers to Atlanta in one day with limited cost. To this

Captain James R. Sandford, Company B, had his leg amputated after being wounded at Dug Gap, May 8, 1864. *John W. Kuhl Collection.*

day there is no clear explanation as to why the Confederates did not defend Snake Creek Gap. Perhaps the best answer comes from a historian who claims that in 25 years of study, he had found "no evidence that the Rebel high command knew of Snake Creek Gap."[50] Certainly this would not surprise anyone driving through the gap today. All that makes the passage possible is a slightly lower elevation than the rest of the ridge and the absence of solid rock like that at Dug Gap. Although the Union march through Snake Creek Gap was unopposed, the assault on Dug Gap contributed to the success of the flanking movement. Severely outnumbered, Joseph Johnston's ability to withstand threats to his defensive position was limited. As a result, the tenacity of the Union attack at Dug Gap lessened, at the very least, any threat to McPherson's movement through Snake Creek Gap.

When the 33rd withdrew from the heights of Rocky Face Ridge, they had to leave behind their dead and some of their wounded. Among the dead were the aforementioned Captain Bartlett, who was from Centerville (now Roseland), and Lieutenant Miller, who was from Newark. Bartlett, a Princeton graduate, left behind a widow and four daughters.[51] Also killed during the assault were Mark Bradley and George Beyer of Company G, Lorenzo Schnarr and Frederick Witt from Company A, Casper Schafer of Company B and Walter Brown of Company D.[52] In addition to these fatalities, a total of 25 officers and men were wounded including Captain Sandford, severely wounded in the right leg, and 2nd Lieutenant Smith, severely wounded in the arm. Both officers were from Newark.[53] While both Sandford and Smith still were alive, their problems and those of the rest of the seriously wounded had only begun. Like Louis Mangold at Missionary Ridge, they were about to experience firsthand the inadequacies of medical care in the 1860s. Unfortunately for the participants, the war occurred at the end of the medical "middle ages," just prior to major breakthroughs in germ theory.

Wounds to the head, neck and abdomen were almost always fatal, but fortunately they were not the most common types of wounds. This dubious distinction belonged to wounds of the arms and legs, which had a positive survival rate of seven to one. The pain of being wounded was bad enough, but the suffering caused by the wound was magnified by the fact that a musket ball wound was worse than those caused by modern bullets. Modern bullets are sterilized by the heat produced by travel at high speeds, but musket balls were not sterilized in this way and almost always brought clothing, skin, and dirt into the wound. Such wounds caused more pain, bleeding, and almost always infection.[54]

After being removed from the battle, the wounded were taken to the foot of the mountain on stretchers or blankets, which did nothing for their condition. Once that ordeal was over, they were moved by ambulance (at that time, a horse-drawn wagon) to the field hospital about one mile away. On the way to the field hospital, the only care that was typically provided was to try to stop the bleeding. Upon arrival at the field hospital, the first step was triage. For those with wounds of the extremities, like Sandford and Smith, the options were limited to amputation or resection. Resection involved the surgical removal of a section of bone, which could leave the patient with a useless limb. Furthermore, the splintering of bones by minie balls carried the potential for chronic bone infection. While the surgeons and doctors did not understand what caused these infections, they did observe the results of the two types of treatment, which led to the more frequent use of amputation.[55]

Amputation was, therefore, the course of treatment chosen for Captain Sandford, who would have waited his turn on the operating table. Although, mercifully, anesthesia in the form of chloroform was available, the operation itself "violated every canon of modern asepsis." Nothing was sterilized; not the hands of the surgeon, his clothing, his instruments or anything he handled during the operation. Not surprisingly this led to an "appalling ratio of wound infections," followed by "an even more appalling mortality rate." When the patient did avoid infection, there was still the risk of a secondary hemorrhage, which was often fatal.[56] Captain Sandford survived the experience and was discharged in September.[57] For some reason, 2nd Lieutenant Smith received the less popular treatment, resection of the radius. Even though Smith survived the procedure, in July Chaplain Faull reported that the result of the wound and the surgery was the "probable imperfect use of his arm forever." Ultimately Smith was discharged for disability at the very end of the war in April of 1865.[58]

Four of the wounded that were brought off of the mountain ultimately died. The first was Henry DeCosta, who died a week later at Resaca. DeCosta was followed by Francis McPartland, who died at Chattanooga on May 24, and John Mullen, who died at Nashville on July 13. The last of these fatalities was George Conklin, who lingered on until September 5, when he died in the hospital at Louisville. Another of the wounded, Abraham Heiss, a Dutch immigrant, spent months in the hospital but survived a wound to his shoulder. Heiss was hampered by the effects of his wound for the rest of his life. Of the severely wounded who had to be left on the mountain, at least two were taken to Confederate hospitals in Atlanta. One of these, John Nix, died there on July 20, the same day that the regiment saw their fiercest combat of the war.[59]

The other badly wounded man was Sergeant John Fenner, who had written to his mother about the drunken brawl during winter quarters. There was apparently correspondence about Fenner's fate, but only two letters from the regiment to Fenner's family survive. William Jones wrote in response to a letter from the family on July 6 and reported that Fenner had been wounded, taken prisoner, and moved to Atlanta. Jones concluded with an incredible combination of optimism and ignorance by writing, "I am very happy to inform you that I expect he will recover soon, but I am not certain how bad the wound is." In a second letter, written to Fenner's mother on August 10, Adjutant Pierson at least had the sense to say only what he knew, that Fenner had been captured at Rocky Face Ridge. One can imagine the anxiety of Fenner's family, still unable to learn his fate two to three months after the battle. The story does not have a happy ending. Fenner, who had been wounded in both legs, died in Atlanta on May 28 and was buried in the National Cemetery at Marietta, Georgia. Fenner had written to his mother at the end of December, praying that "the Lord hasten the day when this war shall no longer torture the bodies of the poor soldiers and the hearts of their families." Fenner's suffering was over, but the pain in the hearts of his family had just begun.[60]

VI

"More like hell than God's beautiful earth"

While the 33rd was engaged at Dug Gap, McPherson's Army of the Tennessee moved through Snake Creek Gap, making Rocky Face Ridge no longer tenable as a Confederate defensive position. Even more important, McPherson was in a position to cut off the Confederates from both the railroad and their route of retreat. Unfortunately, he failed to take advantage of the situation and the Union Army missed a golden opportunity. Some of McPherson's units advanced to within one mile of the railroad village of Resaca on May 9 and found the village only defended by a small Confederate force. Although the Confederates were incapable of stopping the Union troops, McPherson was confused about the actual strength of the enemy and was afraid of being cut off, himself. Finally, the Union general decided that an attack was too dangerous and ordered a withdrawal back to the entrance of Snake Creek Gap. McPherson notified Sherman of his actions and awaited further orders.[1]

As McPherson hesitated near Resaca, the Union army north of Rocky Face Ridge exchanged artillery fire with the Confederates. There were a few skirmishes, but there was no renewal of the prior day's assault.[2] Indeed, the Union leadership was still concerned that the Confederates might launch an attack of their own. The 33rd remained in their camp from May 8 through May 11 and performed some picket duty.[3] The regiment now had a new commander, Colonel Mindil having left the regiment on May 9. Mindil had been ordered to the hospital in Chattanooga for treatment of an injury, so Lieutenant Colonel Fouratt took charge of the regiment.[4] While Mindil recovered, he was assigned to temporary duty as the head of a board of examination for those seeking commissions with U.S. colored troops. Since Mindil would be away through July, Fouratt would command the 33rd for the remainder of the regiment's combat service.

After Sherman learned of the missed opportunity at Resaca on May 10, he still wanted to try to cut off the Confederates' route of retreat. To this end, he sent almost the entire army through Snake Creek Gap in the hope that there was still time to get between the main Confederate force and Resaca. Sherman ordered the XX Corps to lead the movement, but the opportunity was gone. By the time the bulk of the Union Army got through the gap, the Confederates were at Resaca in force.[5] Since Geary's division was the last part of the XX Corps to move, the 33rd New Jersey relieved the 20th Connecticut on May 11 so that regiment could join their division for the movement through Snake Creek Gap. During this period, the 20th Connecticut had been guarding Boyd's Trail, which connected Mill Creek Gap with Dug Gap on the northern side of Rocky Face Ridge. The assignment required manning a long circular picket line that guarded the trail from both sides. In addition the regiment occupied a fortified position on a "hog back" hill overlooking the trail where it met the main road. In order to undertake this assignment, Lieutenant Colonel Fouratt had to lead the regiment on a two and one-half mile march. Since Fouratt had little knowledge of the countryside, the regiment moved carefully with "skirmishers and flankers well out." Guided by the brigade engineering officer, the 33rd arrived at 10:00 A.M. without incident and relieved the Connecticut regiment. After the regiment went into position, Fouratt became concerned that they had to carry out this assignment with 450 men, about half the strength of the Connecticut regiment. Although there was some minimal, ineffective artillery firing at night, there was no real danger as the Confederates had turned their attention to Resaca.[6] The night passed safely, but a change in the weather made things "excessively wet, cold and unpleasant."[7]

The Second Division of the XX Corps moved towards Snake Creek Gap at noon on May 12, but the 33rd was not relieved from their assignment in time to move with them.[8] Marching on their own, the regiment proceeded into the narrow pass, trying to catch up with the division.[9] The march was another experience of the rural South. Snake Creek Gap was described as a "wild, densely, wooded, narrow and picturesque pass" with few signs of habitation and "penetrated only by the midday sun."[10] While in the gap, the 33rd passed the other two New Jersey regiments in Sherman's army, the 13th and 35th regiments. When they saw each other, "you may be sure," William Lambert told the readers of the *Daily Advertiser*, "the meeting of the three representations of Jersey was hearty and the greetings loud."[11] Hundreds of miles from New Jersey, in the wilds of northern Georgia, any remembrance of home must have boosted everyone's morale. Although the inadequate road and volume of traffic made the march difficult, the 33rd rejoined the division during the afternoon just past the end of the gap.[12] By nightfall, the Second Division was encamped in Sugar Valley on the far side of Rocky Face Ridge.[13]

After the bulk of his command had passed through the gap, Sherman advanced his army slowly towards Resaca on May 13. The road through Sugar Valley was no better than the road in the gap and they did not reach Resaca until late afternoon. Like many villages between Chattanooga and Atlanta, Resaca was little more than a few buildings surrounding the railroad. In an ironic twist for any officers who took part in the Mexican War, the village was named after the battle of Resaca de Palma in that war. The Federals advanced to a position on a range of hills on the western side of the valley and found the 50,000-man Confederate army in strong positions on the hills of the eastern side. Although the Confederates were well dug in with both flanks protected by rivers, their defensive position did have a major weakness on the left. At that point, any crossing of the Oostanaula River would threaten the entire Confederate position, much as the flanking movement through Snake Creek Gap had done at Rocky Face Ridge. Sherman believed that the Confederates would retreat south rather than fight at Resaca, so he was more concerned about pursuit. When Sherman issued his orders for an attack on May 14, the plan was similar to that at Dug Gap. While an attack kept the Confederates busy, a crossing of the Oostanaula would be attempted four miles southwest of Resaca at Lay's Ferry. If successful, the operation would once again put the Confederates in danger of being cut off from both the railroad and their line of retreat.[14]

As the Union army moved into position, the Second Division of the XX Corps was placed in reserve behind Butterfield's division.[15] The 33rd and the rest of the Second Brigade camped for the night behind breastworks on the left of the division. Although the battle would begin the next day, the regiment would remain in this position until about 10:00 P.M. the next evening.[16] The battle of Resaca was fairly unusual for the Atlanta campaign in that both sides could see the other's lines and both knew a battle of some kind was imminent. Having two battles in a week must have clearly shown the men in both armies that unlike prior campaigns, this campaign would be one of continuous fighting. Unlike the mountainous terrain at Rocky Face Ridge, the country around Resaca consisted primarily of hills, pine forests, gullies and heavy underbrush. However, like the terrain at Dug Gap, all of these features favored the defenders.[17]

The Union attack began at about 11:00 A.M. on May 14 and the advance was confused from the start. Although Sherman thought the attack was directed towards the Confederate right, the attack was actually much closer to the center. Uncoordinated and greatly hampered by the terrain, the assault lasted about four hours and did little more than hit up against the Confederate line. During this attack, the commanders on both sides realized that the Federal plans and troop dispositions had not taken into account how far the Confederate right extended. Sherman now knew that he had to extend the Union left both to protect the army and also to give more time for the crossing at Lay's Ferry. Acting on similar knowledge, Johnston ordered General Hood to attack the dangerously exposed Union left and cut them off from Snake Creek Gap. Because General Alpheus Williams' division of the XX Corps was on its way to strengthen the Union left, Hood attacked the same position at about 5:00 P.M. Hood's attack was successful at first, but the Confederates were driven back by a strategically placed artillery battery. When a second attack was launched, Williams' division was in place and they stopped the Confederate assault, preventing the flanker (Sherman) from being outflanked.[18]

Throughout the day, the 33rd had observed the day's action safely, and no doubt gratefully, from their reserve position. However, they were not to remain in reserve for long, as the movement of Williams' division was the beginning of the shift of the entire XX Corps to the Union left. The movement of the Second Division began with the First and Third Brigades so that the 33rd and the rest of the Second Brigade were left to hold breastworks previously maintained by an entire division. Finally, beginning at about 10:00 P.M. on May 14, the Second Brigade followed the other brigades past the rear of the Union army. They eventually occupied a new position on the Dalton and Resaca road, having taken almost five hours to march four miles.[19] The march over the broken terrain must have been as difficult as it was time consuming. Since they had seen the failure of the previous day's attack, the men must have understood that the move was in preparation for a new attack, one in which they would participate. Once they finally got into position, the men got what rest they could. Daylight and combat were not far away.

By shifting the XX Corps, Sherman now had two corps, the XX under Hooker and the IV under Howard on the Union left. With his left now strengthened, Sherman's plan for May 15 was for Hooker and Howard to attack the Confederate right or center right. Specifically, the two Federal corps were to press down the Resaca road to Resaca itself. Hooker and Howard took almost the entire morning to get into position and the attack did not begin until 1:00 P.M. Howard attacked first to mask the main thrust by Hooker, but Howard's attack went nowhere and the IV Corps fell back.[20] Instead of masking Hooker's attack, Howard's failed assault gave the Confederates a clear picture of Union intentions. This was not good news for the attackers, including the 33rd New Jersey.

The attack began with the XX Corps facing southeast across the Dalton-Resaca road. Williams' division was on the left, Butterfield's in the center and Geary's division, including the 33rd, was on the right. The plan was for the attack itself to be made to the west of the aforementioned road. The objective was a prominent hill that anchored the Confederate line. Each of the divisions consisted of three brigades, so some 12,000 men would participate in the attack. When the attack began, the brigades were formed in a column of regiments since, in theory, such a large number of troops across a small front would overwhelm any human obstacles in their path. In this formation, Lieutenant Colonel Fouratt as regimental commander was behind the center of the regiment. Although other senior officers would typically be at each end of the formation, at this point the regiment was short on senior officers. The 33rd had lost their colonel to injury and their major to illness so the position on one wing was taken by the very inexperienced adjutant, Stephen Pierson. On the other wing, the responsibility would have gone to the senior captain, most likely Thomas O'Connor. All other company commanders were in front of their companies with the noncommissioned officers in position to close up the ranks as necessary. By this stage of the war all officers were on foot, thus reducing their visibility as targets. At the front of the regiment were two enlisted men carrying the national and state colors. The colors had an important symbolic role, but from a practical standpoint they also served as a rallying point during the "lethal chaos" of battle.[21]

The 33rd did not form up until about 12:30, so they had once again spent a long time waiting for the battle.[22] It was one thing to "hurry up and wait" for a march or other duty. Doing so with a battle imminent quickened the pulse, dried the throat and moistened the palms. Even after waiting until 12:30 to fall in, there was another hour's wait before the regiment and the rest of the Second Division moved forward. While the terrain itself was a problem, the lack of any reconnaissance of the Confederate position made the confusion even worse.[23] The objective of the attack was "a collection of detached eminencies of considerable altitude" with the hollows and

Union troops removing captured Confederate cannon at Resaca. *Harper's Weekly.*

ravines in between full of dense woods and underbrush.[24] Under these conditions it was not a surprise that units got off course and the attack was fragmented. Although the 33rd came under musket and artillery fire early on, most of the fire was too high and the only damage was to the tops of surrounding pine trees.[25]

Confederate general Joseph Johnston had a reputation for constructing strong defensive positions, and the Confederate right at Resaca was no exception. The main line was set up along a ridge that was more a series of hills than one continuous ridge. Many of the hills had spurs extending in all directions and the defenders used these effectively for cross and enfilading fire.[26] Between this defensive line and the attackers was a series of hills with densely wooded slopes. In preparing their defenses, the Confederates cleared the slopes to their immediate front, but not those closest to the Union lines. As a result the natural terrain slowed down and broke up the force of the Union attack while the cleared areas provided open fields of fire for the Confederates.[27]

The Confederate position was already a strong one, but just prior to the attack a new artillery position was established about 80 yards to the front of the main line. Taking advantage of "a sort of natural fort sunk in the side of the hill," a four-gun battery was placed in this position. When the attack began the battery was functioning, but the work to protect the position had not been completed.[28] Completed or

Contemporary picture of the battlefield at Resaca. *George Barnard, Library of Congress.*

not, almost all the Union accounts claimed the fire from the battery took a terrible toll on the attackers. According to Adjutant Pierson, the position was such that the cannons sent "a raking fire right or left."[29] Even more importantly, the adjutant of the 111th Pennsylvania believed that the battery "defended the key of the enemy's position at that point."[30] Given the effectiveness of the fire and the location, the battery was to be the focal point of the fighting, all day and evening.

Since there were so many things working against the attackers, the force of the Union attack was quickly broken up. The situation became so confused that the after-action reports of the Union commanders are almost impossible to follow. Indeed, one participant noted that, "a close examination of the officer's reports reveals that many were as confused after Resaca as they were at the time of the engagement."[31] Confused as it was, the Union advance was able to drive the Confederates from three lines of rifle pits back to the main line. After the disjointed attack reached some temporary cover behind a hill, there was an opportunity to reform. At this point, the 33rd was placed in the first line along with the 134th New York, the 109th Pennsylvania, and the 119th New York.[32]

When the assault resumed, the first line was ordered, reportedly by General Hooker himself,[33] to take the four-gun battery and the Confederate works "at all hazards." Martin Denniston reported that the regiment "made a rush, yelling and

Contemporary picture of the battlefield at Resaca, another view. *George Barnard, Library of Congress.*

hooting, guns roaring, bullets singing and whizzing among us." As the Union advance reached the top of the intervening hill, some of the attackers lay down and took cover. But according to Denniston, Lieutenant Colonel Fouratt, commanding the regiment in combat for the first time, kept the men moving forward. As the regiment continued the attack, those who remained in a prone position offered moral support, shouting as they passed, "Go in Jersies, we will follow you."[34] Although verbal and moral support was fine, joining in the attack would have been preferable. Once the regiment moved down the hill and into a cleared hollow, the Confederate lines were in plain sight, especially the four-gun battery on a 150-foot-high hill, some 150 yards away.[35]

The Confederate gunners now had unobstructed targets well within range, and shells came at the attackers full force along with musket fire from the main lines.[36] According to William Lloyd, "it was hardly possible for a man to live through the storm of lead that was poured upon us."[37] During this firestorm of canon and minie balls, Captain Nathaniel Bray suffered a thigh wound from which he would fully recover.[38] Not as fortunate were Patrick Donnelly of Company F, Aaron Earl of Company E and George Hetherton of Company H, all of whom were killed. In addition to Bray, another 23 members of the regiment were wounded. Among the wounded was James McSorley who was shot in the hip. While McSorley would survive the battle and the war, the wound itself would never heal. Total disabled from his service to his country, McSorley would die from his wound in early 1869. While most of the other wounded would recover, Andrew McGlynchy of Company F died the next day and Britton Drake of Company H succumbed on July 1.[39]

Martin Denniston survived the attack, but he continued to have close calls like the one at Dug Gap. When a "dreadful volley" hit the attackers, Denniston and the others hit the ground probably with or without orders. As Denniston did so, he asked rhetorically, "didn't I hug the ground close?"[40] Denniston at least held his ground. A portion of the 33rd fell back in disorder into the left wing of the 109th Pennsylvania, which was supporting the 33rd. Although this wreaked havoc on that portion of the Pennsylvanians' line, their right wing was able to continue the advance.[41] Some Union regiments fell back slightly to a more protected position, but the overall result was a dangerous stalemate near the four-gun battery.[42] Those that did not fall back simply kept firing from where they lay on the ground.[43] The combined Union fire was effective enough to drive off the Confederate gunners and prevent removal of the guns. However, the closeness to the main line enabled the Confederates to bring a lethal fire on any Union soldier foolhardy enough to approach the cannons.[44]

The two sides were now no more than 50 yards apart, so the less protected Federal troops had a stark choice: lie still or die. This was in some ways worse than the tension of the charge. One participant recalled, "The suspense was dreadful. ... It was a long afternoon and told heavily on the patience of the men."[45] When the Confederates tried to outflank the position of the 33rd and the 109th Pennsylvania, the threat was "handsomely repulsed by the 33rd NJ."[46] A second assault by the Confederates after dark was not dealt with so handsomely. Confederate fire from an unseen source was too much for some of the men, including Martin Denniston. An unauthorized retreat began back down the hill. Denniston joined in and "did not stop until I got behind a log."[47] That Denniston would write about running away to a Paterson newspaper showed how things had changed since 1861. At the beginning of the war, soldiers could not even acknowledge their fears much less give in to them. Such a letter then would have been unthinkable, but the experience of almost three years of war apparently had given the men some latitude in expressing their fears.[48] In any event, the retreat did not last long. The men were reformed and led back up the hill.[49]

Although these counterattacks failed, the Confederate leadership still believed that the guns could be retaken. They claimed to be waiting for the relative safety of darkness.[50] By this point however, some ten Union regiments—almost half of a division—were in position facing the guns.[51] In addition, the Second Division commander, John Geary, saw political value in capturing the guns and was willing to wait.[52] Echoing this sentiment was William Lambert, who wrote, "We could afford to wait and wait long and patiently, we did."[53] The lovely moonlit night presented a terrible contrast. Above was a peaceful evening sky, lit by the moon and the stars, while all around them was the carnage of the battlefield. William Lloyd wrote his wife that he "never saw so many dead men in my life." Not sparing Mary any details, he described the dead bodies, "some with their heads mostly shot off, some with their legs and arms off, more with their insides blowed out."[54] While both sides waited,

Union bands played "Yankee Doodle" in attempt both to sustain the Union men and demoralize the Confederates.[55]

Finally, after what must have seemed like an eternity, Geary ordered the removal of the guns. Since the guns were still covered by deadly Confederate fire, the only relatively safe way to remove them was to dig a road or tunnel up to the front of the battery. After this was completed, the earthworks, logs, and stones could be removed and the cannons dragged out. When the execution of this plan began, the Confederates began firing in response. The main Union line thought the Confederate fire signaled an attack and opened fire. As a result, both enemy and friendly fire hit the position,[56] with the Confederate fire alone lighting up "the whole crest of the hill."[57] Although the fireworks lasted only about 20 minutes, Lieutenant Colonel Kilpatrick of the Fifth Ohio said they were the most "miserable 20 minutes in my life." The fire then died out and the work resumed.[58] After two hours of work, the road was completed. Kilpatrick then asked for 50 men without arms to help remove the guns. In response, "Fifty men of the 33rd New Jersey reported promptly." Promptly or not, by the time the detail arrived, two of the guns were out and the men from the regiment helped with the other two.[59] The regiment having played a dual role in this engagement, William Lambert was able to claim that the 33rd had shared both "the glory and danger of the charge" as well as the "satisfaction of the capture."[60] Regardless of the glory and the satisfaction, the men had to be exhausted. Their second battle, like the first, had begun in daylight and ended after dark. Drained both physically and emotionally, they used the rest of the night to get what sleep they could.

After the initial ordeal was over, the removal of the guns was completed without any significant Confederate fire. However, the lack of opposition was due more to the fact that the Confederates themselves were in the process of withdrawing across the Oostanaula. Late in the afternoon of May 15, Confederate general Johnston had learned that the Federal right had crossed the Oostanaula at Lay's Ferry. As at Rocky Face Ridge, Sherman's army had completed another successful flanking maneuver that threatened the Confederate rear. When the Confederates retreated they took everything of substance with them except for the four cannons,[61] the "loss of life it would have cost to withdraw them being considered worth more than the guns," according to Confederate General Hood.[62] Interestingly, the four guns were a portion of Corput's battery that had fired on the 33rd from Tunnel Hill at Chattanooga.[63] They were also the only cannons lost by Johnston during the Atlanta campaign.[64] When one participant saw the guns the next day, he reported that the wooden carriages and boxes had been destroyed by gunfire. The guns themselves were so full of lead marks that they looked like "a man's face recovering from small pox."[65] Apparently not having seen enough the first time, William Lloyd went back to the battlefield itself and called it "a sickening sight."[66]

Resaca, like Dug Gap, ended for the 33rd New Jersey as a bloody standoff. In both cases, the fighting was stopped due to a successful flanking movement elsewhere. Similarly, it is fair to believe that the efforts of the 33rd and the rest of the Union force at Resaca were necessary to occupy the limited Confederate defenders. The importance of these attacks to the success of the flanking movement however, does not excuse the lack of reconnaissance on strong defensive positions, most likely leading to excessive casualties. One historian termed Hooker's attack "a bloody failure," the only success being the neutralizing of "four semi obsolescent cannons." In total the XX Corps suffered about 1,200 casualties at Resaca, about 30 percent of the Union total.[67] Although the 33rd was fortunate that only five of their almost 30 casualties would die, this was little consolation to those five families. Once again, as at Dug Gap, the regiment had acquitted themselves well. A portion of the regiment had fallen back twice, but this was no disgrace and the men regrouped both times. Even though the Atlanta campaign was only two weeks old, the soldiers were rapidly becoming veteran volunteers in fact as well as in name.

After both armies crossed the Oostanaula River, the Atlanta campaign entered very different terrain. The 30 to 40 miles between the Oostanaula and the next natural barrier, the Etowah River, was much less restricted by natural features. However, once across the Etowah, the armies would again move into mountains covered with heavy forests. Since he was well aware of the terrain, Sherman hoped to overtake and defeat the Confederates between the two rivers. Sherman, therefore, ordered a rapid pursuit of the Confederates, but Johnson continued to retreat. Johnston's goal was to find a place where he could make a stand and stop Sherman with heavy losses.[68]

When the Union pursuit began on May 16, the bulk of Sherman's army, including the XX Corps, was still north of the Oostanaula. The crossing was complicated by the fact that the Oostanaula was formed out of the junction of the Connasauga and Coosawattee rivers. As a result, the XX Corps had first to move east to cross the Connasauga and then south to cross the Coosawattee.[69] The 33rd and the rest of the Second Division began the march, moving three miles southeast parallel to the Connasauga River. The plan was to cross at Newton's Ferry, but this was not possible and the division moved further east to Fite's Ferry. Half of the men (the lucky half) crossed on the ferryboat while the other half removed their clothes and waded across the three-foot deep river, holding their clothes out of the water. No member of the 33rd recorded which group the regiment was in, so it is likely they were part of the lucky group. Based on past experience we can be confident that William Lloyd would have shared such an adventure with Mary. The day was warm, so even those in the water did not have too difficult a time. Once across the Connasauga, the division moved to McClure's Ferry on the 100-yard-wide Coosawattee, which was crossed on two old ferryboats, two companies at a time. After they had crossed, the 33rd and the rest of the Second Brigade camped near Bryant's Farm, about one mile from the ferry.[70]

The crossings took a significant amount of time and the entire XX Corps was not across the Coosawattee until the early afternoon of May 17. By this time, Sherman's advance units had reached Adairsville, about 16 miles south of Resaca. Johnston had originally planned to make a stand in a narrow valley north of Adairsville, but upon personal inspection he decided the valley was too wide and continued the retreat. Once Johnston arrived at Adairsville itself, he believed that he had found the right place. Two roads went south out of Adairsville, one 11 miles southeast to Cassville, the other following the railroad to Kingston, seven miles west of Cassville. Johnston believed that if he divided his army and sent part on the Cassville road and part on the Kingston road, Sherman would do the same. Once the much larger Union army was thus divided, Johnston would reunite his command at Cassville and attack the portion of the Union army approaching that village. Sherman reacted just as Johnston had anticipated and the 33rd found themselves part of the force moving towards Cassville and danger.[71]

Over the next two days, the 33rd marched 12 miles a day, passing through Adairsville and camping on the second day north of Cassville.[72] The area had larger farms and more abundant crops so the men found the country much "improved" over that north of Resaca.[73] More importantly, from a practical standpoint, the route of march was flatter. Carrying knapsacks as well as muskets and haversacks in warm weather, the men appreciated anything that made the march easier. The entire XX Corps was near Cassville on the 18, blissfully ignorant of the fact that Johnston's entire army was in position one mile northwest of Cassville. In the Confederate defenses along Two Mile Creek Johnston had assembled the largest Confederate force ever in the west — over 70,000 men.[74]

On a hot, muggy May 17, the 33rd and the rest of the Second Brigade broke camp just after 6:00 A.M. and headed towards Cassville.[75] The Confederates were prepared at midmorning to launch their attack on the unsuspecting Federal troops, but luck or chance intervened on the Union side. While preparing to attack, the Confederates saw a large number of troops headed towards their right flank. The Union force was a portion of Sherman's cavalry on an entirely different mission, but the possible threat to their flank forced Johnston to cancel the planned attack. The retreat began again, this time to a new position about one-half mile southeast of Cassville. One historian called this unintentional intervention "the most valuable service that will be performed by Sherman's cavalry during the entire campaign."[76]

The new Confederate position was about three miles long, primarily on a 140-foot-high ridge, and was initially considered to be very strong. However, when the artillery of the XX Corps opened up on the position with devastating fire, generals John Bell Hood and Leonidas Polk quickly came to a different conclusion. Both generals implored Johnston to withdraw, but at first he disagreed. Once it became clear, however, that the two commanders did not believe in the position, Johnston decided that the position could not be held. Johnston again ordered a night retreat, this time south of the Etowah River.[77] Although the continued Confederate retreat was good news for the Union army, their failure to overtake the Confederates before they reached the Etowah meant there was hard fighting ahead on terrain that favored the defense.

At the time, the men of the 33rd probably had no idea of their good fortune in avoiding the Confederate trap. What they did know was that they continued in pursuit of the Confederates. When William Lloyd had time to write to Mary, he reported, "we came up with the enemy again and they are in full retreat." Lloyd said the men were tired from 16 consecutive days of marching and fighting, but that he had stood "the scorching sun better than I thought I could." Noting that he and Mary had now been married for one year, he commented dryly, "Then I was by your side as happy as a lark, and today I am hunting the rebels in Georgia, a slight change." He hoped and prayed that they would be together on their next anniversary.[78] As Lloyd wrote this letter, the Confederates had completed crossing the Etowah. Once the pursuing Federals got to the river, they were less than 50 miles from Atlanta.[79]

After the Confederates finished crossing the Etowah, Johnston's army moved to the area around Allatoona, a small railroad village near the pass of the same name. Allatoona Pass itself was a long narrow gorge surrounded by high hills, a defensive position stronger even than Mill Creek Gap. Since Sherman was familiar with the terrain from prior service in Georgia, he knew full well the folly of attacking such a position. As soon as the Union Army was across the Etowah, Sherman intended to send his command due south towards the village of Dallas. Once at Dallas, the army would proceed east to Marietta, cross the Chattahoochee River and move on Atlanta. Although this was another flanking movement, the maneuver would cover a much larger area than anything Sherman had tried thus far. However, what was especially significant about the plan was the logistical implication of separation from the railroad.[80]

Before crossing the Etowah, Sherman gave the army a respite from the campaign. Since this was the first break after leaving winter quarters, the men put the time to good use: resting, eating, reading, and writing letters.[81] Even though the army was in some extremely rural sections of Georgia, the men still got mail delivery almost every day.[82] This was also the first time that the men had a chance to boil their clothes, the only way to rid themselves, at least temporarily, of lice.[83] William Lloyd wrote Mary that the rest was in preparation for a 20-day march. Since Atlanta was only 50 miles away, Lloyd speculated about other possible destinations including Louisiana and South Carolina. By this point Lloyd was willing to march almost anywhere as long as they could avoid another battle. "It is," he told Mary, "an awful thing to be in battle."[84]

What Lloyd had not considered in his speculations was that the route of the army was no longer directly towards Atlanta. When Sherman decided upon this plan, it marked the first and only time during the campaign that Sherman's army operated out of direct contact with their supply lifeline, the railroad. The preparations for a 20-day march referred to the number of days of rations to be carried by the army.[85] Relying on the rations they would carry with them meant that for the first time in the campaign, the 33rd would subsist solely on the standard field rations of hardtack, salt pork, sugar, coffee, and salt. Of all of these, coffee was especially valued by the men, and the boiling of it had the added benefit of sanitizing the often polluted water. Less popular but still of value was hardtack, a flour and water biscuit typically one-half inch thick and about three inches by three inches. Although nine or ten crackers were considered to be a full ration, there was seldom a shortage, as many men would not eat them. Hardtack was nutritious but did little to satisfy hunger from a battle or a hard day's march. It was often too hard to eat or full of maggots or weevils. It was said that one of the benefits of eating hardtack in the dark was the inability to tell whether weevils were present.[86]

Although there were not many good things about hardtack, it was nowhere near as bad as the two meat rations, salt horse and salt pork. Salt horse or "pickled beef" was prepared so that it would last for at least two years. Soldiers could only attempt to eat this delicacy after the meat had been soaked in water for a long period of time.

While that process might have made salt horse somewhat edible, a side result was the removal of both the salt and the juices. Since there was such a lengthy preparation time, salt horse was seldom used except in camp, with the result that salt pork became the only practical meat option in the field. About the only advantage of salt pork was that it could be cooked in a number of different ways or even eaten raw. On the downside however, salt pork was often "black as a shoe on the outside" and frequently "yellow with putrefaction" on the inside.[87] Modern attempts to recreate this tasty morsel have resulted in something that reportedly tastes "like a soggy cube of salt, soaked in grease."[88]

This was clearly a disgusting diet, but that alone was not its greatest disadvantage for the men of the 33rd. In fact, the foul nature of the diet "did not cause a tithe of the sickness and misery" caused by a lack of balance in the diet, especially the lack of fresh vegetables. After the men went without vegetables for long periods of time during a campaign, the insufficiency led to scurvy. Scurvy caused much of the illness and fatalities attributed to "chronic diarrhea and debility."[89] One attempt to deal with this problem was the provision of desiccated vegetables, which the men came to call "desecrated vegetables." Forced to subsist on food of this nature, it is not surprising that one veteran noted, "We ignored the existence of such a thing as a stomach."[90]

Fortified with four days of such sustenance in their haversacks, the 33rd broke camp at 6:00 A.M. on Mary 23.[91] When the regiment passed through Cassville, they found what was described as a fair sized town of 50 houses to be deserted. Cassville was the last village of any size that the 33rd would see for some time. After moving through Cassville, the regiment and the rest of the XX Corps crossed the Etowah during the afternoon. Since all the bridges had been destroyed, the Corps crossed on pontoon bridges near Milam's Bridge. The men then marched for another mile or so before making camp in some woods; over the course of the day they had covered 15 miles.[92]

When Sherman planned this new flanking movement, he did not believe the army would encounter any major resistance before Marietta. However, Johnston had figured out that heading for Marietta by way of Dallas was Sherman's logical next move. The same day that the 33rd crossed the Etowah, Johnston ordered generals William Hardee and Leonidas Polk to move their commands to Dallas. Although both armies had to travel about the same distance, the Confederates were already across the Etowah and were not slowed down by supply wagons. Since the Confederates also marched at night, they reached Dallas first.

As the Union march resumed the next day, the troops passed through rolling countryside with rich soil and many farms. In issuing orders for this phase of the campaign, Sherman for the first time permitted foraging, with the restriction that "indiscriminate plunder must not be allowed." Even with this distinction, or perhaps in spite of it, the opportunity provided by the rich countryside resulted in foraging both authorized and not. The opportunity did not last long. As Sherman's army moved towards Dallas on dusty roads in hot weather, the terrain soon changed to a series of "mounds, knobs, hills and mountains." Like the terrain north of Resaca, these elevations were covered with pine trees and the typical thick underbrush. Foraging came to a grinding halt as the few farms they encountered consisted primarily of squalid log cabins occupied by poor whites.[93]

When the 33rd and the rest of the Second Brigade broke camp at 6:00 A.M. on May 24,[94] they were no longer headed towards Dallas. Picket fire had been heard to the east during the night and the Second Division was assigned to cover the march of the First and Third Divisions. Along with the rest of the division, the 33rd moved about a mile to the east to Raccoon Creek where they remained until the XXIII Corps relieved them. When the regiment resumed the march south, they were clearly back in terrain similar to that of northern Georgia. The route of march moved through fields and woods and then climbed a spur of the Allatoona mountain range.[95] After this the regiment continued over a range of rough hills to Burnt Hickory where they camped for the night. The hard day of marching under a hot sun must have left a tired regiment by nightfall. That the men got much rest was doubtful, as a heavy rain fell all night. It would be some time before they would have much rest of any kind.[96]

At Burnt Hickory, the 33rd and the rest of the XX Corps were only seven miles from Dallas.[97] From this point on the terrain became even more of a problem. Although the Chattahoochee was the only remaining river between Sherman's army and Atlanta, most of the entire distance to the river was "an almost unbroken forest interspersed with dense green thickets." Very few roads existed and they were little more than "mere by-ways"; there was even some quicksand in low lying areas that would have slowed Sherman's command down even if there was no opposition.[98] But there was opposition; Sherman had been receiving reports that the Confederates were moving their army to Dallas. Since Sherman did not or would not believe these reports, he issued orders for May 25 for the army to move on past Dallas. However, Johnston had now even further strengthened his army at Dallas by bringing Hood's division there as well. Once in the area, Hood moved towards New Hope Church, a rough log Methodist meeting house at a crossroads northeast of Dallas, only 25 miles from Atlanta.[99]

When the 33rd broke camp about 6:00 A.M. on May 25,[100] the Second Division was in the lead as the XX Corps moved towards Dallas.[101] They reached Pumpkin Vine Creek at midmorning, just in time to save a burning bridge at Owen's Mill.[102] After they crossed the bridge the troops came to a road, not on Union maps, that split off to the east from the main Dallas road. Hooker, who was with Geary at the head of the Second Division, mistakenly believed that this road also led to Dallas, so he divided his command. While Hooker, Geary, and the Second Division moved down the new road, the other two divisions continued on the main road to Dallas, which was, in reality, the only road to Dallas. After the Second Division moved about one and one-half miles they encountered significant Confederate opposition. When some Confederates were taken prisoner, the division's real situation became clear. The Confederate prisoners told Hooker and Geary that Hood was at New Hope Church with the rest of the army close by. Since the Second Division was five miles from the rest of the Army of the Cumberland this was especially bad news. If the Confederates attacked, there was little to prevent Hood from crushing Geary's division before help arrived. While the rest of the XX Corps was being recalled, Geary quickly deployed his men.[103]

New Hope Church battlefield. *George Barnard, Library of Congress.*

Just like their commanders, the members of the 33rd were not expecting any significant Confederate opposition. In fact, the support elements of the regiment including the surgeons, the quartermaster, and the officer's servants, were so oblivious to any danger that they marched with the regiment rather than at the rear. When they heard the sound of musket fire from the front and not too distant, they were jolted out of their false sense of security. Quickly, the noncombatants went scurrying to the rear through the woods and bushes on both sides of the road, saddlebags and equipment flapping. As they withdrew with more speed than dignity, they were encouraged by shouts of "Go it Doc" or "Go it Jim." Along with this gallows humor, however, Adjutant Pierson recalled that "the effect was perceptible" on the men themselves. Although the line had spread out during the march, it closed up rapidly while the men began to check their weapons.[104] Unlike their previous experiences of combat, this time the regiment would go into battle with little time for preparation or anxiety.

The Second Brigade deployed in support of the First Brigade in a line formed at a right angle to what was still mistakenly believed to be the road to Dallas. The

The "Hellhole" at New Hope Church. *George Barnard, Library of Congress.*

119th New York and the 134th New York were positioned on the right of the road with the 33rd in support. On the other side of the road were the 73rd and 109th Pennsylvania with the 154th New York in support. After about an hour, the Third Brigade came up to take a position parallel to the Second Brigade. About 2 P.M., in an effort to extend the Union left, the 33rd and 154th New York were moved from their reserve positions. Since there was no Federal unit to the 33rd's immediate left, they were in an exposed, dangerous position, but fortunately the Confederates did not attack.[105]

In keeping with standard practice under Joseph Johnston, the Confederates had established a strong defensive position. Running parallel to a branch of Pumpkin Vine Creek were a series of ridges with trees at the top but fairly open valleys to the front. When Geary's advance had reached the top of one of these ridges, the Confederates were in position on the far side. There is some disagreement between Union and Confederate sources as to the extent that the Confederates had established strong defensive works. Almost all of the Confederate reports claimed that Hood's units had little or no chance to erect proper breastworks, but at least one Union commander strongly disputed this claim.[106] Regardless of the degree of preparation of the Confederate defenses, the good news for the Second Division was that the rest of the XX Corps arrived between 4 and 5 P.M. Upon arrival, the First Division was placed to the front of the Second Division while the Third was placed to the left and rear. Since

Charles J. Field, 1st lt. and captain, Company E, died of wounds received at Dallas, Georgia, May 28, 1864. *U.S. Army Military History Institute.*

Sherman still did not believe that there was any significant Confederate opposition in the area, he ordered Hooker to attack. Just past 5 P.M., the Union attack moved forward. The First Division advanced first with the Second and Third divisions starting a few minutes later. The advance was not made any easier by the first mile of rocky ground, which was covered with dense woods and underbrush.[107]

In spite of the rough terrain, Stephen Pierson claimed the men moved forward "with as good a front and line as I ever saw the regiment present." As they advanced, the regiment drove back a heavy Confederate skirmish line to the "fresh red earth" of the Confederate main defensive line. Pierson then reported, "in the next instant, the storm of shot, shell, shrapnel and minie burst upon us." The Confederate fire was so heavy that tree limbs were shot off and fell on members of the regiment. Although "the shriek of shot and shell and vicious song of the minie bullet" was bad enough, worse was the accompanying "sickening thud which told that it has found its mark in the body of a man in blue."[108] A sergeant in the 123rd New York recalled that "the noise was deafening, the air was filled with the fumes of burning powder."[109] Despite the storm of shot and shell, William Lambert reported that the entire Second Division finally fixed bayonets and charged right "up to the muzzle of the enemy's guns."[110]

As the day gave into night, nature herself became part of the "lethal chaos" of the battlefield. A tremendous thunderstorm broke over the battlefield. One observer said it was "a furious storm, the rain came down in torrents, the lightening was blinding."[111] When darkness closed in, Lambert found the scene to be simultaneously "grand and awful" with the flashes of light from the cannons and muskets complimented by "the vivid glare of the lightening." At the same time, the "roaring rumble of the thunder in the heavens" matched the noise from the man-made weapons. Almost drowned out by all of this noise were "the hoarse cheers and yells of the opposing lines; the loud voices of command." It was, Lambert concluded, "more like hell than God's beautiful earth."[112]

Finally, darkness along with the storm brought the fighting to an end. Although both Lambert and Lieutenant Colonel Fouratt claimed, in Fouratt's words, that "only by the intervention of darkness were they [the Confederates] saved from rout," the reality was somewhat different.[113] The strength of the Confederate positions, augmented by their artillery, and the inability of Hooker to effectively use his four-to-one numerical advantage prevented the success of the Union attack.[114] However, although the Union attack failed, it was not followed by a withdrawal. The Federal forces stayed in place and Pierson reported that at some points the two lines were as close as "the width of the Morristown green," back in New Jersey.[115] As at Resaca, a deadly stalemate had occurred; unlike Resaca, this would last for days, not hours.

After it became clear that there would not be any more significant action that night, the 33rd and the rest of the division dug in. According to Pierson, the men worked in the dark, first with their hands and then with some shovels that were brought up from the rear. Those not fortunate enough to get a shovel used bayonets and tin cups. While the digging was going on, trees were cut down in the ravine behind the regiment's position and brought forward for breastworks.[116] When daylight came, the bulk of the Federal troops occupied a wide defensive trench. A breastwork of logs protected the trench, three or four feet high and covered with dirt, with a head log at the top. Unlike the rest of the logs, the head log was supported by poles slanted to the rear so that, the heavy log would not fall on the men if dislodged. In addition, the head log also had a small opening for musket firing.[117]

After some defensive works were finally in place, the men tried to rest in the pouring rain. Lambert reported that the night was long, but "slowly, chilly and wearily, the night passed into morning." When daylight finally came it "revealed two strong lines of works less than three hundred yards apart."[118] Since a minie ball could pierce a six-inch pine board at twice that distance, the men stayed low. On May 26 there were no major assaults, but musket and artillery fire continued all day and into the evening. Throughout the day, the balance of the Union Army came into position.[119] At noon the 33rd was finally relieved by units of the IV Corps. The regiment then moved to a position behind a well-protected knoll at the rear of the brigade.[120] Although the men must have been glad to get off the front line, this was only a temporary respite.

By this point the two armies were drawn up in opposing lines that extended for ten miles through the dense pine forest around New Hope Church. The 33rd and the rest of the Army of the Cumberland were at the center of the Federal line. On the right but not connected was McPherson's Army of the Ohio, while Howard's IV Corps and two divisions of the XXIII Corps were on the left. On May 27, Sherman accepted the fact that the entire Confederate army was present, which made his plan to push on to Marietta impossible to execute. Instead Sherman decided to have the units on the Union left drive back the Confederate right. While this took place, a connection was to be established between the Army of the Cumberland in the center and the Army of the Ohio on the Union right. Unfortunately, Howard's attack on the Confederate right was stopped cold at the battle of Pickett's Mill and his force had to dig in at the starting point of their attack.

The situation got worse on the 28th, when Sherman received more bad news. Rations were becoming a problem. Although a 20-day supply of rations had been ordered for the advance, the bulk of the food was carried in division and corps wagons. Since the area had "no roads of any consequence," getting these supplies to the front line was very difficult. This made clear, if it was ever in doubt, the extent to which the army was dependent on the railroad. In response to the situation, Sherman decided to reconnect to the railroad at Acworth. Acworth was not as far south as Marietta, but it was still past the strong defensive position at Allatoona. In order to do this, Sherman had to clear the route to the railroad at Acworth and connect the Army of the Ohio with the Army of the Cumberland. The connection was the first step, but Confederate attacks and heavy skirmishing on the 28th and 29th delayed the move until May 31.[121]

Throughout this period, the 33rd and the rest of the troops at the Union center were engaged in "a type of fighting that hitherto had been unprecedented in this or any other war except during sieges." Musket fire was exchanged almost constantly, supplemented by sharpshooter and artillery fire.[122] On the Second Division's part of the front, the distance between the lines ranged from 80 to 300 yards. Since the situation was extremely stressful, Geary established a routine whereby two-thirds of

Private James McSorley, Company E, wounded at Resaca. *Stickel Family Collection.*

each brigade was on line at a time with the other one-third in reserve.¹²³ The regiment thus alternated between the skirmish line, the breastworks and a reserve position so that Lambert noted that the period "passed in dangerous monotony."¹²⁴ According to Stephen Pierson, during this period there was "no such thing as a truce or armistice, even for burying the dead." When the weather turned warm again, "the bodies lay there and festered, blue and gray side by side."¹²⁵ Never one to withhold any part of his experience from his wife, William Lloyd wrote about how "some of our dead lay rotting twenty feet in front of us" and were "completely eaten up with maggots."[126] Rations were limited to coffee that was boiled in the ravine and brought up in canteens plus the aforementioned delicacies, hardtack and salt pork. The regiment was in constant danger, in uncomfortable conditions with stifling heat; it was no wonder that Pierson called this period "the hardest seven days that I remember in my army experience."[127]

Perhaps the only positive note was that both sides had dug in so effectively that there were limited casualties.[128] During this period the 33rd suffered a total of seven fatalities. As Captain Field was posting a skirmish line on May 28, he was shot through the right thigh.[129] The wound was ultimately fatal and Field died in the hospital at Lookout Valley on June 5. William Wheeler was killed during the original fighting on May 25 and Joseph Kelly was killed on May 28. Like Field, both Leonard Onderdonk and Joseph Felty were fatally wounded. Also killed during this time were Henry Clark and James Hughes.[130] Although the fatalities were limited to these seven, another 27 men were wounded and eventually recovered.[131]

On the night of May 31, the Army of the Ohio began a division-by-division withdrawal on the Union right. The withdrawn divisions replaced units to their left, enabling similar withdrawals along the Union line so that McPherson's command could gradually connect to the main line from the left. After this movement was completed the army would make a successful connection with the railroad at Acworth.[132] On the next day, a hot and sultry June 1, Stephen Pierson heard cheers from far down the line taken up brigade by brigade. Looking down from the breastworks into the ravine, Pierson saw General Joshua Logan at the head of a column of the XV Corps. No explanation was necessary and "never before or since were comrades welcomed more cordially than we men of the east welcomed the men of the west that morning."[133] When the XX Corps withdrew from their position, they moved to the left or northeast for six miles, and camped behind the Union left at Pickett's Mill. While these movements were going on, that same day another Union force took control of the abandoned Confederate position at Allatoona Pass. This ensured the availability of the railroad between the Etowah and Sherman's new destination at Acworth.[134]

After what was probably a relatively quiet night's rest, the 33rd and the rest of the brigade moved the next day at 11:30 A.M. and proceeded two more miles to the left.[135] The regiment then took reserve positions during "a most terrific thunderstorm of rain and hail."[136] On the following day, June 3, the Confederates accepted the obvious and stopped any effort to contest the Union move to Acworth. Instead they once again withdrew to a new defensive line, this time near Lost Mountain. Although the rain continued, so did the Union movement so that by June 5, Sherman's army was in and around Acworth.[137] When the 33rd occupied their new position, Lambert observed happily that "for the first time in twelve long days, we passed a peaceful day out of the hearing of the continual pop, whizzing chug of the bullets."[138]

Although Sherman had been unsuccessful in reaching Marietta, he had, once again, flanked the Confederates out of a strong defensive position. It is unlikely that the men of the 33rd ever forgot their experiences at New Hope Church. Others in Geary's command who had served at Chancellorsville and Gettysburg claimed that the fighting in the wilderness of Georgia was harder than those historic battles. For good reason, the area where the 33rd fought would be known simply as the "Hell Hole."[139] William Lambert rejoiced over their deliverance, but he did not forget to mourn those who did not survive. Lambert said that, without denigrating any other officer in the regiment, all believed that Captain Field "was the best line officer in the 33rd Regiment." Lambert was also proud of the regiment's record thus far in the campaign and promised New Jersey would have "no cause to regret her 33rd."[140] As Lambert and the rest of the regiment rested and dried out, they had no idea that the worst of the Atlanta campaign was yet to come.

VII

"A very hard day"

Finally out of the constant danger of the "Hell Hole," the officers and men of the 33rd New Jersey enjoyed the relatively safe but wet environment around Acworth. Since the beginning of the Atlanta campaign less than one month before, the regiment had been in three battles. The 33rd had left Lookout Valley with 550 officers and men, but combat, disease, and the elements had begun to eat away at the regiment's strength. In less than 30 days the 33rd had suffered 26 combat related deaths plus 68 wounded. Although some of the wounded were still on duty, at least a dozen had been lost for the rest of the campaign.[1] It is difficult to determine the number of men lost to disease and fatigue, but there were claims that both factors cost the regiment 100 men over the course of the campaign.[2] If these losses were spread out somewhat evenly, then one quarter would have occurred during the campaign's first month. On this basis, the regiment's total strength was down by between 60 and 70 men.

Although more personally real for the regiment, the 33rd's losses were only a small portion of the total Union losses of 12,000 killed, wounded, and missing out of an original force of 100,000. Proportionately, this was lower than the 9,000 Confederate losses out of their maximum strength of 65–75,000. This ratio of combat losses increased the Union manpower advantage, and the imminent arrival of three new Union divisions would make the situation even worse for the Confederates. There were no reinforcements of any significance available to Joseph Johnston and his army. While the manpower disadvantage was bad enough, the Union armies had already driven 80 miles into Georgia, forcing the Confederates to abandon six strong defensive positions. The campaign was going well for Sherman, but these accomplishments had a cost. The physical and psychological strain from the struggle around New Hope Church had taken a toll beyond Confederate bullets. In addition to the wounded, men were now being sent to the rear due to physical exhaustion. Straggling had also become a concern, to the point that Sherman issued an order for stragglers to be shot.

Even though Sherman had been thwarted in the flanking movement through

Dallas, his goals remained the same; Marietta, the Chattahoochee River, and then Atlanta. However, Union tactics would change because Sherman was no longer willing to risk losing contact with the railroad. The revised plan was to push straight ahead rather than try any more broad flanking movements. With a renewed sense of his dependence on the railroad, Sherman decided to wait at Acworth until the railroad bridge across the Etowah River was repaired. In addition to strengthening the supply route, the delay also allowed time for the arrival of two divisions of the XVII Corps, which took place on June 8. When Sherman received word on June 9 that the railroad bridge would be completed on schedule, he issued orders for all Union armies to move forward the next day.[3]

Along with the rest of the Second Brigade, the 33rd was in position near the Widow Hull's plantation about four miles southwest of Acworth.[4] While the 33rd certainly enjoyed this brief break in the campaign, the respite was marred by seven straight days of rain, which made the regiment's camp "but one mud hole."[5] The regiment could now compare Georgia mud with that of Tennessee and would have ample opportunity to sample that of the Carolinas as well. The regiment's tents probably offered some protection at first, but the longer the rain continued, the worse their situation would have become. Just lighting a fire would have been difficult, and once lit, keeping fires going would also have been a problem. Lighter equipment was at risk of floating away, while heavier items might get sucked into the mud. Under these conditions any kind of duty would have been both onerous and miserable. Exposure to the elements also increased the risk of disease, and scurvy was reportedly a problem. In spite of all these problems, the men were reported to be in good spirits while bearing "their hardships cheerfully."[6] However, morale could not have been helped by word of Captain Field's death in Chattanooga or of Charles Nolan of Company F being taken prisoner on June 5. Nolan was sent to Andersonville prison where he died in September.[7] He would not be the last member of the 33rd to suffer and die there. During this same period Michael Phalon died of disease.

When the Union advance began on June 10, Sherman's command was moving against a new Confederate defensive line between Gilgal Church and Brush Mountain, north of Marietta. Even though the rain continued for the seventh straight day, the movement began on schedule with the Army of the Cumberland in its usual position in the center. Late that morning Union advance units encountered Confederate skirmishers a mile from Pine Mountain, the apex of a salient in front of the Confederate main line. Although the position was one mile from the main defensive lines, the Confederates hoped the Union force would attack. Thomas instead ordered his men to dig in even though this meant the day's advance covered only three miles.[8] This at least represented minimal movement; some units like the 33rd New Jersey did not move at all. Although the advance began on June 10, the regiment would stay in its position near Widow Hull's plantation until June 14.[9]

The rain continued for three more days, for a total of 11 consecutive days of rain and little movement. This must have greatly frustrated Sherman, but one piece of good news was the opening of the railroad a day ahead of schedule. After the rain finally stopped on June 14 the roads began to dry out, signaling the real resumption of the campaign. Later that morning Union artillery opened fire on the Confederate

William Cochrane, 1st lt., Company K; captain, Company G; killed in action at Pine Knob, June 16, 1864. *From the Collections of the New Jersey Historical Society.*

position on Pine Mountain, killing General Leonidas Polk. The overall effectiveness of the artillery fire convinced Johnston that Pine Mountain was untenable as a defensive position. Once darkness fell, the Confederates withdrew to a new position.[10]

When the rain stopped on June 14, the 33rd and the rest of the Second Brigade moved for the first time. They advanced to a new position in front of Pine Mountain and were able to occupy the former position of the IV Corps without having to erect new breastworks.[11] The terrain continued to consist primarily of hilly country with dense forests, but the roads, which were poor under any circumstances, were worse due to the heavy rains.[12] The overall isolation of the area was well illustrated by the comments of one elderly lady who charged that the Union had reached so low as to employ foreign soldiers. After all, she asked a Union correspondent, "wasn't them fellers here to-day from a place called New Jersey?"[13]

Once the Confederate evacuation of Pine Mountain was discovered on June 15, Sherman reached the mistaken and perhaps wishful conclusion that the Confederates were retreating. Based on this belief, Sherman ordered Thomas to push forward between Pine Mountain and Kennesaw Mountain against the center of the Confederate line.[14] As part of this movement, the 33rd and the rest of the Second Brigade first moved one and one-half miles forward to the right of Pine Mountain and then proceeded to make a connection with the Third Brigade. Once this connection was made, Geary's command moved forward about noon and bypassed Pine Mountain itself. After crossing two streams, the Second Division halted in a new position in the woods to the right side of Pine Mountain. Each brigade was formed in two lines and the 33rd was lucky enough to be in the second line in a reserve position. However, prior experience must have told the men that once again they were going into battle, their fourth of the campaign.[15]

The wooded area where the division had halted consisted of a series of steep ridges with intervening narrow ravines. However, the ground was not totally consistent as there were a number of spurs running off the ridges. The Second Division did not have too long to wait. General Hooker ordered a 2:00 P.M. attack on the Confederate position to the front. When the 33rd and the rest of the Second Brigade moved forward at 2:15, they crossed the first ravine without significant resistance and waited on the first ridge for the other two brigades to come on line. After all of the brigades reached this position, the entire division moved forward against the main Confederate line on a ridge known as Pine Knob. The advance came under sharp skirmish fire, but the Confederate skirmishers fell back until the attackers came within 200 yards of the main line. Then "the action really began," as the Confederates opened up with deadly musket and artillery fire from well established defensive positions. Since the Union advance could go no further, the men dug in as best they could. Although both of division's flanks were exposed, Confederate counterattacks on both ends were beaten back.[16]

When the attack began, the 33rd was somewhat protected due to the regiment's position in the second line. At some point between 5:00 P.M. and midnight, the 33rd moved up to the front line and came under Confederate fire.[17] The regiment and the entire Second Brigade was in an especially vulnerable position, subject to both artillery and musket fire from three sides and so close to the enemy that Union voices carried into the Confederate works.[18] This was the first and only time during the campaign that the regiment failed to prepare breastworks in the presence of the enemy, which made an already dangerous situation even worse.[19] Such defenses were important, even though General Geary claimed that the close proximity to the Confederate main line made the work dangerous. According to Geary, "The sound of an ax was the signal for a volley of bullets and canister from the enemy." Eventually, in spite of these dangers, trees were cut down in the rear and with "the active use of the spade, a tolerable line" was established.[20] However, for some reason this did not happen on the 33rd's portion of the line.

Regimental adjutant Stephen Pierson claimed that breastworks were not constructed due to reports that the regiment was going to move. Although it is hard to imagine where they would go in the face of such strong opposition, Lieutenant Colonel Fouratt apparently believed the reports, since he ordered Pierson to wake the regiment. Most of the men had lain down where they stood with their weapons at their sides. After Pierson had woken the men, he came to "a row of men stretched out with singular regularity." Since he got no response when he shook these men, Pierson pulled the blanket off one to find "he was dead — they were all dead!," awaiting burial. All in all, said Pierson, it was "a very gruesome experience." After four battles within six weeks, Pierson had apparently been cured of the macabre humor he had exhibited at Dug Gap.

The anticipated order to move never came, and daybreak found the 33rd in a very exposed position. Pierson reported, "The rebel fire was terribly accurate and demoralizing," a redundant statement if there ever was one. The Confederates were firing from protected positions on the unprotected "Jerseymen" so the scene must have resembled a shooting gallery, but the targets in blue were alive, at least for the moment. The regiment's losses piled up as the day went on and the situation got worse in the afternoon when they came under enfilade fire from the right flank. Since this had the potential for disaster, the brigade commander, Colonel Patrick Jones, ordered two companies of the 33rd to advance and stop the Confederate fire. Lieutenant Colonel Fouratt sent Pierson with the two companies and also accompanied them himself. After the movement had almost stopped the Confederate fire, Pierson, "rather foolishly, stood up." Although Pierson had survived a similar mistake at Dug Gap, he was not so lucky this time and was hit by a Confederate bullet in the chest that produced a "stinging sickening sensation." As Fouratt placed Pierson against a tree, Fouratt was afraid that the wound was fatal, but the bullet had passed through his body without hitting his lungs. Pierson was evacuated to the rear and his white appearance led Doctor Reiley, the regimental surgeon, to give Pierson a big drink of whiskey. Pierson claimed this was the first time he had tasted whiskey and the strong drink went to his head. After his wound was dressed, Pierson "was fighting mad, and they tell me my one desire was to get out and kill the fellow who had shot me." Someone had to be detailed to make sure that Pierson did not act on this desire. Although the use of whiskey was problematic, Doctor Reiley was smart enough not to send Pierson to the hospital and he remained with the regiment on light duty and would completely recover.[21]

Although Pierson was fortunate to survive his foolishness, not as lucky was Lieutenant William Cochrane, who was killed on the skirmish line. Since the death of Captain Bartlett at Dug Gap, Cochrane had been in command of Company G (he originally joined with Company K as a 1st lieutenant). At Pine Knob, Cochrane was firing from behind a tree and moved to the other side of the tree to avoid a Confederate sharpshooter. When he moved, Cochrane exposed himself to another Confederate who put a fatal bullet just below Cochrane's left collarbone, which went through or near his heart. Chaplain John Faull, who "loved him as a man and a soldier," reported that Cochrane was buried under a large chestnut tree. In a sad footnote, Cochrane's commission as captain arrived two days after his death.[22] The fighting went on until dark when the Confederates once again evacuated their position. Even though the situation had been extremely difficult, the performance of the 33rd was widely praised. William Lambert said that the regiment's conduct "excelled that of any former occasion."[23] In eliminating the threat from the enfilade fire, Captain O'Connor reported that the two companies "saved the integrity of the line." Praise was also received from a more objective source: Colonel Lockman of the 119th New York stated that the 33rd provided "very efficient assistance" and that "in a measure the success of the movement is due to them."[24]

However, such "efficient assistance" had a high cost. The regiment suffered its highest casualties of the war, the highest of any regiment engaged at Pine Knob.[25] Including those who would subsequently die of their wounds, the 33rd lost 19 dead and 37 wounded. In addition to Lieutenant Cochrane, the following were killed during the long night and day at Pine Knob: William Harker, John Gastlin, Peter Murray, Frederick Weigamonn, Livsey Walsh, Charles Locke, John McArdle, Abraham Vanderhoff, Thomas Eaves, Joseph Hennessy and Lemuel Letts. Thomas Eaves was a Paterson man. Captain Courtois wrote that he was "beloved by all in the regiment." Now he was buried where he fell, "another sacrifice to this accursed rebellion." Perhaps in as much surprise as relief, Courtois noted laconically, "I am still alive." In addition to those killed on the battlefield, Thomas Sands, George Stoll, John Gutherie, Edwin Ryan, Tallmand Hickerson, Newton Dutcher, and Thomas Farrell were wounded and died within the next 30 days. The regiment also lost a man to disease when John Personett died at Chattanooga on June 17.[26]

When the Confederates withdrew on June 16, the retreat was caused by a wise decision by General Thomas to disobey orders. Since Sherman still believed on the night of June 15 that the Confederates had withdrawn, he ordered Thomas to attack the following day. However, Thomas ignored the order and attempted to break the Confederate defenses with his artillery. The artillery fire along with some minor flanking movements put the Confederate left at risk, and Johnston ordered a retreat for after dark on the night of the 16. After Sherman received word of the withdrawal, he ordered Thomas to resume the pursuit the next morning.[27] Once the Confederates withdrew, the entire Second Division moved forward on June 17 and occupied the Confederate defensive position. They did not remain there long, as Geary's command was on the move again by 10:00 A.M. When the Second Brigade advanced in two lines, they moved through some dense woods into an open area on the Marietta and Dallas road and formed in line on some low ground between Darby's Farm and Mud Creek.[28] William Lambert was impressed with the creativity used in naming the creek; he claimed that names in Georgia were "almost as euphonious as those in Virginia."[29] More pertinent at the moment was not the creek's name but the surrounding terrain, which rose sharply from the creek to a hill. In keeping with their standard operating procedure, the Confederates had used the hill to establish a strong defensive positon.[30]

After the division's experiences at Dug Gap and Resaca, General Geary was probably cautious about attacks against higher ground. While the bulk of the division stayed in place, Geary deployed his artillery in an attempt to break the Confederate defensive line. Once the Union batteries got into position, they opened an effective destructive fire on the Confederates. The greatest impact was on the rebel artillery, with a number of guns destroyed or put out of action through the destruction of their protecting embrasures.[31] Back in the Union ranks, "SH" found the Union artillery fire a sight "of great interest and excitement"[32] and certainly better than a direct infantry assault. Although the regiment was not engaged, Everett Horton of Company E received a wound that would prove fatal when Horton died on July 25 in the army hospital at Jeffersonville, Indiana.[33]

While the Second Division was engaged near Darby's Farm, Union artillery fire on another part of the front convinced Johnston of fatal flaws in the Confederate defensive position. Although a withdrawal was necessary, the movement could not take place until new defensive positions were established. Fortunately for the Confederates, the rain returned on the night of June 17–18, making offensive action impossible.[34] The 33rd could not have been in a worse position for bad weather. The ground was already wet and swampy and the men were out in the open without shelter, exposed to the rain and cold winds. Mud Creek overflowed its banks, adding to the general misery. On the skirmish line and in the rifle pits, the men suffered from cramps, a new and unexpected ailment.[35] After 11 straight days of rain at the beginning of the month and now this, the men must have thought the weather was fighting for the Confederates.

The bad weather covered the Confederate withdrawal to their strongest position of the campaign. The new Confederate lines were seven miles long and "anchored and dominated by Kennesaw," a two-mile ridge with three prominent peaks ranging from 200 to almost 700 feet high. When Sherman learned of the evacuation, he again jumped to the erroneous conclusion that the Confederates were retreating across the Chattahoochee River. The renewed Federal pursuit soon learned the truth as they approached Kennesaw Mountain.[36] Fortunately for the 33rd and the rest of the XX Corps, their route of pursuit was to the right of Kennesaw. After the Second Division skirmishers discovered the Confederate evacuation, the division was in pursuit on the Dallas and Marietta road by 7:00 A.M. the next morning. Everyone was glad to get across Mud Creek on a rebuilt bridge, but the march was soon delayed by flood damage to the bridge at Nose's Creek. Once the division got over that creek, they advanced about one mile before reaching the new Confederate defensive line. As the division went on the line, the Second Brigade was assigned a reserve position behind the First and Third Brigades. Although the regiment was out of the swampy position at Mud Creek, the men were no drier; heavy rain continued all day.[37]

Conditions were no better on the next day, June 20, another day of rain and mud.[38] During the morning, the 33rd and the rest of the Second Brigade relieved the Third Brigade. The Second Brigade remained in this position overnight while the other two brigades moved to the right. The next morning, the Second Brigade moved three miles to the right and was reunited with the division.[39] At some point during that day, William Lloyd found time to write to Mary. The strain was beginning to tell on Lloyd, who wrote pessimistically, "We are fighting everyday and I suppose we will be for a long time." On top of the pessimism were clear signs of fatigue: "I am tired of this war, I have seen enough bloodshed." Constantly in combat situations, frequently in rain and mud, there had to be many in the regiment who shared Lloyd's sentiments. During the skirmishing near Pine Knob, Lloyd had apparently almost been taken prisoner. He told Mary that a dozen Confederates had gotten to within 10 feet of him. Although the number of Confederates and the distance were probably exaggerated, Lloyd knew the likely fate of prisoners of war. He fired and ran, while the enemy, regardless of their number and distance, fired and missed.[40]

When the next day brought more rain, everyone was probably disgusted but not surprised. Sherman, who was definitely disgusted, ordered his commanders not even to bother trying offensive operations. For almost a month, the armies had done little more than march, fight, eat, and sleep; they had frequently done so in water and mud. By this point, the unhealthy conditions were producing pneumonia, influenza, and rheumatism, which were sending more men to the rear than Confederate bullets. After the rain mercifully stopped on June 22, Sherman ordered Hooker and the XX Corps to advance towards Marietta. In the early afternoon they moved forward from Nose's Creek with Geary's division in the center. As the advance neared Kolb's Farm on Powder Springs Road, they came under Confederate picket fire and then heavy artillery fire. This was obviously of some concern, but of even greater concern were the claims of two Confederate prisoners of war. The captured Confederates said

James T. Gibson, 1st lt. and captain, Company D. *New Jersey State Archives, Department of State.*

that two Confederate corps under Hood and Hardee were preparing to attack from the woods to the immediate front. Since they would have been vastly outnumbered by what was perhaps the whole Confederate army, Hooker and Schofield, who were on Hooker's right, quickly ordered their men to dig in. While they did so, two regiments were sent forward to make a reconnaissance. They did, in fact, encounter large number of Confederates in the woods forming for an attack.[41]

Although the Confederate force was large, there was only one corps, not two. About 5:00 P.M., Hood's corps moved forward in an attempt to attack the Union flank. As soon as the Confederate troops came out of the woods, Union artillery opened up a lethal crossfire.[42] On this rare occasion, the bulk of the 33rd were fortunate to be spectators rather than participants. The scene provided the recovering adjutant, Stephen Pierson, with his first but not his last "good view of a rebel charge." When the attack began, Pierson said the advance was a "beautiful sight" as the Confederates "swept forward" in an almost perfect line. However, the combination of artillery fire from the front by Williams' division and from the flank by Geary's artillery was "more than men could stand."[43] Under this withering fire, Chaplain Faull reported, the net result was "not more a tithe of them going by the route they had so boldly come in an hour before." Faull, who was obviously no pacifist, walked over the field the next morning and graphically described the landscape as being "covered with blood and brains."[44] Even though most of the 33rd just watched this engagement, the regiment did some skirmishing with some wounded, but no fatalities.[45] Since total Confederate losses were 1,500 compared to 250 for the Union, it is no wonder that Kolb's Farm has been described as "more a one sided slaughter than it is a battle."[46]

While the Union forces had clearly prevailed, their commanders took no chances. By the next morning both Geary's and Williams' divisions had established "full fledged breastworks" on the north side of Powder Springs Road. The Union advance on this part of the front had focused on the possibility of flanking the Confederate left. Since the movement had indicated that the Confederate line was extended at least a mile past the Union right, Sherman decided that nothing could be accomplished on that flank. This conclusion was incorrect, but Sherman's choice of an alternative was even worse: a frontal assault on Confederate fortifications, something he had avoided up to this point. The frontal attack would be made at 8:00 A.M. on June 27 against the main Confederate position on Kennesaw Mountain. At the same time, Schofield was ordered to make a side maneuver on the far right to continue to probe the Confederate left. All of the attacks on Kennesaw Mountain ended in bloody failure; Union losses totaled 3,000 compared to only 700 for the Confederates. Too late to prevent this disaster, word was received that it was indeed possible to turn the Confederate left. This required a stronger force than Schofield had in place so Sherman decided that the quickest and most effective plan was to move McPherson's army from the far left to the far right of the Union position. As McPherson's command was not connected to the railroad, the movement had to wait until the troops received sufficient supplies for ten days.[47]

When the carnage on Kennesaw Mountain took place, the 33rd was extremely fortunate to avoid any part in the assault. While the main attack took place, the regiment and the rest of the division was ordered to move forward in support. As the division formed in a mass formation, the 33rd and the rest of the Second Brigade were in the front. The advance began at 8:00 A.M., first over open ground and then into some woods. After this, the regiment fixed bayonets and charged at the double quick. The attack apparently took the Confederates by surprise and the 33rd captured a number of prisoners without suffering any casualties. Probably as dangerous as the attack was digging in under artillery fire, but again, no casualties were reported. Once in this position, the regiment remained there until the night of June 30.[48]

Since the regiment now had a brief respite from both movement and fighting, William Lloyd had another opportunity to write to Mary. Although the regiment had avoided the slaughter at Kennesaw Mountain, Lloyd's morale had still not improved. His clothes were worn out from the campaign and the combination of heat and fighting had done the same to his morale and stamina. While the regiment was still in Georgia, Lloyd was sure that "we are just as near hell as I want to be." Lloyd may have been tired, but he was not too worn out to take some verbal shots at Company H commander, Captain Barent Frazer, who was never one of Lloyd's favorites. After Frazer had suffered a leg wound, his behavior convinced Lloyd that Frazer "aint no man and no soldier." Lloyd was sure that Frazer would find a way to get home as soon as the campaign was over, but he was nowhere near as sanguine about his own return home. Lloyd wished he could be back home to go to the country with Mary, but he noted dryly, "I don't think I will." Atlanta was still Lloyd's immediate destination, but at this point he thought the only ones who would live to get there "will have to dig their way."[49]

At the same time that Lloyd was writing to Mary, Sherman received correspondence of a more strategic nature. A telegram from the army chief of staff, General Henry Halleck, signaled a major change in both the strategy and the importance of the Atlanta campaign. From the beginning, one of Sherman's tasks had been to keep Johnston from sending troops to aid Lee against Grant in Virginia. Since Grant and Lee were now stalemated near Petersburg and Richmond, Grant told Sherman, through Halleck, that Sherman no longer needed to be concerned with that part of his mission. As a result Sherman was even freer to concentrate on capturing Atlanta. Perhaps more significantly, with Grant unable to defeat Lee, the success or failure of the Atlanta campaign became even more important as a potential decisive factor in the presidential election.[50]

Two days later, on June 30, McPherson was ready to begin his flanking movement around the Confederate left.[51] While that movement began, the Second Brigade moved four miles to the right across the Sandtown Road. The shift of the Second Brigade began at 7:00 P.M. on June 30 and was completed the next day. As part of this overall movement, the 33rd moved two miles to the right.[52] The continued pressure on the left of the already extended Confederate line convinced Johnston that the current position was no longer tenable. As a result, he issued orders to abandon the strong Kennesaw Mountain positions during the night of July 2–3. Although the new Confederate defenses were some six miles south of Marietta, the position was still north of the Chattahoochee River.[53]

As the Army of the Cumberland pursued the retreating Confederates through

Marietta, they encountered resistance south of the town.[54] The pursuit by the Second Division began at daylight, and skirmishing started almost as soon as the division passed through the abandoned Confederate works. After moving through "thickly wooded, broken country," the advance encountered a hastily constructed Confederate defensive line. The combination of artillery fire and a charge by skirmishers drove the Confederates from this new position. The advance of five miles may not have seemed like much, but the progress was significant compared to the limited results of the past month. During the day, the 33rd captured some of the total of 170 prisoners captured by the Second Division. Many of the Confederates had simply had enough and used the retreat to give up the cause. By late afternoon on the eve of the ultimate Union holiday, the regiment had come up against a strong Confederate defensive position.[55]

This Fourth of July in the deep South was an exceptionally hot day.[56] In recognition of the occasion, the officers of the 33rd paused to celebrate the founding of the nation they were fighting to preserve. Perhaps they appreciated the irony, and took satisfaction in doing so deep in the part of the country that was trying to destroy that nation. According to Chaplain Faull, the men passed the day thinking of the past and dreaming of the future. The specialty of the day in the officer's mess was ham soup, and Faull asked, "Who of all the learned in the art of cookery ever heard of ham soup." Prepared by "Mike, an Irishman of the first style," the dish was praised by the officers as "bully."[57] Apparently similar bounty was not available to the enlisted men; William Lloyd told Mary that he had to make do with "2 drinks of whiskey, one chew of tobacco, one cracker and a cup of coffee without sugar."[58]

Even though the holiday was observed, the day did not pass without a call to duty. About 5 P.M., the regiment was ordered to take a house where Confederate fire was, according to Adjutant Pierson, "annoying someone, somewhere." The 33rd went to take this objective, but on arrival they found that the XIV Corps had already done the job. Before this, however, an artillery shell landed in the soft mud near Pierson and the spray "literally covered me with mud; face, eyes, nose, ears, clothes, horse, and all were plastered." The combination of mud and other debris made Pierson think "I was dead: but I was only very dirty." Although Pierson was not sure where the shells hit, he was "very glad that I did not know by experience."[59] Apparently Pierson was not the only one who was "plastered." William Lloyd reported that the officers in charge of the operation were drunk, one so badly that he could not stay on his horse.[60]

The new Confederate defensive line was still north of the Chattahoochee, but the position was only six miles from Atlanta, less than one day's march. Sherman's headquarters was now at Vining's Station, where he considered how to cross the Chattahoochee without heavy losses. The preferred strategy continued to be flanking movements, but any such initiative required repair of the railroad between Marietta and Vining's Station. Another problem was the water level of the Chattahoochee; the river swollen by the heavy June rains would have to drop somewhat to permit a crossing. Repairs to the railroad were completed on July 7 and this was followed by Federal crossings of the Chattahoochee on July 8 and 9. With Union troops across the river at two different points, one upstream and one downstream, Johnston ordered another retreat, this time two miles south of the river.[61]

The Confederate retreat across the Chattahoochee was followed by the longest break in the entire campaign, a respite that lasted until July 17. Since leaving Acworth some 30 days before, the Union army had suffered 9,000 combat losses and an equal number of losses from disease and illness. The men, their uniforms and their equipment were worn out, and the army had advanced only 15 miles. Scurvy, diarrhea, malaria, and typhoid fever had become major problems; less lethal but no more pleasant were lice, chiggers, flies, and the heat. At least the ensuing period of inactivity allowed some time for rest, resupply, and some decent food.[62] The 33rd had actually reached the banks of the Chattahoochee before the break in the campaign began. While resting and refitting, the regiment received fresh vegetables, which dealt with the problem of scurvy.[63] Among those using the time to write home was, of course, William Lloyd. Illness had now caught up with Lloyd, who had been sick since the prior evening. Perhaps depressed by his illness, Lloyd now wondered if the campaign had really just begun. He was afraid that it would take the army as long to go the last few miles to Atlanta as they had taken to reach the Chattahoochee. Although Lloyd may have thought he was being pessimistic, his prediction was remarkably on target. One thing Lloyd was sure of: he was tired of "living in dirt and filth of every kind." Now that he had had the benefit of this experience, he was sure he would know how to appreciate a good home, should he be spared to return.[64]

Despite Lloyd's negative outlook, the proximity to Atlanta along with rest and fresh rations probably helped morale. Chaplain Faull tried to close a letter on a positive note by writing, "We can see Atlanta from the high ground in our vicinity with its towers and steeples and warehouses." Faull also took this opportunity to vent his feelings about what he had seen and experienced in the South. Although the Southerners had created an image of "the princely magnificence in which they live," the reality, Faull claimed, was something else. Similar to Lambert's comments about Tennessee, Faull noted that the grand names of towns suggested thousands of residents. In almost every case, said Faull, they instead found "a most forsaken hamlet, made up of a dirty log tavern, a blacksmith shop, and a couple of houses of the same cast and character." Even Marietta, which Faull characterized as "a very pretty town," paled in comparison to Morristown back home in New Jersey. Faull was especially shocked by the lack of education even among those who considered themselves "the first families of their neighborhoods." Consistently the regiment encountered "houses poorly built, farms poorly cultivated and all in a state in keeping with a low standard of intelligence and moral purpose." This entire deplorable situation, Faull believed, was "due to the peculiar institution," i.e., slavery.[65]

Although the long period of rest was badly needed by the army, the inactivity was primarily due to Sherman's plans for the final stage of the campaign. As soon as the army was across the Chattahoochee, the first step was to cut Atlanta's railroad connection to Montgomery, Alabama. When this was accomplished, the army would pretend to advance on Atlanta from the right or south, but would actually move to the left. With this shift completed, the Union armies would attack Atlanta or the communication lines to the east of the city. Since the first step, the feint to the south, would take a Union cavalry division five days, all other offensive action had to wait on this essential piece of Sherman's plan. Sherman was not the only one making deci-

A contemporary view of the battlefield at Peachtree Creek. *George Barnard, Library of Congress.*

sions during this period. Confederate president Jefferson Davis had finally had more than enough of Joseph Johnston's constant retreats. After Davis replaced Johnston with John Bell Hood on July 17, Hood must have clearly understood that his primary responsibility was to attack.[66]

Under Sherman's plan, McPherson's Army of the Tennessee was to move east of Atlanta, while Schofield's Army of the Ohio and Thomas' Army of the Cumberland moved on the city from the north. Should the Confederates move against McPherson, the way would be open for Thomas and Schofield to take Atlanta. On the other hand, if the Confederates simply stayed where they were, then McPherson was to cut the communications to the east. After the communications to the east and west were cut, the Confederates would have no choice but to evacuate Atlanta.[67] The movement got underway for the 33rd and the rest of the Second Division on July 17. Late that afternoon, the regiment crossed the Chattahoochee on a pontoon bridge at Pace's Ferry. Once the crossing was finished just before dark, the division moved two miles south of the river and camped to the west of Nancy's Creek. According to Captain O'Connor, the rest period had done wonders for the regiment, which was now "as well and determined as the day, we started."[68] No doubt the men's physical condition had improved, but even the most optimistic of them had to believe that hard fighting lay ahead. What they did not know was how soon the fighting would happen and how hard it would be.

On the following morning, the Second Brigade including the 33rd moved forward on a reconnaissance toward Nancy's Creek. Although they moved in a line of battle through dense woods, they did not meet any opposition. When the reconnaissance was complete, the rest of the Second Division moved forward at noon and crossed Nancy's Creek on two bridges. Besides some skirmishing with Confederate cavalry, there was no other contact with the enemy. The advance stopped at the junction of the Buckhead road with the Howell Mill road, and the 33rd camped in the woods. Camp was not made, however, until the men put up breastworks. The painful lessons of Pine Knob did not have to be learned more than once.[69]

Once the Army of the Cumberland was in and around Buckhead, Sherman was now ready for the advance on Atlanta from the north and east. Thomas was ordered to push south across Peach-

Thomas O'Connor, captain, Company F; major, HQ. *From the Collections of the New Jersey Historical Society.*

tree Creek, but unknown to Sherman the Confederates had their own plans for Peachtree Creek. As the Union forces advanced from the north and east, a gap had opened between the Union armies. Hood was aware of the gap and he designed a plan for offensive action. Two Confederate corps were to attack the Army of the Cumberland after they had crossed Peachtree Creek, but before they had dug in. The goal was to drive Thomas' army "into the pocket formed by the junction of the Creek with the Chattahoochee" so that the river and the creek would block any chance of retreat. Thomas would then be separated from the rest of Union army and his choice would be between surrendering or being destroyed. Hood ordered the attack to begin at 1 P.M. on July 20.[70]

While Hood was making his preparations for the attack, the Second Division was crossing Peachtree Creek. The creek was not named after peach trees, but from an Indian story of a giant "pitch" tree that had once been on its banks. Peachtree Creek was an obstacle not because of its depth or width but because of high, steep banks with significant undergrowth, which had the potential to hamper any movement forward or backward. More symbolically, Peachtree Creek was the last natural barrier to Atlanta, five miles away.[71] When the Second Division arrived at Howell's Mill near the creek at about 10:00 A.M., they found some Confederate units on the far bank with the bridge partially destroyed.[72] Meeting some units from the XIV Corps, Geary moved the Second Division to the left about three-quarters of a mile from the mill. A plan for crossing was worked out, while the troops were massed in the surrounding woods. On the far side of the 20-foot-wide creek was a prominent hill where the Confederates had dug in. At about 3:00 P.M., Second Division artillery and heavy skirmish fire opened up on the hill. While this fire kept the Confederates busy, a footbridge was constructed on which Ireland's brigade crossed rapidly and took the hill. Immediately thereafter, the other two brigades followed and dug in. When Geary's skirmishers pushed forward, they hit a Confederate picket line about one-quarter of a mile from the new position.[73]

The next day, July 20 — the worst day in the history of the 33rd — was "fiercely hot." Since only part of the XX Corps had crossed on the 19th, the first order of business was for the rest of Hooker's command to cross. The terrain to the front of the Union position was the typical pattern of low hills and ridges intersected by ravines with the usual pine forest and dense underbrush. Although there were some open fields near the creek, overall visibility was sufficiently limited that neither army could see the other. However, the Confederates knew the location of the Union army, while the Federal forces were ignorant of both the Confederate position and their movements. The advantage was clearly with the Southerners. As the day developed there was, however, one positive factor in favor of the Union army. McPherson's command was advancing from the east, closing in on Atlanta "in overwhelming strength." This force could take Atlanta even before the Confederates attacked, so Hood had no choice but to move his remaining forces to the right. This also meant that the two attacking units had to be moved to the right. Although Hood still planned to attack at 1:00 P.M., further problems developed as the units on the right first moved too slowly and then went a mile further than ordered. Since the units in the center also moved further than ordered, the Confederates were still moving into position when they should have been attacking.[74]

While the Confederate attack was being delayed, the other two divisions of the XX Corps crossed Peachtree Creek and formed on the right and left of Geary's Second Division. Then at about 10:00 A.M., Geary's division moved forward with Candy's brigade in the lead followed by the Second Brigade including the 33rd. The division crossed two ridges and then drove Confederate skirmishers off a third ridge. Since the third ridge was a relatively strong position, the Second Division halted at about noon to wait for the First and Third Divisions to catch up. In establishing this position, Geary brought up all of his artillery and formed his three brigades in a mass formation. At the front of the mass formation was Candy's brigade, supported by Jones' Second Brigade formed in two lines with Ireland's brigade further behind. The division was in an exposed position with basically nothing more than skirmishers from the other two divisions on both flanks.[75]

Finally at about 3:00 P.M., Hardee's command, the right portion of the Confederate attacking force, was in position. The left portion of the attacking force under General Alexander Stewart had thinned out, their line being stretched further to the right. When Hardee ordered his attack to begin at 4:00 P.M., the delays had not hurt the Confederates significantly. Although the entire Union force was on the south side of Peachtree Creek, they had not dug in or prepared defenses. Both of Geary's flanks were insecure and the other two divisions were not even in a combat formation, so the XX Corps was especially vulnerable. The sequence of the attack was to be from the right to left so that the Union left would be forced into the pocket described earlier. Although the delay did not hurt the Confederates on the right, the failure to make a reconnaissance did. When part of the Confederate force on the right got lost and could not find the Union position, it was driven back having met with little success.[76]

Meanwhile, the 33rd's luck had run out. To the front of the Second Division's position was a "high, narrow, timbered hill" about 300 yards from the main line.[77] When Geary ordered Colonel Jones, commander of the Second Brigade, to send out his largest regiment to prepare the hill for an artillery battery, the 33rd was that regiment.[78] Up to then the situation had been very quiet; mail had just been handed out and Adjutant Pierson was reading a letter from his father.[79] Lieutenant Colonel Fouratt ordered the regiment to fall in, and they marched 100 yards to the right of the breastworks and then up a road toward the hill. One participant remembered that "the most undisturbed quiet reigned along the line" with the only sounds being the commands of the officers, the noise of the marching men and occasional picket fire on the flanks.[80] Although it was quiet, Stephen Pierson found the atmosphere "ominously still." On his way forward, Pierson passed Lieutenant Colonel Jackson of the 134th New York, who grimly shook hands and said goodbye. When Pierson laughed in response, Jackson said, "There'll be trouble out there."[81]

As the 33rd marched towards the hill, they encountered no opposition. Immediately in front of the hill, they halted and formed a line of battle.[82] While the regiment waited, Fouratt as well as General Geary and Colonel Jones looked over the ground. On the way to the hill, Geary had met three Confederate prisoners going to the Union rear. The Confederates were "quite communicative, saying there were no large bodies of troops within two miles." Reassured by this false information, Geary ordered Fouratt to proceed.[83] Fouratt then led the 33rd to the knoll, where they prepared to stack arms before working on the fortifications. When Geary's skirmishers tried to move forward at the front of the hill, they were suddenly hit with a volley of musket fire. Since the skirmishers were so close to the hill, some of the bullets reached the regiment's position. Pierson was then ordered by Fouratt to ride to an open area to the left for a clearer view. When he did so, Pierson, who apparently enjoyed watching Confederate attacks, said that he "saw a beautiful sight. Down the great open fields they were coming, thousands of them, men in gray by Brigade front, flags flying." Unlike that of Kolb's Farm, this charge was of more than academic interest to Pierson; he stopped only long enough to get the full picture and headed back to report.[84]

By the time Pierson reached the hill, his report was probably superfluous. Coming out of the woods to the front was a large Confederate force delivering a "rapid

and effective fire." Added to the din of the musket fire was the piercing rebel yell. Somehow the regiment maintained their poise and returned "their fire with vim." Although this briefly halted the first line, the attack simply moved down the ravine on the regiment's right. When Fouratt tried to deploy two companies to protect the flank, the Confederates brushed them aside.[85] As the Confederates passed to the right and rear of the regiment "pouring in a heavy fire from those quarters," another large group of Confederates appeared on the regiment's left.[86] Although taking fire from three sides for almost 45 minutes, the regiment held on as best they could.[87] By this point the 33rd was in danger of being completely surrounded. The Confederates were already shouting orders for the regiment to surrender its colors. Faced with no practical alternative, Lieutenant Colonel Fouratt ordered the regiment to "fall back fighting."[88]

Orlando Guerin, private, Company E; quartermaster and sgt., HQ; 2nd lt., Company I. *U.S. Army Military History Institute.*

Falling back did not help much, however, as the Confederates continued to move forward, almost trampling the retreating regiment. Although the regiment maintained some level of order at first, confusion quickly took over. Since Pierson was still weak from his wound at Pine Knob, he had trouble keeping up and finally fell to the ground exhausted. A Confederate saw him and said, "Get out of that you Yankee son of a gun." Pierson recalled, laconically, "I got out." When he reached the main line, Pierson met his omniscient friend, Lieutenant Colonel Jackson, who queried, "Where are they Adjutant?" "Deploy quickly," said Pierson, "they are right here." But Jackson was wounded before he could even give an order, which just added to the confusion.[89] Another beneficiary of Confederate mercy was Captain George Harris

Opposite: George M. Harris, 1st lt., Company A; captain, Company E; escaped death or capture at Peachtree Creek through Confederate assistance. *U.S. Army Military History Institute.*

(who had joined Company A as a 1st lieutenant) of Company E. After receiving a scalp wound on the left side of his head, Harris was helped over the breastworks by a Confederate. According to Harris, this was the second time that he had received such assistance.[90]

Although Fouratt had heard the Confederate shouts for the regiment to surrender their colors, he claimed defiantly, "With this order we would not comply."[91] However, when the retreat moved through a ravine where the air was "literally full of bullets," a symbolic but important disaster struck.[92] When the color guard stopped in the mistaken belief that a halt had been ordered, they were separated from the regiment, which was fatal.[93] The bearer of the state flag was killed along with a member of the color guard, while other members of the color guard were captured.[94] While all this was going on, the state flag was captured by John Abernathy of the 27th Alabama.[95] Fouratt noted sadly that, given the situation, "to recover the colors was impossible."[96]

The attacking Confederates and the retreating 33rd reached the main Union line almost simultaneously.[97] Along with the 33rd, the 134th and 154th New York fell back in confusion to the bottom of the ridge.[98] Since the Second Division's position was without breastworks and had little support on the right flank, the situation was quite grave. When Pierson arrived within Union lines he thought the battle was lost, but he then saw General Hooker advancing, not retreating. According to Pierson, Hooker said, "Boys, I guess we will stop here," and Pierson, said "stop there we did."[99] Hooker personally rallied both Candy's and Jones' brigades.[100] In response, the Second Division units wheeled to the right and fired on the Confederates in the gap between them and where Williams' division should have been. As they poured enfilade fire on the Confederates and held on, Williams' division finally came up and opened fire from the other side. The Confederates were then caught in a crossfire where they were "mowed down wholesale." Union artillery also took a terrible toll on the attacking Confederates.[101]

Finally, the Confederate attack was driven back. The Confederates were planning a second attack, but Hood was forced to turn his attention to McPherson's advance on his right flank. Although McPherson's command was now within three miles of the center of Atlanta, as at Resaca, McPherson advanced too cautiously and halted. However, a second Confederate attack at Peachtree Creek would have had little chance of success. The Federal troops were now digging in and the element of surprise was gone. The Confederate attack at Peachtree had failed. Although the Confederates had had numerical superiority on the right portion of the front, the attack had been uncoordinated and ineffective. On the left, the element of surprise had helped the Confederates, but an attack of four brigades against nine lacked the numbers to ultimately be successful.[102]

As twilight settled on the battlefield, Pierson approached Bundy's battery of the division artillery. The battery had been part of the devastating Union artillery fire in spite of equally fierce Confederate musket fire. The musket fire was so intense that the spokes of the wheels of the Union artillery carriage had been cut in two. A sergeant, "black and grimy from the fight," told Pierson, "Your stocking legs saved us." Apparently when the powder in cartridges became spoiled, members of the regiment would save the musket balls. When the men had accumulated enough to fill a stocking, they would give them to the artillery battery. At the point when they were hardest pressed during the battle, the artillerymen had loaded the stockings in the guns and fired at point blank range with terrible effect. "It was awful, Adjutant," said the sergeant. Pierson noted that the bodies of the Confederate dead to the front of the battery were "mute evidence of the truth of the Sergeant's story."[103]

While the attacking Confederates had suffered terrible losses, the 33rd themselves had also suffered horribly. A total of 21 men had been killed during the battle or would die from their wounds. Company A suffered only one fatality, Isaac Knight, while Company B had four: Robert Harrison, Bartholomew Cunningham, James Losey, and James McCombs. Although Company C was spared, Company D lost John Vorhees, Peter Wenckler and Alexander McGill. McGill, who was from Paterson, had had part of his skull shot away at Second Manassas. McGill had rejoined his original unit at Fredericksburg, but due to his wound he could not tolerate the loud noise of battle. McGill had then been discharged and returned to his old job as a molder in Paterson. When the 33rd was formed, he believed he was cured and volunteered again. Left behind were a wife and child "deprived of his watchful care." Company E suffered three fatalities, James Lathrop, James Fortune, and Benjamin Wilson, while Company F had one, Ezra Conklin. Although William Lloyd's Company H had only one fatality, Hugh Shields, Company I had four men killed: Charles Anys (originally a member of Company D), Martin Braan (also a member of Company D), Frederick Ehrnest (originally with Company E), and Thomas Williams. The balance of the fatalities came from Company K: William Green, John Long, William Thompson, and Patrick Travers.[104] In addition to the dead, the regiment reported over 30 men missing, many of whom were on their way to Andersonville Prison. Another 20 or more had been wounded.[105]

Also heartfelt was the loss of the state colors. William Lambert reported the loss to the Newark *Daily Advertiser* "with deepest regret, but without shame or sense of disgrace."[106] When Lieutenant Colonel Fouratt wrote of the loss to the state adjutant general, he did so "with feelings of deepest sorrow," but added, "we feel it to be no fault of ours."[107] In support of their position, Lambert and Fouratt quoted the corps, division, and brigade commanders as stressing that under these circumstances the loss was no disgrace. In fact, both Hooker and Geary expressed wonder that the regiment was able to bring back as many men as they did as well as the national colors. This was all true, but Lambert had to have bitter memories of his own words to the readers of the *Daily Advertiser* when the regiment was given the flag back in Lookout Valley. Then, Lambert had pledged that the flag would be returned to New Jersey with "no mark or association" that would make the state reluctant to claim the regiment as their own. There was, however, something appropriate in the loss of such an important symbol on the regiment's worst day of the war. Every minute that the 33rd held up the main attack at Peachtree Creek contributed to stopping a Confederate breakthrough. Placed through no fault of their own in an impossible situation, the regiment had done their duty. The cost of that duty was lost lives and a lost symbol. It was, Georg Muller told his parents, "a very hard day."[108]

VIII

"The old flag floats over Atlanta"

If life is unfair, little in life is less fair than war. In every war some go through combat unscathed to live long and full lives, while others, for no reason besides luck or chance, die without ever having a chance to live. Although this disparity exists in every battle in every war, the difference was especially pronounced for the 33rd New Jersey after the battle of Peachtree Creek. Those who emerged safe, but shaken, could not have known that they had fought their last battle. Although another full year would pass before the regiment returned to Newark, as a unit they would not see combat again. This reality, unknown at the time, magnified the sacrifices of the regiment's dead, who were buried on the field the next day under another scorching Georgia sun.[1]

The living and the dead were not, however, the only groups left in the aftermath of the battle. While the sufferings of the dead were over, those who were taken prisoner or were badly wounded had more to endure. It is to these two groups that we turn our attention before returning to the end of the Atlanta campaign. Probably the worse off of the two groups were the enlisted prisoners on their way to Andersonville prison in southwestern Georgia. Located some 40 miles east of the Chattahoochee River, Andersonville's official name was Camp Sumter. When the Confederate leadership decided to open this new facility in late 1863, they believed that both existing and new prisoners would be more secure in a location further away from the fighting. Although it seems ludicrous in retrospect, the Confederates also believed that it would be easier to supply Andersonville due to the close proximity to the corn growing section of Georgia. Both of these beliefs were wrong, the second one tragically so.

Construction began in January of 1864 of a facility intended to hold 10,000 men. Almost from the beginning the Confederates had difficulty in getting supplies. This began with a lack of lumber that prevented the building of barracks. The second alternative, that of using tents to house the prisoners, also proved impractical. As a result, the prisoners who began arriving in February of 1864 were on their own to arrange protection from the elements. What happened at Andersonville was doubly tragic because of the combination of the things the Confederates could not control and the things they could control, but did not. While the inability to provide housing was bad enough, the situation was made much worse by the failure of the Confederate authorities to lay out a system of roads and rows where the men would build their shelters. Without any such plan or system, it was impossible to maintain any kind of sanitary standards.

At the end of March, Henry Wirz, who would pay the ultimate price for the suffering at Andersonville, was placed in charge of the interior of the prison. Additional prisoners arrived throughout the spring, and the planned capacity of the camp was exceeded by May. The already high mortality rate among the prisoners was increased by the additional strain on the camp's limited resources. On June 17, the day after the 33rd was engaged at Pine Knob, there were more than 21,500 prisoners at Andersonville, twice the intended capacity. When the prisoners from Peachtree Creek arrived some six weeks later, there were almost 30,000 prisoners at Andersonville.

Probably the best description of Andersonville is the same phrase that best describes Civil War combat: "lethal chaos." "Of the three basic necessities—food, shelter and clothing—the only one which Confederate authorities provided for the Andersonville prisoners was food." Since there were no barracks or tents, the men had to construct their own shelters with whatever supplies they could find. As for clothing, they only had that which they wore and had no way of getting any replacements. Some food was provided, but the rations were at best monotonous and soon became scarce. Originally, the Confederates intended to issue cooked rations, but they did not have adequate facilities to do so. Instead, they issued uncooked rations to the men, who had no regular source of fuel for cooking. Incredibly, better food was available from appointed sutlers at prices such as $12 for a gallon of molasses. This was almost a month's pay for soldiers, many of whom had not been paid in months, so it was not a practical alternative. The presence of a sutler at a place like Andersonville suggests that the Confederates were unwilling to take extraordinary measures to deal with extraordinary problems.

The lack of adequate rations and protection from the elements made it very difficult for the men to maintain their health in what had to be the unhealthiest environment imaginable. Some of the prisoners transferred from other prisons were already infected with diseases such as smallpox. Since no plan was ever implemented for the disposal of human waste, the creek running through camp was thoroughly polluted. The resulting combination of little food of poor quality, the absence of discipline or planning about hygiene, and the lack of soap, or clean water increased dramatically every soldier's chance of becoming sick. Besides smallpox, also present were typhoid fever, scurvy, gangrene, and malaria, with dysentery and diarrhea so commonplace that almost everyone was affected. Going to the hospital did not help. The lack of facilities and medicine combined with the inadequate knowledge of hygiene made admission to the hospital little more than a death sentence.[2]

Under these circumstances, maintaining any semblance of morale was almost impossible. In combat a soldier could at least take actions on his own behalf. At Andersonville, a man could only wait and hope or, more likely, wait and die. After prisoner exchanges ended in early July, there was precious little hope left. Successful escape was almost impossible due to the remoteness of the location and the efficiency of the dogs used in the pursuit. The dogs reduced the number of successful escapes, but this would not be forgotten when Sherman's army marched through Georgia that fall. By August, the prison population had reached almost 33,000 with almost 3,000 deaths that month, a mortality rate of 9 percent.[3]

Some members of the 33rd did end up at Andersonville, but there is no certainty about the exact number. Although the different reports of the battle at Peachtree Creek indicated almost 40 officers and men missing, this was clearly postbattle confusion.[4] For example, George Harris, Robert Harrison, and James Lathrop were listed as missing, but Harrison and Lathrop were dead and although Harris was wounded, he was back within Union lines. Furthermore, some of the missing were officers, but only enlisted men were sent to Andersonville. What is certain is that at least 12 members of the 33rd were imprisoned there and six of them died, a mortality rate of 50 percent. Peter Ray, Theodore Cadmus, David Wolf, Charles Williamson, James Murphy, and Thomas Eaton were the six fortunate enough to survive. The story of James Murphy of Company C is especially interesting. Taken prisoner just after the fall of Atlanta on September 4, Murphy was sent to Andersonville where he enlisted in the Tenth Tennessee Rebel Infantry. While nothing is known about Murphy's decision, it is not unfair to think that he chose this course over the deadly environment of Andersonville. Murphy was "recaptured" by Union troops in December of 1864 and transferred to the Fifth U.S. Infantry at the end of the war. The latter move suggests that his expedient decision at Andersonville was not held against him.[5] Wolf and Williamson were paroled after the fall of Atlanta in September, which limited their stay at Andersonville to about six weeks.[6]

Of the six who were not so fortunate, the first to die was John Mailey, a musician from Company E, who died on June 16. From that point there were no fatalities until September 1 when Amzi Willis of Company I (originally a member of Company E) died of dropsy. Next was Charles Nolan of Company F who succumbed on September 14. Nolan had been taken prisoner on June 5, apparently during the movement from New Hope Church to Acworth. There was a third fatality that month when John Higgins of Company G died from diarrhea on September 28. Like Wolf and Eaton, Higgins had been taken prisoner at Peachtree Creek. The other fatality among those taken prisoner at Peachtree Creek was Charles Anys. Anys lingered on at Andersonville long after the facility had effectively been closed as a prisoner of war camp, finally dying from his wounds on February 13, 1865. It is hard to imagine a worse place to try to recover from wounds than Andersonville.[7]

There was also a surprise awaiting the men of the 33rd at Andersonville. According to the regiment's records, Jeremiah Dodge of Company H had deserted on December 10, 1863, at Cleveland, Tennessee, during the Knoxville relief expedition.[8] However, when Corporal Thomas Eaton of Company H arrived at Andersonville on July 27, he met Dodge. Whether Dodge had deserted or not (which seems unlikely given the remote location), he had been a Confederate prisoner since December of

1863. Dodge approached Eaton in September "in a very feeble condition," and, convinced that he had only a few days to live, gave Eaton three photos for his family. Since Dodge lived in another part of the camp, Eaton never saw him again. Dodge died without identification and "was buried among the unknown dead."[9] Exposed to the blazing sun or bad weather, with little or no food, water or medicine, it is hard to understand how Eaton, Cadmus, Ray or anyone else survived. When these three arrived at a Union army hospital in May of 1865, they were "sun-browned and emaciated."[10]

Among the many by-products of the success of Sherman's Atlanta campaign was the threat to the security of Andersonville as prisoner of war camp. Shortly after the battle of Peachtree Creek, the Confederate government decided that no new prisoners should be sent there.

Private Theodore Johnson, Company H. *Robert Jones Collection.*

When Atlanta fell in September, the Confederates began moving the prisoners to new locations in South Carolina. By the end of September, the bulk of the prisoners were gone except for unfortunate ones like Charles Anys. From February 24 to September 21 of 1864 almost 9,500 prisoners died; a total of 13,000 died there through the war. After the war ended, Captain Wirz became Andersonville's last fatality when he was hung for conspiracy and murder. The controversy about what happened at Andersonville will probably go on forever. However, it is hard to disagree with the opinion that "if the Confederacy could no longer provide for its prisoners and was yet unwilling to surrender it should have released them on parole." It is unlikely that anyone can "grasp or convey an accurate picture of the horrors of Andersonville Prison or the suffering endured by the men confined there during that awful summer of 1864."[11]

The period was also extremely difficult for the severely wounded or the sick that were evacuated to hospitals in the rear. After they had endured the journey itself, they were then exposed to the multiple inadequacies of Civil War medicine. In June, the Newark *Daily Advertiser* reported that the newspaper had received a letter from several wounded New Jersey soldiers complaining about the conditions at the Totten General Hospital in Louisville, Kentucky. As a significant number of New Jersey soldiers began to arrive at western hospitals, a new situation had developed. All but four of New Jersey's Civil War infantry regiments served in the east, where the hospitals were in places like Washington, D.C., Philadelphia or even Newark. This made it relatively easy for officials or even families to check on the care given to the sick and wounded. This was much more difficult in the west. In their letter, the soldiers asked for the appointment of a state agent to act on their behalf such as some western states and New York had already done in Louisville. The *Daily Advertiser* wholeheartedly concurred, concluding it "would seem only proper that some state provision be made for their comfort."[12]

State officials must have agreed, because on July 19, the Jersey City *American Standard* reported that Mr. C.D. Deshler, state military agent, would shortly leave for the west.[13] A newspaperman from Newark,[14] Deshler invited written inquiries about sick or wounded soldiers from the 13th, 33rd, 34th and 35th infantry regiments and the Second Cavalry. Such inquiries, Deshler promised, would "be cheerfully attended to by him, to the extent of his ability."[15] Deshler then undertook what was at least a two-month trip visiting hospitals throughout the west. When he arrived, one of the first problems he encountered was men "grieving because they fail to hear from home, sometimes by [a] period of four months." Considering the importance of mail to Civil War soldiers, "grieving" was probably not an exaggeration. Deshler attributed the problem to a lack of specific addresses, so his letters to the New Jersey newspapers listed all soldiers by hospital, ward, and even tent so that the men would receive "the best of medicines, 'word from home.'" While trying to get the mail straightened out, Deshler was also at work to obtain furloughs home for those who requested them.[16]

Deshler traveled to Louisville in August and visited soldiers at five different locations in and around the city. Overall, Deshler praised these facilities, especially Jefferson General Hospital. Located three miles east of Louisville at Jefferson, Indiana, this hospital was "a model institution in every respect." The hospital had some 24 permanent wards, each capable of holding 80 patients. The wards were arranged like the spokes of a wheel extending off common facilities at the center. Since Deshler praised the cleanliness of the hospital, it would appear that some lessons had been learned, even if not fully understood. At Totten Hospital his visit confirmed the reports that had prompted his mission. Little more than "a field hospital" with nothing other than tents for accommodations, Totten was "the most poorly managed of all the hospitals I have yet visited." Not surprisingly, the men from New Jersey and other states unfortunate enough to be there were "loud in their complaints." After Deshler made a report to the local authorities, he received assurances that things would improve.[17]

By the end of August, Deshler was in Nashville where he found "another army of sick and wounded soldiers." Considering the inadequacies of Civil War medicine, Deshler must have had incredible patience and compassion. Since there were some 14 or 15 hospitals in and around Nashville,[18] the number of occupants must have indeed seemed like an army. By September, Deshler had visited 275 New Jersey men and had also, along with other state agents, obtained approval for a number of reforms. Although western soldiers hospitalized in the east could be transferred to western hospitals, for some reason the same was not true for eastern soldiers hospitalized in the west. As an alternative, Deshler was able to obtain furloughs for New Jersey soldiers in western hospitals who were unfit for duty. Other successes of the state agents included two months' pay for soldiers who had not been paid and new clothing for wounded soldiers going home on leave.[19]

Deshler reported on the condition of every soldier he saw in person and in at least one case he made a more detailed report. This was the case of Charles Stanley from Newark, who had enlisted as a drummer boy in Company B at the age of 16. Stanley begged to fight in one unnamed battle and he reportedly fought like a veteran until he was wounded so badly that his arm had to be amputated above the elbow. His behavior both on the battlefield and in the hospital earned him the praise of his companions. In reporting this story, Deshler urged the people of Newark to reward Stanley's "genuine courage" by either adopting him or training him for a trade as "the fit return for his lost arm."[20] After Stanley was discharged at Ward Army Hospital in Newark in May of 1865, perhaps the people of Newark responded to Deshler's request.[21]

During the time he was in Nashville, Deshler received a letter from Captain O'Connor, now in command of the regiment. The 33rd had left Lookout Valley with 550 men, but O'Connor reported that in early August the regiment had a strength of only 230 with just 187 present for duty. Thus far in the campaign, O'Connor claimed that the regiment had suffered combat losses of 234 and 100 "sick and worn out." While these numbers cannot be exact, they give a general sense of the losses suffered by the 33rd since May 1. Deshler's reports consist of line after line about soldiers from the 33rd in the different hospitals, not including officers, who apparently could take of themselves. Perhaps reflecting on his experience and O'Connor's letter, Deshler said that in talking to soldiers from other states, "no organization in the Western Army has a prouder name or is more cordially praised than the 33rd New Jersey."[22]

Although they were no doubt proud of their record, the regiment's reputation was probably the furthest thing from the minds of the men as they regrouped after the onslaught at Peachtree Creek. Since there were still fears of another Confederate attack, the depleted ranks of the 33rd spent the night of July 20 building defensive works. After the defenses were in place, the next day was occupied primarily with the grisly job of burying both the Union and Confederate dead.[23] By the time the work was done, burial details from the Second Division of the XX Corps reported burying over 400 Confederate dead. When division skirmishers moved forward about 400 yards in the early morning, they found that the Confederates were still there.[24] The Union forces had prevailed at Peachtree Creek, but the dynamics had changed. For the first time in the campaign, the Confederates had taken the offensive. If they had done so once, they could do so again.

Hood intended to make up for the missed opportunities of July 20. However, this time the area of operations was to be the Federal left off to the east of Atlanta, the location of the greatest danger to the city. Although it had only made a half-hearted advance on the prior day, McPherson's Army of the Tennessee was within artillery range of the city. McPherson was almost in position to cut the railroad to Macon, Atlanta's last fully functioning rail connection. While the greatest danger was on that front, there was also an opportunity since the end of McPherson's line was exposed and vulnerable to attack. If the Confederates turned the Union flank, they

1st Lt. J. Warren Kitchell, Company I. *U.S. Army Military History Institute.*

could defeat McPherson and then go on to surround Thomas as they had tried to do on July 20. However, time was not on Hood's side. He had to act before the Union forces connected and, even more important, before the supply line was cut. McPherson was already aware of the risk to his flank and was trying to protect it. Hoping that his plan could still work, Hood ordered the attack for daylight on July 22.

At the same time that Hood was making his plans, Sherman had to deal with the dynamics of the new situation. No matter what Hood did, it was obvious that Sherman had to eliminate the gap between his forces. After dark on the 21st, Confederate forces began moving through Atlanta to get in position for the attack. When Sherman received word of this, he once again drew the mistaken conclusion that the Confederates were retreating. Although the Confederate movement started late and was slow, by daylight on the 22nd Confederate general Hardee believed his men were in position to attack the Federal left and rear. However, the Confederate troops were having great difficulty moving over terrain that was either swampy or full of briar patches. Now on the offensive, the Confederates were experiencing the same kind of problems that had plagued Union offensives throughout the campaign. As at Peachtree Creek, the advance was disorganized and blind so that the attack had to be delayed until early afternoon.

The whole premise of Hood's plan was an unopposed advance to attack the Union rear. When the Confederates finally attacked, however, they found the premise was not valid. Not only were the Union troops there, but they were prepared for an attack. Through midafternoon, the Confederates made a series of attacks, but each was beaten back. Although the Union defenders prevailed, there was a major loss in Union leadership with the death of General McPherson. The Confederate attacks continued until dark, but they achieved only one breakthrough, which they failed to exploit. After the last attack was driven back, what was to be known as the battle of Atlanta was over. In the bloodiest battle of the entire campaign the Confederates had accomplished nothing.[25] In one historian's view, Hood had "tried to do too much with too little in too short a time."[26]

Over on the Union right, where the 33rd was, Sherman could have been accused of using his troops in a piecemeal fashion. While the fighting raged on the Union left, only 10,000 Confederates along a four-mile front opposed Thomas' force of 40,000 men. Although they might have taken Atlanta or at least relieved some pressure on the Union left, Sherman provided no direction to Thomas.[27] When the Second Division skirmishers advanced at 5:00 A.M. they found that the Confederates had withdrawn. An hour later, the entire corps moved forward through woods and "very broken country." During the movement, the Second and Third Brigades moved in parallel columns with the First Brigade following behind. After passing through the Confederate works and moving to the right, they reached the road from Howell's Mill to Atlanta. The First and Third Brigades followed the road, but the Second Brigade including the 33rd had to move through the woods.

After the three brigades came together again near the junction with the Marietta road, they drove some Confederate skirmishers into the main defensive line. By 10:00 A.M., the division had taken a position on a ridge facing south only 1,000 yards away from Confederate forts on Marietta Street. By this point in the campaign, the

Thomas H. Lee, 1st lt., Company H; captain, Company G. *U.S. Army Military History Institute.*

troops did not have to be told what to do next. Within two hours breastworks had been constructed and the artillery was in place. During the afternoon, the work continued and by dark the works were complete. In their new positions, the division and the regiment were only two miles from Atlanta.[28] The 33rd was so close to the city that Captain Lambert reported, "The spires and larger buildings of the city are in plain view from our position." Speculating confidently, he added, "We judge not many days will elapse ere the starry banner waves over each."[29]

Although the regiment was close to Atlanta that did not mean that all was well within the Union lines. William Lloyd wrote to Mary that like many days that summer, July 28 was "burning, scorching blistering." Lloyd knew that even animals had ways of dealing with such heat, but he was painfully aware that "we poor devils have to stand it."[30] Georg Muller's endurance was also weakening; he wrote his parents, "I wish this thing would be over with, I am so sick of it."[31] When the heavy rains of June were followed by hot, scorching weather during July, massive numbers of insects "infected the lines like a plague." The lack of a balanced diet was causing outbreaks of scurvy, subjecting many of the men to "dry itching sores" on their arms and legs. Sometimes the means of prevention may have seemed worse than the disease itself. Alternatives included eating dried potatoes which when cooked tasked like "pine shavings," or drinking tea made from the roots of the sassafras bush. Although several weeks of drinking this beverage instead of coffee apparently solved the problem, the experience was also "enough of it for a lifetime."[32] Whether from scurvy or some insect borne disease, Lieutenant Colonel Fouratt was hospitalized due to illness.[33] Since the regiment had not had a major after Major Peloubet's resignation, command fell to Captain O'Connor.

After the attack on his left had been repulsed, Sherman was determined to regain the initiative by moving the Army of the Tennessee from the left to the right wing. Once this was complete, this force would move south and attack Atlanta from the west. Sherman believed that Hood would then be forced either to retreat or to come out and fight. Before this move got underway, however, Sherman needed a replacement for McPherson as commander of the Army of the Tennessee. Sherman's recommendation, which Lincoln approved, was to promote General Howard instead of General Hooker or General Logan. Hooker's response was to resign in protest, so the XX Corps including the 33rd New Jersey got a new commander, General Henry Slocum. While Slocum traveled from Mississippi to take command, General Alpheus Williams, a division commander in the XX Corps, was placed in temporary command.[34]

As the Army of the Tennessee prepared for their move, a regular pattern developed on the 33rd's front. Artillery fire was exchanged and skirmishing took place each day. There were several unsuccessful Confederate attempts to drive in the Union pickets. On July 24, the XX Corps began establishing new works some 600 yards closer to the Confederate lines, which were finished and occupied two days later. Advancing the position was always important, but the real importance of the move was that the area covered by the corps was considerably shorter. Since the new line could be held by two of the three divisions, each division could have a turn off of the firing line.[35] Other than this, conditions had not improved dramatically for the regiment, but they had at least avoided any major engagements. Each day without combat restored to some extent their ability to withstand life in the trenches.

Now under the command of General Howard, the Army of the Tennessee began their move on July 27. The plan was to outflank the Confederate left and take the railroad north of East Point. Sherman, who was present during the move, believed that Hood would then evacuate Atlanta. While this movement was underway, Sherman sent his cavalry on a raid south of Atlanta to disrupt the railroad to Macon and possibly free the prisoners at Andersonville. Since the Army of the Tennessee was to move on the far side of a ridge parallel to the Confederate lines, Sherman hoped the ridge would screen the movement and at least delay any Confederate response. However, Howard and his command moved very cautiously and, therefore, very slowly. When Hood received word that the Army of the Tennessee had left their former position, he correctly analyzed Sherman's intentions. In response, Hood extended the Confederate left in anticipation of outflanking the Union right and attacking from the rear on July 29.

Howard's march on the next day, July 28, reached Ezra Church, named after a small Methodist chapel. When the Union advance came into contact with some Confederate skirmishers and were then hit by artillery fire, Howard correctly anticipated an attack and had his men dig in. Twice the Confederates attacked, once at 12:30 P.M. and a second time at 2:00 P.M., but both times they were driven back. The Confederates suffered terrible losses, some five times the Union losses. Although Hood had ordered the attack, this time the primary responsibility for its failure did not lie with Hood. At Ezra Church, the major problem was the decision of the commander, General Stephen Lee, to launch the attack a day earlier than planned. Regardless of who was at fault, the Confederate losses were a major blow to morale and effectively ended Confederate offensive action in the Atlanta campaign.

Although the Union troops had defeated the Confederates with heavy losses,

Sherman was no closer to taking Atlanta. Once again, they had failed to cut the railroad and the simultaneous cavalry offensive was a total failure. More seriously, time was not on Sherman's side. Atlanta was the only theater of the war where a major Union victory seemed at all possible, but any such victory would be useless if it came after the presidential election. The balloting for the election began in October. If the Confederates could deny the Union any major victories for two to three months, they believed they could win the war through the election. As a result the campaign and the Union cause itself now depended on Sherman and his men.

On the Confederate side, Hood had finally realized that no additional offensive action was feasible against a Union army that was united and dug in. By this point, the Confederate forces were down to 56,000 men of whom only 33,000 were front line troops. Since Hood had taken command on July 18, the Confederates had lost 12,000 men killed, wounded, and missing including many good officers who could not be replaced. While desertion had again become a problem, the bulk of the Confederate forces were not ready to give up. However, they could not be asked to make any more frontal assaults. Hood's only possible strategy was to try to hold on to Atlanta and wait Sherman out. Hood also decided to use his cavalry to try to do the same thing to Sherman that Sherman wanted to do to him: cut his vital supply line.

At the beginning of August, Sherman still believed his best option was to outflank the Confederate left. Now he planned to move Schofield's relatively small Army of the Ohio to the Union right. Their goal would be the same as Howard's, to reach the railroad near East Point. With added strength on the Union right wing, Sherman believed he could stretch the Confederate defenses so they could not defend both Atlanta and their extended left. After Schofield's command passed around the Union right on August 2 and reached the north fork of Utoy Creek, they moved through a heavily forested and sparsely populated countryside. Although the effort to take the railroad was to begin on August 4, the offensive was delayed due to infighting among the Union commanders. When the movement resumed the next day, the Union troops were stopped cold by Confederate artillery fire. Another attempt the next day also failed. Even though the Union forces did reach the end of the Confederate left, the Confederates withdrew into new lines that still protected the railroad. The Confederate forces were reduced, but Sherman was wrong. They still had the capacity to defend Atlanta and their left flank.[36]

Like the Confederates, the Union forces had also suffered significant losses in manpower. The Army of the Cumberland, which included the 33rd, had 20,000 fewer combat troops than at the beginning of the campaign. Since July 1 alone, the overall Union strength was down by 15,000 men.[37] The action on the 33rd's portion of the front had been limited to exchanges of artillery fire plus some skirmishing. Even General Geary, who was prone to long reports, noted laconically that on July 30 and 31 there was "nothing of interest to record."[38] Probably because things were relatively quiet, Georg Muller felt that morale had improved significantly. Repeating what was clearly some wishful thinking, Muller noted talk of a peace agreement, which he told his parents was "my only wish, I am sick of the butchering." Muller went on to say something that had implications for Sherman's future plans: "If they ever place our regiment a few more times into such a battle [as Peachtree Creek] then all of a sudden there will be nothing left of it."³⁹

Sherman knew better than to even consider a frontal assault on any part of Atlanta's defenses. Sherman was correct in thinking that the Confederate defenses around Atlanta were excellent, but he mistakenly believed that their troop strength was equal to that of the Union army. After the last two failures, Sherman thought there were now four alternative approaches to taking Atlanta. Two of these consisted of variations of continuing to move gradually to the right; however, Sherman was concerned that he was already overextended in that direction. While the best alternative was to move the whole army to the right, Sherman believed the army needed rest before attempting such a maneuver. Given the experience of the similar move towards Dallas, he was also understandably concerned about leaving the railroad. As a result, Sherman chose the last alternative, using artillery fire to bomb Atlanta into submission.

When the sustained bombing campaign began on August 9, some 3,000 shells were fired into Atlanta, but there was little damage and no casualties. The Confederate soldiers were well protected in their defenses, and the 5,000 remaining civilians had taken precautions including the construction of bomb shelters. While the bombing campaign went on, Hood's counterstrategy of a cavalry attack on the Federal supply line began on August 10. By the 12th, Sherman was frustrated by the lack of progress from the bombing. Added to the pressure of the political situation was the reality that supplies had begun to run low. Given the level of supplies in the depots at Nashville and Chattanooga and the current rate of use, all food supplies would be exhausted by September 15. The next day, Sherman informed Halleck that he intended to leave one corps on the Chattahoochee and implement his large scale flanking movement with a mobile force of 60,000. However, after Sherman learned of the Confederate cavalry raid and its failure, he decided to use his own cavalry in a similar operation to cut the railroad to Macon. The flanking maneuver, which was to begin on August 18, was suspended and the cavalry raid ordered instead. But even with the absence of the Confederate cavalry, Sherman's cavalry was unable to accomplish their mission. When Sherman learned of the failure of the Union cavalry raid on August 23, there was less than four weeks left before the Union food supplies would run out.⁴⁰

During this period, Colonel Mindil returned from duty in Chattanooga, arriving in camp near Atlanta on August 7. After dining with General Geary that night, the next day he was placed in command of the Second Brigade.⁴¹ Since Lieutenant Colonel Fouratt was still absent, this meant that Captain O'Connor remained in command of the 33rd. As part of the artillery bombardment, the men of the Second Division had constructed an embrasure for siege artillery on the division left. These guns had been part of the firing that began on August 9, firing 50 rounds per gun. Although the Confederates were badly outgunned, the Union artillery offensive did bring some Confederate fire in response.⁴² The defensive works usually protected the men, but Stephen Pierson reported that carelessness led to some problems. In one instance, two soldiers were sitting around a stump on which they had placed a can of hot coffee. When a shell exploded nearby, a piece passed over the stump and missed the men but sent the coffee flying. Once over their shock, the men "began to curse the Rebs for spoiling their breakfast." On other occasions, spent or unexploded shells would roll down a long slope at the regiment's rear. Although the shells seemed to roll very slowly, a soldier once put his foot out to stop one and "the momentum broke his leg."[43]

Even though there was little combat activity during this period, the regiment suffered five deaths. James Donald was taken prisoner and ultimately died in the Confederate prison camp at Millen, Georgia. Disease was also active, taking the lives of Cornelius Lyons, John Herman, and Andrew Hessdorfer.[44] Even duty away from the regiment was not necessarily safe. Michael Kiefer, who was serving with the pioneer corps, died on August 14. While sitting by or near his tent inside the breastworks, Kiefer was hit by a shot and died the next day without regaining consciousness. Kiefer was an immigrant from Bavaria who lived in Verona, about ten miles west of Newark. Although he had listed his age as 42 when he enlisted, Kiefer was in reality ten years older. He left behind a widow and a large family.[45] After Kiefer's death, Chaplain Faull reported that the regiment was down to 240 men. As his contribution towards the morale of the men, Faull continued to hold religious services within the breastworks. After a service on August 14, he reported that attendance was good at the service with the men listening "attentively to the entire address." No doubt in an effort to maintain everyone's morale, Faull concluded on a positive note, "The work goes on and no one doubts the ultimate success of our labors."[46]

Although Faull tried to remain optimistic, William Lloyd was not as positive when he wrote to Mary. According to Lloyd, the regiment was lying in the trenches before Atlanta, "almost burnt to death with the sun." Mary had been delaying a summer trip to the country in the hope of receiving some of Lloyd's pay, but he told her not to bother, as he had still not been paid. Since he was owed almost ten months' pay, Lloyd was probably equally pessimistic both about getting paid and taking Atlanta. After he heard about Mary's plans for the country, he was even more conscious of the disparity between their situations. Lloyd wished he could go on a Jersey picnic with her and also wondered facetiously how the guests "would like to join the picnic that I am enjoying down in Dixie." Although this was a rhetorical question, Lloyd knew the answer: "Not much I guess." However, at the end of the letter, Lloyd expressed some patriotic sentiments, noting that he "never shirked the flag and colors that gave me birth and my parents protection." Perhaps reflecting on the sacrifices of the Union soldiers, he promised, "As long as I am in the American army, I will do an American duty and that is protect my flag, the stars and stripes."[47]

This patriotic mood did not last long. Within a week Lloyd wrote again, complaining that he had "nothing else to employ my time, but scribble, scribble." With all this time on his hands, Lloyd had more opportunities to contrast his lot with that of his wife in the country. Once again, he was "sick of it" for he had "got my fill this time and it serves me just right." Perhaps the sun had caused his bad mood as a few days later he told Mary he had had a slight case of sunstroke. By now, however, he had improved enough to be back on duty, which was light at present. Mary had apparently suggested that Lloyd apply for a furlough, but Lloyd told her this was impossible. At this point, the only way to get a furlough was to be wounded and Lloyd was not that desperate. What really worried him was not being paid, since his wife needed the money for the upcoming winter. Lloyd claimed that when and if he was paid, he would keep only a small amount for himself, as all he needed to buy was tobacco. Separated from almost any kind of civilian life for four months, Lloyd felt, "I don't know what money is any more."[48]

Besides his finances, Lloyd was unhappy about a number of other things beginning with life in Company H. He was the only sergeant who had been with the regiment since the beginning, currently the only one of five fit for duty. He felt that all the easy duty went to his colleague, Sergeant Upton, but "when there is danger it is Sergeant Lloyd." Not surprisingly, Lloyd attributed this favoritism to Captain Frazer, who Lloyd continued to deride as "a damn little shyster." Among the current rumors was one that 600 recruits would be joining the

Captain William McCoy, Company K. *U.S. Army Military History Institute.*

33rd, so the regiment would need eight more lieutenants. Lloyd was sure he could get one of these positions if he got help from friends at home. When the regiment was finally reinforced, though, Lloyd was not promoted. Not sparing anyone from his frustration, Lloyd even lashed out at the Confederates for not coming out of their works for a fair fight.[49] Even though Lloyd may have been an extreme case, the combined stress of inactivity and being at risk in the trenches could only be borne for a limited period of time. At least Georg Muller had good news to tell his parents. He was now detached from the regiment and serving as a guard with the brigade quartermaster. Since Muller no longer had to "listen to the whistling and chirping of the bullets around my ears," he was obviously happy about the new duty. Even so Muller was still suffering from the effects of the campaign; he had lost almost 20 pounds since leaving Lookout Valley in May.[50] Little did Lloyd, Muller or anyone else in the 33rd know, but the campaign was almost over.

Lloyd wrote his latest letter on August 24, which was also the last day of the bombardment of Atlanta. The bombardment ended because the strategy had failed and also because Sherman had to take decisive action. After the cavalry raid failed,

Sherman returned to his plan to leave a corps on the Chattahoochee and take the rest of the army to the far right of Atlanta. Although such a movement took the troops out of the safety of their trenches, the men were ready for the maneuver. The campaign had now been going on for almost four months. If Atlanta was not taken soon, it would be too late. In preparation, Sherman sent his excess wagons, supplies and horses across the Chattahoochee. They would be guarded there by the one remaining corps, which would also guard the supply line to Chattanooga. In a well deserved piece of good fortune, the XX Corps and, therefore, the 33rd New Jersey were chosen to fill that role. While they stood guard, the rest of the army along with wagons containing 100 rounds per man and 15 days of rations and forage would take part in the maneuver.[51]

Preparations for the XX Corps' part in the movement began at daylight on August 25 when Geary sent one regiment and the pioneer corps from each brigade to Pace's Ferry. After they arrived, these units began to build new defensive works on the east bank of the river. That night the XX Corps began moving to the new position, which covered the railroad bridge and other crossings of the Chattahoochee. The Second Division was ready to move on schedule, but they were delayed by the movement of the IV Corps, which was behind schedule. At midnight Geary felt they could wait no longer so he ordered the division to proceed over the main road and a new one prepared by the pioneer corps. Once they arrived at Pace's Ferry at 4:00 A.M., the division went into new positions with the Third Brigade on the left, the Second including the 33rd in the center and the First Brigade on the right. The pickets, who had been left behind, rejoined the division at 6:00 A.M., completing the withdrawal and march of nine miles without the loss of men or supplies.[52] (According to one member of the 33rd—obviously not William Lloyd—the safe movement of the brigade's pickets was due to their being led by Captain Barent Frazer. This man wrote that Frazer's behavior "endears him to all who come in contact with him.")[53] The new position was "a series of wooded ridges parallel to and a quarter of a mile from the riverbank." As they occupied these positions, the prevailing sentiment was probably relief that the march ended in new works not in an attack.[54]

During the night of August 26, the southward march of the rest of the Union army began. When the Confederates learned of the withdrawal of the XX and IV Corps, there were many in Atlanta who wanted to believe that the Federal troops were retreating. Hood, however, recognized the likelihood of a massive shift to his left, but did not know the specifics. After several days of marching, on August 30 Sherman ordered the advance to continue to the area around Jonesboro. On the following day, August 31, Sherman wanted to occupy Jonesboro and destroy the railroad to Macon. The best chance to take Jonesboro without a fight actually came on the 30th, but the Union troops moved too slowly. Hood had always thought the railroad at Jonesboro was a logical target, but it was not until 6:00 P.M. on the 30th that he suspected that such a large portion of Sherman's army was so close to Jonesboro. If Johnston had still been the Confederate commander, he would probably have retreated, but Hood had one more attack left in him. The Confederates were ordered to attack the Federal troops as soon as possible. Recognizing the gravity of the situation, Hood also prepared to evacuate Atlanta if the attack failed.

The slow and cautious movement of Howard's Army of the Tennessee had failed to take Jonesboro on the 30th. The opportunity was gone by the next day, when the Confederate troops had arrived. Recognizing that the chance was lost, Howard ordered his men to dig in, in the hope that the Confederates would attack. Delays on the part of the Confederates gave the Union troops additional time to prepare their defenses. By the time a Confederate force of 20,000 men was finally ready to attack at 3:00 P.M., the Union troops had dug in and set up their artillery. Although the forces were of equal size, the Federal troops were both in better condition and in a stronger position. As with Hood's other offensives, the attack failed. Sherman got the news of this action and

Thomas Morton, corporal, Company H; 2nd lt., Company G. *From the Collections of The New Jersey Historical Society.*

then, more important, the news he really wanted. Schofield's Army of the Ohio was on the Macon railroad, a mile from the village of Rough and Ready. Arriving there just about the time of the Confederate attack at Jonesboro, Schofield's troops were already tearing up track. Atlanta was now cut off from Macon, the city's last source of supply; this was indeed great news. Another opportunity also presented itself: Sherman's army was now in between the two halves of the depleted Confederate army, in a position not just to capture Atlanta, but the Confederate army as well. In perhaps the ultimate irony of the campaign, that very day the Democratic National Convention nominated former Union general George McClellan for president on a platform committed to peace due to the failure of the war effort.[55]

Far to the north in Newark, the antiwar *Daily Journal* reported enthusiastically on the city's reaction to the McClellan nomination. According to the paper, "the whole populace was fired with enthusiasm" with the firing of cannons, the raising of flags, and large crowds of happy people. Rhetorically the paper asked, "Did any one hear or see any demonstration whatever when the result of the recent Baltimore Convention was announced?"[56] There would soon be a very different celebration in Newark.

Sherman ordered an attack on the Confederate force at Jonesboro on September 1. The attack was unsuccessful and the Confederate army would live to fight another day. That night deafening explosions were heard from Atlanta; it was the destruction of Hood's ammunition train, part of the evacuation of Atlanta.[57] Sherman planned to advance against the Confederates again on September 2. In addition, he ordered the XX Corps to press towards Atlanta without endangering the position on the Chattahoochee.[58] General Slocum, who had now taken command of the XX Corps, ordered Geary to send a reconnaissance party towards Atlanta. Geary sent sections of four regiments and some cavalry on this mission under the command of Lieutenant Colonel Walker. William Lambert was also part of the group. Walker's command left at 6:00 A.M. on the Buckhead Road and advanced towards Nancy's Creek. When they arrived at Howell's Mill, the Union force learned that Confederate cavalry had left a few hours before. At Peachtree Creek they found the bridge destroyed, but the infantry crossed on a large log while the cavalry forded the creek.[59] At about 10:30 A.M., they met a similar reconnaissance party from the Third Brigade[60] under the command of Colonel Coburn, who had already received the surrender of Atlanta from the city's mayor. The two groups proceeded into the city, and units from the Second Division reached city hall first at about noon where they raised the flags of the 111th Pennsylvania and the 60th New York.[61] Lambert, who was with this column, reported that the entrance into the city was "unmarked by the pomp and exciting circumstance." Even though there was no cannon fire, church bells, or martial music of any kind, Lambert felt none of that was needed since "the proud faces of the men ... were full of eloquence, silent, but powerful."[62]

After Geary learned of the Confederate evacuation of Atlanta, he ordered the balance of the Second and Third Brigades into the city while the First Brigade maintained the position at Pace's Ferry.[63] When the two brigades along with other units from the XX Corps arrived around dark, they were serenaded by Union bands playing "Rally Round the Flag" and "Yankee Doodle."[64] In general, the Union troops respected private property and the citizens who had remained in the city were not harmed. Earlier that day the pursuit of the retreating Confederates had continued to a point one mile north of Lovejoy's Station. An attack there failed and Sherman called off further action until he learned what had happened in Atlanta. Once word of the Confederate withdrawal was received just before breakfast the next day, Sherman decided to end the campaign.[65]

As the news of the fall of Atlanta spread throughout the Northern states, celebrations broke out almost everywhere. In spite of the sentiments of the *Daily Journal*, Newarkers did their share of celebrating with flags flying throughout the city, and a 100-gun salute was fired at 6:00 P.M. According to the *Daily Advertiser*, the only response of the "sympathizers with the rebellion" was to doubt that the news was true.[66] In Washington, Lincoln asked that thanks be given to God. He was right to be thankful. With the news from Atlanta, the administration's election prospects had turned from sure defeat to sure victory. Unlike Gettysburg, Atlanta needed no interpretation; "the fall of Atlanta means that the war can be won — indeed that it is being won."[67]

Thanks were also due to the officers and men of the 33rd New Jersey and all members of the Union Army. When William Lambert wrote his final letter about the Atlanta campaign on September 9, it was one year to the day since the regiment had left Newark. Probably no regiment left home under less auspicious circumstances, with massive desertions, and men shot by other Union soldiers. But those who had stayed the course had served, and with distinction. William Lambert wrote, "The suffering of its wounded; the living deaths of its captured; the graves of its dead marking the battlefields from Mill Creek to Atlanta give ample token" of the regiment's service. Lambert, comparing the 33rd to the ultimate Union standard, asked rhetorically, "Is not the soldier of to-day the worthy son of 76?" Many campaigns, battles or even portions of battles have been claimed as the decisive event in the Civil War. The Atlanta campaign was not the one decisive event of the entire war, but it was the Confederacy's last opportunity to win the war. That opportunity was now gone. Or, in the words of William Lambert, "The long campaign is ended; the hardships have not been in vain; the victory has been won, and the old flag floats over Atlanta."[68]

IX

"A hard campaign and we expect nothing else"

The officers and men of the 33rd New Jersey had endured the dangers and hardships of the Atlanta campaign for four long months. It would not have been surprising, therefore, if during the first few days in Atlanta they had a hard time realizing that the goal had been achieved. Some members of the regiment must have woken up in the night and had to reassure themselves that they were really in Atlanta, that the "long campaign" was indeed over. This, at least, was a pleasant reality to accept. There was another reality that was clear to all, but difficult to face: the human cost of taking Atlanta. All told, Sherman's army had suffered 4,500 deaths, an equal number taken prisoner, 23,000 wounded, and 55,000 hospitalized from both wounds and disease. Within the XX Corps, the 33rd's division, the Second Division was one-half of its original strength.[1] The 33rd had incurred more than its share of these losses. Within the Second Brigade, the regiment had suffered the highest number of men killed, wounded, and missing, a total of 239. Indeed, the 33rd had twice as many deaths as any other regiment, three times as many men missing, and twice the aggregate losses of any other regiment in the brigade.[2] Engaged in five battles throughout the campaign, the 33rd's heavy losses at Pine Knob and Peachtree Creek placed the regiment first in the brigade in total suffering.

With losses of this magnitude, there was no question that the regiment's strength had been severely depleted. Captain O'Connor had reported the effective strength at 187 in August[3] and Stephen Pierson claimed that only slightly more than 100 marched into Atlanta in early September.[4] Whatever the real number, the regiment was badly in need of reinforcements. The 33rd's stay in Atlanta provided an opportunity for this to happen. As the regiment was persevering through the Atlanta campaign, back in New Jersey the continuing demand for soldiers had forced the implementation of the draft. The long avoided draft finally took place in May of 1864. However, in sharp contrast to the summer of 1863, there was little reaction or interest. Since a number

Map of the Savannah campaign. *Andrea LaConte Magno.*

of municipalities including Newark and Jersey City had agreed to pay the commutation fee for any citizen unlucky enough to be drafted, the lack of a strong reaction was not surprising. Municipal payment of commutation was further supplemented by "insurance societies" where groups of eligible men pooled their resources for commutation of any member who was drafted.[5]

Although payment of the commutation fee was an escape route, the reprieve was only good for that particular draft. And after the commutation fee was eliminated in July of 1864, the only legitimate options were serving or hiring a substitute to take one's place.[6] While some may have been uncertain about serving, one member of the

33rd had no such uncertainty. Apparently Georg Muller learned from his parents that "Sean has been recruited." Muller wrote that Sean should have been smarter than he (Muller) had been. Muller claimed that if he ever came home, "Uncle Sam can wait a long time to get me under his fingers."[7] Since the lack of a commutation fee eliminated any ceiling on the cost of hiring a substitute,[8] the cost soared. This, in turn, produced a new element in what was almost a shadow economy, brokers who found substitutes for those with money. Although some 32,000 New Jersey men were drafted, amazingly only 951 ever served. Instead over 5,400 draftees hired substitutes to take their places while others avoided serving by failing the medical exam, paying the commutation fee or simply failing to report.[9]

The elimination of the large up-front cash bounties that played havoc with the formation of the 33rd did not, however, end the problem of desertion. Close to 400 men were mustered into the 33rd from August to November, but over 100 or almost 30 percent deserted before they actually reached the regiment. This was slightly higher than the ratio of deserters from the regiment's original roster. Since more than 75 percent of those who deserted were substitutes, this suggests that some substitutes functioned much like bounty jumpers. They collected a fee that was probably higher

Private Daniel Algood, Company C. *U.S. Army Military History Institute.*

than any bounty and then deserted. Other than the deserters, more than 200 new men joined the regiment. More than half were substitutes, only 24 were draftees and the balance was recruits.[10] Although the new manpower was welcome, Colonel Mindil reported that many of the substitutes were foreigners without training, who could not speak English.[11]

After Atlanta fell, the situation for both commanders changed dramatically. Sherman now had to hold Atlanta instead of conquering it. However, he was still dependent on a single 300-mile supply line stretching back to Nashville. On the Confederate side, since Hood no longer had to defend Atlanta, he had more flexibility for his movements. As soon as Sherman took control of Atlanta, one of his first steps was to propose a ten-day truce to expel the civilian population of Atlanta. Although this was harsh, the order was given both to limit the demands on Union supplies and to allow Atlanta to be held by a small Federal force. Since Hood had no choice, he accepted Sherman's proposal, but protested the cruelty of the action. Sherman was unmoved by the protest and told Hood to "talk thus to the marines, but not to me." The choice for the unfortunate citizens of Atlanta was between going north or being taken to Rough and Ready for relocation within the Confederacy. While this forced relocation took place, a new and shorter line of defense works was constructed around Atlanta.[12]

Private Morgan P. Daniels, Company C. *U.S. Army Military History Institute.*

At least one member of the 33rd was involved in the movement of civilians from Atlanta. James Struble had been detached from the regiment and now had "a good position in the Ambulance Corps." Struble reported that he had made the 12-mile trip to Rough and Ready five times, arriving at the transfer point about 4:00 P.M. and remaining there until the next morning. Since he was there overnight, Struble had plenty of opportunity for conversation with Confederate officers and enlisted men.

The officers wanted to know who would be elected president, but the more pragmatic enlisted men wanted to know "how soon we should have Peace." According to Struble, the Confederate officers echoed Jefferson Davis' response to a peace initiative, "Independence or extermination." Although the Confederates pretended not to care who won the election, Struble could tell that they still hoped for a McClellan victory. Apparently Struble had some political wisdom, as he accurately predicted to the Confederates that while McClellan would win in New Jersey, Lincoln would be re-elected.[13]

While the Union troops rested and probably gave little thought to the future, Sherman had been thinking about the next step for some time. As early as May when asked about post-Atlanta plans, Sherman responded simply, "Salt Water."[14] Once in Atlanta, Sherman knew that the 300-mile supply line to Nashville could not be relied on for future offensive action.[15] Furthermore, the failure to destroy Hood's army meant there were some 40,000 Confederate troops at Lovejoy's Station, 30 miles southeast of Atlanta. Sherman used September for rest, reorganization, and planning so the initiative went over to Hood.[16] Even with the initiative, however, Hood's options were limited. Since he did not have sufficient manpower to attack Atlanta, Hood's only real alternative was to try to do with his entire army what his cavalry could not do earlier, cut the Union supply line. Hood's command was also positioned at Lovejoy Station to protect Andersonville prison from Union attack.[17] After those prisoners were relocated to other Confederate prisons, Hood was able on September 21 to move his army to Palmetto Station, 25 miles southwest of Atlanta.[18] Palmetto Station was to serve as the base for the Hood's army to cross the Chattahoochee and attack the Union supply line. Confederate president Jefferson Davis traveled to Palmetto in late September, approved the plan and then gave a speech with the details. Unfortunately for the Confederates, the speech was reported in Southern newspapers, which were available to Sherman.[18]

Whether through these newspaper accounts or plain common sense, Sherman was not surprised when Hood's Army of Tennessee crossed the Chattahoochee on September 29 and 30. In fact, Sherman had already sent two divisions to Chattanooga as a precaution.[19] After Hood moved northward during the early days of October, Sherman left Atlanta in pursuit with a force of 40,000 men.[20] Fortunately for the 33rd New Jersey, they and the rest of the XX Corps were left behind to guard Atlanta. Hood began his campaign by attacking Union positions on the Western and Atlantic Railroad. Although most of the Confederate attacks were successful, their attack on the Union position at Allatoona Pass was driven back.[21] In spite of this defeat, Hood continued to move northward through Resaca and Snake Creek Gap where the Atlanta campaign began. Eventually the Confederates took a defensive position at LaFayette, Georgia, about 20 miles from the Chickamauga battlefield. However, when the Union pursuit arrived on October 17, Hood had withdrawn into Alabama.[22] Sherman continued the pursuit to Gaylesville, Alabama, but gave up as Hood continued to move westward.[23]

The pursuit of the Confederates must have been incredibly frustrating for the pursuers, from Sherman down to the enlisted ranks. Sherman's army had just completed four months of hard campaigning through northern Georgia. To now be forced to go back and fight over the same ground had to be one of the most depressing things imaginable. Although the enlisted men could do little but get frustrated, Sherman, could do something about it. As early as September 10, Sherman had written to Grant suggesting a march across Georgia towards Augusta or Columbus. Even before he pursued Hood on October 1, Sherman again wrote to Grant specifically proposing that Thomas be left in Tennessee to deal with Hood. Sherman then wanted to destroy Atlanta and march across Georgia to either Savannah or Charleston. A primary goal of such a campaign would be to cause "irreparable damage" throughout Georgia. Sherman continued his pleas even while in pursuit of Hood. On October 9, he wrote Grant, "I can make this march and make georgia howl!" Added to the proposal was another of Sherman's ideas, that he should destroy the railroad from Chattanooga before leaving Atlanta, literally burning his bridges and his railroad behind him.[24]

Although Grant's initial response was to state his preference for destroying Hood's army, he expressed trust in Sherman's judgment about the best way to proceed. By November 2, Sherman was even more certain of the wisdom of his proposal. To continue to chase Hood's more mobile force lost all the benefits of taking Atlanta in the first place.[25] Moreover, Hood's actions had eliminated the Confederate's ability to block the march, and Thomas was in place to deal with Hood in Tennessee.[26] Ultimately, Grant recognized the wisdom of this argument and gave Sherman the answer he wanted: "Go on as you propose."[27] After he had Grant's approval, Sherman and his army, excluding Thomas' two corps, returned to Atlanta to begin preparations for the march.[28]

Meanwhile back in Atlanta, the 33rd had enjoyed almost two months of garrison life. The regiment's camp in Atlanta was to the right of the McDonough Road, about one and one-half miles from the courthouse.[29] Georg Muller described Atlanta to his parents as a city somewhat larger than Orange, New Jersey. Although Atlanta was considered to be a city, Muller felt Atlanta was more like a village since there were no sidewalks and only one block "where the houses are attached." Muller's assignment was, as a guard with the brigade quartermaster, which he found "a very good place."[30] The regiment had initially enjoyed a period of rest, but the 33rd was now busy "devoting its time to drill and parades" as well as receiving new uniforms and equipment. Since Colonel Patrick Jones had returned to command the Second Brigade, Colonel Mindil was back in command of the regiment.[31] After some prisoner exchanges took place in September, a few of the men taken prisoner at Peachtree Creek returned to the regiment. One of the returnees was Charles Williamson of Company D, who had been wounded in the left side and arm. Captain Courtois reported to the Paterson *Daily Press* that Williamson, despite being wounded and taken prisoner, was now doing well. Courtois was sure this would be "a piece of rather good news" to his mother.[32] Another casualty of Peachtree Creek, Lieutenant George Harris was sent home to New Jersey to recover from his wounds.[33] Less fortunate than Williamson and Harris were Jacob Ernst, John Braan, and Jeremiah Connor, all of whom died of disease. In addition, a sentry in Louisville killed Charles Brogan of Company E and Herman Bimble was killed at Murfreesboro, Tennessee.[34]

The slower pace of garrison life also allowed time for entertainment. A member of another New Jersey regiment reported that "the National Minstrels" performed in the evenings at a cost of 50–75 cents per person and put on "quite a creditable show." For those with more sophisticated tastes, the band of the 33rd Massachusetts put on concerts of both sacred and secular music. Even though the latter events had a higher admission charge of $1, they were still reported to be crowded.³⁵ All was not rest and recreation. Rations were not plentiful and Hood's offensive had disrupted the main supply line. Magnifying these difficulties was the fact that the XX Corps was also responsible for feeding some 13,000 sick and wounded. These demands and the supply shortages led to four major foraging raids by a force of 3,000 men, each lasting two to three days.³⁶ In describing these raids for his wife, General Geary noted that they had ravaged the countryside for 25–30 miles around Atlanta. One of the raids brought back 2,400 wagons of corn plus plentiful supplies of cattle, hogs, and sheep. Setting the tone for the coming campaign, Geary commented, "We take everything from the people without remorse."³⁷

John Smith, 1st sgt., Company I; 1st lt., Company A and Company F. *U.S. Army Military History Institute.*

In what may or may not have been a good thing, William Lloyd was once again in contact with his wife, Mary. By the end of October, Lloyd had apparently regained his sense of humor to some degree. When he described his "southern home," he noted that the sun's rays shined through "the cracks of my humble hovel." Lloyd had gotten up hours before daylight to prepare for a long march, but the orders had been countermanded. Suddenly the letter ended, as Lloyd wrote, "I must go, Good-bye." Taking up the letter again at 7:00 P.M. that night, Lloyd explained that the order had not been countermanded as he had thought. Within five minutes of his breaking away from the letter, they were on the march. One hour later Lloyd and the rest of Company H were fighting with Confederate cavalry near East Point. Apparently the Jer-

Private Charles Snyder, Company C. *U.S. Army Military History Institute.*

seymen had been tearing up the Macon railroad when the cavalry came on the scene. It is hard to know how extensive this action was, but according to Lloyd, "Company H was heroes of the day."

Hood's offensive had cut communications to the north so this was Lloyd's first letter to Mary in a month. According to Lloyd, the raids on the supply line had been effective, causing the men to go on half rations, although this had recently been increased to three-quarters. Conditions were even worse for the animals. Lloyd claimed that 20 mules a day were dying of starvation. Lloyd was no military strategist, but he was smart enough to realize that if the railroad could not be kept open, the city would have to be abandoned. Proud of the last campaign, Lloyd felt that to abandon Atlanta "would be an awful disgrace to us." One Confederate raid on the railroad had caused even greater problems. A chaplain from the 134th New York had been taken prisoner off a train with $9,000 in soldier's pay.[38] This was very bad news for families who needed the money for the upcoming winter.

Lloyd wrote again on November 3 and told Mary that they expected to leave Atlanta the next day. Although there were rumors that Sherman's army was headed for Mobile, Alabama, Lloyd did not believe it. One thing he was sure of, however, was that it would be "a hard campaign and we expect nothing else." Unlike the unlucky members of the 134th New York, the 33rd still had not been paid. Since many of the men's families back in New Jersey had no other means of support, this was a serious matter. Lloyd himself claimed that he had not "had a cent from the government" in over a year. Recent reports or rumors indicated that the 33rd was to receive ten months' pay shortly, and Lloyd promised to send the bulk of his pay home to Mary. Even though the regiment did not move on November 4 as Lloyd had reported, his prediction of a move was not far off.[39] At about 3:00 P.M. on November 5, the entire second Brigade was ordered to break camp in an hour. They then marched one mile to a new camp still near the McDonough road, about two and one-half miles from the city. However, the move was a false start, and the brigade and the regiment returned to the old camp the next day.[40]

They would not be there for long. When Lloyd wrote to Mary on November 11 speculating about an imminent move towards Savannah, it was the last letter he would write from Atlanta. Lloyd was well aware that they would be going on "a long journey and right through the heart of the Confederacy." Based on these factors, Lloyd predicted that the journey would take until January and warned Mary that she would not hear from him during the campaign. To make matters more difficult, the regiment would leave Atlanta without being paid. Lloyd attributed this most recent delay to the fact that New Jersey had gone for McClellan in the presidential election. Since Company H had gained 24 new members, another lieutenant's position was indeed available, but it went to Lloyd's longtime rival, Phil Upton. Undoubtedly with some bitterness, Lloyd predicted that Upton "will lose more by it than he will make." Lloyd also hinted at his own political viewpoint when he asked Mary to tell someone that there were still plenty of opportunities for soldiers in "Lincoln's 8 years war." Sensitive to possible civilian hypocrisy, Lloyd noted that "Jeff" probably voted for Lincoln, "but he ain't willing to serve his country and support his administration by taking his rifle."[41] During the regiment's stay in Atlanta, both Lloyd and Georg Muller asked their families to send them some white stars, the symbol of the Second Division of the XX Corps, for their uniforms.[42] Even though both men complained about their lot, they had also developed a sense of unit pride.

Lincoln had won re-election with a 400,000-vote popular majority. However, the narrow margins of victory in three major states, New York, Pennsylvania, and Indiana, underscored the importance of the successful Atlanta campaign.[43] There were two major factors that had given McClellan a special advantage in New Jersey. After McClellan had been replaced as commander of the Army of the Potomac, he had lived in New Jersey, this no doubt gave him some additional votes. Even more in McClellan's favor was the fact that New Jersey did not permit their soldiers in the field to vote, which cost Lincoln votes. In terms of the regiment's feelings, we have only Lloyd's negative comments along with James Struble's implication that he favored Lincoln. However, one member of Sherman's staff claimed, "One in ten would be a large estimate of the McClellan men in the army. This is true even of the New Jersey Regiments."[44]

Once Sherman had received Grant's approval, he turned his full attention to the preparations for the march. Since there would be no supply line, Sherman needed "a lean picked force." The army had to be able to live off what could be foraged and constantly "move on as it 'ate out.'" There was only one major risk to the campaign: a delay in the march that exhausted supplies and prevented access to new ones. This was most likely to be caused by extended fighting or bad weather. Since there was no significant Confederate opposition, the major concern was the possibility of bad weather.⁴⁵ Preparations began with restrictions on the number of wagons and artillery pieces to accompany the army, which also eliminated the men that would have accompanied them. As a further precaution, Sherman ordered extensive medical exams to screen out men with even the slightest health problems. This process was more rigorous than enlistment exams and contributed to the low rate of illness suffered during the campaign. Those who passed this test felt their value as soldiers had been reaffirmed, which improved their morale. After this process was complete, those who remained were very much a veteran army.⁴⁶ Going against the trend was the 33rd, which was probably one of the few regiments that had a majority of new, inexperienced members. During the first two weeks in November there was a great deal of activity as railroad trains moved out of Atlanta with the sick and unfit as well as extra equipment. While these men and equipment left, other trains were coming in with reinforcements and soldiers who had recovered from wounds and illness, as well as rations and ammunition.⁴⁷

After the movements in and out of Atlanta were complete, Sherman recalled all the detachments guarding the railroad line to Chattanooga. Left behind were small groups to destroy the railroad bridges as part of Sherman's plan to destroy his own supply line.⁴⁸ On November 12, the last train pulled out of Atlanta, so long that multiple engines were required to pull the cars. Besides the men and equipment aboard, the train also carried the army's last letters home as well as large amounts of cash from those troops who had been paid. Once the train had passed out of Atlanta, the railroad was destroyed and the telegraph lines to the north were cut.⁴⁹ A few days later, on November 15, Sherman ordered the destruction of all railroad buildings, machine shops, warehouses, and any other building of any possible use to the Confederates. After darkness fell there were bursts of black dense smoke followed by "tongues of flame" and then "huge waves of fire roll up into the sky." Sherman himself estimated that the flames could be seen for 50 miles. When the work of destruction was complete, "skeletons of great warehouses stand out in relief against and amidst sheets of roaring, blazing furious flames." According to one of Sherman's staff officers, the whole sight was "dreadful to look upon."⁵⁰

To march across Georgia, Sherman had an army of just over 60,000 men. More than 55,000 of that number were infantry from the XIV, XV, XVII and XX corps. The balance consisted of cavalry and a small amount of artillery. The four infantry corps were divided into two wings with the right wing consisting of the XV and XVII corps under the command of General Howard. Howard's counterpart, commanding the left wing, was General Slocum, with the XIV and XX corps. The 33rd New Jersey continued to be part of the XX Corps, now commanded by General Alpheus Williams. As in the Atlanta campaign, the regiment would be part of the second Brigade (commanded by Colonel Jones) of the Second Division (commanded by General Geary). In addition to the 33rd, the second Brigade consisted of the 119th, the 134th, and the 154th New York as well as the 73rd and 109th Pennsylvania. In opposition the Confederates could muster cavalry and militia units totaling no more than 8,500 men.⁵¹

A successful march across Georgia would further divide the already shrunken Confederacy and cut off Lee's army in Virginia from supplies in Georgia and Florida. While these military objectives were significant by themselves, the demoralizing effect

Charles Sutton, 2nd lt. and captain, Company C, had a confrontation with General John Geary, commander of the Second Division of the XX Corps during the march to Savannah, November 1864. *U.S. Army Military History Institute.*

of a successful march on the Southern people was equally important.[52] The first objective of the march was to get the Union army to the center of Georgia between Augusta and Macon. Once this was accomplished, the Confederates would be forced to divide their already small forces between these two locations as well as Millen, Savannah and Charleston. To do this Sherman's army had to march from Atlanta to

Milledgeville, the capital of Georgia, about 100 miles from Atlanta. In order to execute this plan, the two wings of Sherman's army would take separate routes. The left wing would move east towards Madison and Augusta while the right wing would go southeast towards Jonesboro and Macon. By having the two wings take separate routes, Sherman could threaten both Augusta and Macon and then have both wings converge on Milledgeville. This phase of the campaign was to be completed in seven days, requiring the army to march an average of 15 miles per day.[53]

The cutting of the telegraph lines to the north marked the beginning of the first of two long periods when the 33rd would be out of communication with the North. For almost all of the Savannah campaign (the official name for the march to the sea) and the Carolina campaign, the army also could not send or receive mail. This had an impact on the campaigns themselves, which will be discussed later, but also has an impact on the ability to tell the regiment's story. Since the regiment was unable to send mail there are no personal letters or letters to newspapers as sources of information about the regiment's experiences. In fact, for the Savannah campaign, the only eyewitness material that survive are a letter written after the campaign to the Paterson *Daily Register* by "SH" and Colonel Mindil's relatively brief report in the *Official Records*. There are, however, accounts from members of other units that give some sense of the regiment's experience.

The march to the sea began for the 33rd and the rest of the Second Division at 7:00 A.M. on November 15. After the regiment broke camp, they marched slowly through Atlanta, most of which was either still on fire or in ruins. So slow was the pace of the march that they did not pass the outer defenses of Atlanta until 1:00 P.M. Perhaps thinking of the 33rd as modern day Israelites in the wilderness, "SH" reported they saw "columns of smoke at day and the light of fires at night."[54] However, the 33rd and the rest of the Second Division had to deal with more mundane and irritating obstacles than those that faced the Israelites, such as traffic. When the column moved out on the Decatur road, they had to wait for several hours for the preceding units. After stopping for the noonday meal at Decatur, the division left the road and took to the fields so that the lead units were able to stay parallel to the First Division trains. Although this may have speeded up the march somewhat, the head of the column did not camp until 11:00 P.M. near Stone Mountain.[55] The 33rd was not at the head of the column, and the regiment did not make camp until 2:00 A.M.[56] If William Lloyd had expected a "hard campaign," the first day probably did not disappoint him. In addition to problems with traffic and bad roads, General Geary complained about "the miserable character of the animals in our trains." Although the only positive feature of the day was good weather, the division did make the required 15 miles.[57]

Stone Mountain itself was something of a surprise to the Northerners, especially when compared to mountains back home. This mountain stood isolated as a huge round stone without trees or vegetation of any kind. Since the first night out was cool, tents were put up as close to the campfires as was safe. Even so, the cold kept some of the men from sleeping and fires were started again as early as 3:00 A.M.[58] In order to spread out the good and bad aspects of the march, the plan was to rotate the marching order of divisions, brigades, and regiments.[59] The First Division was in the lead on the first day, so the Second Division took the lead on November 16, as did the second Brigade within the Second Division. This was not good news for the 33rd, as their late arrival in camp was followed by an early march the next morning. The regiment broke camp at 8:00 A.M. and crossed the Yellow River at noon at Rock Ridge. Although the required 15 miles were covered, the poor roads and the poor quality of the animals slowed down the march.[60] While the early start must have been hard on the men, the advantage was that they made camp relatively early around 4:00 P.M., about five miles past Yellow River on the Sheffield road. Before leaving Stone Mountain, Sherman's orders for the campaign were read; they included authorization "to forage liberally." Unlike other orders, this was one that the men complied with cheerfully. Already on the second day, "the crowing of a rooster, the squeal of a pig or the quack of a duck was its own signal of death." Less mobile targets like sweet potatoes "disappeared at a greater rate than a bushel per minute."[61] However, the early foraging was not very fruitful, as the XX Corps' earlier supply raids had covered most of this area.[62]

When the army reached untapped areas the next day, the available resources were significantly better so that by the 18th "the men were living in plenty." Of greater significance was the resolution of one of the few problems facing Sherman's army. Since the condition of the mules and horses that accompanied the army was quite poor, sufficient animals were confiscated throughout the first week to provide adequate transportation. Had this not happened, the army might have been hard pressed to continue to move the supply trains at the scheduled rate.[63] The 33rd broke camp by 6:30 A.M. on the 17th and passed through the small village of Sheffield before crossing the Ulcofauhachee River. After they made camp two miles from Social Circle, the regiment helped burn some cotton gins as well as some cotton warehouses.[64] Everything seemed to be going well due to the improvement in the roads and the country had since leaving Atlanta.[65]

On the 18th, as the army began to live "in plenty," the Second Division was busy both marching and destroying. The 33rd was on the move at 5:30 A.M., the beginning of a long day that did not end until they made camp some 12 hours later, one mile from Madison. During the day, the Second Division destroyed the railroad east of Social Circle and also destroyed the depot, the water tank, and some other railroad buildings at Rutledge Station.[66] By this point in the war, the destruction of railroad track had become something of a fine art. If the work was not done properly, the damage could be repaired relatively quickly. The preferred approach began with placing a regiment or more on one side of the track. On command, the men would pick up the wooden ties at one end and flip them over. Once the impact loosened the rails from the ties, the wood ties were detached from the rails and set on fire along with any available telegraph poles. When the fire was hot enough, the rails were placed on top and then twisted out of shape, making it very difficult and time consuming to undo the damage. Sometimes as an added touch and a symbolic message, the rails were twisted into the shape of the letters "US." Throughout the march, the railroad was a major target of the army. Over 300 miles of track were destroyed.[67]

Although the next day brought the first rainfall of the march, the precipitation lasted for only about an hour.[68] During the day, the Second Division was detached

Sgt. Dennis Dease, Company A. *U.S. Army Military History Institute.*

from the rest of the corps for some special work of destruction. Unencumbered of their trains, Geary's more mobile command was on the road by 5:00 A.M. They passed through Madison before daylight and marched on a road parallel to the railroad.[69] "SH" was impressed with Madison, believing the town "must have been inhabited by a wealthy class of rebs" due to the "large stately residences."[70] After having dinner at Buckhead Station, the men destroyed all of the buildings before moving one mile further to destroy the railroad. While at Buckhead Station, the division had one of their few contacts with Confederate troops, a group of scouts. After the division had driven these across the Oconee River, they burned the railroad bridge for good measure. The division then moved on to Blue Spring, again destroying railroad track, a total of five miles for the day.

After this hard day's work, camp was made on the plantation of Confederate Colonel Lee Jordan.[71] Since the property of Confederate leaders was a special target of Sherman's army, Jordan's plantation received no mercy.[72] With plenty of understatement "SH" noted, "It was needless to say that his well stocked farm poultry and sweet potatoes suffered from the hands of our men."[73] At night, the men burned barns and other buildings that contained an estimated 280 bales of cotton and 50,000 bushels of corn. Before leaving the next morning, other buildings, cotton gins, and storehouses were put to the torch. The total value of the destruction was estimated at $20,000 (in 1864 dollars).[74]

When the Second Division resumed their march on November 20, they were headed in a more southerly direction to rejoin the rest of the corps.[75] Breaking camp at 7:00 A.M. in rainy weather, they marched over wet and swampy roads towards the Oconee River. Once they reached the river, the troops marched parallel to it, coming under some sporadic fire from the Confederate cavalry on the far bank. At Park's Mill, they burned the mill and also destroyed some flatboats. After leaving Park's Mill, they crossed Sugar Creek, passed through Glade's Crossroads, continually moving to the left. Camp was made for the night at about 6:00 P.M. near Denham's tannery, reported to be one of the largest in the South. The day's march had covered about ten miles and had yielded forage as well as additional mules and horses.[76]

General Geary's official account of the day's operations includes many of the above details, but nothing about an apparently unpleasant encounter with Captain Charles Sutton of the 33rd. A series of court-martial specifications against Geary claimed that on the road to Eatonton that morning, Geary had for some reason become infuriated with Sutton. At first, Geary's anger took the form of verbal abuse including calling Sutton a "God damned liar." He concluded by saying, "I'll get off my horse and kick your ass." Since Geary stood six foot four, this was not an idle threat. Allegedly, Geary followed through on his threat by seizing Sutton by the neck, shaking him, and then throwing the unfortunate captain on the ground. According to witnesses, Geary then had Sutton placed under arrest and marched at the head of the column, under guard, with his hands tied behind his back. In addition to Sutton, four witnesses signed the charges against Geary, which were then endorsed by both Colonel Mindil and the second Brigade commander, Colonel Patrick Jones. Mindil claimed that this was just one of many incidents and recommended that Geary be placed under arrest, but Jones endorsed only the request for a court-martial. In a somewhat ironic use of the chain of command, Geary himself sent the charges on to headquarters without comment. Although there is no record of what happened to the charges, Geary remained in command of the division for the balance of the war and Sutton continued to command Company C.[77] The incident could not have left any of the participants in an especially good mood. When this was followed by a night of heavy rain, the fate of Denham's tannery and factory was solidified. Although the Second Division destroyed everything the next day, the 33rd probably did not play a significant role in the destruction. While the bulk of the division did not resume the march until 8:00 A.M., the regiment was on its way at 6:00 A.M. Since the rain continued throughout the day, the roads became "deep" and the streams swollen with rainwater. As the red clay soil became wet, it turned into a combination of liquid and a wax- or molasseslike substance. Once they were underway, the division proceeded on the road to Philadelphia Church and from there took the Milledgeville road. After they crossed Crooked Creek, the division finally camped for the night at the fork of the road leading to Dennis' Mill and Walker's Ferry. Even though the countryside was rich with forage, the cold rain made the march difficult and unpleasant. Although the rain finally stopped at night, the weather turned even colder.[78]

Thus far, the 33rd and the rest of the Second Division had passed through countryside with large plantations or mansions surrounded by broad fields. Most of the terrain was relatively flat especially compared to northern Georgia. Provisions were so plentiful that "foraging was simply choosing."[79] Many of the white residents fled at the approach of Sherman's army, so the bulk of the people the army encountered were blacks. For most of the soldiers this was their first significant contact with blacks and, in general, the soldiers treated them "reasonably well."[80] Since for the blacks Sherman's army was an army of liberation, they greeted the arrival of the Union troops with unrestrained rejoicing. Some blacks simply knelt in prayer by the side of the road, praising God with tears in their eyes. Not surprisingly, whenever necessary, "every black man's poor cabin was a city of refuge to a hunted or imperiled Union soldier."[81] Sherman's march was the "first effective implementation of Lincoln's Emancipation Proclamation," so the reaction of the blacks should not be a surprise. One can only try to imagine the reaction of those who had lived in both bondage and hope to the sight of a column of blue uniforms, a living symbol that everything had changed. The march was, in fact, the first change in the lives of blacks in Georgia since the 1600s.[82]

The morning of November 22 was the coldest day of the march thus far[83] and also marked the end of the first phase of the campaign. When the division moved at 6:00 A.M., the men were probably glad to be on the move to generate some body heat. Since the division could not cross Little River at their current location, they took the road to Dennis Station. At Dennis' Mill, the division crossed a stream called Rooly Creek. After a foot bridge was constructed for the infantry, the animals, artillery, and wagons forded the stream. As the bridge was being built, the rest of the division put the time to good use, burning the mill, a cotton gin and press as well as large amounts of grain and cotton. Upon leaving Dennis' Mill, the division continued to follow the path of the railroad and rejoined the rest of the XX Corps.[84] Due to the timing of the movement, the 33rd could only stop for a hasty dinner.[85] Upon arrival at Little River, they were ordered to proceed to Milledgeville, the objective of the first phase of the campaign. The crossing of Little River on a pontoon bridge was difficult for the trains, so the division did not reach Milledgeville until dark. When they finally got to Milledgeville, they passed through the town, crossed the Oconee River on a large bridge and camped some two miles past the river. After a long day's march that covered 20 miles, the night was "intensely cold."[86]

Milledgeville was a "pleasant looking town" of about 3,000 residents on a bluff on the western side of the Oconee River.[87] The town was also the capital of Georgia, so Milledgeville would not receive any mercy from Sherman's army. Since the left wing of Sherman's army only passed through Milledgeville on November 22, the 33rd and the Second Division did not spend any time there. The troops, who did, held a mock session of the Georgia legislature to revoke Georgia's secession from the Union, plundered the state house and state library, and burned the arsenal. On that same day, elements of the right wing fought the only "battle" of the campaign when they ran into Georgia state troops at Griswoldville. For some reason, the state troops attacked the much stronger Union force and they were driven back with heavy losses.[88] Having reached their goal, the regiment got a day of rest on November 23 while the balance of the army converged on Milledgeville.[89]

How had the men of the 33rd fared on the first part of the march? Beyond the fact that there were no combat losses, everything else is speculation. Since William Lloyd could name Savannah as the ultimate goal of the march, most of the men must have had some sense of where they were headed. However, they probably did not have any knowledge of the strength, or lack thereof, of Confederate opposition, so they were probably somewhat apprehensive as the campaign began. When they encountered no opposition, lived well off the land, and enjoyed relatively favorable weather, the apprehension must have died away. Apprehension was presumably replaced by a spirit of adventure, some enjoyment, and some satisfaction in advancing the Union cause in a relatively safe way. The first phase of the campaign had been a total success; more marching and the city of Savannah still lay ahead. Although the regiment was still a long way from home, from a military standpoint they were a lot closer than they had been for some time.

X

"The destroying flame scarcely attracted our attention"

With the first stage of the march successfully completed, Sherman issued orders for the second stage to begin on November 24. The right wing was to leave Milledgeville, moving parallel to the railroad but south of it to a position opposite Sandersonville. During the march, the troops were to continue to destroy both the railroad and the telegraph. While the right wing proceeded by this route, the left wing was to move from Milledgeville to the railroad opposite Sandersonville and from there destroy the railroad to the Ogeechee River. Sherman believed the destruction of the railroad was of major strategic importance and had to be done thoroughly, so he reduced the rate of march to ten miles a day. Simultaneous with the infantry movements, the cavalry was also to destroy some railroad and then move on the prisoner of war camp at Millen. Sherman, at least on paper, also tried to tighten up on foraging, which was to be limited to official parties. Although trying to offer some protection to civilians, Sherman also authorized commanders to deal harshly with any civilians who tried to interfere with the army's movements.[1] At the end of the second stage of the campaign, the army was to come together near Millen.[2]

As part of the preparation for the second part of the campaign, new orders were issued for the formation to be used on the march. When the march resumed, two brigades, a section of artillery, the corps' pioneer battalion, and the pontoon train were to be at least two miles ahead of the main column. By placing these units at the head of the column, the army would be prepared to deal with any obstacles, human or natural, without delay. At the other end of the column, a rear guard of two brigades and an artillery battery were to be at least one mile behind the main column. This, in turn, prevented or limited harassment from the rear. In between the advance and rear guards, the remaining troops were to guard the trains, but more important, help them maintain the rate of march.[3] The march had been successful so far and Sherman wanted it to remain so.

These orders made some adjustments to the march, but a more or less regular routine had already developed. Each evening the specific route was set for the four columns of the army. The columns were to be close enough to support one another, but also far enough apart to obtain sufficient forage. Spreading out the columns also widened the path of destruction, which was typically 30–40 miles wide in total and sometimes 12 miles long.[4] By dividing the army in this way, Sherman also helped to defeat the real threats to the march, which were not the Confederates, but the weather and hunger. On the individual level, the men, almost all of whom had been through the rigors of the Atlanta campaign, knew to carry as little as possible. Each man carried his musket, bayonet, and 80 rounds of ammunition, half in his cartridge box and the other half in his pockets. In addition, the men also carried their haversacks, which contained food and eating utensils. During the first three weeks of the campaign, foraging was so plentiful that the only food the men usually carried was coffee, hardtack, salt, and sugar. The final portion of the men's load consisted of rubber and woolen blankets and one half of a tent. Although these latter items were not that important during the Atlanta campaign, they were definitely needed now.[5]

Each day on the march began with the sounds of reveille even before there was light in the sky. The men slept all over the landscape, on the sides of hills, in valleys, and in their tents, wrapping themselves in blankets and sleeping on beds of evergreen boughs. After company roll call was complete, the fires were restarted with any surviving fence posts the most popular sources of fuel. The fires provided warmth and were used to boil coffee for breakfast, which was no doubt supplemented by whatever had been brought in by the foragers. While the rest of the column prepared for the march, the lead elements for that day — including pioneers, pickets, and skirmishers as well as the lead regiment — had been on the march since before dawn. The lead units typically met the previous night's pickets waiting for their units to pass by. Frequently large numbers of blacks would also be waiting with the pickets. When the main column got underway, the men marched four abreast with the soldiers setting their own pace and choosing the shoulder for carrying their arms. Since, as a rule, the artillery and wagons had the right of way, the infantry often marched in the fields. Although the march usually continued for 50 minutes followed by a ten-minute rest, the practice of the XX Corps was a five- to ten-minute rest every three miles. One further break from the march was the noon dinner stop, which ordinarily lasted from 40 minutes to an hour. The preferred position in the march was at the head of the column, while being at the rear with the wagons was referred to as the "Abomination of Abominations."[6]

Being on the road before dawn was not always pleasant, but the reward for the lead units was stopping to make camp not long after noon. This was even more pleasant because unlike on the Atlanta campaign, the first task was not building earthworks, but preparing supper. Since the units at the rear of the column had to escort the supply wagons, they frequently did not reach camp until dark.[7] When the army went into camp, each unit divided itself on an informal basis into small groups or messes. These groups shared the camping chores including cutting tent poles, getting water, wood, and bedding, and cooking. With fair weather for most of the march, there was time for recreation after supper. The XX Corps had a reputation for enjoying cockfighting, usually with the fruits of the day's foraging. Preparations for sleeping began with the men placing straw or pine needles on the ground inside of their tents. Rubber blankets were then put on top of these materials as a mattress. A fire was kept going at one end of the tent, and the men also kept warm by sleeping in their clothes. Since the army had a different campsite each night, the hygiene problems of long-term campsites were avoided. The health of the army was further helped by the more balanced diet, especially the meat that was provided through foraging. All told, there was little illness on the march. Many men actually put on weight, in sharp contrast to the prior two campaigns.[8]

Like the beginning of the march, the second phase began in excellent weather under a clear blue sky in bracing cold air.[9] Furthermore, the roads were good and the left wing moved through dense pine forests over hilly terrain. However, when the Second Division tried to move at 7:00 A.M., the road ahead was blocked with supply trains. Delays caused by roads blocked with supply trains were first experienced during the Savannah campaign, but would become an even greater problem during the march through the Carolinas. Due to these delays, the march did not effectively get underway until 10:00 A.M. The 33rd and the rest of the second Brigade, drew the undesirable job of guarding the wagon train. In spite of these obstacles, by the time the division made camp near Gum Creek, they had exceeded the daily quota by covering 14 miles.[10]

Assistant Surgeon Charles W. Stickney. *U. S. Army Military History Institute.*

The next day, November 25 was one of the more difficult days on the march.

Even though the division made an early move, starting at 6:30 A.M., they found the road blocked by wagon trains after only going one-half mile. After a delay of almost three hours, the march resumed at 9:00 A.M. The division passed through the village of Hebron and then reached Buffalo Creek. The terrain was swampy, a preview of what the army would encounter in the "low country" of South Carolina. When they reached the creek, they found the First Division and their trains at the creek waiting to cross. Although named a creek, the body of water was one-half mile wide, surrounded by a swamp and heavy woods. To further complicate the crossing, the stream consisted of eight separate channels, each with a bridge varying in length from 30 to 100 feet. The bridges were connected by earthen causeways. All eight of the bridges had been destroyed so there was a lengthy delay to repair or replace them, which lasted until 2:00 P.M. After the repairs were finally complete, the crossing of the First Division took so long that the Second Division was forced to cross in the dark. Once across, the division moved about one and one-half miles over swampy ground before camping for the night. Both the crossing in the dark and the march over swampy ground were described as "very laborious," but the division still covered nine miles, just under the daily goal of ten.[11]

After the nighttime crossing, there was little rest for the regiment, which resumed the march at 6:00 A.M. Like the prior two days, the early start was followed by a lengthy delay. Although morale was still probably high at this point, the early departures followed by long delays had to be frustrating. This time, they went only two miles before spending two hours waiting for the trains in front of them to move. When the march finally resumed, the division proceeded for only two more miles and had to stop again behind the First Division trains. This time, there was at least a better reason for stopping since there was some skirmishing going on with Confederate cavalry. The skirmishing continued through the village of Sandersonville, where Union troops were fired on from the courthouse. In retaliation and probably also to send a message, Sherman ordered the building burnt to the ground. Once the regiment and the rest of the Second Division reached Sandersonville, they were given a new assignment. Leaving their supply trains with the Third Division, the unencumbered Second Division moved towards Tennille, the location of Station Number 13 on the Georgia Central Railroad. During the rest of the day, the men destroyed two miles of railroad track to the east and then camped for the night about four miles east of Tennille. Although the work of destruction took time, the march was not significantly delayed, and the division covered 13 miles.[12]

The destruction of the railroad resumed the next morning. Another four miles were destroyed to a point about seven miles from Station Number 13. When this work was complete, the division resumed the march, reaching Davisborough where camp was made about 9:00 P.M. A total of 12 miles had been covered, with the division continuing to meet or exceed the daily goal. Still separated from the rest of the XX Corps, the division itself was divided the next day. The second Brigade drew the assignment of escorting the corps trains to Station Number 11. Since the bulk of the Second Division's trains had already been left with the Third Division, this duty should not have been too onerous. While the second Brigade and the 33rd escorted the trains, the rest of the division destroyed five miles of track and also skirmished with some Confederates. The work was not dangerous, but the conditions were probably not very pleasant; this section of railroad was located in a continuous morass called Williamson's Creek or Swamp. After the division had completed their mission of destruction, they returned to Davisborough.

The second Brigade's one-day reprieve from railroad destruction, lasted only one day. On November 29, the 33rd and the rest of the second Brigade was ordered to proceed to Station 10½ on the Macon and Savannah Railroad. Once there, they were to destroy one mile of track to the west and everything to the east including the railroad bridge as far as the Ogeechee River. The work was reportedly completed in "a very effectual manner." The countryside on both sides of the Ogeechee was "an extensive swamp" with thick tangled growth, but the roads were passable so that movement was not too difficult. While the second Brigade completed this assignment, the rest of the division continued the march. By the end of the next day they had reached the village of Louisville. The second Brigade was ordered to rejoin the division that afternoon (November 30) and they did so by a "tedious night march of about fifteen miles" by way of Watkins Bridge. They ultimately reached the Second Division's

Private Franklin R. Taylor, Company A. *U.S. Army Military History Institute.*

camp around midnight.[13] Since leaving Atlanta two weeks before, the regiment had been marching or destroying property for all but one day. Even though they were probably tired, the men were used to hard physical labor, and certainly nothing they had encountered was as bad as combat.

Once again, the 33rd's late arrival in camp was followed by an early march. The first day of December saw the division on the move at 7:00 A.M. on the road to Millen. Although it was December, the weather was perfect, clear, and warm; too warm, in fact, for capes or overcoats. During the day the division crossed Big, Dry, Spring and Baker's creeks. None of these were apparently as difficult as Buffalo Creek, suggesting that "Creek" was a relative term. While the terrain continued to be swampy, the roads were still good, but in a sign of things to come, foraging was not as good as it had been. The division stayed on schedule, covering 13 miles, camping one and one-half miles from Bark Camp Creek. On the next day, December 2, the Second Division led the advance. This was to be the last day of the second stage of the campaign. Moving at 6:00 A.M., they crossed Bark Camp Creek and moved towards Buck Head Creek—not particularly creative names, but an improvement over Mud Creek in northern Georgia. Fortunately, the route of march was along an excellent road on higher and drier ground on the crest of a low ridge. When the division arrived at Buck Head Creek at noon, they found the bridge destroyed and Confederate pickets on the far bank. After the Confederates were driven off, the bridge was rebuilt. The division began crossing at 3:00 P.M. and made camp on the east side of the creek near Buck Head Church. Once again the weather was warm and clear; in fact, there had been no rain since November 21.[14] This was the only one of the 33rd's four campaigns where the weather could have been said to be on the Union side.

By that night, December 2, elements of the XX Corps arrived four miles north of Millen, marking the end of the second phase of the campaign. There had been no real opposition during this period, which at least partially explains why this was the worst phase of the campaign for pillaging. One name for foragers was "bummers," which was applied to groups ranging from unauthorized foragers to the entire army. The combination of little opposition and lax discipline allowed these groups to wander far from the army with devastating effect.

After the entire army gathered at Millen, Sherman issued orders for the third and final phase of the campaign. All four corps were to march on Savannah by separate main roads, with the XX Corps to take the middle road between the Ogeechee and Savannah rivers.[15]

The Second Division began the final phase of the march at 11:00 am. on December 3 at the rear of the XX Corps north of Millen. During the day, the division marched by the empty prisoner of war camp at Millen. The camp encompassed 15 acres of earthen huts made by the prisoners in a largely futile attempt to protect themselves from the elements. According to General Geary, the atmosphere was "foul and fetid" and proved that "the worst accounts of the sufferings of our prisoners... were by no means exaggerated."[16] The regiment having only heard about Andersonville, seeing Millen had to make the sufferings of their comrades more real especially as one member of the 33rd, James Donald, had died there.[17] Since the prisoners and their captors were gone, there was little that could be done for or to humans, but there were many bloodhounds in the area. One participant on the march noted that "all bloodhounds were shot on sight."[18] Even more forcefully, one of Sherman's staff officers claimed that "everything in the shape of a dog has been killed." The army was determined to ensure that "no more flying fugitives, white men or negroes, shall be followed by hounds."[19]

After passing the prisoner of war camp, the Second Division crossed a creek and then entered an "almost impassable swamp." The swamp was reached about dark so that moving the trains over the poor roads was difficult. However, in spite of these problems, the division still covered the desired ten miles. Although camp was made within three miles of Big Horse Creek, some portions of the division spent little time there, as the rear units did not reach the campsite until 6:30 A.M. That unfortunate group probably did little but briefly get off their feet, as the march was resumed at 7:30 A.M. Still at the rear of the corps, the men were probably expecting a difficult day and they were not disappointed. When the lead units crossed Crooked Run, the eastern side was found to be so swampy that corduroying was necessary. Corduroying involved taking tree limbs and other pieces of wood and placing them across the road so that wagons could get enough traction to move forward. This was the division's first significant experience with corduroying, but it would become a way of life in the Carolinas. The time spent corduroying meant that the Second Division did not begin crossing until after dark after the Third Division had finished. As a result the Second Division had to endure a second consecutive nighttime crossing. However, everything was delayed so badly that only part of the division could cross that night. Among the units unable to cross that night were the 33rd and the rest of the second Brigade. The cumulative effect of all of these difficulties was that for one of the few times during the campaign the division failed to reach the ten-mile goal, covering only four miles.

General Geary, no doubt anxious to make up for this lost time, had the division on the move by 6:30 A.M. the next day, December 5. After the crossing of Crooked Run was finally complete, the division moved on, crossing Little Horse Creek, the south fork of the Little Ogeechee and the Little Ogeechee itself. The route of march continued through swamps, and corduroying was once again the order of the day. At the south fork of the Little Ogeechee, the division found a large sawmill, which they destroyed. The weather continued to be warm, but the country was very poor, which hampered foraging. On the next day the division was second in the line of march and the men got something of a break, not moving until 8:00 A.M. When they did get underway, they moved through somewhat better country with improved foraging. However, the terrain continued to be swampy and corduroying continued throughout the day. Delays continued to be a problem. The division was forced to halt twice to wait for supply trains to move and managed only a "tedious march" of six to seven miles.[20]

Even though the swamp crossings had been difficult, at least thus far they had not been made worse by the weather. This changed on December 7 when rain made the bad terrain worse so that wagons got stuck in the mud, some every 100 yards. Since the 33rd was on wagon guard, "it was a very wearysome day's work."[21] The route of march continued "through a succession of terrible swamps," so General Geary had the division trains divided among the units to literally share the load. The roads were so bad that at one point "twenty-four loaded wagons sunk to the wagon beds," with the mules sometimes sinking out of sight. The load sharing prevented the loss of much time, and the roads improved as the division moved towards Turkey Creek. After the rain stopped and the weather became sunny and warm, the situation improved even more. By 2:00 P.M., the division reached Turkey Creek, a wide stream over which the pioneer corps had built a bridge. Although the division did not get to cross until 5:00 P.M., they made an additional three miles over excellent roads and covered 15 miles during the day despite all of the problems of the morning.[22] The 33rd made camp near Springfield, which "SH" found to be a "small antiquated village."[23]

With the army now closing in on Savannah, Geary was ordered on the next day to leave the Second Division trains with the Third Division and move in advance of the XX Corps. On the move at 6:00 A.M., they took a route south by east from Springfield. After a six-mile march, the division then took a road to the right in search of a middle road to Monteith. Although the division marched for seven miles, they finally camped in the woods without finding the middle road. While the roads themselves had been passable, there had been some man-made interference in the form of trees felled across the road, which were removed with little difficulty. Since there were a number of plantations along the route of march, there was ample forage for the division. The weather had also improved, and the day's march covered 13 miles before camp was made near Zion Church. In spite of how well the march had gone, the regiment must by now have been anxious for the campaign to end. At this point in its third week, the march had gotten progressively harder and the novelty must have long since worn out.

On December 9, the Second Division began the march at 8:30 A.M., following behind the First Division. When they hit the Louisville road, they turned to the left and took the main road to the station. Five miles to the west of Monteith Station, the division ran up against some of the worst obstacles of the march in Monteith Swamp. The swamp itself was almost two miles wide, and trees had been felled across the route of march. At the eastern end of the swamp were two small redoubts and rifle pits occupied by two pieces of light artillery plus a small number of infantry. While the Second Division waited, the First Division began to maneuver to take the position.[24] Eventually the 33rd and the rest of the second Brigade were ordered forward at the double to support the First Division. "SH" reported that, although the Confederate position was a mile away, "It was wonderful how cheerfully each man complied" in spite of all the marching they had done.[25] However, the support from the second Brigade was ultimately not needed to disperse the Confederates. Although the Confederate force was not much of an obstacle to the XX Corps, the action did delay the march. After covering six miles, the division was fortunate to find a dry campground in between two portions of the swamp.

The march to the sea effectively ended on the next day, December 10. When the movement towards Monteith Station began at 10:00 A.M., the Second Division was third in the order of march, guarding the XX Corps trains. The road was a good one, and when the division reached Monteith Station they were no more than 10 miles

John Z. Taylor, 1st sgt., Company E; 2nd lt., Company F. *U.S. Army Military History Institute.*

from Savannah. After dinner, the division moved towards Savannah on the Augusta road. Heavy artillery fire to the right indicated that the rest of the army was closing in on Savannah. The day's march continued for another five miles, and camp was made near the Five Mile post. Now only five miles from Savannah, the army had successfully completed their march across Georgia.[26] The army was now so close to their goal that December 11 was spent maneuvering into position for operations against Savannah. Early that day, Barnum's third Brigade of the Second Division was sent to reconnoiter between the Augusta road and the Savannah River. They quickly found the Confederate positions and at 10:00 A.M., the rest of the division came into line along an old rice-field dike. While the third Brigade was on the left against the Savannah River, Pardee's first Brigade was to their right in a position that extended to the Augusta road. For the moment, the 33rd and the rest of the second Brigade had avoided the front line. They were in reserve some 500 yards behind the main line of the third Brigade. In that position they were responsible for guarding the nearby division artillery and the west bank of the river.

Although most of the Second Division's position was concealed by trees, the left portion of the line was in the open, 250 yards from a large Confederate defensive work holding seven heavy guns. To the front of the Union position were open fields with a clear view of the Confederate trenches. Immediately in front of the Confederate trenches were large rice fields that had been flooded by the Confederates with water from a canal. The canal itself was 25 feet wide and five to six feet deep, and was located in between the rice fields and Geary's line, further strengthening the Confederate defenses. In order to control the canal, the Confederates had placed artillery in a large defensive work that controlled both the sluice gates and the mouth of the canal. In addition, the Confederates had three other defensive works on this part of the line, all with heavy artillery. Even though the 33rd was in a reserve position, they had to have been able to see that a direct assault on this position would be difficult and costly. Although the guns from all four positions kept up a steady fire, they did no real damage. Opposite the division's left in the Savannah River was Hutchinson's Island. This island, which was unoccupied, extended down past the lower end of Savannah and contained 900 acres of rice fields and a rice mill.[27]

Before discussing the siege of Savannah, two other topics require attention. The first is the most controversial of the campaign and one of the most controversial of the war: the foraging, pillaging, and destruction that took place throughout the march across Georgia. From the Southern point of view the march was such a heinous war crime and badge of suffering that "communities from Texas to Virginia swear that Sherman's army marched through them.[28] Although Sherman clearly intended for the army to live off the land, his self-proclaimed desire to make "Georgia howl" makes it clear that he was after more than supplies. The goal of the march was not just to move the army from Atlanta to Savannah; the plan was also to demoralize the Southern people. By graphically showing the South that "war and individual ruin are synonymous terms," the Union armies hoped to eliminate or seriously damage the Confederate will to fight.[29]

These strategic motives, combined with the combat experiences of Union soldiers, increased the potential for devastation dramatically. The men in the 33rd, for example, were far away from home and had been so for over a year. During that time, they had seen many of their comrades die from Confederate bullets as well as disease. They were also well aware of the sufferings of their fellow soldiers at Andersonville and other prisoner of war camps. Historians such as Gerald Linderman and James McPherson have shown that no matter how disillusioned the soldiers became, their loyalty to their comrades remained high.[30] Given this background, it would have been unrealistic to expect the men not to take actions that would help win the war and gain some measure of revenge. Such inclinations were abetted by the fact that the army was totally out of contact with the North. One of the major controls on behavior during the Civil War was the knowledge that other members of the regiment could and did report both good and bad behavior to those back home. After all communications to the North were cut, this moral oversight ceased to exist until the campaign was over.[31] If these factors were not enough, there was also the behavior of the "bad apples." These were the unauthorized "bummers," some of whom were not even part of the army, men prepared to vandalize and steal for purely selfish reasons. Finally, the very nature of foraging also contributed to the damage, as small groups without supervision operated far beyond Union lines. All of these elements combined made it easy for foraging to become the destruction of property instead of the gathering of food.

Although the devastation to Georgia's economy cannot be denied, any evaluation of the campaign must consider both what Sherman's men did and what they did not do. From the state and the people, Sherman's men took an estimated 6,900 mules and horses, 13,300 cattle, 10.4 million pounds of grain, and 10.7 million pounds of fodder. All told, this was the equivalent of 6 million rations of beef, bread, sugar, and coffee.[32] Not included in these totals is any measure of the property, both civilian and government, that was burned or destroyed. When he wrote his report after the campaign, Sherman himself estimated the total damage at $100 million[33] (in 1864 dollars). This was not just taking what the army needed, a chaplain in the XX Corps noted: "The question, I think, is never asked how much the farmer needs for his subsistence, but all is taken — literally everything." Frequently soldiers took more than they needed or wanted only to discard items along the way. From the chaplain's point of view, the damage was real and had to be seen to be believed: "No one without being here, can form a proper idea of the devastation that will be found in our track."[34] However, it should also be noted that as a rule the army did not directly harm the civilian population, even though there was little to prevent them from doing so. In addition, there seems to be little disagreement that outrages against women were extremely limited.[35] In the final analysis, the march was a tactic of war, one that worked very effectively with limited loss of life on both sides. By its very nature, however, there were abuses that went beyond what was reasonable.

How much did the men of the 33rd participate in this? While the limited number of eyewitness accounts make it difficult to generalize, one historian has argued, "Virtually every man in Sherman's army, at one time or another participated in a foraging expedition."[36] When Colonel Mindil wrote his official report on the campaign, he listed eight men whom he considered to be deserters. According to Mindil, they were "all troublesome characters," who despite all the efforts of their officers were constant stragglers ultimately captured by the enemy. On the regiment's returns, Mindil had listed the men as deserters so if exchanged they could be tried for desertion; this suggests they were involved in some activity beyond regular duty.[37] After the campaign was over, William Lloyd wrote to Mary and lamented the silk dresses, shoes, muslin, and silver platters he could have brought her, but could not carry.[38]

Another eyewitness, "SH," claimed that at times "no restraint was placed on the men while foraging" and that every plantation was searched and things taken. He further reported that things got so bad that guards had to be placed on houses, although to his knowledge no occupied homes were destroyed. However, when it came to the railroad and other property useful to the Confederacy, destruction was so frequent that "the destroying flame scarcely attracted our attention."[39] The most reasonable conclusion is that the behavior of the 33rd was no better or worse than the typical Union regiment.

While the march through Georgia was taking place, there was significant military action in Tennessee that began when Hood entered the state on November 22 with a force of 40,000 men. Although the opposing Union force under Thomas consisted of 55,000 men, they were divided. Hood hoped to defeat the first portion under Schofield and then go on to deal with Thomas. However, Schofield somehow escaped from the trap set for him and went on to Franklin, Tennessee. When Hood attacked the dug-in Union troops there on November 30, the Confederates suffered a devastating defeat losing 6,000 killed and wounded, including some of their leading generals. Total Confederate casualties were three times that of Pickett's charge at Gettysburg. After this disaster, Hood moved with what was left of his army to the outskirts of Nashville, where he dug in and waited. Thomas' force attacked the Confederates on December 15–16, routed them and drove Hood's army back across the Tennessee River. Hood now had less than 20,000 men, and the Army of Tennessee had been eliminated as an effective fighting force.[40]

Before Thomas' attack, Hood ordered his cavalry commander, General Nathan Forrest, plus some infantry to move against Fort Rosecrans at Murfreesboro. After the Confederates arrived outside the fort on December 4, they believed it was too strong to assault. Instead they hoped to cut off the Union supply line and force the Federal troops to come out and fight. On December 7, the Union commander, General Lovell Rousseau, ordered General Robert Milroy to conduct a reconnaissance in force against the Confederates. Although the Confederates deployed to trap the Union force, Milroy outmaneuvered them and formed in a line of battle. When the Union front line launched a spontaneous attack, a portion of the Confederate force broke and ran. By the time the engagement was over, the Union men had taken over 200 prisoners and captured two "twelve pounder Napoleons."[41] Even though this small action took place hundreds of miles from the 33rd New Jersey's location, the relevance to regiment's story lies in the participation of one William Magee of Company C of the regiment. Magee had enlisted in the regiment as a drummer boy at the age of 15, but his height made him appear older than his age. For some reason, Magee was not with the 33rd; he ended up at Murfreesboro where he was credited with playing a major part in the charge that captured the two Confederate artillery pieces.[42] Although Magee's actual role is not clear, what is certain is that on February 7, 1866, William Magee was awarded the Medal of Honor for his role in the battle of Murfreesboro.[43]

Meanwhile, in eastern Georgia, Sherman and his army were faced with the challenge of taking Savannah. The primary obstacle was not Confederate manpower but the local terrain, which had been used to create a strong defensive position. Savan-

1st Lt. Henry F. Sherwood, Company C. *U.S. Army Military History Institute.*

nah was surrounded by marshes, rice fields, and canals, so the only land approaches were five causeways, dry routes of access through the low lying wet countryside. Three of these causeways consisted of wagon roads; the other two carried the railroad lines into the city. Given the limited access, the Confederates had been able to establish a strong defensive network of forts and rifle pits across the causeways about four miles from the city. To further strengthen the defenses, the Confederates had used the floodgates under their control to flood the lowlands in front of their positions. Although the Confederate defenses under General Hardee consisted of only 9,000 men, mostly state militia, the strong defensive positions made a frontal assault almost impossible. While Sherman was concerned about the strong defenses, another problem was that the army was face to face with the greatest danger of the whole campaign: running out of food. Throughout the march to the sea, the key factor was movement, which made available new sources of food for Sherman's 60,000 men. However, once the army had reached its goal, there was nowhere else to go. If the army did not take Savannah or find another source of supply, it would be in serious trouble.[44]

After he finished analyzing the situation, Sherman decided to "invest the city from the north and west" while connecting with the Union fleet in Ossabaw Sound.[45] Connecting with the fleet would both secure a supply route and ultimately make Savannah untenable for the Confederates. In fact, Hardee had been directed by the Confederate authorities to prepare an escape route and to avoid having his army captured at all costs.[46] The key to opening communications with the fleet was the capture of Fort McAllister on the south bank of the Ogeechee River, some 14 miles below Savannah. Since the Confederates recognized the importance of this position, they had constructed a massive earthwork fort that had been impervious to all Federal attacks by water. In addition, the fort could not be destroyed or captured by artillery fire, leaving an infantry assault as the only alternative.[47] Units from the right wing attacked the fort on December 13 and successfully captured it at about 5 P.M. At almost exactly the same time, the Union tug boat *Dandelion* arrived, thus establishing contact with the fleet. Sherman then met with Admiral Dahlgren and other naval commanders to plan further operations. Since the Confederate defenses were so strong, Sherman planned to bring large siege guns to Savannah and then take the city by assault. When Sherman formally demanded the surrender of Savannah on December 17, Hardee refused.[48]

While all of this had been going on, the men of the Second Division of the XX Corps on the far left of the Union line had been busy improving their position. These activities were made somewhat more difficult by Confederate artillery fire that began on December 12, but there was little actual damage. Although the Union response was limited to sharpshooter fire, this was actually more effective than the Confederate artillery. When the Confederates temporarily landed a force on Hutchinson's Island, Geary sent some troops to the island, both to prevent a reoccurrence and to secure the left wing. In addition an artillery battery was placed near the position of the 33rd to cover both the river and part of the island.[49] Even though the connection to the fleet had been made, this did not help immediately as an overland supply route had to be created. Food and forage were running low. The men sustained themselves on the local rice crop for almost two weeks, while wondering why the Confederates had not destroyed the rice.[50] On December 14, a Confederate gunboat came up Black River behind Hutchinson's Island and fired into the second Brigade's position.[51] During this attack, the 33rd suffered their only casualty of the campaign. Private Terrence Sweeney of Company D suffered contused wounds of both thighs, but would completely recover.[52]

By the next day, the Confederates were firing an average of 300 shells a day into the Union lines, but the artillery fire was doing little damage. During the night of December 16, work began on positions for the new siege guns. The work continued the next day only 250 yards from the most advanced Confederate fort and within their plain sight. While the work was important, there was an interruption at 11:00 A.M., when "a large mail arrived for us and caused almost universal rejoicing." This was the first mail the men had received in six weeks; it was a portion of the 20 tons of mail the fleet had delivered to Sherman's army.[53] William Lloyd must have received some of the mail as he took time to write to Mary, probably his first letter to her since leaving Atlanta. Noting that he had one foot in South Carolina and one in Georgia, he reported that he was in good health, as "the campaign hasn't hurt me in the least." As Lloyd had predicted there had been hard marching but no fighting, and now he was apparently part of the groups building the forts. Reflecting the supply situation, Lloyd confirmed that "our grub has been rather short" and claimed he was actually looking forward to some hardtack. Even though it was almost Christmas time, Lloyd reported that the weather was as warm as the summer. Lloyd predicted that as soon as the siege guns were in place, "you can look for good news from this quarter."[54] Such news would come more quickly than everyone including General Sherman would have thought possible.

Corduroying of the roads to the rear was completed on December 18, allowing for the overland delivery of supplies.[55] That same day, Sherman left by boat for another conference with Admiral Dahlgren. The campaign would be over before he returned.[56] On the next day, General Slocum held a conference with his commanders to develop a plan for an assault once the heavy guns were in place. The Second Division had by now completed work on one fort with two more in progress. Throughout this period the Confederate artillery fire continued and was now having some impact. Preparations for the assault continued on December 20 with the men constructing straw fascines to fill up the ditches in front of the Confederate defenses. Also under construction were bamboo fascines made from materials from the pontoon bridging equipment. Fascines were bundles of straw or bamboo tied together at close intervals, which could be used as temporary bridging material. However, the Union forces were not the only ones building something. The Confederates completed a pontoon bridge from Savannah into South Carolina about two and one-half miles from the far left of the Second Division.[57]

That night heavy Confederate artillery fire was accompanied by the sounds of men and wagons moving over the pontoon bridge. After the fire stopped at about 3:00 A.M., elements of the third Brigade advanced about 20 minutes later to the outer Confederate works and found them empty. By 3:40 A.M., the Federal troops found the main works were also deserted. General Geary sent the news on to headquarters and accompanied the third Brigade as they pushed towards Savannah. Near the city limits, they met the mayor and alderman of the city under a flag of truce, and Geary accepted the surrender at 4:30 A.M. The lead units hung the national colors as well as those of the Second Division on the U.S. customs house before the sun was up. Since the city was now at risk from a "lawless mob of low whites and negroes," Geary was placed in command of the city and his men restored order. The 33rd entered into the city at about 8:00 A.M. and established a permanent camp on the city's parade ground.[58]

Against its wishes, Georgia had now rejoined the Union. While the campaign had not been anywhere near as long or as difficult as the struggle for Atlanta, the significance of the success of Sherman's army cannot be overstated. The war and the cost of secession had been brought deep within the South, and there would be a limit to how much more of this the Confederacy could withstand. After he arrived in Savannah, Sherman sent to President Lincoln a well known telegram that began, "I beg to present to you, as a Christmas gift, the city of Savannah." In his less well known reply on December 26, Lincoln acknowledged the gift and the fears that he, and, others had for the campaign. Keeping with the spirit of the season, Lincoln noted that the army's success brought "those who sat in darkness to see a great light." He then asked prophetically, "But what next?"[59]

XI

"There will be no rest"

It is understandable that Sherman and Lincoln used images of Christmas to describe the successful Savannah campaign, but mention of the holiday most likely did not help the morale of the officers and men of the 33rd New Jersey. Although all were glad to have arrived safely in Savannah, they knew all too well that this was the second Christmas spent far from home. Christmas day itself in Savannah was rainy, but in spite of the inclement weather, the men were called out to hear the reading of Sherman's message of congratulations. While some men enjoyed a good holiday meal,[1] for others it was "a lean and hungry Christmas" with little more than rations of boiled rice and beef.[2] William Lloyd told Mary that he had a "very dull Christmas" since he "went to bed almost broken hearted" after a meal of mush and molasses. All was not lost, however, as some friends eventually came to his tent "with a bottle and some segars" and they spent several hours drinking, smoking, and singing.[3] To a man, they must have hoped and prayed that this was the last Christmas apart from their loved ones.

Although Lloyd had some complaints about Christmas, he was fairly positive when he wrote to Mary on December 26. Lloyd claimed he was happy to be safe "in a beautiful city" and to "bear the honor with the heroes of another victory."[4] The successful campaign may have accounted for part of Lloyd's good humor, but even more important was the fact that at long last, the regiment had been paid: almost $60,000 on Christmas day itself.[5] Although this might have been thought of as a Christmas present, the money was no gift; the men had earned every penny and were really owed interest. Lloyd had received just over $200, but he only sent $20 home in the mail, believing that there was too much risk in sending larger amounts.[6] Chaplain Faull returned home to New Jersey on leave in early January and many of the men apparently sent their pay home with him. In total, Faull was entrusted with $20,000, most of which he delivered to Marcus Ward in Newark for the men's families. Since travel was difficult and the danger of theft magnified by the war, the faith of the men and the bravery of Faull was remarkable. Faull also took with him an

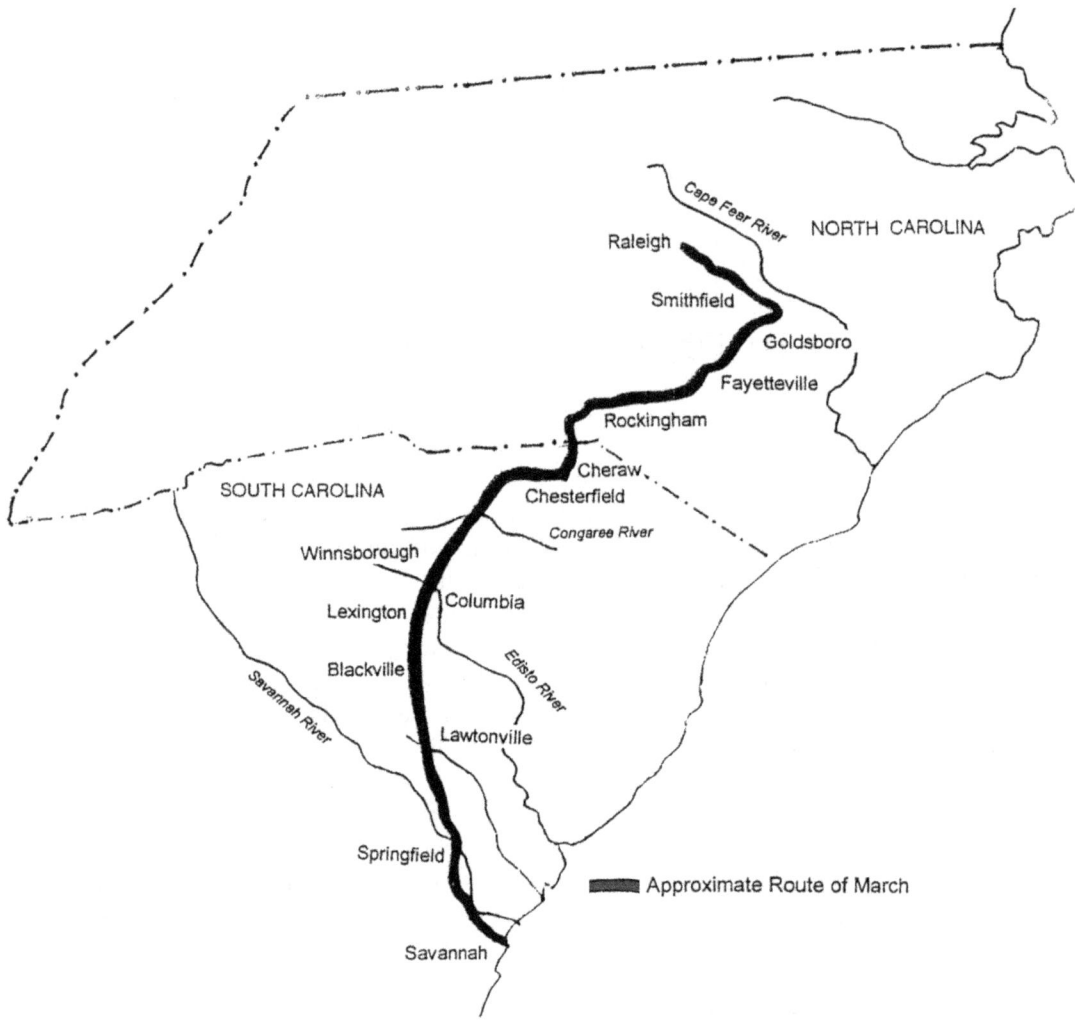

Map of the Carolina campaign. *Andrea LaConte Magno.*

escaped slave who had become attached to Captain Nathaniel Bray. Bray had sent the man along with Faull to join Bray's family in Branchville, where he became an employee. The winter climate in New Jersey must have been harsher than what the man was used to, but this was probably more than offset by freedom and a paid job.[7]

William Lloyd noted in his letter that the regiment was on provost duty in Savannah. Whether because the Second Division was the initial Union force in the city or because of General Geary's prior experience in government, Geary had been placed in charge of the city. As a result, the Second Division functioned as the police force and reportedly brought order to Savannah. Although Savannah was a Southern city like Atlanta, the atmosphere was much more hospitable.[8] No doubt this was to some extent due to the fact that little if any damage was done to the city.[9] The population was basically friendly, especially after some 200 "irreconcilables" were sent to Charleston.[10] Savannah was a valuable port and supply base for the Union army, so there was no question of destroying the city; this had a corollary effect of protecting private property. However, the influx of war refugees had created major shortages of food and fuel. At first army supplies were used to help feed the civilian population. Subsequently, there were substantial donations from the North.[11] Thinking about the future, William Lloyd speculated hopefully on a rumor that the regiment would stay in Savannah as part of the occupying force since he believed that "we have done our part, in Sherman's great movements."[12]

As in Atlanta, the stay in Savannah provided an opportunity for resupply. Throughout this period, duty was typical for garrison life including drill and dress parades with classes, concerts, and theatrical performances available as evening diversions. In a city the size of Savannah, there were also less desirable diversions including bordellos and gambling.[13] Since the 33rd had been assigned to provost duty, they were kept especially busy. Georg Muller told his parents that the regiment had little rest as they were always moving their camp to different locations throughout the city. Muller was impressed with Savannah, which he found to be about as large as Newark with "almost all very beautiful buildings." Perhaps used to the more consistently harsh winters of the North, Muller found the weather in Savannah "unstable," alternating between warm and cold with rain, but no snow.[14] During December, the regiment suffered five fatalities from disease as Martin Van Buren, John Strube, David Russell, Thomas Caldwell, and James Adams all died that month. Another fatality was Peter Wenckler, who died on December 15 after being wounded and taken prisoner at Peachtree Creek. How Wenckler came to be in Savannah is not clear. He may have been imprisoned at Andersonville or perhaps Millen and then evacuated to a Confederate hospital in Savannah.[15]

While William Lloyd had been in a relatively positive frame of mind on December 26, the good mood did not last long as he wrote a very bitter letter to Mary two days later. Lloyd was again pursuing a commission, but he had received no response from Captain Frazer other than being told not to bother Colonel Mindil. This led Lloyd to observe, "The officers in the Regiment is the God dammdest meanest lot of curs this side of Hell." With this preamble, Lloyd then recited how he had been in every battle, done every kind of duty, was never drunk or disorderly, and never talked back to officers. Yet in spite of this exemplary service, he got little praise and less recognition. Even though Lloyd had been in every battle, the idea that he was a model soldier is somewhat hard to accept. Lloyd was so frustrated with the situation that he wanted to give up being a sergeant and go back into the ranks. Another even more preferable alternative was getting out of the army entirely. To that end, Lloyd urged his friends at home to get him out of the army by whatever means necessary. Perhaps recognizing that he had gotten carried away, Lloyd apologized to Mary for his language, attributing it to the soldier's status as "white slaves." Once he had gotten all of this off his chest, Lloyd closed by wishing her a "Happy New Year."[16]

When Lloyd wrote again on January 1, the coming of the New Year had apparently improved his mood somewhat. He hoped that 1865 would bring peace, the restoration of the Union, and his return home, although probably not in that order.

While he assumed Mary had enjoyed a proper New Year's dinner of goose, he was left with mush and fat pork. Lloyd was not that disappointed, since he and some friends had acquired five canteens of whiskey. Thus fortified, Lloyd reported that "we had a merry old time," which consisted primarily of breaking furniture. As part of the celebration, Lloyd fired his musket with the result that his tent caught on fire and almost burned down. However, Lloyd wasn't concerned; "New Year's don't come, but once a year, and tents are cheap." Besides passing on the news of this celebration, Lloyd also sent Mary the bulk of his pay. His good spirits had not evaporated some ten days later. According to Lloyd, Savannah was a "wonderful city," and he was fine except for a lack of rations. He was even philosophical about this since there was "no use in growling, for I have got use to doing without."[17]

In this same letter, Lloyd noted that the rest of the army was gradually moving by boat transports to Hilton Head in South Carolina. While as usual there was speculation about the regiment's future, there was very little in the way of facts. Although he originally had wished that the regiment would continue to be on garrison duty in Savannah, Lloyd was now more realistic as he hoped their destination was Richmond and with it the end of the war.[18] Certainly the movement of other troops into South Carolina indicated that the regiment's stay in Savannah would be briefer than their time in Atlanta. During the next ten days, there was a change in both the regiment's location and the weather. By January 20, the 33rd was on Hutchinson's Island in the Savannah River guarding the pontoon bridge to South Carolina. Georg Muller had earlier complained that the weather was inconsistent, but the weather was now consistently bad. Sherman's army was plagued with rain that made the roads "utterly impassable."[19] Lloyd wrote to Mary from the regiment's new location and noted that the rain had turned the rice field on Hutchinson's Island into a rice swamp.[20] The regiment returned to their old camp after a few days, while the rain persisted.[21]

The purpose of the 33rd's temporary assignment on Hutchinson's Island was to support the beginning of a new campaign. Once Savannah had been taken in December, Lincoln's response to Sherman's news of the victory had included the prophetic question, "But what next?" While Lincoln may have had ideas of his own, he added that the best approach would be for him to leave the answer to Sherman and Grant.[22] In fact, Grant and Sherman had been in contact about the next step even before Savannah fell. After communications were reopened in December, Grant had sent Sherman a dispatch stating that once Savannah was taken, Grant wanted Sherman's army brought to Virginia by boat. A staff officer who was present when Sherman read this message reported that Sherman "was almost sick with anxiety and outrage." Although Sherman was in agreement that Virginia should be the destination, he did not want to get there by boat. Instead, Sherman wanted to replicate the Savannah campaign by marching through the Carolinas. Beginning the next day, Sherman began arguing for this. Grant ultimately agreed, especially after the army chief of staff, General Halleck, determined that the necessary shipping would take two months to arrange. In agreeing to Sherman's proposal, Grant emphasized his desire for Sherman to be underway as soon as possible.[23]

There would be some clear similarities between the Carolinas campaign and the Savannah campaign. As in the Savannah campaign, the army consisted of about

60,000 men and was divided into a left and a right wing. Once again the 33rd New Jersey would be part of the Second Division of XX Corps in the left wing. When the army left Savannah, they would be completely cut off from supply bases and communications as they had been after leaving Atlanta. Since there would be no access to Union supplies until reaching the Cape Fear River in North Carolina, foraging would once again be the order of the day. Sherman tried, at least in theory, to tighten up the practice. In the Carolinas, foraging parties were to be commanded by officers, the foragers were not to enter houses, and they were to leave the residents food for their own use. The authority to burn property was given only to corps commanders, which meant, theoretically, that only four people in the army could make that decision. Although the destruction of property was supposed to be limited to retaliation for resistance to the army's march, the practice would be somewhat different. As a result, the same debates that began during the Savannah campaign would be extended to the march through the Carolinas. At least one new element was present; the feeling of the men towards South Carolina, the place where secession had been born.[24] A chaplain in the XX Corps reported that every soldier "feels a sort of hatred against this state." The sentiment was clearly, "Let South Carolina know what war is."[25]

In planning the march through the Carolinas, the route was determined by the topography. The sea coast of Georgia and South Carolina was full of rivers and swamps that were easy to defend. Sherman planned to avoid this problem by moving into the interior of South Carolina and then approaching the upper portions of these rivers where they would be easier to cross.[26] Since the interior of the state was more fertile, this alternative would also offer better forage for the army.[27] The proposed route of march might have seemed to be the easier option, but there were still plenty of swamps and low lying land in the army's path. Furthermore, in this new campaign, the army would have to cross almost all of the major water obstacles instead of marching parallel to them as in the prior campaign. Success was, therefore, going to depend in large measure on bridge building and the pioneer corps. This factor was taken into account in planning for the campaign, especially with the provision of extra axes. There was little that could be done about another key factor, the weather. Sherman's army had been incredibly fortunate with the weather during the march to Savannah. Should this good fortune not continue, especially given the water obstacles, there would be major problems.[28]

The strategy for the campaign was relatively straightforward. While the left wing feinted toward Augusta, Georgia, the right wing would do the same towards Charleston, South Carolina. After creating confusion about their intentions, the two wings would head directly for Columbia, the capital of South Carolina. From there they would move on to Goldsboro, North Carolina. Once at Goldsboro, the army would connect to supply bases on the North Carolina coast by means of railroads from New Bern and Wilmington. At Goldsboro, Sherman's army would be within striking distance of Virginia for the beginning of the spring and summer campaigns of 1865.

Preliminary movements of troops of the right wing into South Carolina began at the end of December with a goal of beginning the campaign by January 15. Since the left wing was to feint towards Augusta, Georgia, the troops were to move up both banks of the Savannah River until they reached Sister's Ferry. After they arrived there, the troops on the Georgia side would then cross into South Carolina with the entire left wing to reunite at Robertsville, South Carolina. Once this connection was made, the left wing would march north to where the Charleston and Augusta railroad crossed the Edisto River. While the left wing was threatening Augusta, the right wing was to move to Beaufort, South Carolina, by boat and thereby threaten Charleston. When this feint was completed, the right wing would go west and meet the left wing north of the Charleston and Augusta Railroad. After the standard destruction of the railroad, both wings would head for Columbia.[29]

Since the only remaining major Confederate army was under siege at Petersburg, the military obstacles facing Sherman's army were not formidable. Any forces left to defend the Carolinas were scattered from Virginia to Tennessee, including the last remnants of the Army of Tennessee. During the first part of the campaign, the Confederate forces were concentrated too slowly and Sherman's army moved too rapidly for any effective Confederate defense of South Carolina.[30] While Sherman was successful with the things he could control, his luck with the weather ran out in the Carolinas. In planning the march of the left wing up the Savannah River, the XX Corps including the 33rd New Jersey was supposed to be on the Carolina side of the river. Although the first and third divisions of the XX Corps had crossed the river by January 17, heavy rains had swollen the river significantly. The pontoon bridge was swept away by the floodwaters and the causeway, used by the Confederate troops escaping Savannah, was now under four feet of water. The flood left the entire Second Division and a portion of the Third Division and their train on the wrong side of the river. General Geary was ordered to take command of all these units and to follow the XIV Corps up the Georgia side of the river for a crossing at Sister's Ferry.[31]

It was relatively easy to make this adjustment to the route of march, but the weather had just begun wreaking havoc with Sherman's plans. After General Geary turned over the command of Savannah on January 19, torrential rains set in that continued day and night through January 23. The flooding was so bad that the river overflowed both banks and the division could not move at all.[32] The only positive note was that during this period of bad weather they were still in Savannah, where conditions had to be better than on the march. At this point the division had approximately 5,300 men, probably about one-half of their original strength.[33] The men of the 33rd had been issued eight days' rations, and Georg Muller believed that their destination was Charleston. Although Muller did not know the plans for the campaign, he did know what to expect. In his last letter prior to leaving Savannah, he told his parents, "As long as we are with Sherman, there will be no rest until the war is over."[34]

When the rain finally stopped on January 24, the weather turned clear and cold. On January 25 General Geary was ordered to begin the march to Sister's Ferry on the next day, but the order was countermanded. Finally on January 26, a firm order was received for the march to begin at 8:00 A.M. on the 27th. Since Colonel Mindil was now commander of the second Brigade, Lieutenant Colonel Fouratt, back from sick leave, had resumed command of the regiment. In addition to the 33rd, the second Brigade consisted of the 73rd and 109th Pennsylvania and the 119th, 134th, and 154th New York. The entire brigade consisted of 72 officers and 1,145 enlisted men, which shows how much the army had been worn down by combat and disease. The total strength of 1,247 was only about 20 or 25 percent greater than the authorized strength of many regiments. In anticipation of what lay ahead, a pioneer company of 30 men and a tool wagon accompanied each brigade. During the Carolina campaign, tools would be far more important than muskets.[35]

At 8:00 A.M. on January 27, the 33rd New Jersey and the rest of the Second Division began the almost 40-mile journey from Savannah to Sister's Ferry.[36] After leaving their camp near the jail, the second Brigade moved through the streets of Savannah to the Augusta road where they met the first and third brigades. By the time the second Brigade arrived, the first Brigade was already underway on the road along the west bank of the Savannah River. The second Brigade then followed them with the third Brigade following behind with the wagon trains.[37] Since the terrain dictated the route of march through the Carolinas, the Second Division actually had to march back towards Atlanta to get into position for the start of the campaign. As a result, the 33rd was experiencing in a small way what the rest of Sherman's army had been through when they followed Hood's army back into northern Georgia. Far worse was the physical burden of escorting both their own and other unit's supply wagons, some 300 in all. Even though the weather continued to be cold, the roads had not sufficiently hardened, so as the day went on the ground was broken up by the wagons and deteriorated badly. Due to these conditions, the brigade only made 12 miles that day in spite of an early start. While the Second Division began making camp at 3:00 P.M., the trains did not finish the march until dark.[38] One of the many disadvantages of a winter campaign was the limited daylight; many marches began and ended in the dark. After camp was made for the night, 100 men from the second Brigade were assigned to picket duty under the command of Captain Thomas Lee of the 33rd.[39]

The march resumed in the dark at 6:00 A.M. on January 26. After breaking camp, the Second Division followed the Augusta road for four miles, but then broke off the deception and turned left on the McCall road. The division proceeded to within three and one-half miles of Springfield and camp was made about 2:00 P.M. on the Widow Bird's plantation. The cold weather had moderated somewhat around the middle of the day and the division made 14 miles over bad roads that required a lot of corduroying.[40] Corduroying was to be a way of life during the Carolina campaign, but the task was less difficult if there were fence rails or other lumber available. If wood was not readily available, the men had to cut down trees, trim them of their branches, and then drag them to the site. In the swamps of Carolina, trees frequently had to be cut down in knee-deep mud and then placed in roadbeds submerged in water of similar depth. On especially bad areas of road, the corduroying process had to be repeated.[41]

When the 33rd and the rest of the brigade broke camp at 6:30 A.M. the next day, they were last in the line of march with the added burden of the division trains. After passing through the town of Springfield about 8:00 A.M., the Second Division forded Jack's Creek, probably no pleasant task in January.[42] Back in December, "SH" had

XIV and XX Corps crossing the Savannah River at Sister's Ferry. *Harper's Weekly.*

found Springfield to be "a small antiquated village." One would imagine that the town did not look any better the second time around especially in winter.[43] About one mile past the creek, the division turned to the right toward Sister's Ferry. The route of march then went through a bad swamp at Ebenezer Creek where once again the road had to be corduroyed. Even though the march was difficult, the Second Division covered 12 miles and camped at 2:00 P.M. within three miles of the ferry. The regiment now had a wait of five days.

Before any crossing of the Savannah River could be made, engineers had to build 1,000 feet of wooden and pontoon bridges. This alone would have been time consuming, but on the South Carolina side of the river, the road was under water for two miles, in some places up to 12 feet deep. To add to the difficulties, the Confederates had put a large number of logs on this part of the road, mixed with torpedoes (mines). Removal of these explosive devices was both difficult and dangerous; at least two men were severely injured.[44] On the same day that the 33rd arrived at Sister's Ferry, another member of the regiment lost his life in combat. While detached from the regiment, Sergeant Lucius Hull was killed by Confederate guerrillas at Tunnel Hill, Georgia. The tragedy of Hull's death was further magnified by the fact that his wife had predeceased him, leaving four orphan children back in Newark.[45] Although combat fatalities were limited, disease continued to claim its quota as

Michael O'Connor, Charles Riker, John Lee, William Jackson, James Hand, and Francis Moakler all succumbed in January.[46]

One person who had reason to be grateful for the unscheduled respite at Sister's Ferry was Chaplain John Faull. The delay in the regiment's movements allowed Faull to rejoin them before they got too far into South Carolina. Faull had been absent for 33 days on his visit home to New Jersey. The trip had required 25 days of travel, culminating in a five-day ocean voyage from New York to Hilton Head, South Carolina. Since the voyage had been over rough seas, Faull and everyone else had to pay "devotions ... over the bulwarks." Apparently these experiences had helped to solidify Faull's attitude towards the Confederacy. He now predicted to readers of the Sussex *Register* that "South Carolina is now about to taste the sweet fruits of her own works, and to be made to feel the hand of war."[47]

At Sister's Ferry, the weather improved dramatically. It became clear and mild, making the situation easier both for those who waited and those who worked on the bridges. No doubt trying to maintain some military discipline, Colonel Mindil reviewed the brigade on February 1.[48]

The regiment would now be out of contact with the North until they got close to the coast of North Carolina. As in the Savannah campaign, this severely limited eyewitness accounts by members of the regiment. Before the brigade moved, an additional "Jersey flavor" was added on February 2 when the 13th New Jersey was temporarily attached to the brigade by General Geary.[49] Although the rain resumed on February 2, by the evening of the next day conditions were adequate for the cavalry to begin crossing the river.[50] The entire Second Division moved towards the ferry on February 4, but their crossing was delayed until 10:00 A.M. by the crossing of the cavalry supply trains. Mercifully, there was a break in the weather as the rain stopped, if only temporarily. When the Second Division finally began crossing, the second Brigade was second in line and started crossing at 11:00 A.M. Once across the river, they marched for two miles and drew five days' rations at a temporary supply point.[51] The significance of the crossing was not lost upon many Union soldiers, who reportedly gave three cheers as they stepped on to South Carolina soil for the first time.[52]

After drawing supplies, the 33rd did not resume the march until 5:00 P.M., when they moved towards Robertsville camping near there well past dark. Although the weather was clear and warm, Nathaniel Bray claimed that the road from the river was the worst he had ever seen. Chaplain Faull finally caught up with the regiment that day, ending his long return journey. When Geary's command reached Robertsville, they found that the town had already been visited by other Union troops and consisted "chiefly of standing chimneys and ash heaps."[53] Near Robertsville was another physical barrier, the Great Black Swamp, with three miles of roads that were "utterly impassable for trains." Meeting another major obstacle so shortly after the prolonged crossing of the river was not a good omen. The 250 wagons of the cavalry supply train had now been assigned to the Second Division in addition to the extra wagons they were already escorting. Since the swamp was such a formidable obstacle, Geary left the third Brigade with the trains on the far side of the swamp and assigned details from the other units to corduroy the roads throughout the night.[54] The corduroying process was never easy, but doing it at night in the muck and mire of a swamp must have made railroad destruction or breastworks building seem like easy duty.

Ultimately, it took some 1,500 men all of the morning of February 5 to finish corduroying the road through the swamp. After the work was complete, the trains began crossing at noon and the whole division was underway by 1:00 P.M. Once they got through the swamp, the division camped at a crossroads near Trowell's Farm, about eight miles past Robertsville. At Trowell's Farm, some blacks showed General Geary the bodies of three Union soldiers. The blacks claimed that Mr. Trowell had pointed out the soldiers to Confederate cavalry. It appeared to Geary that the soldiers had then been shot down "in cold blood." His response was to place Trowell under arrest as an accessory to murder and to order the destruction of his property. The fate of Trowell's Farm and Robertsville was a bad sign for other villages and towns located in the army's path. After the ordeal of corduroying the swamp in the dark, it is hard to imagine how anyone had any strength left for a day's march. Once the division got out of the swamp, the roads improved and the weather was clear and warm. The division covered a total of nine miles.[55]

The weather continued to be favorable the next day, which was a help to the 33rd and the rest of the second Brigade as they were once again burdened with the division's wagon trains.[56] When the division passed through Lawtonville and moved towards Beech Branch, they again encountered roads that were in very bad condition. The units of the second Brigade made camp for the night four and one-half miles past Lawtonville on the Buford's Bridge road. Although the countryside consisted of substantial plantations that had been abandoned by their owners, there was not much available for the foragers, preceding divisions having already visited these locations.[57] Foragers who took more than they needed probably hurt fellow Union soldiers as much as they did the Confederates. The weather, which had been favorable for a few days, deteriorated that night when a heavy rain began falling.[58]

The heavy rain continued on February 7 so that roads, which were already bad, became worse and required extensive corduroying. At noon, the division reached Coosawhatchie Swamp, which was badly swollen by the heavy rains. Geary and his command were now faced with crossing 300 yards of water, three and one-half feet deep, with a "treacherous bottom." Since no bridge of any kind existed, Geary assigned 600 men to build one and to corduroy the approach to the bridge. When the crossing began at 4:00 P.M., there was very little daylight left. Three brigades, the artillery, and most of the supply train crossed during the night. All of this traffic caused the "treacherous bottom" to degenerate even further into "deep holes of a quicksand nature." Throughout the night, men had to be sent into the waist-deep water to place trees and logs on the submerged road and then somehow pin them down so that they would not float away. The weather was cold with heavy rain all day and all night. Under these conditions, it was amazing that the division was able to move six and one-half miles. Commenting on the day's results, Geary noted with some understatement that the weather had added to "the discomforts of the situation."[59] Although the 33rd and the rest of the left wing were barely into South Carolina, they had already experienced more problems than they had encountered during the entire Savannah campaign. Most Civil War armies did not even attempt campaigning during the winter. The fact that Sherman's army did so successfully is a tribute to their tenacity.

The efforts to cross the division's supply trains went on all night, affirming Georg Muller's prediction that there would be no rest during this campaign. Geary had received orders from left wing commander General Slocum to move forward quickly, so the march for Buford's Bridge began at 6:00 A.M. on February 8. The men were wet, cold, covered with mud, and exhausted; they must have moved forward on sheer willpower. The rain had stopped and, while the weather remained cold and the roads were muddy, the route of march had been corduroyed to some degree by the preceding columns. Perhaps being spared the task of corduroying the road made up to some extent for the forage lost to the advance units. Once Geary's command arrived at Buford's Bridge, the task was to cross the Big Salkehatchie, a stream that was wide, deep, and swampy. Through the swampy areas were a series of causeways connected by 23 small bridges. The total network was one-half mile long. Although there was a line of defensive works on the northern side that could have effectively prevented the crossing, the works were unoccupied. While the crossing was difficult, three brigades and most of the trains were across by dark, with the 33rd itself crossing at dark. Since the division was spared the time consuming process of corduroying, the rate of march was better and they covered 14 miles over the course of the day.

When the march resumed at 9:00 A.M. on February 9, the division moved over good roads through well cultivated country. For the first time during the campaign, the division's foragers found plenty of supplies and "all returned well laden." The weather was still far from ideal, it being cold enough for snow to fall for the only time during the campaign. Although the regiment's experiences in Tennessee had been compared to Valley Forge and Morristown, snow in South Carolina probably made the men wonder if they were going to more closely repeat the revolutionary experience. However, regardless of the weather, the division made 18 miles over the course of the day and camped relatively early at 3:00 P.M., one mile from Blackville. After they got to Blackville, the division was reunited with the rest of the XX Corps, which had traveled up the South Carolina side of the Savannah River. By this point, everyone in Geary's command had to be exhausted. This must have been recognized to some extent, as the division was assigned to stay in place and guard the supply wagons. While the men of the Second Division tried to get some rest, the balance of the XX Corps destroyed the railroad. Although the Second Division was ordered to move to Duncan's Bridge about 1:00 P.M., the 33rd and the rest of the second Brigade was left behind to guard the train and the village of Blackville.[60] This was probably not too challenging, as there was "not much left to show how much of a village it had been." Captain Bray and his "mess" were able, though, to occupy a hotel owned by a Mrs. Struble; an improvement, no doubt, over the usual accommodations.[61]

The majority of the Second Division crossed Duncan's Bridge before dark on February 10, but the artillery and the horses had to remain on the south bank until the bridge was repaired. In actuality, Duncan's Bridge was six bridges connected by causeways about one mile in length; three of the bridges across the two main channels of the South Edisto had been destroyed and needed extensive repairs. As a result, the crossing was not finished on February 11. The division spent the day repairing

The XX Corps entering Blackville, South Carolina. *Harper's Weekly*.

the bridges and corduroying the causeways. No one could have been happy about having to do this work, but at least the countryside along the river continued to be a productive area for foraging.[62] The importance of this cannot be overestimated; the men apparently tolerated the weather and the exhausting work if they had adequate rations.[63] While this work proceeded, the somewhat rested second Brigade including the 33rd made a ten-mile march and rejoined the division by the end of the day.[64] The final march on Columbia, the capital of South Carolina and the birthplace of secession, was about to begin, and there was only one more river to cross. Getting this far had been an accomplishment, something one historian attributed to " 'Yankee' ingenuity, strong backs, excessive profanity and a considerable amount of whiskey."[65]

The morning of February 12 saw the reunited Second Division headed for a crossing of the North Edisto River at Jeffcoat's Bridge. During the day, Geary's command encountered Confederate opposition for one of the few times during the campaign, when shots were exchanged with some Confederate cavalry. Then when the division reached the river, they found that Jeffcoat's Bridge had been burned and some Confederate troops were in defensive positions on the north bank of the river. Even though the terrain consisted of a swamp with dense tangled undergrowth, Geary sent skirmishers from the first Brigade out on both flanks, which drove the Confederates out of their position. On the far side of the crossing was a large swamp with a causeway leading through it. At the end of the causeway the Confederates had additional defensive positions with artillery covering the division's route of march. Since the swamp was too deep for a flanking maneuver, the division dug in and waited. By dark all Confederate fire had stopped and the bridge repair work was completed by 1:00 A.M. When the Union skirmishers went forward, they found the Confederate defensive position abandoned. Although there had been delays at the bridge, good time had been made during the day. The 33rd itself covered 15 miles before reaching the river at 4:00 P.M.

While the 33rd and the rest of the second Brigade were crossing the river just before day break on February 13, up ahead the division skirmishers encountered more Confederate opposition. This time some Confederate skirmishers had dug in at a bridge across a small stream, but the defenders were soon driven out of these works and fell back to a rail barricade. The Second Division soon forced the Confederates out of this position as well. Although the regiment and the rest of the second Brigade rushed forward in support of the first Brigade, no assistance was needed. In the skirmishing at the North Edisto, the Second Division lost three men killed and ten men wounded. Geary then ordered a halt at this point to let the other two divisions of the XX Corps pass so the men would have a chance to have breakfast, having no doubt worked up a good appetite. Once the other divisions were past, the Second Division was ordered to escort the corps' trains to a camp some four miles ahead. The terrain north of the Edisto was hillier with sandy soil, which must have slowed down the rate of march as the rear of the train did not reach camp until 11:00 P.M.

The resumption of the march on February 14 was marred by bad weather, the troops encountering both rain and cold temperatures. The regiment and the Second Division had the added burden of escorting the trains of the First Division as well as their own. Encumbered in this fashion, they were only able to make about seven miles that day. During the march, they followed the direct road to Columbia until the road intersected with roads to Orangeburg and Lexington. At this point, the division turned to the left and made camp after a day of marching through poor country with little forage. Since they had spent a full day escorting the trains of two divisions, the Second Division was rewarded on February 15 by marching unencumbered at the head of the corps. The weather somewhat offset this advantage: Captain Bray wrote, "The rain is falling copiously." Such consistently bad weather must have stretched the creative limits of those trying to accurately describe the campaign. The route of march followed the Lexington Road towards Congaree Creek, where there was again opposition from Confederate cavalry. When the division arrived at the creek, the scene was almost a repeat of that at the Edisto, with Confederate defenders dug in on the far side of the creek. In response, skirmishers once again set out through swampy, dense thickets surrounding a four- to five-foot-deep stream to outflank the Confederates. Once the skirmishers were across the stream, they charged from the rear while a force from the division simultaneously charged from the front. As a result of the combined action, the bridge was taken without Union casualties and was repaired without slowing down the march. Skirmishing with Confederate cavalry continued throughout the day. Finally about two miles from Lexington, the Confederates were driven back towards Columbia. When the 33rd went into camp at about 3:00 P.M., they had covered nine miles.[66] By this time, the entire left wing was encamped around Lexington, some 20 miles from Columbia.

The right wing of the army was also converging on Columbia, so by February 16, the entire army was on the left bank of the Congaree River. Although Columbia, "the cradle of secession," was directly to the east in plain view, the Congaree was too broad to ford and the only bridge had been destroyed. Sherman ordered the XV Corps to occupy Columbia. The plan was for them to do this by heading north and crossing the confluence of the Saluda and Broad rivers above Columbia. Once across, they were to make the short march south to Columbia and destroy all public buildings, the railroad and factories, but spare private property.[67] While this was tak-

Nathaniel Bray, captain, Company I; major, HQ; maintained a diary of the Carolina campaign. *New Jersey State Archives, Department of State.*

ing place, Sherman directed the left wing to cross the Saluda River at Zion Church, take the road leading to Winnsborough and destroy the railroad and bridges around Alston. Since they were busy on this assignment, the left wing did not enter Columbia and had no role in what happened there.[68]

When the left wing resumed the march on February 16, the Second Division was once again in charge of the trains of the XX Corps, moving at about 10:00 A.M. at the rear of the corps. As they crossed the construction site of a new railroad, they confiscated a large number of axes and pickaxes. Given the nature of the campaign thus far, and what was to come, this equipment was more valuable than new muskets. After they left the railroad, the division rejoined the corps, which was camped four and one-half miles from Columbia. Since there had been increased cavalry activity, the 33rd put up a "slight line of works."[69] While the regiment was digging in around Columbia, the Newark *Daily Advertiser* noted that one of the regiment's most illustrious members, Robert Harriot a.k.a. "Mickey Free," was home on leave from Chattanooga.[70] "Free" had apparently had more than enough of combat and campaigning.

As the XV Corps closed in on Columbia on February 17, the day of reckoning had come for the city and its inhabitants. On that morning, the authorities tried to avoid or limit the damage by surrendering the city. As with other places "visited" by Sherman's army, there was and always will be debate about what happened at Columbia. Although Sherman's orders made his public intentions clear, whether his private intentions included the destruction of the city will never be known. Some fires were already underway when the army entered the city, the retreating Confederates having set bales of cotton on fire. Unfortunately, cotton was not the only thing stockpiled in Columbia: the city was "virtually one vast warehouse filled with spirituous liquors." After these fell into the hands of the advance Union units who had had little sleep or food during the prior 24 hours, drunken pillaging broke out and continued throughout the day. Even so, most fires were put out by the middle of the afternoon, but after dark, vast new fires broke out accompanied by strong winds, which turned the city into an inferno. Whether these new fires were a series of independent acts or a concerted effort, they were intentionally set by Union soldiers and by dawn most of Columbia was in ashes. The XV Corps remained in Columbia for two more days to finish destroying public property, finally leaving on February 20. When they left the city, they were sent off with hisses and boos from a population that no doubt believed there was little more Sherman and his men could do to them.[71]

XII

"Haul up, stuck in the mud"

Although they left no written testimony, it is not unreasonable to believe that the members of the 33rd New Jersey approved of the destruction of Columbia. Separated from their families and homes for over a year, witnesses to death and suffering, the men of the 33rd were not likely candidates to have mercy for the place where secession began. However, it is an academic point since the 33rd was not at Columbia. While the city was being destroyed, the regiment and the rest of the left wing were on their way towards Winnsborough. The Second Division moved at 9:00 A.M. on February 17 their first destination being Leaphart's Mill on Twelve-Mile Creek. On arrival, however, they found the XIV Corps blocking the way. Since there was nothing to do but wait, they made camp for the night after only making five miles. Geary's command moved early the next day towards the Saluda River in hope of making up for lost time, but once again they had to wait, this time for supply trains to cross ahead of them. Finally, at 11:00 A.M., the Second Division began crossing the river on the way to Broad River, near Wateree Creek, where the entire left wing was to cross. They were delayed again by the wagon train of the XIV Corps and camped for the night at Ravencroft's Mill after covering eight miles. After leaving Columbia, most of the conditions on the march had improved. The weather was described as "delightful" and they were moving over good roads. However, one problem reported by Captain Bray was that both forage and subsistence were "quite scarce."

The wait for the advancing units continued on the 19th, so the Second Division did not move until 2:00 P.M. At least the men waited in warm and pleasant weather. It must have seemed like a harbinger of spring to the regiment. After they got underway, the division moved for two miles before most of Geary's command turned to the right on the road leading to Freshly's Mill. While this movement was underway, the 33rd and the rest of the second Brigade stayed on the original road to protect against a possible Confederate attack. Although there was no Confederate attack, there was something blocking the division's progress: the slow-moving trains of the First Division. Much of the delay was due to road conditions, as the Second Division had to do "considerable corduroying," which enabled their supply trains to move without difficulty. The 33rd was fortunate to avoid the corduroying work by serving as an unneeded security force. It was not until 9:00 P.M., well after dark, that the second Brigade was ordered to rejoin the division. The ensuing four-mile march was made over what Captain Bray called "the worst corduroy road I ever saw." When division camped for the night they had made only five miles due to the late start and the delays on the way.

On the following day, as the XV Corps left what remained of Columbia, there were further delays. The Second Division did not move until 2:00 P.M. After crossing the Broad River on a long pontoon bridge, they headed towards Winnsborough. Just past the river, they crossed the Abbeville Railroad, which was of such inferior quality that it was apparently not even worth destroying. The division continued their march on an unused and muddy road across both woods and fields up to Little River. When they arrived there, they found the river was indeed little, only a 30-yard-wide stream and, therefore, not a major obstacle. After this crossing, the division reached the main road to Winnsborough. The excellent nature of the road made for an easier march, but the terrain became quite hilly. By the time Geary's command camped for the night, they were within nine miles of Winnsborough after marching through rich countryside with good forage.

When the Second Division of the XX Corps reached Winnsborough on February 21, the fate of this "pretty town of about 2,500" was very different from that of Columbia. In what must have seemed like a rare occurrence, the men of the 33rd and the rest of the division had the advantage of leading the corps unburdened by supply trains. After breaking camp at 6:30 A.M., they reached Winnsborough by 11:00 A.M. without encountering any Confederate opposition. When smoke was seen rising above the village, the lead elements of the division rushed forward and with some difficulty put out the fire. Upon General Geary's arrival, he found the town full of foragers, probably both authorized and unauthorized, and sent them back to their commands. General Ario Pardee and the first Brigade were placed in charge of the town. At the same time the other two brigades including the 33rd devoted themselves to tearing up the Greensboro and Columbia Railroad to the north of the town. During the course of the afternoon, a total of three and one-half miles of track was torn up and burned, a change of pace from corduroying and moving wagons through the mud. Even with devoting the afternoon to railroad destruction, the division was still able to cover nine miles on the day's march. To make the day a complete success, the division foragers had another productive day.

After the destruction of the railroad was finished on the following day, the two brigades had destroyed a total of seven and one-half miles of track. While this was going on, the first Brigade continued to guard Winnsborough until the rest of the left wing passed through the town. This was finished by 4:30 P.M., and the first Brigade also resumed the march, heading toward Rocky Mount Post Office and North Carolina. During the time the first Brigade had been in Winnsborough, there was little, if any, destruction of private property. The mayor of the town had been given a note from Confederate general Wade Hampton guaranteeing safe passage for any Union soldiers left behind to protect the town. When the townspeople begged for such protection, Geary agreed and assigned two members of his provost guard to remain

The XIV Corps crossing the Catawba at Rocky Hill, South Carolina. *Harper's Weekly.*

behind. One hopes they were volunteers. The two men then helped the citizens drive off any Union stragglers until the Confederate cavalry arrived the next morning. The Confederates honored Hampton's pledge and the residents heaped praise on the two men, who returned safely to the division. Considering what had happened at Columbia and other places, this incident was, as Geary noted, "a remarkable one." After the railroad destruction was complete, the balance of the division including the 33rd spent the rest of the day and evening marching to rejoin Geary and the first Brigade at Wateree Church. The 33rd did not stop marching until after midnight, having covered 15 miles. The men of the regiment must have been exhausted as they did their best to make camp in the dark. Although they may not have had a full night's rest, they needed all they could get for what lay just ahead.[1]

Both wings of the army had been on this phase of the march since February 20, heading east towards the next water obstacle on the way to Cheraw, the Catawba River. The right wing was to cross the river at Peay's Ferry, which they did with little difficulty; the left wing was to cross at Rocky Mount, which would become a nightmare. When the Second Division reached Rocky Mount Post Office at 3:00 P.M. on the 23rd, the troops of both the first and third divisions had already crossed on a pontoon bridge and the First Division trains were in the process of crossing. Even after everything he and his men had been through, Geary would write that this crossing was "one of the most difficult imaginable."[2]

All of the troops, animals, and wagons had to cross on a single pontoon bridge across a river 250 yards wide, but crossing the river was only the first problem. Once across the river, the route of march followed a very narrow road up a steep hill that the prior trains had only been able to climb with extensive assistance.[3] By now the road was a quagmire, in some places with mud three feet deep.[4] Since they were the last division of the corps to cross, the Second Division did not even start crossing until dark, when a cold rain developed and continued all night. One participant described the night as being as "black as a pocket." The troops, including the 33rd, were divided up 12 men to a wagon and, by an incredible effort of all involved, a good portion of the train had crossed by 10:00 P.M. Tearing up railroad tracks must have seemed like time off compared to this. When they had to make way for Union cavalry, the rest of the Second Division was forced to wait until morning in unimaginable conditions. Most of those who had crossed camped three miles from the river on the road to Hanging Rock Post Office, but the 33rd did not even get that far, camping one mile past the river. Not without some irony Geary noted, "The day's work was an excessively fatiguing one." Although not life threatening, performing arduous work in such horrible conditions must be recognized for the level of perseverance and commitment to duty it required.[5]

While the 33rd had been fortunate enough both to cross the river and climb the steep hill on the 23rd, the remainder of the Second Division trains could not cross until the next morning. When they were finally ready to cross, the entire road up the hill had become impassable and had to be completely corduroyed. Even those portions of the division that had already crossed made little progress as preceding traffic, bad road conditions, and more rain combined to slow down the march. Like the steep hill behind them, the next four miles had to be corduroyed as the heavy rain had turned the ground into quicksand. The weather turned colder towards nightfall.[6] The XX corps were more fortunate than the XIV Corps, which had been following them. The waters of the rain swollen river swept away the pontoon bridge leaving the XIV Corps on the wrong side of the river, unable to cross until February 26. During the period the XIV Corps was waiting to cross, conditions were so bad that the XX Corps took four days to go the 20 miles to Hanging Rock. In addition to annoying Sherman, the situation gave the Confederates some hope that the weather might actually stop the Union army.[7]

The 33rd and the rest of the Second Division spent February 25 in camp since the XVII Corps was on the wrong road and took most of the day to get out of the way. Although the regiment did not march that day, not everyone stayed in camp. Lieutenant Colonel Fouratt organized a mounted foraging party, but no report of the results has survived. Even this duty must have been an improvement as they got to ride rather than walk. February 25 may have been a day of rest from marching, but the conditions in camp could not have been too pleasant as the weather was cold with heavy rain until midnight. By this point, the men and everything they carried must have been completely waterlogged. When the division moved at 7:00 A.M. on the following day, they were encumbered with both their own trains and those of the Third Division. When they reached Hanging Rock Post Office at 1:30 P.M., the weather had finally changed and was now warm and clear. The roads were still a problem, and two-thirds of the way had to be corduroyed. There were plenty of fence rails avail-

Hanging Rock. *Harper's Weekly.*

able so less effort was required to obtain the necessary materials. The roads past the Catawba River consisted of a crust with quicksand underneath, so that any wagon or animal that went off the corduroy sank three feet or more deep in the mire. In spite of the conditions and all of the time spent corduroying, the division covered nine miles that day.[8]

Hanging Rock was not, as one might think, the location of a local gallows. Rather, it was a huge rock that was part of an irregular group of rocks piled one on top of the other. Hanging Rock itself was estimated to be 20 feet in diameter and could provide shelter for several people. Another rock in the group rested on a third rock that supported it only in two places. The unique setting gave the mistaken impression that the second rock could easily be pushed over; one eyewitness claimed that the rock looked like a ship resting on the top of a cliff.[9] The image could have been a subconscious wish for another means of transportation over the waterlogged landscape. When the water level on the Catawba finally went down sufficiently on the 26th, the XIV Corps began crossing at midnight. While the left wing was encountering all these problems, the right wing crossed at Peay's Ferry on February 23 with little difficulty.[10]

Although the warm weather continued on the 27th, the skies threatened the return of the rain. When the Second Division crossed Hanging Rock Creek at 2:00 P.M., for a change they had an easy crossing, fording a river with a smooth rocky bottom. This might have been taken for granted on prior campaigns, but now the easy crossing was gratefully appreciated. Since the division had gotten off to a late start, they only made three miles before stopping for the night. The 33rd had a short night's sleep, then were ordered to move at 4:00 A.M. to guard a position at Little Lynch's Creek. Even though the rest of the division had a little more sleep, they too made an early start, leaving camp unencumbered at about 6:30 A.M. The lack of supply wagons may have caused some soldiers to look forward to an easier day's march. Since the division was in the lead, the men of the main body had to corduroy much of the road, which continued to be full of quicksand. The men of the 33rd probably did not mind their early move, which allowed them to avoid corduroying duty. By the time the division completed their march at about noon close to Clyburn's Store, the 33rd had rejoined them after a march of nine miles. The men's morale got a boost when they were mustered for pay. The route of march did not yield much in the way of forage, so the division could no longer rely on foraging parties on foot. Instead the responsibility was turned over to mounted parties organized by brigade. These mounted parties also acted as de facto cavalry patrols. On the last day of February, these groups worked at some mills to grind corn and also captured several important bridges.[11] During February the regiment suffered only two deaths, Japhet Bartlett and Samuel Madden, both from disease. The low number of fatalities, in spite of the harsh conditions, supported the belief that Civil War armies were healthier when on the move, no matter how difficult the conditions.[12]

By this point, the destruction that Sherman's men had left in their path had damaged Confederate military capacity on several levels, not the least of which was an increase in desertions. Since the cause was clearly becoming lost, Confederate soldiers were more willing to desert to protect or preserve whatever might be left at home. Although the Confederate military leadership remained confused at the end of February as to Sherman's ultimate goal, by the beginning of March they knew that it was not Charlotte. When several days later Union newspapers reported the establishment of a supply base at New Bern, North Carolina, the Confederate authorities had confirmation that the march's ultimate goal was Goldsboro. Simultaneous with this news came the final change in Confederate commanders. General Joseph Johnston, Sherman's old adversary from the Atlanta campaign, was brought back for a last stand. Johnston's first order of business was to bring together in North Carolina all of the available troops. Johnston could potentially draw on close to 40,000 troops; however, they were spread out over a wide area. There were no supplies available, so the Confederate troops would also have live off the land. Johnston's plan was to unite his troops and then attack one of the wings of Sherman's army.[13]

The 33rd New Jersey began the last month of the Civil War at the rear of the XX Corps. Along with the rest of the Second Division, they crossed Big Buffalo Creek and then Lynch's Creek.[14] Upon arrival at Lynch's Creek, they had the rare luxury of crossing on a bridge, something "so unusual it occasioned much comment." While there was no way to know for sure, there appeared to be some consensus that the Confederates had simply forgotten to destroy the bridge.[15] Although the weather had again turned moist with slight rain throughout the day, there was not much damage to the roads, and the only corduroying was done on hills near creeks. Moving through a poor and sparsely populated countryside, the division made 12 miles that day. The next day, March 2, saw the regiment still at the rear of the corps, escorting the division trains for a second consecutive day. After breaking camp at 9:30 A.M., the division reached Big Black Creek at noon where they found the bridge situation, or the lack thereof, had returned to normal. Since the first and third division trains were already ahead of them waiting for a bridge to be constructed, the Second Division was ordered to make camp for the night. All told, the division's progress was only six miles, a tedious march over barren country in cold and rainy weather.[16]

The division got off to an early start the next day, moving at 6:30 A.M., but the day was one of constant delays behind the trains of other divisions. Captain Bray reported that the roads were "worse today than any time since the campaign began." The required corduroying and bridge repair slowed down the march a great deal. As a result, the men were on the move until well after dark, reaching the town of Chesterfield Court House at 9:00 P.M. Over the course of the day and evening, they covered 15 miles amid periodic showers that did not end until nightfall.[17] Chesterfield Court House itself was apparently not impressive as it was described as a "dirty little town" with 20 houses, a hotel and, of course, a courthouse.[18] When the march resumed on the following day, March 4, the division escorted the supply trains of the lead division as well as its own. Once again there was plenty of water across the line of march. Three creeks were crossed before reaching Sneedsborough on the plank road to Cheraw. By this point, the roads had deteriorated, being of "the worst description" and consisting almost entirely of quicksand. Although the countryside was poor, the foragers had good luck, which must have been of some consolation to men who spent the day working and marching in mud and quicksand.[19] The men's spirits got a real boost during the day when they entered North Carolina, leaving South Carolina behind.[20]

Although the benefits of entering North Carolina were fairly intangible, the men got something much more tangible on March 5, when they spent all day in camp. The respite from marching was necessary to allow a bridge to be built across the Great Pedee River at Pegues' Ferry. Since the river was 920 feet wide and the pontoon unit was short on supplies, the construction project was no small accomplishment. A further complication was a swift current that made securing the pontoons in the water very difficult. As this was going on, the regiment got a badly needed day of rest, catching up on sleep, drying out, and scraping the mud off of what was left of their uniforms. The division resumed the march at 8:00 A.M. the next morning and reached Cheraw at 12:30 P.M., where they had to wait until 4:00 P.M. for the preceding units to cross the Pedee River. The weather was at least pleasant. The division covered 15 miles for the day, camping some six miles past Cheraw. At this point, both wings of Sherman's army were on their way toward Fayetteville, North Carolina.[21] When the army entered North Carolina, Sherman had issued new orders about foraging and the treatment of the population. North Carolina had been the last state to secede, so there was to be no assumption that all of the residents were enemies. At the same time, foraging had to continue since the army could not expect any Union supplies until crossing the Cape Fear and Neuse rivers. Since the area between the Great Pedee and Fayetteville was poor, this would be a real challenge for Sherman and his army. In addition, for the first time since Atlanta, there was a significant presence of Confederate troops. The terrain in North Carolina was described as "one vast, extensive pine forest" with a number of factories for the manufacture of turpentine, resin,

William Wilson, Jr., corporal and 1st sgt., Company C; 1st lt., Company E; and Captain, Company F. *New Jersey State Archives, Department of State.*

and tar. While there were restrictions on foraging, there was no protection for the factories or the forests, which were set ablaze with regularity.[22]

When the 33rd and the rest of the Second Division broke camp at 6:00 A.M. on March 7, they were at the head of the corps. All other conditions were favorable as the march proceeded over "good roads" in "delightful" weather. Although the march was easier than normal, the day was not free of physical exertion after the division arrived at the Wilmington, Charlotte and Rutherford Railroad. By this time General Geary had become a connoisseur of Southern railroads, and he praised this one for its excellent structure. However, that made no difference to its fate. Some three-quarters of a mile was destroyed. While some of the troops destroyed the railroad, others joined in the destruction of resin factories, including one with 2,000 newly made barrels. Apparently the burning of resin factories had some unintended consequences, when some hot resin overflowed onto the road, requiring the construction of a bridge. After what they had been through, unnecessary bridge construction was the last thing the men needed. Even with the time devoted to destruction, the 33rd made 15 miles and camped within five miles of Rockingham.[23]

By this point, everyone was probably fatalistic about the weather, so they were not surprised that the next day brought another full day of heavy rain. The division did not march until almost noon at the rear of the corps. Given similar past experiences, the men were probably also not surprised that this meant delays. They waited for three hours for the Third Division trains to cross Mark's Creek. While they waited, the roads continued to deteriorate to the point of being almost impassable, so that corduroying was the only solution. With no small amount of understatement, General Geary noted, "Much labor was expended." And not for the first time in the Carolinas, Captain Bray encountered "the worse piece of road I ever saw." The combination of bad weather making bad roads worse had a predictable outcome. Lieutenant Colonel Fouratt reported that the regiment did "make but ten miles and haul up, stuck in the mud."[24] This was a good description of the entire campaign. To some the march through the great pine forest seemed like marching in a tunnel. Life did not improve when they got into camp. One participant noted that some men preferred to spend the night standing by campfires in the pouring rain rather than putting up tents on the soaked ground.[25] It is hard to understand how the men carried on, their constant march through pouring rain broken only by corduroying and pushing wagons out of the mud; then after a day of this kind of labor, having to sleep or trying to sleep in the mud or on rain soaked ground.

The situation did not improve much on March 9, which included the crossing of the appropriately named Drowning Creek. Somehow the regiment made 12 miles over what were described as "horrible roads." By this point, the officers were probably running out of adjectives (or at least printable ones) to describe the road conditions. Probably well aware of the strain on the men, General Geary kept finding alternate routes so that the Second Division "only" had to corduroy two miles of the 12 they covered that day. Another cold rain set in at 3:00 P.M. as the division was making camp near McFarland's Bridge. Some two hours later, with the rain coming down in torrents, almost everything was underwater. Since the adjoining fields had also been turned into quagmires by the rain, the trains could not leave the roads for fear that they would never get out of the mud.[26] Streams were now flooded to the size of rivers and the men were frequently marching through water up to their knees. When the foragers did not come in, the men were left with only the food they had carried with them. Although huge fires were lit to try to help the men dry out, needless to say, "it was a miserable night." The 33rd was assigned to picket duty.[27] But in spite of the rain, the mud, the constant corduroying, and the lack of rations, Sherman's army continued to advance into North Carolina.

Although the rain had stopped the next day, March 10, the roads were again horrible and slowed down the progress of Geary's command. The Second Division crossed the Lumber River at 10:30 in the morning, but a mile past Buffalo Creek they were delayed until 4:00 P.M. by the preceding trains. Buffalo Creek, which was "ordinarily a mere rivulet," was so swollen with rain that the construction of any kind of crossing took hours to build. Even after crossing the creek, there were more swamps to negotiate and the trains ahead of the division kept delaying any progress. Captain Bray reported that the men "worked all afternoon and bivouacked two miles from where we started from."[28] The men may have worked up a good appetite, but there was little available for them as foraging results were limited to "small returns, primarily cow peas and some potatoes." Since the only way cowpeas could be consumed was by boiling them in a thick soup that looked and tasted like yellow mud, they were only eaten "in a starving condition."[29]

The division moved at 6:30 A.M. on March 11 and crossed Nicholson's Creek. At about 10:00 A.M., General Geary received orders to escort the entire corps supply trains as the other two divisions had been ordered to Fayetteville unencumbered by trains. Since the full train consisted of close to 1,000 wagons, this was the last thing the wet, tired, and hungry men needed. The wagons were divided among the three brigades, and the infantry marched off the road to the sides of the wagons. Considering the conditions of the roads, this probably did not make much of a difference. Now triply encumbered, the division crossed Rockfish Creek on a double bridge, Beaver Creek, and Puppy Creek and some others apparently too small to be named. The roads were especially bad near the stream crossings with the usual pockets of quicksand. While the day's march did require several miles of corduroying, the rain finally stopped and the weather was clear and cool. The division made camp for the night at the intersection of the Fayetteville and Albemarle plank road, only 13 miles from Fayetteville. Since the Thirty-thirty was at the rear on supply wagon escort duty, they did not reach camp until 4:00 A.M. the next morning.[30]

James Reiley, surgeon. *John W. Kuhl Collection.*

The other elements of the division got on underway at 5:00 A.M. on March 12 so they must have been breaking camp just as the 33rd was attempting to get a few hours' sleep. While the respite was not long enough to recover from the prior day's ordeal, the regiment got some rest, as they did not break camp until 10:00 A.M. The route of march was on a plank road; the men must have felt as though they were walking on cement compared to the standard fare for this campaign. Captain Bray kept track of the rate of march, noting that they covered five miles in one hour and 20 minutes and then after only a 15-minute rest, marched another five miles in one hour and 30 minutes. Most of the division reached Fayetteville by 1:00 P.M. and made camp southwest of the town, but the 33rd did not arrive until dark due to their late start.[31]

Fayetteville, on the west or right bank of the Cape Fear River, was an important location. The town was home to a number of mills and factories, but more important there was a United States Arsenal located on a hill to the west of the city. The facility contained equipment taken from the famous arsenal at Harpers Ferry, which the Confederates used to make guns and ammunition.[32] Even though sympathy with the rebellion was not to be assumed in North Carolina, Fayetteville was one place where there was no doubt that the inhabitants were enthusiastic supporters of the war. This, combined with the presence of the arsenal and the destruction of the bridge over the Cape Fear River, had earned Fayetteville harsh treatment. Sherman did not disappoint anyone in this regard as he ordered the destruction of the railroad, shops, and factories as well as the arsenal and any weapons or supplies located there. While the destruction was to be widespread and thorough, Sherman did show some compassion, ordering that one mill be left to provide for the residents.[33]

In addition to Fayetteville's real military significance, its location was also important to the morale of Sherman's army. This became clear to everyone on March 12, when the usual noises of the army and the "Sabbath stillness" of a Southern town were interrupted by the "shrill whistle of a steamboat." The source of the noise was the Federal tug *Davidson*, which had come in response to messengers sent from Sherman to General Alfred Terry at Wilmington, North Carolina. Since this was the first communication with Union forces since leaving Savannah, the captain of the tug offered to take back letters from the men. When the tug left at 6:00 P.M., the deck was covered with mail. The tug would return several times, providing other opportunities to send letters.[34] William Lloyd got a chance to send a letter on March 14 as the regiment was preparing to leave Fayetteville. He described the march from Savannah as long and tedious. He was barefoot and felt he was "growing old fast, not in years, but in appearance." Lloyd claimed that the only food they could get was what they stole, but he also seemed tired of the destruction. He claimed, "This is getting to be an awful army, it fears nothing." Lloyd had once again quarreled with the company commander.[35] While the regiment had been marching through the Carolinas, one of their former comrades had managed to get somewhat better duty. According to the Newark *Daily Advertiser*, Mickey Free, whom the paper described as a champion pedestrian, was now at the Ward Hospital in Newark. After Free had gotten himself detached from the regiment and then home on leave, he now apparently found a way to stay there.[36]

While the stay in Fayetteville was brief, re-establishing communications accomplished several important things. Sherman took the opportunity to replace worn out horses and mules, which after six weeks of pulling wagons through mud, water, and swamp probably included almost every animal in the army. A significant number of refugees, both black and white, had been following the army, and Sherman sent them to Wilmington with an escort.[37] As was noted, there were several opportunities to send letters. One participant described the men writing their first letters in six weeks as a sight "which will not soon be forgotten."[38] Some supplies were brought to the army from Wilmington, but they were primarily rations, not the shoes and uniforms that the men really needed.[39] When Sherman had an informal review of the troops as they passed through Fayetteville, the need for new clothing and shoes was obvious to everyone. Although the order was to clean up as best possible, the only thing that was really practical was to scrape mud off the worn out uniforms. Since this only revealed the ragged condition of the uniforms under the dirt or what was left of them, it did very little for the men's appearance. Most of the men had no pants at all below the knee.[40] When the 33rd arrived in Fayetteville on March 12, Captain Bray speculated that they would remain there for a short time for re-supply. How short became clear at 12:00 P.M. the next day, when the regiment and the rest of the second Brigade was ordered to move immediately. The 33rd left Fayetteville on the afternoon of March 13. They first marched past Sherman's reviewing position and then crossed the Cape Fear River on a pontoon bridge. Once across the river, the regiment proceeded for six miles on the Raleigh plank road. Fortunately for the regiment, while in Fayetteville they had gotten some of the new shoes that were available.[41]

Although the 33rd did not get much rest in Fayetteville, they did stay in camp all day on the 14th, probably their first decent rest in some time.[42] The next day, after the whole army was across the Cape Fear River, the march on Goldsboro, the final goal of the campaign, began. More or less simultaneously, the bulk of the Confederate forces began gathering at Smithfield between Raleigh and Goldsboro. Hardee's corps was in advance of the main body, six miles south of Averasboro, trying to find out where the Union army was going and if Sherman's entire command was headed their way.[43] When the Union army left the Fayetteville area, the 33rd and the rest of the Second Division were once again "blessed" with wagon escort duty.[44] In order to increase the mobility of the left wing, each of the two corps had assigned their wagons to a single division. The Second Division was one chosen for the XX Corps.[45] Earlier in the day, Major O'Connor of the 33rd was placed in charge of the division's 250 mounted foragers with orders to function as cavalry in advance of the division. General Geary then assigned one brigade to lead the way with the other two brigades, which included the 33rd, bringing forward the trains. This did not begin until late afternoon and, as might be expected when the regiment was on wagon train escort duty, heavy rain began in the afternoon and lasted all night. Even though the 33rd was on the march until 3:00 A.M., they only covered seven miles over a plank road in fairly poor condition.[46]

The following day, March 16, saw the first combat of the campaign when the first and third divisions of the XX Corps came up against Confederate troops commanded by General Hardee. After the Union troops attacked and failed to drive off the Confederates, Hardee withdrew; he had learned what Johnston wanted to know. It was now clear that Sherman's entire army was headed towards them and that their goal was Goldsboro. Although the battle at Averasboro has been described as "little more than a skirmish," the real significance of the engagement was not so much the fighting or the information the Confederates obtained. The real importance lay in the impact on the two wings of the Union Army. While the left wing had been delayed at Averasboro, the right wing had continued on towards Goldsboro, creating a significant gap between the two wings. Since Johnston's army was smaller than the Sherman's, this gap was just what Johnston needed for his plan to isolate one wing and then attack it. Johnston now had the opportunity he had been looking for, since Sherman did not know where Johnston's army was nor did he have any idea of the Confederate commander's plans. The Confederates could attack one of the columns of Sherman's army before the Union forces reached Goldsboro and reinforcements.[47]

At the same time that the rest of the XX Corps was skirmishing with the Confederates, the 33rd got a brief rest after their 3:00 A.M. arrival. They then continued the march in the ever present rain and the march finally ended at 5:00 A.M. the next morning. Up ahead, the whole column had been delayed at South or Black River due to minor Confederate resistance on the prior day, which delayed the construction of a bridge. Although only 60 yards wide, after all the rain the river was at least 18 feet deep and was continuing to rise. As usual, the rain had made a mess of the roads, which necessitated extensive corduroying of the approaches to the bridge. Since the wagon train now had over 1,000 vehicles with their left flanks exposed to the Confederates, Geary put heavy picket lines at all the crossroads. One piece of good news was that some supply wagons had rejoined the column with rations for men and animals. The heavy rains were accompanied by strong winds, but the rain finally stopped by the end of the day. Because the preceding units so thoroughly blocked the Second Division's route of march, the men got to spend the next day, which was clear and pleasant, in camp.[48]

When the weather was again clear and pleasant on March 18, the two consecutive days of good weather must have seemed like a miracle to the men. Although the weather had improved, there had not been enough time for the roads to follow suit, which made for a long day. The division moved out at 6:00 A.M. on the Tarborough Road toward Bentonville, a route of eight and one-half miles, all of which had to be corduroyed. The work had been done by the troops ahead of the trains, so the trains themselves did not experience the significant delays of prior days. Even with this advantage, the trains still did not reach the camp on Seven-Mile Creek until about 7:30 P.M.[49] As the Union advance was slowly moving forward, Confederate general Johnston began to implement his plan. Johnston estimated that the two wings of the Union Army were one day's march apart so he ordered his army to Bentonville, 20 miles west of Goldsboro.[50]

Although Johnston had only been able to gather 18,000 men from the remnants of various Confederate forces, the shrinking of the Confederate Army had left them with a surplus of generals. To command this relatively small force, the Confederates had two full generals, Johnston and Bragg, as well as four lieutenant generals. Meanwhile, like the Second Division, the unencumbered divisions of the XX Corps had had problems crossing the Black River. Since this put them some eight miles behind the XIV Corps, not only was the left wing separated from the right, the units of the left wing were also separated. Sherman believed that Johnston had 40,000 men, but while he had been warned that the Confederates would make a stand at Bentonville, he refused to believe it. Regardless of what Sherman believed, Johnston had ordered an attack at a point two miles south of Bentonville.

Sunday, March 19, was the third consecutive day of good weather as "it dawned clear and beautiful." If anyone in the units of the left wing thought conditions were too good to be true, they were right. When the XIV Corps broke camp at 7:00 A.M., they soon came into contact with Confederate skirmishers. Although the Union commanders, joined by left wing commander General Slocum, first believed that they were only opposed by Confederate cavalry, the entire Confederate army was only a few miles ahead. Slocum finally realized what was happening from a Union prisoner of war who had been serving in the Confederate army but had now escaped. In response, Slocum decided that the best course of action was to go on the defensive until he heard from Sherman. At the same time that he dispatched messengers to Sherman, Slocum ordered the two unencumbered divisions of the XX Corps to join him. The fighting went on all day within hearing of the right wing, but they continued to march away. Sherman, himself, did not learn of the attack until that night. After he finally learned of the battle, Sherman confirmed Slocum's decision by ordering him to hold on while the rest of the army moved to Bentonville. The Confederates made several attacks on Slocum's defenses during the course of the 19th, but by the end of the day, they were driven back to their original position.[51]

At the rear of the left wing, still on wagon train escort duty, the men of the 33rd and the rest of the Second Division heard heavy firing throughout the day. The regiment crossed Big Cohera Creek and made eight miles for the day. However, the roads continued to be bad and the corduroying tally for the day was three miles, almost half of the distance covered that day. At about 10:00 P.M., General Geary was ordered to send ambulances, supply and ammunition wagons, and all empty wagons to rejoin the corps. Two hours later, orders were received to leave one brigade with the rest of the trains and bring the other two brigades to Bentonville by morning. Fortunately for the 33rd, they and the rest of the 800 men of the second Brigade were selected to remain behind. Train escort duty and the accompanying corduroying were full of tedium and physical exertion, but there was no question that it was still preferable to the dangers of the battlefield. Georg Muller had no doubts about this. When he wrote to his parents he told them, "We were lucky not to have been involved." When Geary and the other two brigades rejoined the corps at 4:30 A.M., they were placed in reserve in anticipation of a Confederate attack. However, the attack never came and by 11:00 A.M., orders were sent back to Colonel Mindil to move the trains towards Goldsboro.[52]

The reason that there was no Confederate attack on the 20th was that the right wing was rapidly approaching the battlefield. The XV Corps was there by noon and the XVII Corps arrived in the afternoon. Even though he had numerical superiority, Sherman did not want a battle. Johnston could no longer afford one. Johnston had, in fact, only remained on the battlefield to remove his wounded. Although skirmishing went on all day, Johnston's attempt to isolate and destroy one wing of Sherman's army had failed.[53] Back in its position some distance from the fighting, the 33rd and the second Brigade received orders to move out by the end of the day and were on the move by twilight. The brigade had created substantial breastworks around the trains, but these would not be needed. They were probably the last major defensive positions the men built. Once underway, the brigade continued to march until midnight, covering seven miles before camping near Falling Creek. One mile of the route of march was through a swamp, all of which had to be corduroyed.[54]

After the Confederate wounded had been removed on March 21, Johnston no longer had any reason to remain at Bentonville, but he did have added incentive to leave. General Schofield and his command had arrived at Goldsboro. Once united with Sherman's forces, the Union army would have 90,000 men in the field. The total of Confederate killed, wounded, and missing was 2,600 compared to 1,500 for the

Union Army. When Johnston ordered a retreat toward Smithfield, there was no longer any Confederate opposition between Sherman's army and Goldsboro.[55]

Separated from the rest of the Second Division, the 33rd and the rest of the second Brigade were ordered to move the trains to a location near the railroad crossing of the Neuse River. A temporary corps' supply depot was to be set up at that point; from there wagons were to be sent to Kingston for supplies.[56] Since the railroad was inadequate, these arrangements would help provide for the army's needs as they gathered around Goldsboro.[57] The brigade and the regiment crossed Falling Creek and reached Grantham's Store, covering only five miles as heavy rains once again accompanied the march. They reached their destination the next afternoon and camp was made near the Wilmington Railroad in order to establish the supply depot.[58] One clear sign of the campaign's progress was that the army was going to use this railroad rather than destroy it. The men probably had to control what was almost a reflex reaction to destroy any railroad they encountered.

As the army gathered around Goldsboro, the campaign was near a successful conclusion. Sherman tried to have a review of the troops for generals Schofield and Terry, who had arrived at Goldsboro with their commands. However, Sherman's army had too much of a "comical appearance" to make a positive impression. Pets and animals that the men had collected along the way, which may have looked better than barefoot soldiers dressed in rags, accompanied them. After two regiments had passed the reviewing stand, Sherman had the good sense to call the whole thing off.[59]

On March 21 after arriving at the temporary supply depot, the 33rd and the brigade remained in camp, but the sick and wounded were sent on to Goldsboro. There was still one last twist to the weather, as strong winds blew sand around like "drifting snow." On the following day, the brigade followed the sick and wounded into Goldsboro. They crossed the Neuse River and camped northeast of the city. Orders to make comfortable camps and get full supplies of clothes and food were well received, but even more welcome was "the pleasant announcement that the campaign was ended."[60]

Another long campaign was over. As the commanders wrote their reports, they could not help but be impressed with what had been accomplished, especially considering the obstacles. Beginning with the First Division's crossing of the Savannah River, the XX Corps' portion of the campaign had lasted 67 days. During that period it had rained 21 days, almost one in every three. While marching 435 miles in 56 days, General Geary estimated that the 33rd and the rest of the Second Division had put down 60 miles of corduroy and destroyed eight and one-quarter miles of railroad. In total, Geary believed that the Second Division by themselves had done almost $3 million worth of damage (in 1865 dollars). In spite of the water, the mud, hunger, and exhaustion, the men and animals had come through the arduous campaign remarkably well. The entire Second Division suffered only five combat deaths during the campaign, along with 18 wounded. While the 33rd did not report any casualties, they did report 15 missing out of a total of 38 for the brigade. Even disease had been kept at bay during the march; the average rate of sickness was just over 2 percent, much better than the norm in camp.[61] The reality, of course, was that marching in almost any conditions was less dangerous than the unhealthy climate of camp.

When he filed his official report for the 33rd, Lieutenant Colonel Fouratt noted that the men had foraged liberally as ordered, but were still sometimes short of food. However, a greater problem was that the regiment had not received adequate supplies before leaving Savannah, especially shoes. The campaign Fouratt reported was full of lengthy difficult marches, often late after dark, in day after day of cold and wet weather. Since this was combined with a lack of food and clothing, the campaign was the hardest the regiment had endured.[62] Reporting unofficially, but with no less feeling, Georg Muller told his parents that during the march "groceries were very scarce." While he had been without shoes for a week, this was probably better than the norm.[63] Certainly both Fouratt and Muller would have agreed with Sherman's postwar comment, "The march to the sea seems have captured everybody, whereas it was child's play compared with the other [the Carolina campaign]."[64] Perhaps sensing this, another participant "hoped the American people will not soon forget the sacrifices made by Sherman's men in the Carolinas."[65]

XIII

"Cries of joyful recognition"

The Carolina campaign, like the Atlanta and Savannah campaigns, was followed by a period of rest and resupply. After the railroad from New Bern was finished on March 25, the first supply trains began arriving in Goldsboro. Sherman's army was now able to resume the regular routines of army life. Among other things, this meant that the men were at long last able to get haircuts as well as clean themselves and their equipment. Although they may not have enjoyed resuming drills, parades, and inspections, they could not object to the mild spring weather. Morale was already high from the success of the campaign and the men's attitude got another boost with the arrival of the first mail in two months. Unlike Savannah, however, there was not much to do in Goldsboro; the town was small and the men had little or no money. In spite of the fact that the men had not been paid in two months, no paymaster was expected and Sherman himself had to borrow $40.[1]

With the reopening of communications to the North, correspondence resumed, both professional and private. Colonel Mindil took the time both to recommend Captain Bray for promotion to major[2] and to work on his own behalf. In a letter to his father, Mindil asked him to arrange for prominent people in Philadelphia to intervene for his promotion to brigadier general. Claiming that the promotion would not cost the government anything, Mindil added modestly, "I have earned it and deserve it more than 50 others who have received it."[3] Although Mindil was probably far from objective in evaluating his own record, he did have strong support from General Geary, who wrote on Mindil's behalf to Secretary of War Stanton. Geary commented favorably on Mindil's service as a staff officer and as a regimental and brigade commander. Geary went on to praise Mindil as "a fine tactician and one of the best drill officers in the Volunteer service." All the generals up the chain of command including both Sherman and Grant added their support.[4]

Although the 33rd's records indicate that close to 300 men were mustered into the regiment between January and April,[5] many of these had been detained for garrison duty at either Chattanooga or Dalton.[6] This had resulted in such confusion about the regiment's roster that Mindil wrote to the state adjutant asking for a visit from the state agent to get the muster rolls in order.[7] Although new members were added to the regiment, death was not yet finished subtracting from their numbers, as four men died from disease during March and April: James Butler, Frederick Burkgard, Thomas Nelson, and Patrick Moran. Moran had contracted his illness as a prisoner of war, although where and when is not clear.[8]

Georg Muller, who was still among the living and glad of it, wrote his parents that the regiment had received new uniforms. While glad to be rid of his rags, Muller felt the new uniforms made the regiment look like new recruits. After what they had been through since 1863, the men wanted their veteran status clearly understood. Although Muller had been through plenty of hardships, army life must have agreed with him to some extent. He informed his parents that he had "grown quite a lot since I left," noting proudly that he was now 5'11".[9] During this period, William Oliver, who had been taken prisoner near Atlanta in August of 1864, was fortunate enough to return home safely. After being paroled in North Carolina, Oliver was home on furlough where the Sussex *Register* reported that his treatment as a POW confirmed "rebel brutality." In spite of his ordeal, Oliver was apparently in relatively good health, recuperating at his home in Hampton Township in Sussex County.[10]

As the men recovered, Sherman and Grant were busy planning what they hoped would be the final phase of the war. The recently completed Carolina campaign had wreaked a 40-mile-wide path of destruction, but Sherman looked at this almost as a secondary accomplishment. Of much more significance for Sherman was moving his army close enough for a joint effort with Grant's army in Virginia.[11] One way to look at both the Savannah and Carolina campaigns is as the movement of Sherman's army from Atlanta to take part in the final defeat of the Confederacy in Virginia. Sherman left Goldsboro on March 25 to meet with Grant on the 27th and 28th, and they also met with President Lincoln. During these discussions, Sherman urged Grant to wait for Sherman's army to arrive in Virginia before launching any major offensive. However, Grant planned to move the next day, while Sherman's army would not be ready to leave Goldsboro for two weeks. Grant was concerned that Lee's army might escape and also believed it essential that the Army of Potomac defeat Lee on their own, so he declined Sherman's request.[12]

While Grant did not agree to wait for Sherman, they did agree on a reorganization of Sherman's army and on a plan for joint operations. The reorganization was necessary primarily because of the connection of Sherman's army with the Army of the Ohio under General Schofield for a combined force of 89,000 men. The left wing of Sherman's army became the Army of Georgia commanded by General Slocum. Included in the Army of Georgia were the XX Corps and the 33rd New Jersey. General Joseph Mower was now in command of the XX Corps in place of General Williams. In between what had been the left and right wings of Sherman's army would be Schofield's Army of the Ohio. The Army of the Tennessee would continue to make up the right wing. The ranks of the army had been swollen with new recruits, motivated by the combination of high bounties and the belief that the war would soon be over.[13]

Although the plan was for Sherman's army to move towards Richmond on April

10, events did not wait for the plan to be implemented. Sherman learned on April 6 that both Petersburg and Richmond had been evacuated and also received orders from Grant that the "strategic points" were now "the Confederate armies of Lee and Johnston." The primary concern was to prevent a connection between the two Confederate armies; Grant would pursue Lee while Sherman would go after Johnston. Sherman's army would still move on April 10, but the immediate destination was now Raleigh in pursuit of Johnston's army located around Smithfield.[14]

Georg Muller told his parents that the news of the fall of Richmond brought "large jubilation here." However, he took a cautious approach, noting, "If this is true I am hoping that I will be in Newark by next fall."[15] Amidst this jubilation, preparations were made for the resumption of the march. Mindil, who had just been put back in command of the regiment, was instead placed in command of the first Brigade on April 9.[16] The second Brigade, including the 33rd, once again found themselves under the command of Colonel Patrick Jones. The army broke camp at 6:30 A.M. on April 10, passed through Goldsboro and followed the Neuse River on the Smithfield Road. At the end of the day they camped on Atkinson's plantation, one mile north of Moccasin Creek. Before even going four miles, the First Division met Confederate pickets "who showed a disposition to dispute our passage with more than their usual tenacity." Even though the 33rd did not encounter any Confederate opposition, the day's march must have seemed like the Carolina campaign all over again, as they crossed at least four creeks or rivers. In one of their last acts of resistance, the Confederates destroyed a dam, flooding the low ground in between Moccasin and Raccoon creeks, so that the last two crossings were especially difficult. In addition, rain fell all day, making for what Lieutenant Colonel Fouratt called "a tedious and wearisome journey." The countryside had improved, though. Newly promoted Major Bray called the area "better than any we passed this side of Savannah."[17]

There was also rain in New Jersey on April 10, but the day was anything but "tedious and wearisome." Word had been received that Lee had surrendered to Grant on the previous day. The Newark *Daily Advertiser* reported that the rain did not in any way lessen the response to the good news. Even in the inclement weather "far up in the misty air from pole and steeple the stars and stripes stream to the breeze." In honor of the occasion, a new 22- by 30-foot flag flew for the first time in front of City Hall. The paper noted that the atmosphere was one of "profound joy and gratitude," especially since "a lasting and honorable peace seems now almost accomplished." Perhaps somewhat ironically, the coming of peace was greeted with gunfire throughout the day, including a 200-gun salute fired at the hospital. The employees of the Morris and Essex Railroad cheered, flew flags, and made their own contribution to the celebratory gunfire. All of these celebrations, official and otherwise, were to climax at 5:00 P.M. with a 300-gun salute accompanied by the ringing of church bells, factory bells, and steam whistles.[18] Major Runyon issued a proclamation urging all citizens to go to their places of worship the next evening both to give thanks and to pray for the restoration of the Union.[19]

When the news reached Paterson, the Paterson *Daily Press* proclaimed the "City Wild with Joy." Businesses and schools closed, and bells were rung, while the fire department made "a joyous run." As in Newark, "a forest of flags made the rainy skies radiant and beautiful." Thousands of working men marched through the streets and the city's cannon club fired their big gun. The paper proclaimed it "a proud day for Paterson and the country."[20] Further north and west in Newton, no special celebrations took place since the citizens had apparently interpreted the evacuation of Richmond as foretelling Lee's surrender. As a result, they had held a celebration on April 7 that was marked by the firing of cannon, the ringing of church bells, and "two or three of the largest bonfires that ever blazed in our village." When the news of Lee's surrender was received, "by common consent" there was no need for a repeat performance.[21]

While all of this celebrating was going on in New Jersey, back in North Carolina, unaware of the good news, Sherman's army continued their pursuit of Johnston. On April 10, the 33rd took part in the left wing's movement toward Smithfield. At the same time, the right wing was moving towards the same goal, but by a more circuitous route. Johnston was uncertain of Sherman's route of march so he had moved his army to Smithfield, where he could block either of the two most likely routes and make a connection with the retreating Lee. After the fall of Richmond, Johnston's problems with desertion had increased significantly. While at Smithfield, Johnston learned that Raleigh was Sherman's destination so the Confederates also moved in that direction.[22]

On April 11, the 33rd had the "honor" to be the lead unit for both the XX Corps and the Second Division. When the regiment passed the First Division's picket line, Lieutenant Colonel Fouratt put three companies in advance as skirmishers, one on each side of the road and one on the road itself.[23] Unfortunately for him, Georg Muller was part of the skirmishing force. He told his parents that as they moved forward, "suddenly the rebels welcomed us with whistling bullets," a sound all too familiar to Muller.[24] Throughout the day, the skirmishers were in constant contact with small parties of Confederate cavalry, especially at bridges and swamps. At some places the Confederates erected barricades, and there was a regular pattern of an exchange of shots followed by a Confederate retreat. While avoiding Confederate bullets, the regiment had to move through waist-deep swamps, but in spite of all these skirmishes, no one was injured. The regiment avoided the ultimate tragedy of a combat death at the very end of the fighting. Ultimately, the Confederates were driven past Smithfield, which the division reached about 2 P.M. Fouratt reported that the regiment's skirmishes were the last ones of the war for the XX Corps and the Second Division. It is very likely that the regiment was involved in one of the last engagements between the main armies.[25]

Sherman finally received the good news from Appomattox that night and the glad tidings were shared with the bulk of the army the next morning.[26] The 2nd Division responded to the announcement "with unbounded enthusiasm."[27] One officer said the news brought tears to the eyes of the men followed by the cheering of 90,000 soldiers. The bands broke out into patriotic songs, colors were unfurled, and even "the very mules brayed their happiness." For a change, the weather was even nice, a warm clear day in good country so that "the earth never seemed fairer to mortal eyes." The men took "water, cold coffee or something warmer" and drank the toast that Washington allegedly shared with his men, "Boys, here's luck." If ever an army slept well, it was Sherman's that night, as "a hundred thousand happy dreams still celebrated the thrilling news." There was no doubt one common theme in those dreams: home.[28] For the men of the 33rd, there had to be great happiness that their long odyssey through the Confederacy was finally nearing its end.

By this point, the only remaining question was whether Johnston would surrender or allow his army to dissolve into small guerrilla bands. Since the Confederates could move more quickly than the Union troops, Sherman was hard pressed to prevent the latter. As a result, Sherman had only one strategy: to move after Johnston as quickly as his army could move. To that end he ordered the supply trains left at the rear and a rapid movement be started towards Raleigh.[29] As part of this plan, the Second Division began moving at about 9:30 on the morning of April 12, having duly celebrating the news of Lee's surrender. The division crossed the Neuse River at Smithfield, which was followed by two crossings of Swift's Creek. After they completed the second crossing, they camped for the night at 6:00 P.M. on Mrs. Saunder's plantation just past the crossing. Everything seemed to be in their favor now as they covered 14 miles on good roads in warm weather. Recording the news from Appomattox in his journal, Major Bray noted without understatement, "This is the happiest day our soldiers ever experienced." When the division resumed the march the next day at 5:30, the rain had returned, but the roads were good and they reached Raleigh at about noon. The 33rd camped on some hills west of the city and remained in the camp the next day along with the rest of the Second Division. During the day, General Geary received orders to march the next day towards Holly Springs, but the orders were countermanded before the march could begin.[30] Sherman had received a letter, from General Johnston requesting a truce as a preliminary step to discussions about an end to the war.[31]

While the 33rd was pursuing the Confederates, a former officer of the regiment was in Washington, where he was an eyewitness to history. Lieutenant John Toffey, who had been disabled since Citico Creek, was serving with the Veteran Reserve Corps at an army hospital. When Toffey learned on Friday, April 14 that President Lincoln and General Grant would be attending Ford's Theater that night, he decided to go as well. Toffey did not so much want to see the play, but the "two *great men*." At about 10:30 P.M., Toffey and the rest of the audience heard a shot fired, which they assumed was part of the play. Only when a man (John Wilkes Booth) jumped onto the stage from the president's box did they realize that something was amiss. Toffey claimed that although he and other officers in the audience were armed, "the thing was done so quick" that they did not have time to react. After he returned to the hospital, Toffey was telling the officer of the day what he had seen when a horse without a rider came down the street. Toffey and a guard stopped the profusely sweating horse and took the animal to Major General Augur's office. After this, Toffey and another officer were then ordered to take a squad of men and search the adjoining houses, but the search did not turn up anything or anyone. According to Toffey, John Wilkes Booth had hired the horse at a local livery stable.[32]

When word of Lincoln's assassination reached Sherman's army on April 17, General Geary reported that the news "produced the deepest grief and indignation."[33] The adjutant of another regiment in the Second Division stated, "The army was never before so furiously aroused."³⁴ The men were clearly outraged, but Sherman had taken precautions before announcing the news, and no damage or harm was done to Raleigh or its inhabitants. Since the day also brought the announcement of the first day of the truce, the temperature was lowered somewhat as the focus shifted away from fighting. Not among the cooler heads was Major Bray, who felt the entire army would now prefer to "carry war to the knife through every town and hamlet in the Confederacy until the last vestige of secession shall be swept from the face of the earth." Sherman also shared the news with Confederate general Joseph Johnston, who was fully aware of the danger the situation posed for the defeated Southerners.³⁵

When Sherman and Johnston did meet on April 17, Sherman offered the same terms that Grant had offered Lee at Appomattox. However, Johnston responded by pointing out that he was in a more favorable position than Lee since his army was not surrounded and could escape. Instead, Johnston proposed a larger peace agreement to include the surrender of not just Johnston's army, but all remaining Confederate forces. The two men met again the following day, and Sherman offered terms that went far beyond anything Lincoln or the government had authorized. Among these terms was a suspicious reference to protecting Confederate property that could have been interpreted to include slaves. Once Johnston agreed to these terms, Sherman sent them on to Washington the next day by means of Major Henry Hitchcock, a member of his staff.³⁶

While the truce was in place, the members of the 33rd and the rest of Sherman's army enjoyed another period of rest. Since the truce also meant a gradual end to foraging, the army went back on army rations of hardtack and salt pork. Not surprisingly, this did not sit too well with the men who had gotten used to a higher standard of living. Although the food was not as good, the only duty was a series of reviews leading up to a review of the full army.³⁷ When William Lloyd wrote to Mary the day after the Second Division had been reviewed, he started out on a wildly optimistic note suggesting this might be his last letter from the army or the South. Lloyd considered the "news of Richmond and Lee" to be "old" and also apparently knew that the terms negotiated by Sherman were under review in Washington. At the review, Lloyd claimed that Geary had told the men that they would be on their way to Washington within eight to ten days. Their stay in the capital was to be highlighted by a grand review that "will be one of the finest things on record." However, the best news of all was that the review would be followed by their return home and muster out of the army. After all of this was completed, Lloyd said he and Mary would "live in peace and happiness evermore."³⁸ Considering what Lloyd had been through, he was entitled to some degree of hyperbole. Mary, on the other hand, probably recognized that there was some period of adjustment ahead.

Colonel Mindil took advantage of the truce to write to the state adjutant general and noted the receipt of the promotions of William Lambert and Nathaniel Bray to major. While Mindil acknowledged that three other captains, McCoy, Frazer, and Courtois, were all senior in rank, Mindil also believed McCoy and Frazer to be "deficient in rank and ability." Since William Lloyd had consistently expressed similar opinions of Frazer, Mindil's letter would probably have been music to his ears. Although Courtois might have been qualified for promotion, he had been absent from the regiment since January 1 and Mindil believed that he had resigned. Probably anticipating the return home to New Jersey, Mindil asked for new state colors to replace those lost at Peachtree Creek.[39]

The lull occasioned by the truce came to an abrupt end on April 24 when Major Hitchcock returned, but not alone. With Hitchcock was General Grant bringing news that the administration had totally rejected the terms Sherman had offered Johnston. Sherman immediately wrote to Johnston to inform the Confederate commander that the only possible terms were those offered to Lee. Furthermore, the truce would end in 48 hours. Sherman ordered all commands to be ready to resume the pursuit of the Confederates.[40] General Geary received orders to have the Second Division prepared to move the next day towards Jones' Crossroads. He put the division on half rations and also authorized the resumption of foraging. While they prepared to move, the men of the 33rd must have wondered if their hopes of peace and a return home had been premature. The division broke camp at 9:45 A.M. and made Jones' Crossroads by 6:00 P.M., marching 12 miles over a hilly and dusty road.[41] Fortunately for everyone, Johnston had the wisdom to see the hopelessness of his position. This was, no doubt, solidified by the fact that over a five-day period some 4,000 Confederates had simply given up and gone home. When the next meeting of the two commanders took place on April 26, an agreement was reached on the basis of the terms that Lee had accepted from Grant. Although the news of the final surrender did not bring the spontaneous celebration that was generated by Lee's surrender, the event did not go unobserved. After the troops learned that this time the war really was over, there were fireworks and torchlight parades, as well as singing and cheering.[42]

Lieutenant Colonel Fouratt was granted 20 days of leave that same day, so the newly promoted Major Bray took command of the regiment as they and the rest of the Second Division were ordered back to Raleigh.[43] Now that the war was really over and the next long march would be toward home, there was a range of emotions in the regiment. Chaplain Faull wrote proudly to the Sussex *Register* of the final victory and proclaimed, "The war is ended, the government is saved, and the traitorous South is taught a lesson of obedience to law that cost her dearly." Faull knew that the regiment, while still mourning Lincoln, had "great cause for rejoicing" and predicted they would be on their way to Washington as soon as possible. Somewhat more realistically than William Lloyd, Faull hoped they would return home to celebrate the fourth of July "under the additional inspiration of a redeemed, regenerated and disenthralled nationality." According to Faull the only thing on the men's minds was "Home Sweet Home."[44]

Such was certainly the case for both Georg Muller and William Lloyd. Muller wrote to his parents of the regiment's jubilation at the announcement of their impending departure for home and told them the first goal was to reach Richmond in 15 days. After Richmond, they were to move on to Washington and the "big review" which would be followed by a train ride back to New Jersey. Muller, like Faull, hoped they would be home for the fourth of July, but he was more realistic than Lloyd since he did not think this was his last letter home.[45] Lloyd did not venture any new predictions about their arrival, but asked Mary to make him some new clothes so that he could "throw the government clothes away."[46] In preparation for the trip home, the regiment turned in all their ammunition except for 25 rounds per man while wagons were loaded with supplies and forage for the departure for Washington on April 30.[47]

The 33rd and the rest of the Second Division left Raleigh for Washington as scheduled on April 30 and arrived there on May 19. Although the march was generally over good roads, the weather became increasingly hotter, making the march more difficult as it progressed. The Second Division crossed the Virginia state line on May 3 and passed through Richmond on May 11, well ahead of the timetable outlined by Georg Muller. On May 15, the first anniversary of the battle of Resaca, the division passed over the Chancellorsville and Spotsylvania Court House battlefields. Many units from the Second Division had seen action at Chancellorsville, so this made for a somewhat macabre reunion. Major Bray had not been present at Spotsylvania Court House, but the hundreds of unburied corpses and the overall destruction led to "the most horrible sights" with "evidence of it being one of the hardest fought battles of the war." Of more historic interest to the 33rd was passing through Catlett's Station, where some 20 months ago they had boarded trains for the trip west only to make the return journey by foot. The division made good time during the march, exceeding 20 miles a day on six separate occasions, but there was some controversy about the rate of march.[48] Some units suffered casualties that were attributed to the hard marching, especially from Raleigh to the Virginia state line. There were reports of rivalries among the different corps commanders including rumors of wagers as to which corps would arrive first.[49] However, other participants claimed that the men themselves forced the pace because of their desire to return home, sometimes having to be restrained by their commanders.[50] Since Major Bray reported that the 33rd's march was easy and the men were well behaved, the regiment apparently did not go through any undue suffering.[51]

After the Second Division covered the last 18 miles on May 19, they went into camp on Gregson's Farm some three and one-half miles from Alexandria. They would remain there until the Grand Review on May 24.[52] Just prior to the big event, the Newark *Daily Advertiser* published news of a former member of the regiment. On May 19, the paper announced that one Francis Tully, "a young man well known in Jersey City," was arrested by the police as a bounty jumper. Tully was formerly a lieutenant with the 33rd, and the paper reported that he was dismissed from the regiment "in consequence of some difficulty." Nor was Tully a one-time offender; the paper reported that he had jumped the bounty three or four times under assumed names. Although there was no report of Tully's fate, the veterans of the regiment must have been glad that at least one scoundrel did not escape the long arm of the law.[53]

While Tully's activities probably would have annoyed the men, other news most likely would have infuriated them. On May 22, the Newark *Daily Advertiser* reported the arrival of 388 paroled prisoners at the hospital at Hilton Head, South Carolina. The majority of the men, the paper claimed, had been at Andersonville, "that rebel prison house, far worse than the 'Black Hole of Calcutta.'" According to the report, the men were in horrible condition, many "mere skeletons with slight covering of muscle." Three of these men, Thomas Eaton, Peter Ray, and Theodore Cadmus, were members of the 33rd New Jersey. Perhaps motivated by this report of Union suffering, that same day the paper called for planning of a fitting welcome for the returning units. Since the government had decided that the regiments would return to their home states to be mustered out, this was especially appropriate. All troops from northern New Jersey would come to Newark, so it was especially important that "Newark not be behind her sister cities in the heartiness of her welcome to the returning veterans."[54]

Back in Washington, the Grand Review of the western armies took place on May 24. Many units ordered to fall in as early as 5:00 A.M. While early departures were nothing new for the men, this would at least be a more pleasant task. The forming of the army was described as being like "the uncoiling of a tremendous python." Although the signal gun to begin the review was fired at 9:00 A.M., the units of the XX Corps did not reach the reviewing stand until the afternoon.[55] In order to give a full flavor of the western armies, the marching columns included pontoon bridges, ambulances, and supply wagons. Many soldiers carried spades and axes, implements that had certainly gotten more recent use than their muskets. Some of the pets acquired on the army's long march through the South were "comfortably fastened" to the saddles of pack horses and mules, including chickens, raccoons, dogs, and goats. Flags and banners were carried proudly, both new ones and some "torn by bullets and reduced to shreds."[56]

The sidewalks along the route of march were "packed to suffocation" and looked to the men like a "sea of fluttering color."[57] Some "sobbing women lifted babies above the crowd to see the troops," while others prayed. Many placed flowers on the muskets of the men or over their necks and the street itself became covered with flowers. Bands played the national anthem and the Battle Hymn of the Republic and the crowds sang along. Not be outdone by the spectators, at various times the ranks themselves erupted into "spontaneous bursts of wild cheering," acknowledging the climax of the long months and years of service. Although the atmosphere was like a circus, the men "were marching as they had never marched before," relieving Sherman, who knew his army all too well.[58]

Reporting specifically on the New Jersey units, the correspondent of the Newark *Daily Advertiser* was very proud of their appearance. The writer noted that the "thinned ranks, bronzed faces, and tattered battle flags attested the hardships they had endured in the nation's service." He also claimed that no portion of any Union army "presented a finer appearance than did the gallant veterans from New Jersey."[59] Other observers noted that the eastern troops in Sherman's army had taken on the appearance of their fellow soldiers from the west. There was a large deputation from New Jersey seated on a platform near Lafayette Square close to the White House. Fittingly, the deputation included Marcus Ward, who been the "soldier's friend" throughout the war. Once past the reviewing stand, the 33rd marched four miles north of the city and camped on the Bladensburg Road. The men may not have realized it, but they had made their last march of any length.[60]

After they arrived at their new camp, the officers and men settled down to complete any remaining business, and more important to await their departure for home. During this period, Colonel Mindil received the news he had been waiting to hear for months if not years. At last he was promoted to brevet brigadier general for "general good conduct during the Savannah and Goldsboro campaigns."[61] Mindil was also busy trying to attend to the needs of some of the men. At least three members of the regiment, Sergeant Edward Barrett, "one of the best soldiers of my regiment," Private James McCormick and Private Patrick McClean, "an excellent soldier," had not yet received their $300 veteran's bounties. McCormick's paperwork had been lost by Captain John Sandford before Sandford was dismissed for his disgraceful behavior in Virginia. Barrett and McClean's records were incomplete for some other reason. McClean's case had become even more poignant since he had been severely wounded and partially disabled. There is no record as to whether the men ever received their bounties.[62]

As June began, William Lloyd reopened the last phase of his correspondence with his long suffering wife, Mary. He acknowledged her most recent letter, the first he received since Raleigh, but he "thought it too hard not to get any word from home" and claimed Mary would feel the same way in his place. His only comment on the Grand Review was to say, "I received many a Bouquet of Roses from the fair hands of the opposite sex," which sounds suspiciously like an attempt to make her feel jealous. However, perhaps recognizing that he was far from perfect, he added that he had some long stories to tell her that "will be good on a winter's night." While Lloyd had no answer to the big question as to the date of their return home, he understandably wanted it to be as soon as possible. At least part of his motivation was allegedly due to the fact that the men in the regiment were "raising the devil here, stealing and selling everything they can get hold of."[63]

Also in early June, the Newark *Daily Advertiser* reported that the eastern troops in Sherman's army were to be detached from their corps and assigned to the Department of Washington. After this has taken place, they were to be sent back to their home states "as rapidly as circumstances may warrant." Although this transfer was made shortly thereafter on June 6, no word was received about their return home. The regiment's camp at Bladensburg was described as "beautifully located" and "a model in point of neatness and taste," which was most likely due to General Mindil's desire to maintain his reputation. While current discipline might have been strict, the camp contained plenty of evidence of past lapses, in the shape of trophies from the Savannah and Carolina campaigns. These trophies included elegant china and quilts, almost all of which had supposedly been hidden in the woods by Southerners; left behind was silverware too heavy to carry. Although unauthorized, these items were present without apology. The highest place of honor in the camp, however, was given to the regiment's battle flag, which was torn to pieces and barely attached to the flagpole. Indeed, a visitor to the camp claimed that the flag, not the plunder found or taken from the South, was the men's proudest possession. While in camp, the regiment received a visit from Marcus Ward and a dress parade was held in his honor, probably one time the men did not begrudge such an event.[64]

The month dragged on with no word of their departure for home, and the men grew increasingly restless and tired of waiting. When Georg Muller wrote to his parents, he indicated that he did not know when they would be coming home. However, he was confident that the officers would keep them in the army as long as possible. The frustration apparently spilled over into the ongoing tensions between

the eastern and western troops. Muller, for one, seemed to consider himself part of the western army. According to Muller, whenever the westerners encountered men from the Army of the Potomac, they would shout, "All quit [sic] on the Potomac." Understandably, this provoked the eastern troops, and they didn't "stop until they demolish each others faces considerably."[65] Not surprisingly, William Lloyd was also getting frustrated; he sent home Mary's picture since he was afraid someone in the "hard crowd" would steal it. In a rare moment of tenderness, he said he would rather lose $25 than the picture. Unlike Muller, Lloyd was not going to sit around and wait; he informed Mary that he was "coming home if I don't stay more than two hours."[66]

While Lloyd intended to return to the regiment after a visit home, the long delay in mustering out led to some more permanent departures: almost 70 members of the regiment deserted during June and July. Most of these were newly enlisted men who had little to lose, but there were about 14 men who had been with the regiment since the beginning.[67] Apparently the pull of home was so great for these men that they were not interested in their final pay or the welcome home ceremonies in Newark. Some other members of the regiment went home on unauthorized leave. These were arrested upon their return and held as deserters. However, Lieutenant Colonel Fouratt sought to have them released. Fouratt believed that their "imprisonment and disgrace" was sufficient punishment and he must have been persuasive, as none of those involved was listed as a deserter on the regiment's final roster.[68] Not surprisingly, William Lloyd joined those on unauthorized leave and equally not surprisingly, he got away with it. After he returned to the regiment, he wrote Mary to say, "Everything is Hunky Dora." The captain had apparently done nothing more than observe that Lloyd had cheek. According to Lloyd, the men were, of course, glad to see him and said there was "no one like Bill Lloyd."[69] That sentiment was no doubt shared by Mary and also by anyone who has read Lloyd's letters.

While they were at Bladensburg, the regiment received good news about their lost state colors. The Ninth New Jersey had found the flag in Charlotte in the Confederate archives. By the end of June the flag was back in Trenton and carried two inscriptions. The first said, "Captured by John Abernathy of Company E, Twenty seventh Alabama regiment in the fight of July 20, 1864." The second, no doubt written with great satisfaction, read "Re-taken by Captain M.C. Runyon of Company G, Ninth New Jersey Volunteers at Charlotte, North Carolina, May 1865."[70] One person who clearly appreciated this news was Chaplain Faull, who realized his goal of celebrating the Fourth of July at home. When the original speaker at the observation in Newton "shrunk from the task," Faull had no such inhibitions and "made a very entertaining, spirited and patriotic speech."[71]

Death did not leave the regiment during the month of June, as there were a total of seven fatalities. Louis Hoffat, who had been with the regiment since 1863 and had survived both combat and the long marches, was killed in some kind of accident near Alexandria on June 24. In addition, William Margeson, Charles Orethle, William Wolf, David Morris, William Kishpaugh, and Emile Troutvetter all died of disease.[72]

By the middle of July, word finally began to reach Newark about the regiment's

Opposite: One of the 33rd New Jersey's battle flags. *U.S. Army Military History Institute.*

impending return home. On July 11, "Adelphia" wrote to the Newark *Daily Journal* that the regiment would leave for home the following Sunday or Monday. This was incorrect, but suggested that the event was not far off. "Adelphia" also cautioned that "the people of Newark not forget us—we have not forgotten them."[73] During this period, John Toffey completed his participation in the Lincoln assassination events by attending the execution of the conspirators. The event moved Toffey to observe, "I do not care to see any more executions except Jeff Davis' I think I could help hang him myself."[74]

The regiment finally boarded trains for the trip home at 8:00 P.M. on July 19. Everyone's mood had to be very different from the last train trip from Washington, headed west in the fall of 1863. Although their total number was 700, this included men from other regiments who had been transferred to the 33rd for the purpose of discharge. On the next day the men had dinner at the Volunteer Refreshment Saloon in Philadelphia and reached New Jersey that afternoon, stopping in Trenton. There they were welcomed by Governor Parker and had supper and breakfast in the city before leaving for Newark at 10:30 A.M. on Friday, July 21. While the train headed north, "a large number of people had gathered around the depot... and had waited patiently for hours." At about 5:30 the firing of a cannon placed near the railroad on South Broad Street signaled the arrival of the regiment. From the sidewalks and windows along the way people waved and cheered for the 33rd. When the train pulled in at the Market Street Depot, they were greeted by an "immense concourse of citizens," a portion of the Veteran Reserve Corps, Hook and Ladder Company No. 1, and Rubsam's Brass Band.[75]

The scene at the depot was one of great jubilation as the men poured out of the freight cars and off the roofs to the greetings of family and friends. "The citizen greeted warmly his old comrade," while "Sister and brother, mother and son rushed into each others arms with cries of joyful recognition." One can only hope that Georg Muller's parents and Mary Lloyd were somewhere in the crowd. Then the regiment formed up for the march to City Hall, preceded by the band, the hook and ladder company and the Veteran Reserve Corps. It was a very different escort from the armed guard that accompanied their last march in Newark. The route of march was up Market Street to Mulberry, south on Mulberry to Walnut Street and then up Walnut to City Hall on Broad Street. At City Hall they were greeted by three cheers and a welcoming speech by Mayor Runyon. General Mindil responded for the regiment, and after the ceremony was over, they marched up Broad Street to Military Park. Broad Street "was fairly alive with welcoming spectators, who crowded the sidewalks and filled the windows and balconies of the houses" with flags flying everywhere. The 33rd reached Military Park about 7:00 P.M., where long tables had been set up under the trees to provide the tired and hungry veterans with a substantial supper at the expense of the city. During the dinner, Mindil escorted Marcus Ward among the tables where he was "greeted with vociferous acclaims of the soldiers."[76]

After the dinner was over, the regiment marched out of the park and down Centre Street to the old hospital building that would serve as a barracks for the night. Since many of the men were permitted to go to their homes, this was apparently offered as a convenience for the men who did not live in Newark. A number of the officers, including Mindil, Lieutenant Colonel Fouratt, and majors Bray and Lambert stayed at Lockwood's Hotel. Although only about 150 out of the 700 men who returned that day were original members of the regiment, those men at least must have realized the tremendous irony of where they spent their last night in the army. Only 22 months ago, they had been at that same hospital, waiting for transportation, when the most embarrassing moments in the regiment's history took place. They had come full circle, welcomed as heroes to spend their last night as a regiment on that very same spot. The next morning the men were furloughed until July 31, when they were to receive their final pay.[77]

The men must have realized fairly quickly that they were back in a world with very different standards of behavior. On July 24, the Newark *Daily Journal* reported that two members of the regiment had been arrested for fighting in William Street. Charles Crock and August Heckinger must have used some of their last pay for fines for their part in the disturbance.[78] While this type of incident was probably to be expected, perhaps of more long term interest was a report in the Hudson County *Democrat* that had originally appeared in the Paterson *Daily Guardian*. General Mindil had apparently made a speech at the Republican State Convention suggesting that the returning soldiers would vote for Marcus Ward in the upcoming election for governor. The Paterson paper claimed to have spoken with some unidentified men from the regiment "who hold him [Mindil] in utter contempt" since he was absent from the regiment at many crucial times and "was far from what a colonel ought to be." Since Mindil was from Pennsylvania, the paper thought it absurd for him to believe he could control the votes of New Jersey soldiers. This commentary notwithstanding, Ward was elected governor.[79]

Ward continued to help New Jersey's soldiers. On August 2, another Paterson paper, the *Daily Press*, reported that due to Ward's efforts, the regiment was to be paid through their date of discharge, giving them 15 days' extra pay. There was, however, the standard delay in payment. This was a special problem for members of the regiment who lived outside of Newark and had no money for their expenses or the trip home. Once again Ward came to the rescue, advancing each man five to 25 dollars against their final pay, which was to be received on August 4 and 5. When the men were paid, there was another sense of coming full circle: they received their pay where their life as regiment began, Camp Frelinghuysen.[80]

By early August, therefore, the 33rd New Jersey had gone out of existence. The war was over; the men were either at their homes or on their way there. Gradually they would adjust to civilian life, resume their careers or professions, or begin new ones.

At this point, some reflection on the regiment's experience is appropriate, including a comparison to other New Jersey and Union regiments and some consideration of the meaning of the 33rd's history. In total, 163 members of the 33rd New Jersey died during the war. The number that died from disease, accidents, and in prisoner of war camps (85) was slightly higher than those who died directly in combat (78). However, one can argue that the deaths in prisoner of war camps, especially at Andersonville, were combat related so that combat deaths really exceeded those from disease or other causes. Simply looking at total numbers, the 33rd ranks 16th in total losses among New Jersey infantry units. However, all but one of the regiments with greater losses served in the east. The one exception, the 34th New Jersey, suffered 170 deaths of which only three were combat related, so the 33rd actually suffered the highest combat casualties of the four New Jersey regiments that served in the west. This includes the 13th New Jersey, which also served in the east and was at risk in the bloody battles on that front.[81]

One certainly has to conclude that the members of the 33rd had a far greater chance of returning home alive and in good health than those who served in Virginia. Does that, however, make the 33rd's service less worthy? Along with the rest of the XI and XII Corps, the regiment was uprooted from Virginia and sent to a part of the country that must have seemed like another planet. After the battles at Chattanooga, they had to endure four months of constant campaigning before they reached Atlanta. Although once they got to Atlanta they would not face combat again, they could not have known this at the time. Then they were effectively given the task of walking home, or at least to the nation's capital. Even though there was no significant military opposition in these later campaigns, there was still the challenge of marching through hostile territory where they could expect little or no outside help. While the Savannah campaign was not terribly difficult, their experiences in the Carolinas are almost impossible to visualize. The ordeal must have been as difficult as that of the Continental Army at Valley Forge or Morristown without the snow. Although none of this can compare to the casualty rates in Virginia during the last year of the war, the regiment was not at fault for serving in a different area under a commander with a different philosophy. Perhaps the fairest and most appropriate approach is to honor the service of all of New Jersey's regiments.

How does the 33rd's experience compare with the typical Union regiment? First, it is important to understand how the 33rd's experience was unique; then a comparison with the more typical Civil War experience is possible. The uniqueness of the 33rd's experience was due to the manner in which the regiment was formed. While the primary issue for the Federal government in 1863 was the need for more men, the primary issue for the state and local governments in New Jersey was to avoid a draft. This led to the payment of large cash bounties at the time of enlistment instead of the Federal practice of staggered payments. Such cash bounties provided the opportunity to steal the equivalent of one year's wages, and the temptation was too great for anyone with the least inclination in that direction. By the time the draft was finally implemented in New Jersey, local governments had learned how to limit the impact of the draft without appealing to the worst instincts of the population.

This knowledge was too late to benefit the 33rd and other regiments formed at that time. The nature of its formation made the regiment's experience different because they left home under a cloud. One can only assume that the hundreds who deserted in the summer and fall of 1863 would not have made very good soldiers, so their loss probably did not hurt the regiment. However, the standard image of the Union regiment leaving home was one of a patriotic send-off with flags flying, bands playing, and crowds cheering. When the 33rd left Newark, they suffered the ignominy of being marched under armed guard to their point of embarkation and suffered three fatalities even before they left the city.

With an understanding of this background, it is possible to compare the 33rd's experience to that of the "typical" Union regiment. In his book *For Cause and Comrades*, James McPherson argues that Civil War soldiers, both North and South, fought, suffered, and died primarily for a cause they believed in and for their closest comrades in arms. For the Union soldier, the cause was essentially preservation of the nation created by the American Revolution. As a result, Union soldiers saw their sacrifices paralleling those of Continental soldiers, in effect preserving their legacy. Although the abolition of slavery was not initially a widely shared motivation, as the war progressed and Northern soldiers spent more time in the South, they came to believe that the Union could not be restored without eliminating slavery. "Comrades" meant, of course, all Union soldiers, but comrades were especially the small group of men with whom one shared food, duty, and danger.[82]

An equally important part of the Civil War soldier's world was the role of courage. Today, there is fairly common acceptance of the idea that courage does not mean or require the absence of fear. However, for Civil War soldiers, courage meant "heroic action undertaken without fear." "To feel fear was to be a coward," so the soldier not only had to do his duty, he had to do so without even feeling or acting afraid. This in turn made it almost impossible to talk about one's fears, which could lead to the revelation that one was afraid and, therefore, a coward.[83] Although today some might find the phrase "Death before dishonor" terribly trite, for the Civil War soldier it was a very real motto. Since sickness might be faked to avoid combat, sick soldiers throughout the war went into battle to avoid any possible label of cowardice.[84] At Citico Creek in November of 1863, John Toffey did so against the doctor's advice and received a wound that ended his active military service.

While cause, comrades and courage were all important, cause and courage make the clearest connection to the uniqueness of the 33rd's experience. Most Union regiments left home with the challenge of demonstrating that their behavior matched both their beliefs and the opinions others held of them. In other words, they had to live up to their reputation.[85] The 33rd, however, was in the unfortunate position of having to live down their reputation as the "mutinous regiment." One can imagine, therefore, the feelings of young officers like William Lambert as they tried to earn a reputation. The 33rd had only just arrived in Virginia and was literally marching around looking for a home, when Lambert started praising their performance, assuring his readers that they would ultimately be proud of the regiment.[86] Such assurances continued after the regiment was transferred to the west. Captain Courtois, Major Peloubet, and unknown writers such as "SH" joined Lambert in praising the regiment's behaviour.[87] This even took the form of a member of Company H claiming that the 33rd was considered the "crack regiment" of the XI Corps before they had even been in a battle. Even though this was clearly an exaggeration, it shows how much importance members of the regiment placed on their reputation.[88]

When the 33rd went into battle at Chattanooga and then into the Atlanta campaign, their commitment to the cause was stressed. At the conclusion of the Knoxville relief expedition, Lambert wrote proudly that the regiment had lived up to the reputation the state's soldiers had always held. The major prior military experience of New Jersey soldiers had obviously been in the American Revolution. However, Lambert made sure no one missed the point by claiming that the suffering on the march had been equal to that at Valley Forge. After the Atlanta campaign ended, Lambert reiterated this point by rhetorically establishing direct symbolic linkage between the members of the regiment and the soldiers of "76."[89] This theme was picked up by Chaplain John Faull, who practically called for vengeance on South Carolina and almost crowed about the defeat of the traitorous South. Faull even provided a litany of the shortcomings of Southern life, all of which he attributed to slavery.[90] Whether or not this was a new idea to Faull, many members of the Union army shared that conclusion.[91]

To fully absolve themselves of their "mutinous" reputation, the members of the 33rd also had to live and die by their society's definition of courage. Since fear was not supposed to be admitted, comments in some letters and newspaper accounts may be somewhat surprising. In describing his behavior at the battle of Resaca, Martin Denniston asked rhetorically, "didn't I hug the ground" and admitted running so that "I did not stop till I got behind a log."[92] While these comments would have probably been unthinkable in 1862, things had changed to some degree by 1864. Georg Muller wrote frequently to his parents wishing that the war and suffering was over, including comments about being afraid to go back to the front and being sick of the butchering.[93] As we have seen, William Lloyd's letters are full of negative comments about every aspect of army life, including the fighting and the bloodshed.[94]

However, at least two things must be kept in mind about this issue. One is that such feelings were more acceptable in 1864 than they would have been earlier in the war. Furthermore, complaints about army life must be separated from one's bottom line beliefs and values. James McPherson probably put this best when he said, "Griping has been a privilege of American soldiers in all wars." The Civil War was no exception to this.[95] While they did plenty of complaining, both Muller and Lloyd took time to talk about courage. When he described the disaster at Peachtree Creek, Muller was careful to defend the regiment's performance by including General Geary's comments about the lost flag. His letters also contain comments about the Confederates retreating or wavering when confronted with the men of the Second Division.[96] William Lloyd was a chronic complainer, but as early as October of 1863 he stated firmly that he would do his best and would not run on the battlefield. After the regiment finally got to Atlanta, Lloyd thought it would be a disgrace should they have to evacuate the city. And by the time the regiment reached Savannah, Lloyd wrote of being one of "the heroes of another victory."[97] The experience of the 33rd was not dissimilar to that of other Union regiments; the difference was that the 33rd did not leave home with any "goodwill" or benefit of the doubt that other regiments had. While the officers and men may have felt that they had to justify themselves even before they had done anything of real significance, the regiment's record is the only justification necessary.

The meaning of the Civil War is a theme beyond this book and the limits of the author, but following closely one regiment's story inevitably leads to some reflection. Two things make such reflection difficult. One is the foreknowledge of the ultimate Union victory, which makes it difficult to think about the possibility of a Union defeat or the implications of such a defeat. The chapter about the fall of Atlanta, specifically the probable defeat of the Union cause if Atlanta was not taken, was written at the height of a civil upheaval in the Balkans. Although it is difficult for us today to visualize more than one country in the continental United States, there is no reason that what is now the United States could not have been divided into multiple countries, much like Europe. Nor is it impossible that the kind of civil strife that has characterized the Balkans for centuries could have continued in the United States. By helping determine, once and for all, that we would be one country, the officers and men of the 33rd deserve our gratitude.

Such reflection is also difficult because the country the Civil War generation lived in, or more specifically the country they came out of, no longer exists. Few people in the United States today would even think of defending slavery or a caste system with an aristocracy. However, in 1861, a large section of this country did not just believe in those things, but were willing to fight a war to defend them. Regardless of whether the goal of the members of the 33rd was to destroy slavery, they were part of that destruction, which makes their sacrifices worthwhile and also demands our gratitude. Slavery was the foundation of a caste system that was not the idealized world of *Gone with the Wind*, but a system totally opposed to the principles that gave this country birth.[98] When Sherman's aide, Henry Hitchcock, met Confederate general Wade Hampton at the end of the war, he knew exactly what he confronted. Hampton, said Hitchcock, was "a man of polished manners, scarcely veiling the arrogance and utter selfishness which marks his class."[99] Reflecting on his travels throughout the Confederacy, Hitchcock wrote, "Talk about negro slavery!—if we haven't seen white slaves from Atlanta to Goldsboro, I don't know what the word means."[100]

When the war ended all of this was destroyed forever. Perhaps this was part of what Lincoln meant by "a new birth of freedom." The officers and men of the 33rd were not perfect and made many mistakes, but they helped make all of this happen. Even though some of them did not really want to be there, ultimately they did their duty. According to Napoleon, one of the keys to military success was getting "the heaviest battalions into the field and keeping them there." The historian Reid Mitchell claims that the Union army prevailed because they were able to do just that, or more specifically, because the volunteer Union soldier agreed to stay there until the end. This was especially true in 1864 when there was little mystery or romance left to the war.[101] As the officers and men of the 33rd New Jersey returned to civilian life in 1865, they did so with the satisfaction of knowing that they had been no small part of that effort.

Appendix: Regimental Roster, by Company

This appendix consists of the rosters of the ten companies that made up the Thirty-third New Jersey. The information was taken from William Stryker's *Records of Officers and Men of New Jersey in the Civil War*. According to Stryker, the regiment was formed by company, beginning with Company A and running through Company I, skipping J, and finishing with Company K.

Each company has been divided into its original membership and those who joined after September 1863. Each member has been listed at his original rank and with the first company that he joined. In addition notations have been made of those who died and those who deserted. For additional information readers are encouraged to consult Stryker's original work.

Code:
KIA — killed in action   DOW — died of wounds
DOD — died of disease   DES — deserted

FIELD AND STAFF

Colonel George W. Mindil
Lieutenant Colonel Enos Fouratt
Major David A. Peloubet
Adjutant William H. Lambert
Sergeant Major Stephen Pierson
Quartermasters James B. Titman and John A. Miller
Surgeon James Reiley
Asst. Surgeons Charles W. Stickney and J. Henry Stiger
Chaplain John Faull
Commissary Sergeant James Allen
Principal Musician William E. Preston

COMPANY A

Original Roster

Captain William G. Boggs (DOW)
1st Lieutenant George M. Harris
2nd Lieutenant William L. Shaw
1st Sergeant Nicholas Aspen

Sergeants: Dennis Dease, John Harmes, John Mooney (DES), David, J. Small, Isaac J. Yeomans

Corporals: Florence Coleman, Jacob Gimming, John W. Jackson, Joseph Kelly (KIA), Barnet Kerrigan, Edward O'Flaherty, Michael Sorrogihn (DES), Christian Switzer, Oliver Van Horn, William Van Houten, David Wolff

Privates

William I. Atkins (DES)
John Barry (1) (DES)
John Barry (2) (DES)
John Blackwell (DES)
John Brett (DES)
Frederick Bright (DES)
Lewis Brown (DES)
John Burke (DES)
Francis Cain
Michael Canfield (DES)
William H. Canfield
Edward Carney
Abraham Cassler
William Cassler
Alfred Chambers (DES)
William Chambers (DES)
Francis Clark
Thomas Conelly (DES)
John Connor (DES)
Patrick Connor (DES)
William H. Cramer
Patrick Devaney
Christian Eckel (DES)
William Edsall (DES)
William Ellen (DES)
Jacob Ellsauser (DES)
David W. Emery (DES)
Francis Englehardt
John Everle (DOW)
Michael Fields
Jacob Fuchs
James Gilroy
John J. Godfrey (DES)

James Gordon (DES)
John H. Gray (DES)
John J. Griffin (DES)
John Hamilton (DES)
John Harper
Patrick Hart
James Harvery (DES)
William Henderson (DES)
Alexander Henry
Robert H. Johnston
Thomas Jones (DES)
George Kattera (DES)
William Kipp
David Kittsmiller
Edmund Kleepis
John E. Kleepis
Isaac Knight (KIA)
John J. Lewis (DES)
Alfred Lockwood (DES)
James A. McCabe (DES)
Justin McCarthy (DES)
Lewis McCully (DES)
Charles McDermott (DES)
Daniel McDonald (DES)
James McLaughlin
John McMahon (DES)
Patrick McManus (DES)
James McRaun (DES)
Charles Mangold
Alfred Moore
John Mortimer (DES)
James Mullaney (DES)
Joseph Murdock (DES)

John Murray (DES)
Frederick O'Brien (DES)
Peter O'Brien (DES)
Michael O'Connor (DOD)
Patrick O'Neil (DES)
Leonard F. Onderdonk (DOW)
George Oswald (DES)
Charles H. Prout
Richard Rachford
Michael Reilly (DES)
Nicholas Rheinheimer (DOD)
Joseph Ribble (DOD)
Mahlon F. Richards
James H. Robinson (DES)
Bartholomew Ryan
Thomas Ryan (DES)
Gustav Schmidt (DES)
Julius Schmidt (DES)
Charles Schultz (DES)
Lorenzo Schnarr (KIA)
Albert Schwartz (DES)
Francis Sheridan (DES)
William Simmonson (DES)
Cyrus Slocum (DES)
Edwin Smith (DES)
George Smith (DES)
James Smith (DES)
William Smith (DES)
Francis Sommers (DES)
John Stanton (DES)
Louis Steinkopf

Michael Sweeney (DES)
Franklin Taylor
George Tribe
George Unger (DES)
James H. Walter (DES)
John Webber
Andrew Weidel
Joseph Weigant
Henry White (DES)
Thomas Williams (DES)
Henry Wilson (DES)
Frederick Witt (KIA)
Frederick Wolf
Charles Wolforth (DES)
William L. Yeomans

Additions to Company A

1st Lieutenant John C. Smith

Corporal Frederick Nirk

Privates

John Aid (DES)
Charles Anderson (DES)
Michael Arnold
Thomas Bailey
John Barry (3) DES
John H. Beach
Joseph Bender
George Blank
Ferdinand Blater
Adophus Bomstine
John Bower
Joseph B. Bowley
John F. Brown (DES)
Frederick Burkgard (DOD)
Charles Brown
William Brown
Edwin Case
Peter Claus
Edwin Connor
William Curtis (DES)
Walter J. Dalton (DES)
Henry Davis
William Davis (DES)
James Delaney (DES)
Louis Dorraine
Daniel Dow (DES)
Thomas J. Drew
Francis Ehrgott
John Foley (DES)
Thomas Ferris (DES)
Robert Foster (DES)
Michael Galey
Con Gallagher
John Galligan
Samuel Gifford
William J. Gleour
Michael Goggins
Thomas Haley
Thomas Henry (DES)
Eugene Jacquet
Joseph Johnston
Joseph Keppel
Monroe King
William Klauser
Christian Kopp
Frederick Kramer (DES)
Peter J. Krug
Frank Kurtzner
Otto Lorenzo (DES)
Gustave Luner
William H. McCarter
Martin McDonald
John Malone
Frederick Martin (DES)
William Marron (DES)
William Metcalf
Conrad Meyer
Martin Miller
John Moore
John Mullen
Herman J. Muller
Lewis Peters (DES)
Charles Rosel
Nicholas Sandstrom
Anthony Schaifer
Leo Schribiger
Joseph R. Sherwood
Antone Silver
Henry A. Smith (DES)
Francis W. Strong
Nelson P. Talberg (DES)
Charles Syealdown
Herman Volmer
Lewis Vogel
John Walter (DES)
James Wood
Joseph Wheeler
Albert Yost
Daniel Young

COMPANY B

Original Roster

Captain James R. Sandford
1st Lieutenant James A. Somerville
2nd Lieutenant James Warner

1st Sergeant Sidney R. Smith
Sergeant Francis J. Mulvey (DOD)

Corporals: Andrew Gallagher, Robert Harrison (KIA), George W. Riker, Frank Sturn

Musicians: Richard Halloway and Terrence Riley

Privates

Louis Auschurtz
Charles Austin (DES)
Edward Barrett
Herman Bimblie (KIA)
Charles Boker (DES)
James Bolin (DES)
James Buchanan
Thomas Caldwell (DOD)
Alonzo S. Chapman (DES)
John L. Chadwick
George W. Chapman
James Clark
James Cole
Henry Collins
Jacob Cook
John Cramer
William H. Craven
Bartholomew Cunningham (KIA)
Patrick Delaney (drowned in Tennessee River)
Bernard Devlin
Terrence Dolan
John Donnelly
Thomas Dryden
Charles Earl
Louis Erdman
James Flinn
Charles Francis (DES)
George W. French (DES)
Frederick W. Francke
George Greinor
Enos Greinor
Frederick Guther
Andrew Hagle (DES)
William Harms
Robert Harriott (alias Mickey Free)
John S. Hastings
Christian Herre
Louis Hoffatt (killed in accident)
Daniel Hogan
Patrick Irvin
Charles Johns (DES)
Matthew Kearney
Michael Kiefer (DOW)
Joseph P. Kiestling
Francis Kielhoffer
William Knapp (DES)
Bartholomew Leate
James H. Losey (DOW)
James McCombs (KIA)
Henry MacDonald
James McMann
William McLaughlin (Died)
Patrick Mahoney
William Martin (DES)
George Miller (Georg Muller)
Robert Monroe (DES)
Robert Myers
Dominick O'Donnelly
Adolph Ortmann (DES)
Charles Parish
Alexander Polson
Henry Richer (DES)
John Riley
Montgomery Rose
Allen T. Sanford
Casper Schafer (KIA)
William Sharp
Alexander Sloan
Charles Smith (DES)
Samuel Smith (DES)
Edward Smith
Charles E. Stanley
George Steadman
Frederick Steward
Theodore Stockwell (DES)
William Sullivan (DES)
David Taylor
John T. Tucker
Daniel B. Van Orden
Edward Wade (DES)
George H. Waters (DOD)
James Watson
John H. Wilson
Charles Williams (DES)

Additions to Company B

Privates

John Anderson (DES)
John Armstrong (DES)
William Atkins
William Barry (DES)
Patrick Bergman
Richard Black
Theodore H. Black
John Blaney (DES)
Henry Blucer (DES)
Jefferson Brutzman
George Burnham
James Carey
Michael Carven
Benjamin Chase
Victor Clemens
John Coldon
John Collins (1)
John Collins (2)
Matthew Cook
John Craft (DES)
Thomas Cragg
Henry Croft
Thomas Daley
James H. Dayton

John Davis
Thomas Davis
John Delaney
John Devenyers (DES)
Alfred Ellsworth (DES)
Louis Faulks
James Ferguson (DES)
Horace B. Fletcher
John H. Gardiner
John Hamann (DES)
John Hamilton
John Hardy
John Harty
Michael Harris
George Harris
Joseph Harris
Charles Hastings (DES)
John M. Headstrom
Hugh Hefferman
Charles F. Hill
John Hinkle
Adolphe Hocke
Henry Howard
Thomas Jones (DES)
Michael Kelly
Charles Kent
Thomas Kelly (DES)
Charles King (DES)
Michael Kinney (DES)
Timothy McCarthy
Robert McCready
Joseph McDermott
James McGuire (DES)
Dennis Madden
Charles H. Martin (DES)
Henry Martin
Thomas Martin
William Martin
Edward Mervion (DES)
John O'Connell (DES)
Charles Parish
William Peterson (DES)
Stephen Pierson (DES)
Otis Philteplace
John Powers
James H. Quinn
William Ray
James M. Riker
John Riley (DES)
Robert Ritter
William Sanders
Adam Schonck
John Shirts
William Simmons
John Smith
George Stephens
James Sullivan (DES)
Michael Sullivan (DES)
George Thompson
Barnett Tona
Cornelius Van Saun
George Wagner (DES)
Henry Walter
Albert Weatherwalks
Charles J. Weyble
John E. Weyble
William C. White
John Wilson
Thomas Wood
John Wyman
John Young (DES)
Ludwic Zister (DES)

Company C

Original Roster

Captain Amzi S. Taylor
1st Lieutenant Henry F. Sherwood
1st Sergeant: Edward King (DES)

Sergeants: Alfred W. Bergen, James Bannan (DES), James Corcoran, John T. Fairchild, Michael Higgins, John J. Mullen (DOW), William H. Wise

Corporals: George Dennis (DES), James F. Dooley (DES), James Dougherty, William H. Harker (KIA), Patrick Hickey, John Lambert, Joseph Riley, Louis Schaffer, William C. Schultz (DES), Charles Wagner, Henry West, Louis Weivland, William Wilson, Jr.

Musicians: William Magee, James H. Harrison, Elsi B. Dawson

Privates

William R. Alexander
Joshua Bertinshaw
George W. Brower (DES)
William Buckley
Enoch W. Bowers
Garret Burns
David Burr
Dennis Cahill
Michael Callegan (DES)
Louis D. Campbell
George W. Caswell (DES)
Thomas Coffee
Owen Commons
John Conover
Louis Croughan

James H. Curran (DES)
George Davidson (DES)
Daniel Desmond
James Donnelly (DES)
Theodore Drake (drowned in Tennessee River)
William Esch
John Felty
George Femmel (DES)
Martin Fox
Joseph Gallian (DES)
John Gastlin (KIA)
Michael Griffin (DES)
Frederick Guther
John Guthrie (DOW)
Mortimer Guthrie
William Harms
George Hastings (DES)
Owen Hennesse
John Henry
Andrew Hessdorfer (DOD)
Joseph Hessdorfer
Benjamin Hook
Patrick Kirwan (DES)
Oscar M. Lathrop (drowned in Tennessee River)
Thomas Lewis
Dennis McAuliffe
Robert McDonald
Joseph D. McIntyre
William McNeil
James Marks (DES)
John Maseker
James May (DES)
Samuel Messenger
George Miller (DES)
Patrick Moran (DOD contracted while POW)
Nathaniel P. Morris
James Murphy
John Murphy (DES)
Peter Murray (KIA)
William Murray
Charles A. Norris
Andrew Probst
Nicholas Redman (DES)
John Riley (DES)
Timothy Riley
Charles Scott
Henry Schwan
Thomas W. Seaman
Dennis Sheridan (DES)
John Shiber (DES)
Arthur Smith (DES)
Charles J. Snyder
August Violet (DES)
Frederick Weigamonn (KIA)
Mattias Weller
Martin Winchell
George Willis

Additions to Company C

Captain Charles A. Sutton

Privates

Aaron C. Ackerman
James Aikens
Daniel Algood
Dominick Babcock
George Ballou
Charles Bostwick
Thomas Cann (DES)
William Carney (DES)
Summer T. Conant
Smith Crane (DES)
Phibbs W. Cullen
Morgan P. Daniels
James Davis (DES)
Martin R. Denniston
George Decker
James Donely (DES)
James Donnelly
John Enyon
Thomas Ferris (DES)
John Flemming
John Gallagher (DES)
John Glazen
James Gray (DES)
William Griswold
William S. Hayden
Patrick Hickey
John J. Howell
Martin Hulbert
Morgan Lake
Christian Lange
William McMannis (DES)
Charles W. Mascar (DES)
Antone Miller
John Mullen
Johannes Olsan
Thomas Parsons
Frederick Rittman
Edgar G. Rockwell
Oloff Salenbourg
Jacob Schaub
Rudolph Schmidt
Walter Scott (DES)
Jesse Sickles
John H. Simmerman
George Slockbower
Charles Smith
Thomas Smith (DES)
Lewis Stage
Clark C. Steelman
George Stimson (DES)
William E. Terill, Jr.
Herman Theune
Dominick Troyer
William Vanneman (DES)
Joseph Veach (DES)
Mathias Wagner
Mark Waldron

Joseph Weyman
John F. Wendelin
Benjamin White

Thomas Williams
Charles Wilson
William Woodring

Francis Wolf
John Wrykerd
Henry Zeller

Company D

Original Roster

Captain Charles Courtois
1st Lieutenant James T. Gibson

2nd Lieutenant William A. Miller
1st Sergeant Charles Downs

Sergeants: Barney Decker, Hudson Davenport, Charles Dougherty

Corporals: William Barry (DOD), John M. Bowen, Thomas Chamberlain, John Craig, John H. Hopper, Alexander McGill (KIA), Robert Patterson, George Quinby, Thomas Reed, John Ruffing, Edwin Ryan (DOW), Thomas Wright.

Musicians: Alfred Dell, William E. Preston

Privates

Anthony Angen
Edward B. Arnold
Charles A. Bailey (DES)
George W. Bailey (DES)
William Banta
Joseph Brant
Charles H. Brown
Levi Brown
Walter W. Brown (KIA, May 8, 1864)
Edward Cameron (DES)
John C. Cannon
Patrick Carroll
Thomas Clark
Cory Clement (DES)
Allen Conklin
Wesley Conklin
John Connell (DES)
Martin Cook
Garrett Davenport
Augustus DeCamp
John Decker
Patrick Dempsey
John Desmond
Thomas Doyle (1)
Thomas Doyle (2) (DES)
Sylvester Falconer

Henry Fanning
Michael Fox
Alexander Freeman
John Gardner
Thomas Gardner (DES)
Abraham Goodwin (DES)
Thomas Hanley
Thomas Hardman
Thomas Heald
Michael Heffrin (DES)
Thomas Henderson (DOD)
Tallman Hickerson (DOW)
James Hogencamp
Emanuel Hollman (DES)
James Hughes (KIA)
Alexander D. Johnson
John T. Kent
Frederick Kensler
James Kenworthy
John Kinstry (DES)
James Knight
Andrew J. Krouse
Henry Lorne (DES)
Andrew Lynch
Thomas Lynch

Henry McGinnis
John McKeon
Barney McNulty
John Maloney
John Masker
Charles Matonia (DOD)
Ferdinand Metel
Joseph Metzler
Garret Miller
William Monaghan
Michael Murphy
Patrick Murphy (DES)
James Nixon (DES)
James Palmer
Isaac C. Parliman
George Pershaw
Michael Phalon (DOD)
Charles Poole
William Post (DOW)
Charles Rickert
John Ryan
Thomas Sands (DOW)
Andrew J. Stiff
Daniel Sullivan
Terrence Sweeny
David Swift
James Van Blarcom

Martin Van Buren (DOD)
Lemuel A. VanBuskirk
Aaron Van Riper
John Vorhees (KIA)
John Welsh
William Welsh
Peter Wenckler (DOW)
Thomas R. Williams

Additions to Company D

Sergeant James Bunce   Corporal John Porter

Privates

Charles Anys (DOW)
John Anys
Angelo Ballman
William Berger (DES)
John Bowman
John Braan (DOD)
Martin Braan (KIA)
Henry Brewster
Aaron Clark
James Clarke (DES)
Frederick Cope
Jesse Cornelius
John Corrighan
Thomas Coulton (DES)
Daniel C. Courtwright
John J. Davis
John Day (DES)
John Dien
Patrick Dillon (DES)
Jeremiah Donovan
John Dutches

Thomas Eaves (KIA)
James Elliott
Wilhelm Faber
John Frass
Luke Freeman
James W. Hand (DOD)
Henry Hanson
John Hicks
Michael Higgins (DES)
John Hurley
James H. Hyde
John Lee (DOD)
David Leslie
John B. Lyman
Hugh Lynch (DES)
John W. Miller (DES)
Henry Pantzer
Charles Petty
John Pira (DES)
Benjamin S. Potter
Jesse H. Reeves

William Retzlorf (DES)
Henry Robinson (DES)
William Rogers (DES)
William Ross
Frederick Rynack (DES)
Frederick Schaber
Valentine Sealand
Horace Sheffer (DES)
Josiah Sherman
Joseph Smith (DES)
John M. Snook
Jacob Sonderker
Samuel S. Stephens
Charles G. Strum
William W. Southgate
Gotfried Unruke
Cornelius Van Heest
Henry C. Ward
George Weatherwalks
Charles H. Williamson
William Wolf (DOD)

COMPANY E

Original Roster

Captain John Sandford   2nd Lieutenant Joseph L. Miller (KIA)
1st Lieutenant Charles J. Field (DOW)

1st Sergeants: John Z. Taylor, John Wilson

Sergeants: John A. Fenner (DOW), James McLaughlin

Corporals: Philip R. Beaufort, William R. Clintock, Martin Grozing, James H. Lathrop (KIA), David Miller, John Williams, George B. Winegar

Musicians: John Mailey (Died as POW), George T. Shelton, Thomas Whalen

Privates

George Abbos
George Bamlie
George Bayne
Harrison Bates (DES)
Benjamin F. Boges (DES)
John Boyd
Charles Brehm (DOD)
William Beyer
Charles Brogan (killed by sentry)
Charles Brown
David Byrns
William H. Chadwick (DES)
George Christian (DES)
Daniel Conklin (DES)
George Conklin (DOW)
Peter Cooper
Michael Coughlin (DES)
Frank Cox (DES)
Charles Davenport
Henry DeCosta (DOW)
Garret Demott
William Dillon
Martin Ditter
Aaron Earl (KIA)
James Fortune (DOW)
Michael Fleming
Charles C. Gallagher (DES)
Barnabas C. Goucher
Patrick Gray (DES)
William Green (DES)
Charles Greiner (DOD)
Orlando K. Guerin
William Hall
Joseph Harrison (DES)
Louis Hausser (DES)
Everett Horton (DOW)
David Hower
Michael Hyland
William Hyatt
John R. Jenkins (DES)
James H. Jones (DES)
Thomas Jones (DES)
William Jones
Thomas Langston (DES)
Thomas McCarroll
James McCormick
Michael McLaughlin
James McSorley
William H. Mittania
James Moan
Hugh Murphy (DES)
James O'Brien (DES)
Joseph Palmer (DES)
Mathew Reagan
William Roain (DOD)
Philip Ryan (DES)
Samuel J. Seering (DOW)
Edward Shields (DES)
Peter Shivers
William Sipp
Joseph Smithurst
John C. Sortsman (DOW)
Landamar Tabersky
Hugh Taggart (DES)
Augustus Tallman
Edward Terry (alias Edgar Andrews)
Abraham S. Titlow
William H. Townley (DOD)
Charles Trumpore (DES)
George Turbitt
Livsey Walsh (KIA)
Thomas Walsh (DES)
Lyman Wilcox
Charles Williams (DES)
Charles Winner
Benjamin Wilson (KIA)
Abel L. Young

Additions to Company E

Privates

Henry Alruth
Elwood Archer
Japhet Bartlett (DOD)
Abraham Benjamin
John Bowman (DES)
Alexander Bush
Israel Card
Isaac Collins
Peter Curran
Peter DeGraw
Thomas Donohue
William C. Fields
Frederick Ehrnest (KIA)
Michael Fitzgerald
Jacob Flukiger
Sylvester Geuscher
Michael Gilday
James Gillen
Thomas Hallahan
John Halloran (DES)
August Hamburg
John Hansis
John M. Haney
Lawrence Harrington
John Hayes
William Howard
John Hustian
Edward Hynes
Joseph Ingersoll
William Jackson (DOD)
Eric Johnson
George S. Johnson
Edward Jones (DES)
Mathew Kale
Garret Kavanaugh (DES)
Dennis Kellaher
Michael Kennedy
Frederick Kloepfer
Joseph Kneader
Christian Lempke (DES)
Carl Linck
Bernhardt Lobes

Thomas Low (DES)
James Lowery
Peter Lowery
Thomas Marooney
John McDonald (DES)
Louis McLennan
Samuel Madden (DOD)
William Meiners (DES)
Louis Martin (DES)
George Miller

Henry Miller
Thomas Mitchell
John Myer (DES)
Thomas Nelson (DOD)
John O'Brien (DES)
Henry Ollas (DES)
Franz Passman
William Price (DES)
Peter Riley (DES)
John Ryonles (DES)

Gustav Schultz
Samuel Smith
William Smith
Philip Specht (DES)
Charles W. Stephens
Martin Van Riper (DOD)
George Ward
John Webb
Samuel Wilberforce
Amzi Willis (DOD)

Company F

Original Roster

Captain Thomas O'Connor
1st Lieutenant George L. Begbie

2nd Lieutenant Alexander Eason
1st Sergeant James J. Deegan

Sergeants: William Hearn, John L. Herman (DOD), William Lynch (DES), Rowland Savage, Charles H. Woodruff

Corporals: Charles Crock, James Donnelly, James Flynn (DES), and William McDonald

Musician: Charles A. Pettit

Privates

Edward Adams
Robert Anderson
Tobias Bacher
Julius F. Bachmeyer
William Barton (DES)
Frederic Bowers
Edward Boylan
Abner Brady (DES)
Joseph Brower (DES)
Hendrick Brown
John Bunt (DES)
Francis A. Carberay
Ezra V. Conklin (KIA)
Sebastian Cook
Patrick Dailey
Patrick Donnelly (KIA)
James Duffy
Henry Ford (DOD)
John Ford (DOD)
Henry Gatfield (DES)
Francis Germain (DES)
Daniel Gerrety

Gabriel Gessler
John Haas (DES)
John Hamill (DES)
August Heckinger
Charles F. Hemle
James Hiler
John Jacobs
Joseph Janaschek
Cornelius Jefferson (DES)
James P. Jones (DOD)
Peter Keilgesner
Henry Kelsall
George H. King
Charles Kolner (DES)
Charles Krebs
Jacob Lanning (DES)
Charles S. Lewis (DES)
James Lewis
John Leighlin
Andrew McGlynchy (DOW)
John McCluskey

Patrick McDermott (DES)
William McDonald
John McJohn
Charles Macguire
John Magee (DES)
Joseph M. Mathews
Patrick Mathews
Francis J. Moakler (DOD)
Allen H. Mordene (DES)
John Morgan (DES)
John Murray (DES)
Charles Nolan (died as POW)
Michael O'Brien
Richard O'Brien
John Outcalt
John W. Peck
Sydney S. Pettit
August Quackenbush
Joseph Quinan (DES)
Jeremiah Quinn (DES)
Michael Regan (DES)

Michael Riley
Thomas Riley
William Rudden (DES)
Peter Schmidt
Erastus H. Schofield
Flut Schem (DES)
Patrick Sheean (DES)

Patrick Smith
Patrick S. Smith
Peter Smith (1)
William Soden
James Splan
Frederick Steel
Montgomery Stogdill

George Stout (DES)
Albert W. Tompkins
John Van Wort
George Van Wort (DES)
Francis Warren
John Welcher
Richard White

Additions to Company F

Privates

Robert M. Babcock
William Bennett
Charles Berg
Joshua Briggs
Patrick Connell
Patrick M. Cronin (DES)
Charles Davis
Simon Decker (DES)
Louis Eberling
William Edwards (DES)
Charles Erman (DES)
John E. Evans (DES)
John Fisner
Henry Fuss
Peter Gabbler
James Glass
John Godfrey

Thomas Griggs
John Grimmel (DES)
Edward F. Groome
John B. Groome
Philip Grub
Ferdinand Hoersch
Lucius Hull (KIA)
Andrew Jackson
Jacob Kohler
Joseph Kompter
Andrew N. Losey (DES)
Sebastan Ludwig (DES)
James McGee
James W. Marshall
Edward Miller
James Morgan
Joel Reeves

James Sands (DES)
Franz Schafer
Albert Schmidt
Paul Schraner
John Smith (1)
John Smith (2)
Peter Smith (2)
James H. Stickle
Frederick Their
William Tittamary (DES)
Casper Vogele
Richard Waters (DES)
Augustus Weber
Charles Wieland (DES)
Thomas A. Williams
Edward C. Wilson (DES)

COMPANY G

Original Roster

Captain Henry C. Bartlett (KIA, May 8, 1864)
1st Lieutenant John J. Toffey
2nd Lieutenant William J. Harrison
1st Sergeant Oscar J. Bucken

Sergeants: Phineas W. Conover, Martin Foster, Nathaniel D. McCoy, John Prescott, Joseph Quinn

Corporals: Patrick Burns, James Louis, Michael Metzger, Richard B. Smith, Abram N. Wade

Musicians: Robert D. Gardner and Allen Ramsey

Wagoner: Michael O'Donnell

Privates

Thomas Allen (DES)
William Anderson (DES)
Orson L. Babbitt
John O. Bailey (DES)
Ferdinand Baisch
Thomas Bell (DES)
George Beyer (KIA)
Mark E. Bradley (KIA)
Dillon Brown (DES)
John Brown (DES)
Robert Burns
John Cain (DES)
Thomas Carroll (DES)
Henry Clark (KIA)
Michael Conlin (DES)
Lawrence Conway
James Donald (died as POW)
James Doyle (DES)
Joseph Eaton
Jacob Ernst (DOD)
Joseph Felty (DOW)
James Finley (DES)
Philip Flood
John Gallon
Alfred Gardner (DES)
Jacob Glenn (DES)
Abraham Heiss
Thomas Hardman
Robert C. Henderson
Joseph Hennessy (KIA)
Michael Herey (DES)
John Higgins (died as POW)
Andrew Hildebrand (DOD)
Robert Hobart
James Joyce
Joseph Kenney (DES)
Joseph Lacy
Niels Larson
Cornelius Lyons (DOD)
Charles McDonald (DES)
Daniel McKenzie
Peter McCoy
Jonathan McGrath (DES)
James McMahon (DES)
Francis McPartland (DOW)
Lewis Mangold (DOW)
Jacob Meyer (DES)
Patrick Morris (DES)
George Mulligan (DES)
John Nix (DOW)
William Ortnea
Benjamin Phillips (DES)
James Phillips (DES)
Sanford Phillips (DES)
Edward W. Pierson (DES)
Charles Reiley (DES)
Edward Reiley
Henry Richardson (DES)
John Scheel
Charles Smith (DES)
Henry Smith (DES)
Michael J. Smith
William Smith
Charles Steer
Henry Steer (DOD)
Charles Sudholtz
Alfred Thomas (DES)
Lawrence Van Nostrand (DOD)
William Wallace (DES)
Peter W. Wiggins (DES)
Amil Wilkie (DES)
John Williams (DES)
George W. Wilson (DES)
John Wilson (DES)
Thomas Wilson (DES)
George M. Wiltz (DES)

Additions to Company G

Privates

Jacob Y. Aber
William Anderson (DES)
George Back
Frederick Gelliete (DES)
Antone Bernhauser
Robert Boone (DES)
William Borden
John Boyman
Francis Brennan
Valentine Brock (DES)
Alexander Brout
George Brown (DES)
James Burk (DES)
Michael Burk (DES)
Charles Burkhardt (DES)
James Burns (DES)
John Carroll
Nehemiah Conklin
Theodore N. Conover (DES)
Adolph DeJapha (DES)
James Dowd (DES)
James Duffy (DES)
Adolph Dursch
Theodore Dust
Andrew Flood
Alexander Fouger (DES)
John Ganning (DES)
Frank Grothe
Daniel Hartford (DES)
Frederick Heile (DES)
Andrew Henderson
John Hoey (DES)
Henry Hamilton
John Jennings (DES)
Andrew Kelly
James King (DES)
Joseph Koener
Charles Krause (DES)
Michael Langwell (DES)
Charles Luckelmacher
Mathias Lyer

Michael McGonigle
John McGinnis (DES)
Christian Mathias
Richard McKelvey
William McKelvey
John McKenna
Carl Metz (DES)
David Morris (DOD)
James Morse (DES)
John Muller (DES)
James O'Meara (DES)
Charles Orethle (DOD)
Frederick Nieuman
Stephen W. Peany
Henry D. Polhemus
William Pomroy (DES)
Thomas Powers
William Ray
Charles Reynolds
Theodore Rodman
William H. Schneider (DES)
James Shehan (DES)
Thomas Shehan (DES)
William Sinclair (DES)
George Smith (DES)
Robert W. Smyth (DES)
Sylvester Stakle (DES)
James Steel
John Struble (DOD)
Thomas Sweeney (DES)
Jerry F. Thompson
Charles Wagner (DES)
Simon Wagner
Frederick Wenning
Joseph Wheeler
Charles White (DES)
James Williams
Charles E. Winters (DES)

Company H

Original Roster

Captain Barent Frazer, Jr.
1st Lieutenant Thomas H. Lee
2nd Lieutenant Joseph P. Couse
1st Sergeant Philip Upton

Sergeants: Joseph Crane, Timothy J. Holly, William H. Lloyd, A.S. Louis Miller, Bernard O. Dougherty, and John A. Shay (accidentally killed)

Corporals: Frank A. Adams (DES), John M. Buxton, Thomas H. Eaton, Erastus Meyers, Oder Quinn, James McLaughlin, Thomas Morton, Francis Smith, and Francis Taylor

Musicians: William C. Hall (DES), John C. Reifler

Privates

Henry Aiken
William Anderson (DES)
William Blank (DES)
James Bligh (DOD)
John Brady (DES)
William Brandt
Louis H. Brown
Oliver E. Brown (DES)
John Burke
John Burns
Abram S. Canfield
Augustus Carson (DES)
Hugh Comstock
Jacob H. Conine
Jeremiah Connor (DOD)
John W. Cooper
Joseph A. Cooper
James Dalton
Newton C. Dealing
Henry Dikeman (DES)
Jeremiah R. Dodge (died as POW at Andersonville prison)
Britton Drake (DOW)
Newton Dutcher (DOW)
Noah C. Estill
Christopher Forrighn
Daniel Fraser (DES)
John T. Harlow
Leonard Hendershot
Peter Hendershot (DES)
George Hetherton (KIA)
William Higgins
Ambrose Hotchkiss
James M. Jarvis
Henry Jennings (DES)
Frank Johnson (DES)
Pierson Johnson
Theodore Johnson
Charles J. Johnston (DES)
Cyrus G. Jones
James C. Jones (DES)
Thomas Keating
Timothy Kenney (DES)
James M. Kidney
George Langley
James Lawton
Lemuel Letts (KIA)
Charles H. Locke (KIA)
Andrew McCabe

Christopher McEvoy
Daniel McNamara
Thomas Marsh (KIA)
John Mooney (DES)
James Moran
Patrick Mulligan (DES)
John Murnin (DES)
Robert Newton
John B. Pittenger
William Oliver
Charles F. Reed (DES)
Hugh Shields (KIA)
Samuel Slacker
Thomas Slate (DES)
William Space
Alma Spangenberg
Otto Spierling
James Spriggins (DES)
James Stoll (accidentally killed)
Augustus Straway
William H. Straway
James A. Struble
Bernard Stykenighter
Henry Thomas (DES)
John Vanderbrock (DES)
Josiah Van Druff
Edward Van Horn
Thomas Ward
Herman C. Wicker (DES)
Charles Williams (DES)
Charles Wright

Additions to Company H

1st Sergeant Joseph Crane

Privates

Francis P. Backter
Lockwood Belden
George Best
Charles H. Chamberlain
Samuel B. Cox
Francis Coxon
James G. Demerest
John Donnelly
James Dougherty
Charles Douvall (DES)
Frederick Eaton
John Fishbock
John Ford
Garret Garrison
Thomas Gebson
Henry Gilman
Charles Haase
Henry C. Halset
Richard Hermann
John Isterstrum
Samuel Johnson (DES)
Michael Kelly (DES)
George King
William B. Kishpaugh (DOD)
William Koelter
Frank Krause (DES)
William B. Lawson
James Leonard (DES)
James Lewis (DES)
William Lewis
Henry Ludwig
John McCabe
William McKee (DES)
Michael McCarty
James McIntyre
Thomas Mick
Jacob Miller
Peter Mola (DES)
Barney Mooney
William Morris (DES)
Bernard Mossacker (DES)
Wallace Newland
John O'Brien (DES)
Thomas O'Brien (DES)
William Parker
Bernard Plag (DES)
William Price (DES)
Augustus Reynolds (DES)
John Robinson (DES)
John Ryder (DES)
John Shaffer
John Shay (DES)
Edward Smith
George H. Stoll (DOW)
George Taylor
Gabriel Tebo
William F. Town
Emile Troutvetter (DOD)
Christian Wegan
Charles Weller
George Wells
Frank Winters

COMPANY I

Original Roster

Captain Samuel F. Waldron (KIA)
1st Lieutenant J. Warren Kitchell

2nd Lieutenant Francis Childs
1st Sergeant John C. Smith

Sergeants: Charles Fengar, William R. Frazer, Theodore Manee, David Russell (DOD), Theodore F. Rogers, and Thomas Shepherd

Corporals: Edward Blake, John Connor, Peter Dieien, Patrick Dillon (DES), Martin Dolphin, George Hager, John McArdle (KIA)

Musicians: William R. Adams, Mark Fohs, John L. Megill

Privates

James Allen
George F. Ballentine
William Bannon
John M. Bennett
Lawrence Bergen
James Butler (DOD)
Samuel D. Coombs
John Collins (DES)
Christopher Devine
Bartholomew Dougherty (DES)
Thomas Dougherty
John Egert (DES)
William Fagan
Thomas Farrell (DOW)
Andrew Folt (DOD)
Andrew Fowler (DES)
Augustus Freunt (DES)
John W. Green
James E. Griffiths (DES)
Michael Haggerty
Robert J. Harrison
Thomas Hayden
William Herbert

Frederick Holland
Henry F. Jones
Joel Jones (DOD)
William Kelly
Martin Krom (DOD)
John Lang (DES)
Edmund Leaver (DOD)
Abraham Lynn
Andrew McCain
John McDonald
Robert McGregor (DES)
Bernard McManus
William McNeil
William Masker (DES)
Nicholas Moore
Michael Murray (DES)
Gilbert Parker (DES)
John Personnet (DOD)
John Phillips
Gottlieb Prob
John G. Probst
Philip Y. Redding
Charles Renhart (DES)
Charles Ryerson

August Shawager (died of gunshot wound)
Edward Smith
James Smith (DES)
Philip Smith (DES)
Richard D. Soden
Michael Stager
John Sullivan (DES)
George Thompson (DES)
Robert Thompson (DES)
Abraham Vanderhoof (KIA)
Patrick Ward (DES)
Joseph Weil
Wilbur Wetsel
Thomas Williams (DES)
August Witte (DES)
Henry Witte (DES)
Louis Witte (drowned in Tennessee River)
Thomas Wood (DES)
William Wright (DES)

Additions to Company I

Captain Nathaniel K. Bray
2nd Lieutenant William L. Geary

Sergeant Levi Smith
Corporal James A. Burr

Privates

Joseph Aspinwell
Edward Barret (DES)
Daniel Berry
Henry Bieber (DES)
Charles Bird
Abner Bishop
Charles Bishop
Lionel Brooks

Milton Brooks
Frank Burns (DES)
John A. Burr
Richard C. Burris
George H. Chapman
John Clark (DES)
Ambi Conklin
Lewis Conklin

Michael Conlon
Joseph Connell (DES)
Erastus DeGraw
Horace Davis
Samuel P. Davis
Frank Dowd (DES)
William Drew
George Ely

Jacob Engle (DES)
John Feeny (DES)
William Fletcher (DES)
James Flood (DES)
Michael Fredericks (DES)
Henry Foster
John Fuller
Michael Galey
John Gaune (DES)
William Hamilton (DES)
John O. Harris (DES)
Louis Hartman (DES)
William Healey (DES)
Thomas Henry (DES)
John Heusefall
Michael Hieylser (DES)
Richard John (DES)
Alfred Johnson (DES)
Henry Johnson (DES)
George Johnston (DES)

John Kelly (DES)
August Kenneye (DES)
John Kennedy (DES)
William King (DES)
James Johnson
William Kaine
Nathaniel Kiser
Joseph Lang
John Leininger
Julius Linderman
Anthony Mares
William Margeson (DOD)
Ernst Mayer
Charles E. Mayo
Ernst H. Meyers
Charles Miller
William Miller
Josiah Mullen
James Murchie
Patrick Murphy (DES)

James Murtough
John Oakley (DES)
Nathan Parliament
George Price (DES)
Henry Proll (DES)
Jacob Riker
John Ryan (DES)
William Ryan
Moody A. Sandburn
August Schuffner (DES)
Herman Seibert
William Shield
David Smith (DES)
Levi Smith
William Stelling
Michael Taggart
John Weiderberger
Peter Wendt
Thomas Williams (KIA)
Charles H. Wood

Company K

Original Roster

Captain William McCoy
1st Lieutenant William H. Cochrane

2nd Lieutenant Francis Tully
1st Sergeant Thomas Duncan

Sergeants: Theodore Cadmus, Michael Donahoe, John O'Neill, James Simpson

Corporals: Patrick Dooley, Oscar Encke, Thomas Fallon, William McFadyen, James Morrissey, John Quinn, Peter S. Ray, Edward Sandalls, Michael Tormey

Privates

James Adams (DOD)
William Anderson (DES)
Chester Andrews
Albert Arnslee (DES)
Hiram Babcock (DOD)
John Bell (DES)
Herman I. Blauvelt
James Booth
James Brady (DES)
Mordecai Y. Bryant
Michael Cannon (DES)
George W. Chase (DES)
James Clarke (DES)

John Clarke (DES)
Timothy Collins (DES)
James Cox
Peter Curran (DES)
Charles H. Davis (DES)
John Dermody (DES)
John Dudley (DES)
Ernest D. Eike
Francis Ernst
John Foley (DES)
Thomas Foster (DES)
Michael Gerherty (DES)
Samuel Gillespie

Albert Goetchins
William F. Green (KIA)
James Green
Robert Hall
James Hamilton (DES)
Gustave Hartman
Charles Hastings (DES)
William Hayden (DES)
James Hays
Thusfey Hyland (DES)
Mathew Kelly
Thomas F. Kenney
John Kerrigan (DES)

Thomas Kiernan
Jacob Kunz (DES)
William Larchland (DES)
John Larkin
Andrew Layden
Mathew Liberty (DES)
William Lockhart (DES)
John Long (KIA)
Frederick H. Lyon
John W. Martling
Daniel McCarron (DES)
Francis McCarty
Patrick McClean
Patrick McDonald (DES)
John McGiff (DES)
James Monahan

Francis Myers (DES)
Patrick Newman (DES)
John O'Brien (DES)
William Ritter (DES)
James Roe
George Roth (DES)
William Sandford (DES)
Patrick Slattery
John Smith
Michael Smith (DES)
Henry Stapleton (DES)
George J. Stock
Daniel B. Stuart
James Sweeney (DES)
George W. Thomas
Thomas Thompson (DES)

William Thompson (KIA)
  (alias John O'Keefe)
James Townley
Patrick Travers (KIA)
John Tyrell (DES)
Anthony Ummersie
Peter Welch
Adam Wetzel
William E. Wheeler
  (KIA)
John Williams (DES)
John Williams, Jr. (DES)
Charles Wilson (DES)
Frederick J. Wilson (DES)
Blakey Windsor

Additions to Company K

2nd Lieutenant Andrew Gallagher

Privates

John Allen
Patrick Ahern (DES)
George Belmont (DES)
Carl Bender (DES)
William Blesse
Jules Boniface
George Bowen
Joseph A. Brown
Richard W. Clarke (DES)
Edward Collier (DES)
John Collins
Thomas Collins (DES)
Michael Cox
William Day (DES)
Philip DeFreese
Charles C. Dawson
Evan B. Edmunds
Thomas Feeley (DES)
William Gibson (DES)
Patrick Gleason (DES)
John E. Haines
Michael Higgins
Philip Hilgar
Henry Hilgiloah
William Hunt

William Johnson (DES)
Edward Knox
James Landford (DES)
Carl J. Lindmark
Thomas Long (DES)
Thomas McCarthy
Edward McDermott
John McGee (DES)
Adolph Machowof
Thomas Matthews (DES)
William Melhorne
Thomas Mitchell (DES)
Timothy Monahan
John F. Morris (DES)
Henry Meyers
James Mulinio
Frank Muller
William Murphy (DES)
John O'Neil (DES)
Thomas O'Rourke (DES)
Isaac Perry
Charles Riker (DOD)
John Riley
Martin Rogan
Thomas Ryan

John Schafer
William Slesser
George Smith
James Smith
John Smith (DES)
William Smith
William J. Smith
Richard Stage
Richard Stewart
Frederick W. Studdiford
Jeremiah Sullivan
Daniel Taylor (DES)
Charles Thompson (DES)
William Thompson (DES)
Ira Van Orden
George Vannatten
Horace Vannatten
John Verricke (DES)
Augustus Vredenburgh
Charles Wagner
William H. Waldron
Andrew Walters (DES)
Frank H. Winters
George T. Wood
Edward Yetman (DES)

Chapter Notes

Introduction

1. John Cunningham, *Newark* (Newark, N.J.: New Jersey Historical Society, 3rd edition, 2002), p. 202.

2. John Boyle, *Soldiers True* (New York, N.J.: Eaton and Mains, 1903), preface.

Chapter I. "I have had uphill work here"

1. Joseph G. Bilby and William C. Goble, *Remember You Are Jerseymen* (Hightstown, N.J.: Longstreet House, 1998), p. 351.

2. Provost General to Mindil, July 7, 1863, New Jersey State Archives.

3. Alan A. Siegel, *For the Glory of the Union: Myth, Reality and the Media in Civil War New Jersey* (Rutherford, NJ: Fairleigh Dickinson University Press, 1984), p. 38.

4. William Gillette, *Jersey Blue: Civil War Politics in New Jersey, 1854–1865* (New Brunswick, NJ: Rutgers University Press, 1995), p. 38.

5. Siegel, *For the Glory of the Union*, p. 38.

6. Gillette, *Jersey Blue*, pp. 1–9, 239–241.

7. Siegel, *For the Glory of the Union*, p. 9.

8. Gillette, *Jersey Blue*, p. 239.

9. Newark *Daily Mercury*, July 27, 1863.

10. James McPherson, *Battle Cry of Freedom* (New York: Oxford University Press, 1988), pp. 600–611; Eugene Murdock, *One Million Men: The Civil War Draft in the North* (Madison: The State Historical Society of Wisconsin, 1971), pp. x, 5–6.

11. Murdock, *One Million Men*, pp. 6–7, 308; Bilby and Goble, *Remember You Are Jerseymen*, pp. 22–29.

12. Gillette, *Jersey Blue*, p. 240.

13. McPherson, *Battle Cry of Freedom*, pp. 609–611; Iver Bernstein, *The New York City Draft Riots* (New York: Oxford University Press, 1990), pp. 17–72.

14. Newark *Daily Journal*, July 13, 1863.

15. Newark *Daily Mercury*, July 14, 1863; Newark *Daily Journal*, July 14, 1863.

16. Newark *Daily Mercury*, July 15, 1863.

17. Newark *Daily Mercury*, July 15, 1863; Newark *Daily Journal*, July 15, 1863; Newark *Daily Advertiser*, July 15, 1863.

18. Gillette, *Jersey Blue*, pp. 241–243.

19. McPherson, *Battle Cry of Freedom*, p. 611.

20. Gillette, *Jersey Blue*, p. 243.

21. Newark *Daily Mercury*, July 11, 1863.

22. Bilby and Goble, *Remember You Are Jerseymen*, p. 345.

23. William S. Stryker, *Record of Officers and Men of New Jersey in the Civil War, 1861–1865, Compiled in the Office of the Adjutant General*, 2 vols. (Trenton, N.J.: John L. Murphy, Steam Book and Job Printer, 1876), pp. 859–880, 959–1003.

24. Bilby and Goble, *Remember You Are Jerseymen*, pp. 347–48.

25. William F. Fox, *Regimental Losses in the American Civil War 1861–65* (Albany, N.Y.: Brandon Printing Company, 1898), pp. 4–5.

26. John Y. Foster, *New Jersey and the Rebellion: A History of the Services of the Troops and People of New Jersey in Aid of the Union Cause* (Newark, N.J.: Dennis and Company, 1868), p. 609.

27. Siegel, *For the Glory of the Union*, p. 41; Murdock, *One Million Men*, p. 7.

28. Newark *Daily Journal*, July 30, 1863.

29. Newark *Daily Mercury*, August 7, 1863, and August 11, 1863; Murdock, *One Million Men*, p. 218.

30. Newark *Daily Mercury*, August 20, 1863.

31. Newark *Daily Advertiser*, August 4, 1863, and August 12, 1863.

32. Mindil to "Your Excellency," August 15, 1863, New Jersey State Archives.

33. Newark *Daily Advertiser*, August 17, 1863.
34. Newark *Daily Mercury*, August 18, 1863, and August 22, 1863.
35. Newark *Daily Advertiser*, August 22, 1863.
36. Newark *Daily Advertiser*, September 1, 1863.
37. Bilby and Goble, *Remember You Are Jerseymen*, pp. 98, 108, 379.
38. Siegel, *For the Glory of the Union*, p. 73; Bilby and Goble, *Remember You Are Jerseymen*, p. 220.
39. Newark *Daily Advertiser*, August 21, 1863.
40. Newark *Daily Advertiser*, August 25, 1863.
41. Newark *Daily Mercury*, August 28, 1863.
42. Newark *Daily Journal*, September 3, 1863.
43. James McPherson, *For Cause and Comrades* (New York: Oxford University Press, 1997), p. 47.
44. Bilby and Goble, *Remember You Are Jerseymen*, p. 377.
45. Newark *Daily Advertiser*, August 13, 1863.
46. Bilby and Goble, *Remember You Are Jerseymen*, p. 378.
47. Regimental Letter Book, General Order 15, September 14, 1864, National Archives.
48. Mindil Autobiographical Statement, New Jersey Historical Society.
49. United States Government, *The War of the Rebellion: A Compilation of the Official Records of the Union and Confederate Armies*, 128 vols. (Washington, D.C.: 1880–1901), hereafter cited as *OR*, ser. I, vol. 11, pt. 1, pp. 491–492, 498; *OR*, ser. I, vol. 11, pt. 1, p. 856; *OR*, ser. I, vol. 11, pt. 2, p. 182.
50. Mindil Medal of Honor Citation, October 25, 1893. Available at http://www.army.mil/cmh=pg/mohciv2.htm.
51. Bilby and Goble, *Remember You Are Jerseymen*, p. 345.
52. Newark *Daily Advertiser*, September 7, 1863.
53. Bilby and Goble, *Remember You Are Jerseymen*, pp. 345–351.
54. Mindil Autobiographical Statement, New Jersey Historical Society; Foster, *New Jersey and the Rebellion*, p. 566.
55. Mindil Autobiographical Statement, New Jersey Historical Society; John J. Pullen, *A Shower of Stars* (Mechanicsburg, Pa.: Stackpole Books, 1997), p. 170.
56. Memorial Service for William Lambert, June 16, 1912, p. 13, U.S. Army Military History Institute, E467.1L38M45.1912.
57. Pullen, *A Shower of Stars*, pp. 67–81, 170–172.
58. Newark *Daily Advertiser*, September 7, 1863.
59. Rogers to Lambert, September 3, 1863, New Jersey State Archives.
60. Newark *Daily Advertiser*, September 7, 1863.
61. Newark *Daily Advertiser*, August 19, 1863; Newark *Daily Mercury*, August 20, 1863.
62. Stryker, *Record of Officers and Men of New Jersey in the Civil War*, pp. 959–1003.
63. Newark *Daily Journal*, September 3, 1863.
64. Stryker, *Record of Officers and Men of New Jersey in the Civil War*, pp. 959–1003.
65. Newark *Daily Journal*, September 17, 1863.
66. Newark *Daily Mercury*, November 11, 1863.
67. Newark *Daily Advertiser*, September 3, 1863 and September 7, 1863.
68. Newark *Daily Journal*, September 7, 1863; Newark *Daily Advertiser*, September 7, 1863.
69. Newark *Daily Journal*, September 8, 1863; Newark *Daily Mercury*, September 8, 1863; Newark *Daily Advertiser*, September 8, 1863.
70. Newark *Daily Journal*, September 8, 1863.
71. Hudson County *Democrat*, September 12, 1863.
72. Siegel, *For the Glory of the Union*, pp. 75–78, 207.
73. Somerset *Messenger*, September 10, 1863.
74. Ella Lonn, *Desertion During the Civil War* (New York: The Century Company, 1928), p. 227.
75. Lonn, *Desertion During the Civil War*, p. 227.
76. Newark *Daily Advertiser*, September 8, 1863.
77. Newark *Daily Journal*, September 8, 1863; Newark *Daily Advertiser*, September 8 and September 9, 1863.
78. Newark *Daily Advertiser*, September 9, 1863; Newark *Daily Mercury*, September 9, 1863.
79. Newark *Daily Advertiser*, September 9, 1863.
80. Newark *Daily Advertiser*, September 9, 1863; Newark *Daily Journal*, September 9, 1863.
81. Newark *Daily Advertiser*, September 9 and September 10, 1863; Newark *Daily Journal*, September 9, 1863; Newark *Daily Mercury*, September 9, 1863.
82. Newark *Daily Advertiser*, September 10, 1863; Newark *Daily Mercury*, September 10, 1863; Newark *Daily Journal*, September 10, 1863.
83. Newark *Daily Advertiser*, September 10, 1863.

Chapter II. "You will no doubt be surprised to know that I am out here"

1. Newark *Daily Advertiser*, October 21, 1863.
2. *OR*, ser. I, vol. 29, pt.2, p.156.
3. Hudson County *Democrat*, October 31, 1863.
4. William Lloyd to Mary Lloyd, September 11, 1863, Western Reserve Historical Society.
5. Newark *Daily Advertiser*, September 14, 1863, September 15, 1863, and September 28, 1863.
6. Stryker, *Record of Officers and Men of New Jersey in the Civil War*, p. 982.
7. Newark *Daily Advertiser*, September 28, 1863.
8. William Lloyd to Mary Lloyd, September 14, 1863, Western Reserve Historical Society.
9. Stryker, *Record of Officers and Men of New Jersey in the Civil War*, pp. 989–990.
10. *Supplement to the Official Records, Record of Events*, vol. 40, pt. 2, p. 679.
11. Hudson County *Democrat*, October 31, 1863.
12. Newark *Daily Advertiser*, September 28, 1863.
13. Hudson County *Democrat*, October 31, 1863.
14. *Supplement to the Official Records, Record of Events*, vol. 40, p. 679.
15. Hudson County *Democrat*, October 31, 1863.

Notes — Chapter II

16. William Lloyd to Mary Lloyd, September 14, 1863, Western Reserve Historical Society.
17. *Supplement to the Official Records, Record of Events*, vol. 40, p. 679.
18. Newark *Daily Advertiser*, September 28, 1863.
19. *OR*, ser. 1, vol. 51, pt. 1, pp. 1089–1091.
20. Newark *Daily Advertiser*, September 28, 1863.
21. Hudson County *Democrat*, October 31, 1863.
22. Newark *Daily Advertiser*, September 28, 1863.
23. Hudson County *Democrat*, October 31, 1863.
24. Newark *Daily Advertiser*, September 28, 1863.
25. Newark *Daily Mercury*, October 17, 1863.
26. William Lloyd to Mary Lloyd, September 18, 1863, Western Reserve Historical Society. Date of letter is probably incorrect as the regiment arrived at Catlett's Station on September 19.
27. Mindil to Howard, September 20, 1863, Regimental Letter Book, National Archives.
28. *OR*, ser. 1, vol. 51, pt. 1, 1091.
29. William Lloyd to Mary Lloyd, September 18, 1863, Western Reserve Historical Society.
30. John J. Pullen, *The Twentieth Maine* (Dayton, Ohio: Morningside House, 1991), p. 19.
31. Hudson County *Democrat*, October 31, 1863.
32. Mindil to Stone, September 21, 1863, Regimental Letter Book, National Archives.
33. John Toffey to parents, October 5, 1863, Rutgers University Special Collections.
34. Mindil to Brown, September 23, 1863, Regimental Letter Book, National Archives.
35. Stryker, *Records of Officers and Men of New Jersey in the Civil War*, p. 976.
36. Mindil to Brown, September 23, 1863, Regimental Letter Book, National Archives.
37. Newark *Daily Journal*, October 20, 1863.
38. Newark *Daily Mercury*, October 17, 1863.
39. Wiley Sword, *Mountains Touched by Fire* (New York: St. Martin's Press, 1995), pp. 36–48.
40. Shelby Foote, *The Civil War: A Narrative, vol. 2, Fredericksburg to Meridian* (New York: Random House, 1963), p. 765.
41. Hudson County *Democrat*, October 31, 1863.
42. *Supplement to the Official Records, Record of Events*, vol. 40, p. 679.
43. Stryker, *Record of Officers and Men of New Jersey in the Civil War*, pp. 959–1003.
44. George Metcalf, Autobiography, (U.S. Army Military History Institute, Harrisburg Civil War Roundtable Collection), p. 115.
45. Mark H. Dunkelman and Michael J. Winey, *The Hardtack Regiment: An Illustrated History of the 154th New York State Volunteer Infantry* (East Brunswick, N.J.: Associated University Presses, 1981), p. 87.
46. George K. Collins, *Memoirs of the 149th Regiment N.Y. Volunteer Infantry* (Hamilton, N.Y.: Edmonston Publishing Inc., 1995), p. 181; Georg Muller to parents, October 13, 1863, New Jersey Historical Society. Georg Muller was a member of Company B. In Stryker's *Records of Officers and Men of New Jersey in the Civil War*, he is listed as George Miller; his letters to his parents are all written in German, which may account for the confusion about his name.
47. Newark *Daily Advertiser*, October 21, 1863.
48. Collins, *Memoirs of the 149th Regiment N.Y. Volunteer Infantry*, pp. 181–182.
49. Newark *Daily Advertiser*, October 21, 1863.
50. Newark *Daily Advertiser*, October 21, 1863.
51. Collins, *Memoirs of the 149th Regiment N.Y. Volunteer Infantry*, p. 183.
52. Newark *Daily Advertiser*, October 21, 1863; John Toffey to parents, October 5, 1863, Rutgers University Special Collections.
53. Collins, *Memoirs of the 149th Regiment N.Y. Volunteer Infantry*, p. 186.
54. Newark *Daily Advertiser*, October 21, 1863.
55. John Toffey to parents, October 5, 1863, Rutgers University Special Collections.
56. Foote, *The Civil War, vol. 2, Fredericksburg to Meridian*, p. 765.
57. Gerald F. Linderman, *Embattled Courage: The Experience of Combat in the American Civil War* (New York: The Free Press, 1987), p. 159.
58. Hudson County *Democrat*, October 31, 1863.
59. Stryker, *Record of Officers and Men of New Jersey in the Civil War*, pp. 959–1003.
60. Newark *Daily Advertiser*, October 21, 1863.
61. Georg Muller to parents, October 13, 1863, New Jersey Historical Society.
62. Paterson *Daily Register*, October 19, 1863.
63. Stryker, *Record of Officers and Men of New Jersey in the Civil War*, p. 963.
64. Newark *Daily Mercury*, October 17, 1863.
65. Paterson *Daily Register*, October 19, 1863.
66. Paterson *Daily Register*, October 19, 1863; Georg Muller to parents, October 13, 1863, New Jersey Historical Society.
67. William Lloyd to Mary Lloyd, October 10, 1863, Western Reserve Historical Society.
68. Newark *Daily Mercury*, October 17, 1863.
69. Newark *Daily Advertiser*, October 19, 1863.
70. Pullen, *The Twentieth Maine*, pp. 33–36.
71. McPherson, *For Cause and Comrades*, pp. 4–5; Stephen Ambrose, *Citizen Soldiers* (New York: Simon and Shuster, 1997), pp. 13–14.
72. Linderman, *Embattled Courage*, pp. 93–94.
73. McPherson, *For Cause and Comrades*, pp. 131–134.
74. McPherson, *For Cause and Comrades*, p. 132.
75. William Lloyd to Mary Lloyd, September, 11, 14, and 18, 1863, October 3, 10, 18 and 27, 1863, Western Reserve Historical Society.
76. William Lloyd to Mary Lloyd, October 3, 27 and 29, 1863, Western Reserve Historical Society.
77. John Fenner to Sister, October 22, 1863, Camden County Historical Society.
78. Paterson *Daily Register*, October 23, 1863.
79. Newark *Daily Advertiser*, October 21 and November 6, 1863.
80. Newark *Daily Mercury*, October 17, 1863.
81. Mindil to Stockton, October 14, 1863, Regimental Letter Book, National Archives.
82. Mindil to Stockton, October 14, 1863, Regimental Letter Book, National Archives.
83. Mindil to Townsend, October 14, 1863, Regimental Letter Book, National Archives.

84. Mindil to Miegs, October 28, 1863, Regimental Letter Book, National Archives.
85. Stryker, *Record of Officers and Men of New Jersey in the Civil War*, pp. 959–1003.
86. William Lloyd to Mary Lloyd, October 10, 1863, Western Reserve Historical Society.
87. Newark *Daily Advertiser,* November 9, 1863.
88. Foster, *New Jersey and the Rebellion*, pp. 611–612.
89. Newark *Daily Advertiser*, November 9, 1863.
90. Foster, *New Jersey and the Rebellion*, p. 612.
91. Newark *Daily Mercury*, November 6, 1863.
92. Newark *Daily Advertiser*, November 9, 1863; Newark *Daily Mercury*, November 6, 1863.
93. Newark *Daily Advertiser*, November 9, 1863.
94. Georg Muller to parents, October 30, 1863, New Jersey Historical Society.
95. William Lloyd to Mary Lloyd, October 27, 1863, Western Reserve Historical Society.
96. Paterson *Daily Register*, November 6, 1863.
97. Foster, *New Jersey and the Rebellion*, p. 612.
98. Paterson *Daily Register*, November 6, 1863.
99. John Toffey to father, October 30, 1863, Rutgers University Special Collections.
100. William Lloyd to Mary Lloyd, October 29, 1863, Western Reserve Historical Society; Georg Muller to parents, October 30, 1863, New Jersey Historical Society.
101. Sword, *Mountains Touched by Fire*, pp. 99–104, 112–147; Peter Cozzens, *The Shipwreck of Their Hopes* (Urbana and Chicago: University of Illinois Press, 1994), pp. 8–22, 48–100.
102. Newark *Daily Advertiser*, November 27, 1863.
103. Georg Muller to Parents, November 15, 1863, New Jersey Historical Society.
104. Newark *Daily Advertiser*, November 27, 1863.
105. Newark *Daily Advertiser*, November 27, 1863.
106. William Lloyd to Mary Lloyd, November 4, 1863, Western Reserve Historical Society.
107. William Lloyd to Mary Lloyd, November 9, 1863, Western Reserve Historical Society.
108. Newark *Daily Journal*, November 18, 1863.
109. William Lloyd to Mary Lloyd, November 9, 1863, Western Reserve Historical Society.
110. William Lloyd to Mary Lloyd, November 9, 1863, Western Reserve Historical Society.
111. Newark *Daily Journal*, November 18, 1863.
112. Newark *Daily Advertiser*, November 27, 1863.
113. Newark *Daily Advertiser*, November 27, 1863.
114. Newark *Daily Journal*, November 18, 1863.
115. Newark *Daily Advertiser*, November 27, 1863.
116. Newark *Daily Journal*, November 18, 1863.
117. Foster, *New Jersey and the Rebellion*, p. 614.
118. Newark *Daily Journal*, November 18, 1863.

Chapter III. "A victory almost over nature herself"

1. Cozzens, *The Shipwreck of Their Hopes*, pp. 7, 15, 115–116.
2. Sword, *Mountains Touched by Fire*, pp. 190–191; Cozzens, *The Shipwreck of Their Hopes*, pp. 72–73.
3. Cozzens, *The Shipwreck of Their Hopes*, pp. 103–105.
4. Cozzens, *The Shipwreck of Their Hopes*, pp. 111–115.
5. John Toffey to brother, November 10, 1863, Rutgers University Special Collections.
6. Newark *Daily Advertiser*, November 27, 1863.
7. Georg Muller to parents, November 15, 1863, New Jersey Historical Society.
8. John Toffey to grandmother, November 18, 1863, Rutgers University Special Collections.
9. Stryker, *Records of Officers and Men of New Jersey in the Civil War*, pp. 975, 979, 982, 985, 993.
10. Cozzens, *The Shipwreck of Their Hopes*, pp. 122–123.
11. Richard A. Baumgartner and Larry Strayer, *Echoes of Battle: The Struggle for Chattanooga* (Huntington, W. V.: Blue Acorn Press, 1996), p. 196.
12. David Peloubet Diary, Rutgers University Special Collections, *OR*, ser. I. vol. 31, pt. 2, p. 362.
13. *OR*, ser. I, vol. 31, pt. 2, p. 362.
14. Newark *Daily Advertiser*, January 7, 1864.
15. David Peloubet Diary, Rutgers University Special Collections.
16. Newark *Daily Advertiser*, January 7, 1864.
17. Cozzens, *The Shipwreck of Their Hopes*, pp. 125–128.
18. Cozzens, *The Shipwreck of Their Hopes*, p. 129.
19. Newark *Daily Advertiser*, January 7, 1864.
20. John Toffey to parents, December 1, 1863, Rutgers University Special Collections.
21. Cozzens, *The Shipwreck of Their Hopes*, pp. 129–133.
22. David Peloubet Diary, Rutgers University Special Collections.
23. Newark *Daily Advertiser*, January 7, 1864.
24. Cozzens, *The Shipwreck of Their Hopes*, pp. 128, 133.
25. *OR*, ser. I, vol. 31, pt. 2, pp. 347, 359, 362, 364.
26. Newark *Daily Advertiser*, January 7, 1864.
27. *OR*, ser. I, vol. 31, pt. 2, p. 362.
28. John Toffey to parents, November 25, 1863 and December 1, 1863, Rutgers University Special Collections.
29. Chief Record and Pension Office to State Adjutant General, September 10, 1897, New Jersey State Archives.
30. *OR*, ser. I, vol. 31, pt. 2, p. 362.
31. Newark *Daily Advertiser*, January 7, 1864.
32. *OR*, ser. I, vol. 31, pt. 2, p. 362.
33. Newark *Daily Advertiser*, January 7, 1864.
34. *OR*, ser. I, vol. 31, pt. 2, p. 362.
35. George Metcalf Autobiography, pp. 136–137, U.S. Army Military History Institute, Harrisburg Civil War Roundtable Collection.
36. Earl J. Hess, *The Union Soldier in Combat* (Lawrence: University Press of Kansas, 1997), p. 47.
37. *OR*, ser. I, vol. 31, pt. 2, p. 348.
38. Newark *Daily Journal*, December 7, 1863.
39. Stryker, *Records of Officers and Men of New*

Notes — Chapter III

Jersey in the Civil War, pp. 975, 989; Newark *Daily Advertiser*, December 5, 1863.
40. Cozzens, *The Shipwreck of Their Hopes*, pp. 137–138, 145–149.
41. Cozzens, *The Shipwreck of Their Hopes*, p. 148.
42. Newark *Daily Advertiser*, January 7, 1864; Cozzens, *The Shipwreck of Their Hopes*, p. 148.
43. David Peloubet Diary, Rutgers University Special Collections.
44. Newark *Daily Advertiser*, January 7, 1864.
45. Cozzens, *The Shipwreck of Their Hopes*, p. 151.
46. Newark *Daily Advertiser*, January 7, 1864.
47. Cozzens, *The Shipwreck of Their Hopes*, pp. 151–154.
48. David Peloubet Diary, Rutgers University Special Collections.
49. Newark *Daily Advertiser*, January 7, 1864.
50. Cozzens, *The Shipwreck of Their Hopes*, pp. 159–200; Sword, *Mountains Touched by Fire*, pp. 202–230.
51. Cozzens, *The Shipwreck of Their Hopes*, pp. 203–216.
52. Newark *Daily Advertiser*, January 7, 1864.
53. Cozzens, *The Shipwreck of Their Hopes*, pp. 216–241.
54. David Peloubet Diary, Rutgers University Special Collections.
55. Cozzens, *The Shipwreck of Their Hopes*, p. 223.
56. David Peloubet Diary, Rutgers University Special Collections.
57. *OR*, ser. I, vol. 31, pt. 2, p. 364.
58. Newark *Daily Advertiser*, December 23, 1863; Stryker, *Records of Officers and Men of New Jersey in the Civil War*, p. 979.
59. *OR*, ser. I, vol. 31, pt. 2, p. 358; Stryker, *Records of Officers and Men of New Jersey in the Civil War*, p. 985.
60. Cozzens, *The Shipwreck of Their Hopes*, pp. 245–350.
61. Cozzens, *The Shipwreck of Their Hopes*, pp. 351–354, 362–363.
62. David Peloubet Diary, Rutgers University Special Collections.
63. Newark *Daily Advertiser*, January 7, 1864.
64. David Peloubet Diary, Rutgers University Special Collections.
65. Newark *Daily Advertiser*, January 7, 1864.
66. George Mindil Diary, New Jersey Historical Society.
67. Newark *Daily Advertiser*, January 7, 1864.
68. Cozzen, *The Shipwreck of Their Hopes*, pp. 366–372.
69. Cozzen, *The Shipwreck of Their Hopes*, p. 386.
70. George Mindil Diary, New Jersey Historical Society.
71. David Peloubet Diary, Rutgers University Special Collections.
72. Cozzens, *The Shipwreck of Their Hopes*, pp. 385–387.
73. *OR*, ser. I, vol. 31, pt. 2, p. 351.
74. George Mindil Diary, New Jersey Historical Society.
75. *OR*, ser. I. vol. 31, pt. 2, p. 351.
76. George Mindil Diary, New Jersey Historical Society.
77. David Peloubet Diary, Rutgers University Special Collections.
78. George Mindil Diary, New Jersey Historical Society.
79. Newark *Daily Advertiser*, January 7, 1864.
80. David Peloubet Diary, Rutgers University Special Collections.
81. Cozzens, *The Shipwreck of Their Hopes*, p. 387.
82. George Mindil Diary, New Jersey Historical Society.
83. *OR*, ser. I. vol. 31, pt. 2, p. 351.
84. George Metcalf Autobiography, U.S. Army Military History Institute, Harrisburg Civil War Roundtable Collection, pp. 143, 148.
85. George Mindil Diary, New Jersey Historical Society.
86. Newark *Daily Advertiser*, January 7, 1864.
87. David Peloubet Diary, Rutgers University Special Collections; George Mindil Diary, New Jersey Historical Society.
88. *OR*, ser. I, vol. 31, pt. 2, p. 351.
89. George Mindil Diary, New Jersey Historical Society.
90. David Peloubet Diary, Rutgers University Special Collections.
91. George Mindil Diary, New Jersey Historical Society.
92. Newark *Daily Advertiser*, January 7, 1864.
93. David Peloubet Diary, Rutgers University Special Collections; George Mindil Diary, New Jersey Historical Society.
94. George Mindil Diary, New Jersey Historical Society.
95. *OR*, ser. I, vol. 31, pt. 2, p. 352.
96. George Mindil Diary, New Jersey Historical Society.
97. David Peloubet Diary, Rutgers University Special Collections.
98. George Mindil Diary, New Jersey Historical Society.
99. *OR*, ser. I, vol. 31, pt. 2, p. 353.
100. Cozzens, *The Shipwreck of Their Hopes*, p. 354.
101. Newark *Daily Advertiser*, January 7, 1864.
102. George Mindil Diary, New Jersey Historical Society.
103. Newark *Daily Advertiser*, January 7, 1864.
104. Newark *Daily Advertiser*, February 3, 1864.
105. Newark *Daily Advertiser*, January 7, 1864.
106. David Peloubet Diary, Rutgers University Special Collections.
107. George Mindil Diary, New Jersey Historical Society.
108. Cozzens, *The Shipwreck of Their Hopes*, pp. 387–388.
109. *OR*, ser. I, vol. 31, pt. 2, p. 354.
110. Newark *Daily Advertiser*, January 7, 1864.
111. George Mindil Diary, New Jersey Historical Society.

112. David Peloubet Diary, Rutgers University Special Collections.
113. George Mindil Diary, New Jersey Historical Society.
114. David Peloubet Diary, Rutgers University Special Collections.
115. George Mindil Diary, New Jersey Historical Society.
116. George Mindil Diary, New Jersey Historical Society.
117. Newark *Daily Advertiser*, January 7, 1864.
118. David Pelobet Diary, Rutgers University Special Collections.
119. George Mindil Diary, New Jersey Historical Society.
120. David Peloubet Diary, Rutgers University Special Collections.
121. David Peloubet Diary, Rutgers University Special Collections.
122. Stryker, *Records of Officers and Men of New Jersey in the Civil War*, p. 989; Thomas Eaton Affidavit, New Jersey State Archives.
123. Newark *Daily Advertiser*, January 7, 1864.
124. David Peloubet Diary, Rutgers University Special Collections.
125. *OR*, ser. I, vol. 31, pt. 2, p. 355.
126. David Peloubet Diary, Rutgers University Special Collections.
127. Newark *Daily Advertiser*, January 7, 1864.
128. *Supplement to the Official Records, Record of Events*, vol. 40, p. 693.
129. Stryker, *Records of Officers and Men of New Jersey in the Civil War*, pp. 967, 985, 989.
130. Cozzens, *The Shipwreck of Their Hopes*, pp. 389–391.
131. Newark *Daily Advertiser*, January 7, 1864.
132. Newark *Daily Advertiser*, January 7, 1864.
133. *Supplement to the Official Records, Record of Events*, vol. 40, p. 693.
134. John Fenner to mother, December 17, 1863, Camden County Historical Society.
135. Thirty-third New Jersey File, Chickamauga and Chattanooga National Military Park Library.

Chapter IV. "I thought I could bear it without a tear"

1. Newark *Daily Journal*, December 2, 1863.
2. Paterson *Daily Press*, December 2, 1863.
3. Newark *Daily Journal*, December 7, 1863.
4. Newark *Daily Mercury*, December 11, 1863.
5. Peloubet to Townsend, December 22, 1863, Regimental Letter Book, National Archives.
6. Newark *Daily Advertiser*, January 4, 1864.
7. Newark *Daily Journal*, January 11, 1864.
8. Newark *Daily Advertiser*, January 16, 1864.
9. Newark *Daily Advertiser*, January 18, 1864.
10. Newark *Daily Advertiser*, January 22, 1864.
11. Mindil to Stockton, December 20, 1863, Regimental Letter Book, National Archives.
12. Mindil to Lincoln, December 29, 1863, New Jersey Historical Society.
13. Mindil to Miegs, December 27, 1863, Regimental Letter Book, National Archives.
14. Mindil to Thomas, December 28, 1863, Regimental Letter Book, National Archives.
15. William Lloyd to Mary Lloyd, December 21, 1863, Western Reserve Historical Society.
16. John Toffey to parents, December 29, 1863, Rutgers University Special Collections.
17. John Toffey to parents, January 13, 1864, Rutgers University Special Collections.
18. John Toffey to grandmother, March 11, 1864, Rutgers University Special Collections.
19. John Toffey to Friend, April 25, 1864, Rutgers University Special Collections.
20. Richard Baumgartner and Larry Strayer, *Echoes of Battle: The Atlanta Campaign* (Huntington, W. V.: Blue Acorn Press, 1991), pp. 12–14.
21. Albert Castel, *Decision in the West* (Lawrence: University Press of Kansas, 1992), p. 1.
22. Dunkelman and Winey, *The Hardtack Regiment*, pp. 98–99.
23. Baumgartner and Strayer, *Echoes of Battle: The Atlanta Campaign*, p. 17.
24. John D. Billings, *Hardtack and Coffee: The Unwritten Story of Army Life* (Lincoln: University of Nebraska Press, 1993), pp. 76–77.
25. George Washington Adams, *Doctors in Blue* (New York: Henry Schuman Inc., 1952), pp. 203–206.
26. Adams, *Doctors in Blue*, pp. 3, 199–200, 202, 222.
27. Stryker, *Records of Officers and Men of New Jersey in the Civil War*, pp. 963, 975, 978–979, 982, 993, 997.
28. Newark *Daily Advertiser*, February 4, 1864.
29. Castel, *Decision in the West*, pp. 16–17.
30. Newark *Daily Advertiser*, February 3, 1864.
31. Paterson *Daily Register*, February 22, 1864.
32. Newark *Daily Advertiser*, March 30, 1864.
33. George Mindil Diary, New Jersey Historical Society.
34. Stryker, *Records of Officers and Men of New Jersey in the Civil War*, pp. 991, 993.
35. Newark *Daily Advertiser*, February 3, 1864.
36. Paterson *Daily Register*, February 4, 1864.
37. Newark *Daily Advertiser*, February 4, 1864.
38. Paterson *Daily Register*, February 4, 1864.
39. Newark *Daily Advertiser*, February 4, 1864.
40. Newark *Daily Advertiser*, February 3, 1864.
41. Newark *Daily Advertiser*, March 3, 1864.
42. *OR*, ser. I, vol. 31, pt. 2, p. 363.
43. Newark *Daily Advertiser*, March 3, 1864.
44. Paterson *Daily Register*, February 4, 1864.
45. George Rolfe Diary, One Hundred and Thirty-sixth New York File, Chickamauga and Chattanooga National Military Park Library.
46. Newark *Daily Advertiser*, February 4, 1864.
47. Paterson *Daily Register*, February 4, 1864.
48. George Rolfe Diary, One Hundred and Thirty-sixth New York File and Martin Bushnell Diary, One Hundred and Fifty-fourth New York file, Chicka-

mauga and Chattanooga National Military Park Library.
49. William Lloyd to Mary Lloyd, January 24, 1864, Western Reserve Historical Society.
50. Georg Muller to parents, February 1, 1864, New Jersey Historical Society.
51. Paterson *Daily Register*, February 22, 1864.
52. Newark *Daily Advertiser*, January 29, 1864.
53. Newark *Daily Advertiser*, March 3, 1864.
54. Peloubet to Fry, February 4, 1864, Regimental Letter Book, National Archives
55. Paterson *Daily Register*, February 22, 1864.
56. Georg Muller to parents, February 28, 1864, New Jersey Historical Society.
57. Newark *Daily Advertiser*, March 3, 1864.
58. William Cochrane to John Toffey, February 21, 1864, Rutgers University Special Collections.
59. Newark *Daily Advertiser*, March 3, 1864.
60. John Fenner to mother, February 26, 1864, Camden County Historical Society.
61. William Lloyd to Mary Lloyd, March 12, 1864, Western Reserve Historical Society.
62. Letter to William Lloyd from regiment, March 8, 1864, signature illegible, Western Reserve Historical Society.
63. William Lloyd to Mary Lloyd, March 12, 1864, Western Reserve Historical Society.
64. William Lloyd to Mary Lloyd, March 14, 1864, Western Reserve Historical Society.
65. William Lloyd to Mary Lloyd, March 14, 1864, Western Reserve Historical Society.
66. Newark *Daily Advertiser*, March 30, 1864.
67. Newark *Daily Advertiser*, March 3, 1864.
68. William Lloyd to Mary Lloyd, March 29, 1864, Western Reserve Historical Society.
69. Newark *Daily Advertiser*, May 2, 1864.
70. Paterson *Daily Register*, April 20, 1864.
71. Georg Muller to parents, April 17, 1864, New Jersey Historical Society, William Lloyd to Mary Lloyd, April 18, 1864, Western Reserve Historical Society.
72. Newark *Daily Advertiser*, May 2, 1864.
73. William Lloyd to Mary Lloyd, April 14, 1864, and April 18, 1864, Western Reserve Historical Society.
74. William Alan Blair, ed., *A Politician Goes to War: The Civil War Letters of John White Geary* (University Park: Pennsylvania State Press, 1995), p. 163.
75. George Mindil Diary, New Jersey Historical Society.
76. Newark *Daily Advertiser*, May 2, 1864.
77. Stryker, *Record of Officers and Men of New Jersey in the Civil War*, pp. 959, 964, 972, 980, 983 and 990.

Chapter V. "Bullets began to rain about me"

1. Castel, *Decision in the West*, pp. 17–18, 26, 29–31, 63–73, 79, 90–97, 112.
2. Lee Kennett, *Marching Through Georgia* (New York: Harper Collins, 1995), pp. 9–10.
3. *History and Tour Book of the Atlanta Campaign* (*Blue and Gray* magazine, 1976), pp. 24–25.
4. Castel, *Decision in the West*, p. 54.
5. Sword, *Mountains Touched by Fire*, pp. 159–160.
6. Castel, *Decision in the West*, p. 117.
7. Stephen Pierson, "From Chattanooga to Atlanta in 1864," New Jersey Historical Society, p. 332.
8. George Mindil Diary, New Jersey Historical Society.
9. *OR*, ser. I, vol. 38, pt. 2, pp. 215, 227.
10. Castel, *Decision in the West*, p. 125.
11. George Mindil Diary, New Jersey Historical Society; *OR*, ser. I, vol. 38, pt. 2, p. 215.
12. *OR*, ser. I, vol. 38, pt. 2, p. 215; Newark *Daily Advertiser*, June 27, 1864.
13. George Mindil Diary, New Jersey Historical Society.
14. Paterson *Daily Press*, June 4, 1864.
15. *OR*, ser. I, vol. 38, pt. 2, p. 216; Newark *Daily Advertiser*, June 27, 1864.
16. Cozzens, *The Shipwreck of Their Hopes*, p. 15; Kennett, *Marching Through Georgia*, p. 9; *History and Tour Guide of the Atlanta Campaign*, pp. 24–25.
17. Castel, *Decision in the West*, pp. 121–123, 126–127.
18. Castel, *Decision in the West*, p. 131.
19. Henry Stone, "Part 1: Opening of the Campaign," in *The Atlanta Papers*, compiled by Sidney C. Kerksis (Dayton, Ohio: Press of the Morningside Bookshop, 1980), p. 15.
20. Baumgartner and Strayer, *Echoes of Battle: The Atlanta Campaign*, p. 69.
21. Castel, *Decision in the West*, pp. 131–132.
22. *OR*, ser. I, vol. 38, pt. 2, pp. 114–115.
23. *OR*, ser. I, vol. 38, pt. 2, pp. 115, 203.
24. Hess, *The Union Soldier in Battle*, pp. 1–21, 45–50; *OR*, ser. I, vol. 38, pt. 2, p. 226.
25. Castel, *Decision in the West*, p. 134.
26. *OR*, ser. I, vol. 38, pt. 2, p. 115.
27. Georg Muller to parents, June 9, 1864, New Jersey Historical Society.
28. *OR*, ser. I, vol. 38, pt. 2, pp. 115–116.
29. *OR*, ser. I, vol. 38, pt. 2, p. 226.
30. Pierson, "From Chattanooga to Atlanta in 1864," New Jersey Historical Society, p. 333.
31. Hightstown *Gazette*, July 28, 1864.
32. *OR*, ser. I, vol. 38, pt. 2, p. 226.
33. Newark *Daily Advertiser*, June 27, 1864.
34. *OR*, ser. I, vol. 38, pt. 2, p. 226.
35. *OR*, ser. I, vol. 38, pt. 2, p. 217.
36. Paterson *Daily Press*, June 4, 1864.
37. Newark *Daily Advertiser*, June 27, 1864.
38. Pierson, "From Chattanooga to Atlanta in 1864," New Jersey Historical Society, p. 334.
39. Newark *Daily Advertiser*, June 27, 1864.
40. Hess, *The Union Soldier in Battle*, pp. 1–29.
41. Newark *Daily Advertiser*, June 27, 1864.
42. McPherson, *For Cause and Comrades*, pp. 39–41.
43. Castel, *Decision in the West*, pp. 133–134.

44. *OR,* ser. I, vol. 38, pt. 2, p. 226
45. Pierson, "From Chattanooga to Atlanta in 1864," New Jersey Historical Society, p. 334.
46. Hess, *The Union Soldier in Battle,* pp. 29–37.
47. *OR,* ser. I. vol. 38, pt. 2, pp. 116, 217, 226
48. Newark *Daily Advertiser,* June 27, 1864.
49. Castel, *Decision in the West,* pp. 134–135.
50. McMurry, *History and Tour Guide of the Atlanta Campaign,* p. 26.
51. Phillip Collins to author, September 1999; Newark *Daily Journal,* May 10, 1864.
52. Styrker, *Records of Officers and Men of New Jersey in the Civil War,* pp. 963, 967, 975.
53. Newark *Daily Journal,* May 8, 1864, and May 10, 1864.
54. Adams, *Doctors in Blue,* pp. 113–115, 228.
55. Adams, *Doctors in Blue,* pp. 66, 116–117, 131–132; *OR,* ser. I, vol. 38, pt. 2, pp. 148–149.
56. Adams, *Doctors in Blue,* pp. 112, 118, 122.
57. Stryker, *Records of Officers and Men of New Jersey in the Civil War,* p. 964.
58. Sussex *Register,* July 1, 1864; Stryker, *Records of Officers and Men of New Jersey in the Civil War,* p. 994.
59. David Hess to author, September 1999; Stryker, *Record of Officers and Men of New Jersey in the Civil War,* pp. 971, 978, 985.
60. William Jones to Dear Sir, June 6, 1864; Stephen Pierson to Mrs. Fenner, August 10,1864, Camden County Historical Society; Stryker, *Records of Officers and Men of New Jersey in the Civil War,* p. 978; John Fenner to mother, December 17, 1864, Camden County Historical Society.

Chapter VI. "More like hell than God's beautiful earth"

1. Castel, *Decision in the West,* pp. 135–143.
2. Castel, *Decision in the West,* p. 140.
3. *OR,* ser. I, vol. 38, pt. 2, pp. 206, 221.
4. Newark *Daily Advertiser,* June 27, 1864; *OR,* ser. I, vol. 38, pt. 2, p. 206.
5. Castel, *Decision in the West,* pp. 142–152.
6. *OR,* ser. I, vol. 38, pt. 2, pp. 221, 447.
7. Daniel P. Conyngham, *Sherman's March Through the South* (New York: Sheldon and Co., 1865), p. 45.
8. Castel, *Decision in the West,* p. 149.
9. *OR,* ser. I, vol. 38, pt. 2, p. 221.
10. Collins, *Memoirs of the 149th Regiment N.Y. Volunteer Infantry,* p. 244.
11. Newark *Daily Advertiser,* June 27, 1864.
12. *OR,* ser. I, vol. 38, pt. 2, p. 221.
13. Castel, *Decision in the West,* p. 149.
14. Castel, *Decision in the West,* pp. 137, 151–154.
15. Castel, *Decision in the West,* p. 153.
16. *OR,* ser. I, vol. 38, pt. 2, p. 221.
17. Castel, *Decision in the West,* p. 152.
18. Castel, *Decision in the West,* pp. 152–166.
19. *OR,* ser. I, vol. 38, pt. 2, pp. 117–118, 206, 221; Castel, *Decision in the West,* p. 168.
20. Castel, *Decision in the West,* pp. 169–173.
21. Castel, *Decision in the West,* pp. 158, 173–176; Pierson, "From Chattanooga to Atlanta in 1864," p. 336, New Jersey Historical Society. Exactly what happened to Major Peloubet is not completely clear. According to William Lambert, he was back in the North on leave during the winter of 1864 after the return of Lieutenant Colonel Fouratt (Newark *Daily Advertiser,* March 30, 1864). Pierson stated that Peloubet was sick during the battle of Resaca and he resigned his position on August 4, 1864, (Stryker, p. 959). He probably never returned from his leave.
22. *OR,* ser. I, vol. 38, pt. 2, p. 221.
23. Castel, *Decision in the West,* p. 174.
24. G.S. Bradley, *The Star Corps* (Milwaukee, Wisconsin: Jermain and Brightman, 1865), p. 98.
25. Pierson, "From Chattanooga to Atlanta in 1864," p. 336, New Jersey Historical Society.
26. *OR,* ser. I, vol. 38, pt. 2, p. 118.
27. Collins, *Memoirs of the 149th Regiment N.Y. Volunteer Infantry,* pp. 247–248.
28. *OR,* ser. I, vol. 38, pt. 2, p. 277; pt. 3, p. 812.
29. Pierson, "From Chattanooga to Atlanta in 1864," p. 336, New Jersey Historical Society.
30. Boyle, *Soldiers True,* p. 206.
31. William M. Anderson, *They Died to Make Men Free: A History of the 19th Michigan Infantry* (Dayton, Ohio: Morningside Press, 1994), p. 333.
32. *OR,* ser. I, vol. 38, pt. 2, p. 206.
33. *OR,* ser. I, vol. 38, pt. 2, pp. 205, 221.
34. Paterson *Daily Press,* June 4, 1864.
35. Collins, *Memoirs of the 149th Regiment N.Y. Volunteer Infantry,* p. 248.
36. Collins, *Memoirs of the 149th Regiment N.Y. Volunteer Infantry,* p. 248.
37. William Lloyd to Mary Lloyd, May 16, 1864, Western Reserve Historical Society.
38. *OR,* ser. I, vol. 38, pt. 2, p. 222.
39. Stryker, *Record of Officers and Men of New Jersey in the Civil War,* pp. 978, 982, 989; *OR,* ser. I, vol. 38, pt. 2, p. 222; James McSorley Pension Records, National Archives.
40. Paterson *Daily Press,* June 4, 1864.
41. *OR,* ser. I, vol. 38, pt. 2, p. 263.
42. Boyle, *Soldiers True,* p. 206.
43. Collins, *Memoirs of the 149th Regiment N.Y. Volunteer Infantry,* p. 248.
44. Newark *Daily Advertiser,* June 27, 1864.
45. Collins, *Memoirs of the 149th Regiment N. Y. Volunteer Infantry,* pp. 249–250.
46. *OR,* ser. I, vol. 38, pt. 2, p. 263.
47. Paterson *Daily Press,* June 4, 1864.
48. Linderman, *Embattled Courage,* pp. 17–33.
49. Paterson *Daily Press,* June 4, 1864.
50. *OR,* ser. I, vol. 38, pt. 2, p. 813.
51. Boyle, *Soldiers True,* pp. 206–207.
52. Castel, *Decision in the West,* p. 179.
53. Newark *Daily Advertiser,* June 27, 1864.
54. William Lloyd to Mary Lloyd, May 21, 1864, Western Reserve Historical Society.
55. Paterson *Daily Press,* June 4, 1864.
56. *OR,* ser. I, vol. 38, pt. 2, pp. 120, 278.

57. Boyle, *Soldiers True*, p. 207.
58. Baumgartner, *Echoes of Battle: The Atlanta Campaign*, p. 92.
59. *OR*, ser. I, vol. 38, pt. 2, p. 164.
60. Newark *Daily Advertiser*, June 27, 1864.
61. Castel, *Decision in the West*, pp. 178–179.
62. *OR*, ser. I, vol. 38, pt. 3, p. 760.
63. McMurry, *History and Tour Guide of the Atlanta Campaign*, p. 45.
64. Shelby Foote, *The Civil War: A Narrative, vol. 3, Red River to Appomatox* (New York: Random House, 1974), p. 334.
65. Collins, *Memoirs of the 149th Regiment N.Y. Volunteer Infantry*, p. 251.
66. William Lloyd to Mary Lloyd, May 21, 1864, Western Reserve Historical Society.
67. Castel, *Decision in the West*, pp. 175, 178.
68. Castel, *Decision in the West*, pp. 186, 192.
69. Castel, *Decision in the West*, p. 190.
70. Collins, *Memoirs of the 149th Regiment N.Y. Volunteer Infantry*, p. 252; *OR*, ser. I, vol. 38, pt. 2, pp. 121, 206.
71. Castel, *Decision in the West*, pp. 193–195, 197–200.
72. *OR*, ser. I, vol. 38, pt. 2, p. 222.
73. Collins, *Memoirs of the 149th Regiment N.Y. Volunteer Infantry*, p. 252.
74. Castel, *Decision in the West*, pp. 197–198.
75. *OR*, ser. I, vol. 38, pt. 2, p. 206.
76. Castel, *Decision in the West*, pp. 200–202.
77. Castel, *Decision in the West*, pp. 203–206.
78. William Lloyd to Mary Lloyd, May 20, 1864, Western Reserve Historical Society.
79. Castel, *Decision in the West*, p. 209.
80. Castel, *Decision in the West*, pp. 209, 213–214.
81. Castel, *Decision in the West*, p. 216.
82. William Lloyd to Mary Lloyd, May 20, 1864, Western Reserve Historical Society.
83. Castel, *Decision in the West*, p. 216.
84. William Lloyd to Mary Lloyd, May 21, 1864, Western Reserve Historical Society.
85. Castel, *Decision in the West*, p. 214.
86. Billings, *Hardtack and Coffee*, pp. 112–116, 129.
87. Adams, *Doctors in Blue*, pp. 207–208.
88. Tony Horowitz, *Confederates in the Attic: Dispatches from the Unfinished Civil War* (New York: Pantheon Books, 1998), p. 257.
89. Adams, *Doctors in Blue*, pp. 208–209, 212.
90. Billings, *Hardtack and Coffee*, pp. 135, 139.
91. *OR*, ser. I, vol. 38, pt. 2, p. 207; Pierson, "From Chattanooga to Atlanta in 1864," New Jersey Historical Society, p. 337.
92. Newark *Daily Advertiser*, June 28, 1864; Collins, *Memoirs of the 149th Regiment N. Y. Volunteer Infantry*, p. 255.
93. Castel, *Decision in the West*, pp. 215–216, 218–220.
94. *OR*, ser. I, vol. 38, pt. 2, p. 207.
95. Collins, *Memoirs of the 149th Regiment N.Y. Volunteer Infantry*, p. 255; *OR*, ser. I, vol. 38, pt. 2, p. 122.
96. Newark *Daily Advertiser*, June 28, 1864.
97. Castel, *Decision in the West*, p. 220.
98. Collins, *Memoirs of the 149th Regiment N.Y. Volunteer Infantry*, p. 255.
99. Castel, *Decision in the West*, pp. 220–221, 226.
100. *OR*, ser. I, vol. 38, pt. 2, p. 207.
101. Castel, *Decision in the West*, p. 221.
102. *OR*, ser. I, vol. 38, pt. 2, pp. 122–123.
103. Castel, *Decision in the West*, pp. 221–222.
104. Pierson, "From Chattanooga to Atlanta in 1864," New Jersey Historical Society, p. 338.
105. *OR*, ser. I, vol. 38, pt. 2, pp. 207, 222.
106. Jacob Cox, *Sherman's Battle for Atlanta* (New York: DaCapo Press, 1994), pp. 68–69, 72; *OR*, ser. I, vol. 38, pt. 3, pp. 817, 828, 830, 833.
107. Castel, *Decision in the West*, p. 223.
108. Pierson, "From Chattanooga to Atlanta in 1864," New Jersey Historical Society, p. 339.
109. Rice Bull, *Soldiering: The Civil War Diary of Rice C. Bull* (Novato, California: Presidio Press, 1977), p. 117.
110. Newark *Daily Advertiser*, June 28, 1864.
111. Bull, *Soldiering*, p. 117.
112. Newark *Daily Advertiser*, June 28, 1864.
113. Newark *Daily Advertiser*, June 28, 1864; *OR*, ser. I, vol. 38, pt. 2, p. 222.
114. Castel, *Decision in the West*, pp. 225–226.
115. Pierson, "From Chattanooga to Atlanta in 1864," New Jersey Historical Society, p. 339.
116. Pierson, "From Chattanooga to Atlanta in 1864," New Jersey Historical Society, p. 339.
117. Castel, *Decision in the West*, p. 228.
118. Newark *Daily Advertiser*, June 28, 1864.
119. Castel, *Decision in the West*, pp. 228–229.
120. *OR*, ser. I, vol. 38, pt. 2, pp. 222–223.
121. Castel, *Decision in the West*, pp. 228–247, 251–252.
122. Castel, *Decision in the West*, pp. 247–248.
123. *OR*, ser. I, vol. 38, pt. 2, p. 124.
124. Newark *Daily Advertiser*, June 28, 1864.
125. Pierson, "From Chattanooga to Atlanta in 1864," New Jersey Historical Society, p. 339.
126. William Lloyd to Mary Lloyd, June 9, 1864, Western Reserve Historical Society.
127. Pierson, "From Chattanooga to Atlanta in 1864," New Jersey Historical Society, pp. 339–340.
128. Castel, *Decision in the West*, p. 249.
129. *OR*, ser. I, vol. 38, pt. 2, p. 223.
130. Stryker, *Record of Officers and Men of New Jersey in the Civil War*, pp. 963, 975–976, 985, 997.
131. *OR*, ser. I, vol. 38, pt. 2, p. 223.
132. Castel, *Decision in the West*, pp. 251–252, 255.
133. Pierson, "From Chattanooga to Atlanta in 1864," New Jersey Historical Society, p. 340.
134. Castel, *Decision in the West*, p. 255.
135. *OR*, ser. I, vol. 38, pt. 2, p. 207; Castel, *Decision in the West*, p. 256.
136. Newark *Daily Advertiser*, June 28, 1864.
137. Castel, *Decision in the West*, pp. 258–260.
138. Newark *Daily Advertiser*, June 28, 1864.
139. Foote, *The Civil War, vol. 3, Red River to Appomattox*, p. 347.
140. Newark *Daily Advertiser*, June 28, 1864, August 15, 1864.

Chapter VII. "A very hard day"

1. Comparison of listing of occupants of army hospitals in the Jersey City *American Standard*, August 22, 1864, with lists of wounded in Newark *Daily Advertiser*, May 19, 1864, June 6, 1864, and June 8, 1864.
2. Newark *Daily Journal*, September 2, 1864.
3. Castel, *Decision in the West*, pp. 262–267.
4. *OR*, ser. I, vol. 38, pt. 2, p. 228.
5. Paterson *Daily Press*, July 9, 1864.
6. *OR*, ser. I, vol. 38, pt. 2, p. 228.
7. Stryker, *Records of Officers and Men of New Jersey in the Civil War*, p. 982.
8. Castel, *Decision in the West*, pp. 267–270.
9. *OR*, ser. I, vol. 38, pt. 2, p. 208.
10. Castel, *Decision in the West*, pp. 272–278.
11. *OR*, ser. I, vol. 38, pt. 2, p. 208.
12. Collins, *Memoirs of the 149th Regiment N.Y. Volunteer Infantry*, p. 264.
13. Conyngham, *Sherman's March Through the South*, pp. 127–128.
14. Castel, *Decision in the West*, pp. 279–280.
15. *OR*, ser. I, vol. 38, pt. 2, pp. 127, 208–209.
16. *OR*, ser. I, vol. 38, pt. 2, pp. 127–128, 208–209.
17. *OR*, ser. I, vol. 38, pt. 2, pp. 209, 228; Newark *Daily Advertiser*, August 15, 1864.
18. *OR*, ser. I, vol. 38, pt. 2, pp. 128, 209.
19. Pierson, "From Chattanooga to Atlanta in 1864," New Jersey Historical Society, p. 342.
20. *OR*, ser. I, vol. 38, pt. 2, p. 128.
21. Pierson, "From Chattanooga to Atlanta in 1864," New Jersey Historical Society, pp. 342–343.
22. *Sussex Register*, July 15, 1864.
23. Newark *Daily Advertiser*, August 15, 1864.
24. *OR*, ser. I, vol. 38, pt. 2, pp. 229, 235.
25. Fox, *Regimental Losses in the Civil War*, p. 450.
26. Stryker, *Records of Officers and Men of New Jersey in the Civil War*, pp. 971–972, 975, 979, 985, 989, 993; Paterson *Daily Press*, July 1, 1864.
27. Castel, *Decision in the West*, pp. 280–281.
28. *OR*, ser. I, vol. 38, pt. 2, pp. 129–130.
29. Newark *Daily Advertiser*, August 14, 1864.
30. *OR*, ser. I, vol. 38, pt. 2, p. 130.
31. *OR*, ser. I, vol. 38, pt. 2, pp. 130–131.
32. Paterson *Daily Register*, July 9, 1864.
33. Stryker, *Records of Officers and Men of New Jersey in the Civil War*, p. 979.
34. Castel, *Decision in the West*, p. 283.
35. *OR*, ser. I, vol. 38, pt. 2, p. 131.
36. Castel, *Decision in the West*, pp. 285–287.
37. *OR*, ser. I. vol. 38, pt. 2, p. 132.
38. Castel, *Decision in the West*, p. 288.
39. *OR*, ser. I, vol. 38, pt. 2, pp. 132, 229.
40. William Lloyd to Mary Lloyd, June 21, 1864, Western Reserve Historical Society.
41. Castel, *Decision in the West*, pp. 289–292.
42. Castel, *Decision in the West*, pp. 292–295.
43. Pierson, "From Chattanooga to Atlanta in 1864," New Jersey Historical Society, p. 344.
44. *Sussex Register*, July 15, 1864.
45. *OR*, ser. I, vol. 38, pt. 2, p. 229.
46. Castel, *Decision in the West*, p. 295.
47. Castel, *Decision in the West*, pp. 299–301, 304, 316–322.
48. *OR*, ser. I, vol. 38, pt. 2, pp. 133–134, 229.
49. William Lloyd to Mary Lloyd, June 28, 1864, Western Reserve Historical Society.
50. Castel, *Decision in the West*, pp. 322–323.
51. Castel, *Decision in the West*, p. 324.
52. *OR*, ser. I, vol. 38, pt. 2, pp. 212, 224, 229.
53. Castel, *Decision in the West*, pp. 327–330.
54. Castel, *Decision in the West*, pp. 330–331.
55. *OR*, ser. I, vol. 38, pt. 2, pp. 134, 229; Castel, *Decision in the West*, pp. 330–331.
56. Castel, *Decision in the West*, p. 331.
57. *Sussex Register*, July 29, 1864.
58. William Lloyd to Mary Lloyd, July 8, 1864, Western Reserve Historical Society.
59. *OR*, ser. I, vol. 38, pt. 2, 229: Pierson, "From Chattanooga to Atlanta in 1864," New Jersey Historical Society, p. 347.
60. William Lloyd to Mary Lloyd, July 8, 1864, Western Reserve Historical Society.
61. Castel, *Decision in the West*, pp. 335–341.
62. Castel, *Decision in the West*, pp. 343, 349–352.
63. *OR*, ser. I, vol. 38, pt. 2, p. 229.
64. William Lloyd to Mary Lloyd, July 8, 1864, Western Reserve Historical Society.
65. *Sussex Register*, July 29, 1864, and August 5, 1864.
66. Castel, *Decision in the West*, pp. 347–350, 360–365.
67. Castel, *Decision in the West*, p. 348.
68. *OR*, ser. I, vol. 38, pt. 2, pp. 136, 230.
69. *OR*, ser. I, vol. 38, pt. 2, p. 136; Hudson *County Democrat*, September 17, 1864.
70. Castel, *Decision in the West*, pp. 365–368.
71. Castel, *Decision in the West*, pp. 365, 367.
72. Collins, *Memoirs of the 149th Regiment N.Y. Volunteer Infantry*, p. 275.
73. *OR*, ser. I, vol. 38, pt. 2, pp. 136–137.
74. Castel, *Decision in the West*, pp. 369, 371–372.
75. *OR*, ser. I, vol. 38, pt. 2, pp. 137–138.
76. Castel, *Decision in the West*, pp. 373–377.
77. *OR*, ser. I, vol. 38, pt. 2, p. 138.
78. Lloyd Document, Western Reserve Historical Society, in the William Lloyd papers. This is a typed account of the battle of Peachtree Creek signed by William Henry Lloyd; however, the style is not like that of Lloyd and some of the words are literally the same as an article in the Newark *Daily Advertiser* of August 2, 1864, reportedly taken from an account in the New York *Times*.
79. Pierson, "From Chattanooga to Atlanta in 1864," New Jersey Historical Society, p. 350.
80. Lloyd Document, Western Reserve Historical Society, p. 4.
81. Pierson, "From Chattanooga to Atlanta in 1864," New Jersey Historical Society, p. 350.
82. Lloyd Document, Western Reserve Historical Society, p. 4, Pierson, "From Chattanooga to Atlanta in 1864," New Jersey Historical Society, p. 350.
83. *OR*, ser. I, vol. 38, pt. 2, pp. 138, 213.
84. Pierson, "From Chattanooga to Atlanta in 1864," New Jersey Historical Society, p. 350.

85. Fouratt to Stockton, July 23, 1864, New Jersey State Archives.
86. Newark *Daily Advertiser*, August 15, 1864.
87. Georg Muller to parents, July 29, 1864, New Jersey Historical Society.
88. Newark *Daily Advertiser*, August 15, 1864.
89. Pierson, "From Chattanooga to Atlanta in 1864," New Jersey Historical Society, pp. 350–351.
90. Newark *Daily Advertiser*, August 1, 1864.
91. *OR*, ser. I, vol. 38, pt. 2, p. 225.
92. Fouratt to Stockton, July 23, 1864, New Jersey State Archives.
93. Newark *Daily Advertiser*, August 15, 1864.
94. Fouratt to Stockton, July 23, 1864, New Jersey State Archives.
95. *OR*, ser. I, vol. 38, pt. 3, p. 896.
96. Fouratt to Stockton, July 23, 1864, New Jersey State Archives.
97. Newark *Daily Advertiser*, August 15, 1864.
98. Dunkelman and Winey, *The Hardtack Regiment*, pp. 118–119.
99. Pierson, "From Chattanooga to Atlanta in 1864," New Jersey Historical Society, p. 351.
100. Castel, *Decision in the West*, p. 377.
101. Conyngham, *Sherman's March Through the South*, p. 164.
102. Castel, *Decision in the West*, pp. 378–379, 382–383.
103. Pierson, "From Chattanooga to Atlanta in 1864," New Jersey Historical Society, p. 352.
104. Stryker, *Records of Officers and Men of New Jersey in the Civil War*, pp. 963, 967, 975, 978–979, 982, 989, 993, 997; Paterson *Daily Press*, August 2, 1864.
105. *OR*, ser. I, vol. 38, pt. 2, p. 231.
106. Newark *Daily Advertiser*, August 15, 1864.
107. Fouratt to Stockton, July 23, 1864, New Jersey State Archives.
108. Newark *Daily Advertiser*, February 3, 1864; Georg Muller to parents, July 29, 1864, New Jersey Historical Society.

Chapter VIII. "The old flag floats over Atlanta"

1. Castel, *Decision in the West*, p. 385.
2. Ovid Futch, *History of Andersonville Prison* (Gainesville, Florida: University of Florida Press, 1968), pp. 1–4, 6–7, 10–18, 30–33, 35, 38–39, 100, 107.
3. Futch, *History of Andersonville Prison*, pp. 43–44, 46, 49.
4. Jersey City *American Standard*, August 15, 1864; Newark *Daily Advertiser*, August 1, 1864.
5. Newark *Daily Advertiser*, May 22, 1865; David Wolf pension records as quoted, John Anderson to author, March 17, 1999; Thomas Eaton statement, New Jersey State Archives; Stryker, *Records of Officers and Men of New Jersey in the Civil War*, p. 971.
6. John Anderson to author, March 17, 1999; Paterson *Daily Press*, October 24, 1864.
7. Stryker, *Records of Officers and Men of New Jersey in the Civil War*, pp. 978, 982, 985, 993.
8. Stryker, *Records of Officers and Men of New Jersey in the Civil War*, p. 989.
9. Thomas Eaton statement, New Jersey State Archives.
10. Newark *Daily Advertiser*, May 22, 1865.
11. Futch, *History of Andersonville Prison*, pp. 44, 84, 95, 106, 113, 117–119. Parole meant a promise not to fight until officially exchanged. See also Horowitz, *Confederates in the Attic*, pp. 312–331.
12. Newark *Daily Advertiser*, June 22, 1864.
13. Jersey City *American Standard*, July 19, 1864.
14. Siegel, *For the Glory of the Union*, p. 46.
15. Jersey City *American Standard*, July 19, 1864.
16. Jersey City *American Standard*, August 22, 1864.
17. Paterson *Daily Press*, August 24, 1864.
18. Jersey City *American Standard*, August 29, 1864.
19. Jersey City *American Standard*, September 15, 1864.
20. Jersey City *American Standard*, September 10, 1864.
21. Stryker, *Records of Officers and Men of New Jersey in the Civil War*, p. 966.
22. Jersey City *American Standard*, August 29, 1864.
23. Castel, *Decision in the West*, pp. 384–385.
24. *OR*, ser. I. vol. 38, pt. 2, p. 141.
25. Castel, *Decision in the West*, pp. 385–413.
26. Castel, *Decision in the West*, p. 413.
27. Castel, *Decision in the West*, p. 414.
28. *OR*, ser. I, vol. 38, pt. 2, pp. 141–142.
29. Newark *Daily Advertiser*, August 15, 1864.
30. William Lloyd to Mary Lloyd, July 28, 1864, Western Reserve Historical Society.
31. Georg Muller to parents, July 29, 1864, New Jersey Historical Society.
32. Boyle, *Soldiers True*, pp. 243–244.
33. Newark *Daily Advertiser*, August 15, 1864.
34. Castel, *Decision in the West*, pp. 417–422.
35. *OR*, ser. I, vol. 38, pt. 2, p. 143.
36. Castel, *Decision in the West*, pp. 424–461.
37. Castel, *Decision in the West*, p. 453.
38. *OR*, ser. I, vol. 38, pt. 2, p. 143.
39. Georg Muller to parents, August 5, 1864, New Jersey Historical Society.
40. Castel, *Decision in the West*, pp. 461–462, 464–475.
41. George Mindil Diary, New Jersey Historical Society.
42. *OR*, ser. I. vol. 38, pt. 2, p. 143.
43. Pierson, "From Chattanooga to Atlanta in 1864," New Jersey Historical Society, p. 354.
44. Stryker, *Records of Officers and Men of New Jersey in the Civil War*, pp. 971, 982, 985.
45. Verona–Cedar Grove *Times*, January 14, 1993; Stryker, *Records of Officers and Men of New Jersey in the Civil War*, p. 967.
46. Sussex *Register*, September 2, 1864.
47. William Lloyd to Mary Lloyd, August 16, 1864, Western Reserve Historical Society.

48. William Lloyd to Mary Lloyd, August 21, 1864, Western Reserve Historical Society.
49. William Lloyd to Mary Lloyd, August 24, 1864, Western Reserve Historical Society.
50. Georg Muller to parents, August 30, 1864, New Jersey Historical Society.
51. Castel, *Decision in the West*, p. 485.
52. *OR*, ser. I, vol. 38, pt. 2, p. 144; Castel, *Decision in the West*, p. 485.
53. Hudson County *Democrat*, September 17, 1864.
54. Newark *Daily Advertiser*, September 23, 1864.
55. Castel, *Decision in the West*, pp. 485–508.
56. Newark *Daily Journal*, September 1, 1864.
57. Castel, *Decision in the West*, pp. 511–524.
58. Castel, *Decision in the West*, pp. 521–522.
59. *OR*, ser. I, vol. 38, pt. 2, pp. 145–146.
60. Newark *Daily Advertiser*, September 23, 1864.
61. Castel, *Decision in the West*, pp. 527–528.
62. Newark *Daily Advertiser*, September 23, 1864.
63. *OR*, ser. I, vol. 38, pt. 2, p. 146.
64. Newark *Daily Advertiser*, September 23, 1864.
65. Castel, *Decision in the West*, pp. 529–533.
66. Newark *Daily Advertiser*, September 3, 1864.
67. Castel, *Decision in the West*, p. 543.
68. Newark *Daily Advertiser*, September 23, 1864.

Chapter IX. "A hard campaign and we expect nothing else"

1. Castel, *Decision in the West*, p. 536.
2. *OR*, ser. I, vol. 38, pt. 2, p. 220.
3. Jersey City *American Standard*, August 29, 1864.
4. Pierson, "From Chattanooga to Atlanta in 1864," New Jersey Historical Society, p. 356.
5. Bilby and Goble, *Remember You Are Jerseymen*, pp. 40–41.
6. Bilby and Goble, *Remember You Are Jerseymen*, pp. 41–42.
7. Georg Muller to parents, September 28, 1864, New Jersey Historical Society.
8. McPherson, *Battle Cry of Freedom*, p. 603.
9. Bilby and Goble, *Remember You Are Jerseymen*, pp. 42–43.
10. Stryker, *Records of Officers and Men of New Jersey in the Civil War*, pp. 959–1003.
11. *OR*, ser. I, vol. 44, p. 299.
12. Castel, *Decision in the West*, pp. 548–549.
13. Sussex *Register*, September 30, 1864.
14. Foote, *The Civil War, vol. 3, Red River to Appomattox*, p. 549.
15. Castel, *Decision in the West*, p. 549.
16. William A. Scaife, *The March to the Sea* (Saline, Michigan: McNaughton and Gunn, Inc., 1993), p. 9.
17. Foote, *The Civil War, vol. 3, Red River to Appomattox*, pp. 603–604.
18. Scaife, *The March to the Sea*, p. 9.
19. Castel, *Decision in the West*, p. 552.
20. Scaife, *The March to the Sea*, p. 16.
21. Castel, *Decision in the West*, p. 552.
22. Foote, *The Civil War, vol. 3, Red River to Appomattox*, p. 613.
23. Scaife, *The March to the Sea*, p. 16.
24. Scaife, *The March to the Sea*, pp. 9–10, 16.
25. Scaife, *The March to the Sea*, p. 16.
26. Castel, *Decision in the West*, p. 553.
27. Scaife, *The March to the Sea*, p. 17.
28. Castel, *Decision in the West*, p. 553.
29. *OR*, ser. I, vol. 44, p. 297.
30. Georg Muller to parents, September 27, 1864, and September 28, 1864, New Jersey Historical Society.
31. *OR*, ser. I, vol. 44, p. 298.
32. Paterson *Daily Press*, October 24, 1864.
33. Mindil to Parker, September 25, 1864, Regimental Letter Book, National Archives.
34. Stryker, *Records of Officers and Men of New Jersey in the Civil War*, pp. 967, 978, 985, 989, 993.
35. Newark *Daily Advertiser*, October 26, 1864.
36. Kennett, *Marching Through Georgia*, pp. 235–236.
37. Geary, *A Politician Goes to War*, p. 235.
38. William Lloyd to Mary Lloyd, October 23, 1864, Western Reserve Historical Society.
39. William Lloyd to Mary Lloyd, November 3, 1864, Western Reserve Historical Society.
40. *OR*, ser. I, vol. 44, pp. 295, 298.
41. William Lloyd to Mary Lloyd, November 11, 1864, Western Reserve Historical Society.
42. William Lloyd to Mary Lloyd, November 3, 1864, Western Reserve Historical Society; Georg Muller to parents, September 28, 1864, New Jersey Historical Society.
43. Castel, *Decision in the West*, p. 554.
44. Henry Hitchcock, *Marching with Sherman* (Lincoln: University of Nebraska Press, 1995), p. 19.
45. Kennett, *Marching Through Georgia*, p. 227.
46. Joseph T. Glatthaar, *The March to the Sea and Beyond* (New York: New York University Press, 1985), pp. 19–20, 23.
47. Castel, *Decision in the West*, p. 554.
48. Castel, *Decision in the West*, p. 554.
49. Kennett, *Marching Through Georgia*, pp. 232–233.
50. Hitchcock, *Marching with Sherman*, pp. 56–57.
51. Scaife, *The March to the Sea*, pp. 19–30, 39.
52. Kennett, *Marching Through Georgia*, p. 226.
53. Scaife, *The March to the Sea*, pp. 30, 35, 40.
54. Paterson *Daily Register*, January 3, 1865.
55. *OR*, ser. I, vol. 44, p. 269.
56. Paterson *Daily Register*, January 3, 1865.
57. *OR*, ser. I, vol. 44, p. 269.
58. Bull, *Soldiering*, pp. 177–179.
59. Glatthaar, *The March to the Sea and Beyond*, p. 103.
60. *OR*, ser. I, vol. 44, pp. 269, 298.
61. Paterson *Daily* Register, January 3, 1865; *OR*, ser. I, vol. 44, p. 298.
62. Kennett, *Marching Through Georgia*, p. 251.
63. Kennett, *Marching Through Georgia*, pp. 251–253.
64. Paterson *Daily Register*, January 3, 1865; *OR*, ser. I, vol. 44, p. 298.
65. *OR*, ser. I, vol. 44, p. 270.

66. *OR*, ser. I, vol. 44, pp. 270, 298.
67. Glatthaar, *The March to the Sea and Beyond*, pp. 137–138.
68. Paterson *Daily Register*, January 3, 1865.
69. *OR*, ser. I, vol. 44, p. 270.
70. Paterson *Daily Register*, January 3, 1865.
71. *OR*, ser. I, vol. 44, p. 270.
72. Kennett, *Marching Through Georgia*, p. 279.
73. Paterson *Daily Register*, January 3, 1865.
74. *OR*, ser. I, vol. 44, p. 270; Paterson *Daily Register*, January 3, 1865.
75. Paterson *Daily Register*, January 3, 1865.
76. *OR*, ser. I, vol. 44, pp. 270, 298.
77. Geary Court Martial Specifications, George Mindil Papers, New Jersey Historical Society; *Records of Officers and Men of New Jersey in the Civil War*, p. 968.
78. *OR*, ser. I, vol. 44, pp. 270, 298; Hitchcock, *Marching with Sherman*, p. 81.
79. Boyle, *Soldiers True*, p. 259.
80. Glatthaar, *The March to the Sea and Beyond*, pp. 52–53.
81. Boyle, *Soldiers True*, pp. 261–263.
82. Burke Davis, *Sherman's March* (New York: Random House, 1980), p. 33.
83. Paterson *Daily Register*, January 3, 1865.
84. *OR*, ser. I, vol. 44, p. 271.
85. Paterson *Daily Register*, January 3, 1865.
86. *OR*, ser. I, vol. 44, pp. 271, 298.
87. Conyngham, *Sherman's March Through the South*, p. 254.
88. Scaife, *The March to the Sea*, pp. 44, 50, 51–57.
89. *OR*, ser. I, vol. 44, p. 298.

Chapter X. "The destroying flame scarcely attracted our attention"

1. *OR*, ser. I, vol. 44, p. 527.
2. Saife, *The March to the Sea*, p. 40.
3. *OR*, ser. I, vol. 44, p. 533.
4. Kennett, *Marching Through Georgia*, pp. 244–245.
5. Glatthaar, *The March to the Sea and Beyond*, pp. 100–102.
6. Collins, *Memoirs of the 149th Regiment N.Y. Volunteer Infantry*, pp. 290–291; Glatthaar, *The March to the Sea and Beyond*, p. 103.
7. Collins, *Memoirs of the 149th Regiment N.Y. Volunteer Infantry*, p. 292; Kennett, *Marching Through Georgia*, p. 244.
8. Glatthaar, *The March to the Sea and Beyond*, pp. 104–105, 117.
9. Hitchcock, *Marching with Sherman*, p. 90.
10. *OR*, ser. I, vol. 44, p. 272; Paterson *Daily Register*, January 3, 1865.
11. *OR*, ser. I, vol. 44, pp. 272, 298.
12. *OR*, ser. I, vol. 44, p. 272; Scaife, *The March to the Sea*, p. 62.
13. *OR*, ser. I, vol. 44, pp. 272–273, 296, 298.
14. *OR*, ser. I, vol. 44, pp. 273–274; Hitchcock, *Marching with Sherman*, pp. 120, 126.
15. Scaife, *The March to the Sea*, pp. 64, 69–70, 85.
16. *OR*, ser. I, vol. 44, p. 274.
17. Stryker, *Records of Officers and Men of New Jersey in the Civil War*, p. 985.
18. Collins, *Memoirs of the 149th Regiment N.Y. Volunteer Infantry*, p. 296.
19. George Nichols, *The Story of the Great March from the Diary of a Staff Officer* (London: Samson Low, Son and Marston, 1865), p. 52.
20. *OR*, ser. I, vol. 44, pp. 274–275, 298.
21. Paterson *Daily Register*, January 3, 1865.
22. *OR*, ser. I, vol. 44, p. 275.
23. Paterson *Daily Register*, January 3, 1865.
24. *OR*, ser. I, vol. 44, pp. 276, 298.
25. Paterson *Daily Register*, January 3, 1865.
26. *OR*, ser. I, vol. 44, p. 276; Paterson *Daily Register*, January 3, 1865.
27. *OR*, ser. I, vol. 44, pp. 276–277, 296.
28. Glatthaar, *The March to the Sea and Beyond*, p. xiii.
29. Reid Mitchell, *The Vacant Chair* (New York: Oxford University Press, 1993), pp. 36, 101.
30. Linderman, *Embattled Courage*, pp. 234–236; McPherson, *For Cause and Comrades*, pp. 85–87.
31. Mitchell, *The Vacant Chair*, pp. 27, 36–37.
32. Glatthaar, *The March to the Sea and Beyond*, p. 130.
33. *OR*, ser. I, vol. 44, p. 13.
34. Bradley, *The Star Corps*, pp. 184, 207.
35. Glatthaar, *The March to the Sea and Beyond*, p. 72.
36. Glatthaar, *The March to the Sea and Beyond*, p. 121.
37. *OR*, ser. I, vol. 44, p. 298.
38. William Lloyd to Mary Lloyd, undated, Western Reserve Historical Society.
39. Paterson *Daily Register*, January 3, 1865.
40. Castel, *Decision in the West*, pp. 555–558.
41. Wiley Sword, *Embrace an Angry Wind* (New York: Harper Collins, 1992), pp. 296–298.
42. Foster, *New Jersey and the Rebellion*, pp. 857–858. According to Foster, Magee was an orderly to a General Van Cleve, who ordered Magee to take a regiment and attack the Confederates. Supposedly the Magee started with the 181st Ohio and after being driven back successfully completed the attack with the 174th Ohio. The account seems hard to believe, yet Magee did indeed receive the Medal of Honor.
43. Medal of Honor citation.
44. Davis, *Sherman's March*, pp. 96–98.
45. *OR*, ser. I, vol. 44, p. 10.
46. Davis, *Sherman's March*, p. 103.
47. Scaife, *The March to the Sea*, pp. 91–97.
48. *OR*, ser. I, vol. 44, pp. 10–11.
49. *OR*, ser. I, vol. 44, pp. 277–278.
50. Bull, *Soldiering*, pp. 197–198.
51. *OR*, ser. I, vol. 44, p. 278.
52. Paterson *Daily Register*, January 3, 1865.
53. *OR*, ser. I, vol. 44, pp. 274, 708.
54. William Lloyd to Mary Lloyd, December 17, 1864, Western Reserve Historical Society.
55. *OR*, ser. I, vol. 44, p. 279.
56. Scaife, *The March to the Sea*, p. 109.

57. *OR*, ser. I, vol. 44, p. 279.
58. *OR*, ser. I, vol. 44, pp. 279–280, 298, 309.
59. *OR*, ser. I, vol. 44, pp. 783, 809.

Chapter XI. "There will be no rest"

1. Davis, *Sherman's March*, p. 122.
2. Bull, *Soldiering*, pp. 201–202.
3. William Lloyd to Mary Lloyd, December 26, 1864, Western Reserve Historical Society.
4. William Lloyd to Mary Lloyd, December 26, 1864, Western Reserve Historical Society.
5. Sussex *Register*, January 15, 1865.
6. William Lloyd to Mary Lloyd, December 26, 1864, Western Reserve Historical Society.
7. Sussex *Register*, January 15, 1865.
8. Davis, *Sherman's March*, p. 128.
9. Conyngham, *Sherman's March Through the South*, pp. 295–299.
10. Boyle, *Soldiers True*, p. 273.
11. Davis, *Sherman's March*, p. 128.
12. William Lloyd to Mary Lloyd, December 26, 1864, Western Reserve Historical Society.
13. Davis, *Sherman's March*, p. 127.
14. Georg Muller to parents, January 25, 1865, New Jersey Historical Society.
15. Stryker, *Records of Officers and Men of New Jersey in the Civil War*, pp. 967, 975, 985, 993, and 997.
16. William Lloyd to Mary Lloyd, December 28, 1864, Western Reserve Historical Society.
17. William Lloyd to Mary Lloyd, January 1, 1865, Western Reserve Historical Society.
18. William Lloyd to Mary Lloyd, January 10, 1865, Western Reserve Historical Society.
19. George Mindil Diary, New Jersey Historical Society.
20. William Lloyd to Mary Lloyd, January 22, 1865, Western Reserve Historical Society.
21. George Mindil Diary, New Jersey Historical Society.
22. *OR*, ser. I, vol. 44, p. 809.
23. Davis, *Sherman's March*, pp. 108–109, 129.
24. John G. Barrett, *Sherman's March Through the Carolinas* (Chapel Hill: The University of North Carolina Press, 1956), pp. 31, 35–38.
25. Bradley, *The Star Corps*, p. 246.
26. Barrett, *Sherman's March Through the Carolinas*, p. 40.
27. Collins, *Memoirs of the 149th Regiment N.Y. Volunteer Infantry*, p. 304.
28. *OR*, ser. I, vol. 47, pt. 1, p. 169; Barrett, *Sherman's March Through the Carolinas*, p. 35.
29. Barrett, *Sherman's March Through the Carolinas*, pp. 39–41.
30. Barrett, *Sherman's March Through the Carolinas*, pp. 48–50.
31. *OR*, ser. I. vol. 47, pt. 1, pp. 17, 581.
32. *OR*, ser. I, vol. 47, pt. 1, p. 681.
33. Boyle, *Soldiers True*, p. 276.
34. Georg Muller to parents, January 25, 1865, New Jersey Historical Society.
35. *OR*, ser. I, vol. 47, pt. 1, pp. 681–682.
36. *OR*, ser. I, vol. 47, pt. 1, p. 682; Boyle, *Soldiers True*, p. 276.
37. Nathaniel Bray Diary, John W. Kuhl Collection.
38. *OR*, ser. I, vol. 47, pt. 1, p. 682; George Mindil Diary, New Jersey Historical Society.
39. Nathaniel Bray Diary, John W. Kuhl Collection.
40. *OR*, ser. I, vol. 47, pt. 1, p. 682.
41. Barrett, *Sherman's March Through the Carolinas*, pp. 35–36.
42. *OR*, ser. I, vol. 47, pt. 1, pp. 682, 731; Nathaniel Bray Diary, John W. Kuhl Collection.
43. Paterson *Daily Register*, January 3, 1865.
44. *OR*, ser. I, vol. 47, pt. 1, pp. 426, 682.
45. Newark *Daily Advertiser*, February 14, 1865.
46. Stryker, *Records of Officers and Men of New Jersey in the Civil War*, pp. 963, 971, 975, 979, 982.
47. Sussex *Register*, February 17, 1865.
48. George Mindil Diary, New Jersey Historical Society.
49. Nathaniel Bray Diary, John W. Kuhl Collection.
50. George Mindil Diary, New Jersey Historical Society; *OR*, ser. I, vol. 47, pt. 1, p. 682.
51. *OR*, ser. I, vol. 47, pt. 1, pp. 682, 734; Nathaniel Bray Diary, John W. Kuhl Collection.
52. Collins, *Memoirs of the 149th Regiment N.Y. Volunteer Infantry*, p. 303.
53. Bull, *Soldiering*, p. 207; Nathaniel Bray Diary, John W. Kuhl Collection.
54. *OR*, ser. I, vol. 47, pt. 1, pp. 682–683.
55. *OR*, ser. I, vol. 47, pt. 1, p. 683.
56. George Mindil Diary, New Jersey Historical Society.
57. *OR*, ser. I, vol. 47, pt. 1, pp. 683, 731.
58. George Mindil Diary, New Jersey Historical Society.
59. *OR*, ser. I, vol. 47, pt. 1, p. 683.
60. *OR*, ser. I, vol. 47, pt. 1, pp. 683, 734.
61. Bull, *Soldiering*, p. 209; Nathaniel Bray Diary, John W. Kuhl Collection.
62. *OR*, ser. I, vol. 47, pt. 1, p. 684.
63. Bull, *Soldiering*, p. 210.
64. *OR*, ser. I, vol. 47, pt. 1, pp. 684, 734.
65. Barrett, *Sherman's March Through the Carolinas*, pp. 51–52.
66. *OR*, ser. I, vol. 47, pt. 1, pp. 684–685, 734; Nathaniel Bray Diary, John W. Kuhl Collection.
67. Barrett, *Sherman's March Through the Carolinas*, pp. 60–62.
68. *OR*, ser. I, vol. 47, pt. 1, p. 21.
69. *OR*, ser. I, vol. 47, pt. 1, pp. 686, 734.
70. Newark *Daily Advertiser*, February 16, 1865.
71. Barrett, *Sherman's March Through the Carolinas*, pp. 71–74.

Chapter XII. "Haul up, stuck in the mud"

1. *OR*, ser. I, vol. 47, pt. 1, pp. 21, 686–688, 734; Nathaniel Bray Diary, John Kuhl Collection.
2. *OR*, ser. I, vol. 47, pt. 1, pp. 22, 688; Barrett,

Sherman's March Through the Carolinas, pp. 98–99, 101.
    3. *OR*, ser. I, vol. 47, pt. 1, p. 688.
    4. Barrett, *Sherman's March Through the Carolinas*, p. 99.
    5. *OR*, ser. I, vol. 47, pt. 1, p. 688, 734; Boyle, *Soldiers True*, p. 283.
    6. *OR*, ser. I, vol. 47, pt. 1, p. 688.
    7. Barrett, *Sherman's March Through the Carolinas*, pp. 99–100.
    8. *OR*, ser. I, vol. 47, pt. 1, pp. 688, 734.
    9. Conyngham, *Sherman's March Through the South*, pp. 352–353.
    10. Barrett, *Sherman's March Through the Carolinas*, pp. 100–101.
    11. *OR*, ser. I, vol. 47, pt. 1, pp. 688–689, 734.
    12. Stryker, *Records of Officers and Men of New Jersey in the Civil War*, pp. 978–979.
    13. Barrett, *Sherman's March Through the Carolinas*, pp. 107, 111–113.
    14. *OR*, ser. I. vol. 47, pt. 1, p. 689.
    15. Collins, *Memoirs of the 149th Regiment N.Y. Volunteer Infantry*, p. 316.
    16. *OR*, ser. I, vol. 47, pt. 1, pp. 689, 735.
    17. *OR*, ser. I, vol. 47, pt. 1, p. 689; Nathaniel Bray Diary, John W. Kuhl Collection.
    18. Barrett, *Sherman's March Through the Carolinas*, p. 106.
    19. *OR*, ser. I. vol. 47, pt. 1, p. 689.
    20. George Mindil Diary, New Jersey Historical Society.
    21. *OR*, ser. I. vol. 47, pt. 1, pp. 23, 427, 690.
    22. Barrett, *Sherman's March Through the Carolinas*, pp. 120–121.
    23. *OR*, ser. I, vol. 47, pt. 1, pp. 690, 735; Nathaniel Bray Diary, John W. Kuhl Collection.
    24. *OR*, ser. I, vol. 47, pt. 1, pp. 690, 735; Nathaniel Bray Diary, John W. Kuhl Collection.
    25. Bull, *Soldiering*, pp. 221–222.
    26. *OR*, ser. I, vol. 47, pt. 1, pp. 585, 690, 735.
    27. Bull, *Soldiering*, p. 223; Nathaniel Bray Diary, John W. Kuhl Collection.
    28. *OR*, ser. I, vol. 47, pt. 1, pp. 585, 690, 735; Nathaniel Bray Diary, John W. Kuhl Collection.
    29. Bull, *Soldiering*, p. 223.
    30. *OR*, ser. I, vol. 47, pt. 1, pp. 691, 735.
    31. *OR*, ser. I, vol. 47, pt. 1, pp. 691, 735; Nathaniel Bray Diary, John W. Kuhl Collection.
    32. Collins, *Memoirs of the 149th Regiment N.Y. Volunteer Infantry*, pp. 308–309.
    33. Barrett, *Sherman's March Through the Carolinas*, pp. 139–141.
    34. Barrett, *Sherman's March Through the Carolinas*, pp. 135–136.
    35. William Lloyd to Mary Lloyd, March 14, 1865, Western Reserve Historical Society.
    36. Newark *Daily Advertiser*, March 14, 1865.
    37. Barrett, *Sherman's March Through the Carolinas*, p. 137.
    38. Collins, *Memoirs of the 149th Regiment N.Y. Volunteer Infantry*, p. 309.
    39. Barrett, *Sherman's March Through the Carolinas*, p. 136.
    40. Bull, *Soldiering*, pp. 224–225.
    41. *OR*, ser. I, vol. 47, pt. 1, pp. 691, 735; Nathaniel Bray Diary, John W. Kuhl Collection.
    42. *OR*, ser. I, vol. 47, pt. 1, p. 735.
    43. Barrett, *Sherman's March Through the Carolinas*, pp. 147–150.
    44. *OR*, ser. I, vol. 47, pt. 1, p. 691.
    45. Barrett, *Sherman's March Through the Carolinas*, pp. 148–149.
    46. *OR*, ser. I, vol. 47, pt. 1, pp. 691–692, 732, 735.
    47. Barrett, *Sherman's March Through the Carolinas*, pp. 154–158.
    48. *OR*, ser. I, vol. 47, pt. 1, pp. 692–693, 735.
    49. *OR*, ser. I, vol. 47, pt. 1, p. 693.
    50. Barrett, *Sherman's March Through the Carolinas*, p. 159.
    51. Barrett, *Sherman's March Through the Carolinas*, pp. 160–167, 176–177.
    52. *OR*, ser. I, vol. 47, pt. 1, pp. 693–694, 735; Georg Muller to parents, April 8, 1865, New Jersey Historical Society.
    53. Barrett, *Sherman's March Through the Carolinas*, pp. 178–180.
    54. *OR*, ser. I, vol. 47, pt. 1, pp. 732–733, 735.
    55. Barrett, *Sherman's March Through the Carolinas*, pp. 181, 184; Davis, *Sherman's March*, p. 241.
    56. *OR*, ser. I, vol. 47, pt. 1, p. 694.
    57. Jacob D. Cox, *Sherman's March to the Sea* (New York: Da Capo Press, 1882, 1994), p. 211.
    58. *OR*, ser. I, vol. 47, pt. 1, pp. 729, 733, 735.
    59. Barrett, *Sherman's March to the Sea*, pp. 186–187.
    60. *OR*, ser. I, vol. 47, pt. 1, pp. 695, 730, 735; Nathaniel Bray Diary, John W. Kuhl Collection.
    61. *OR*, ser. I, vol. 47, pt. 1, pp. 189, 588, 697–698, 733.
    62. *OR*, ser. I, vol. 47, pt. 1, p. 735.
    63. Georg Muller to parents, April 8, 1865, New Jersey Historical Society.
    64. Barrett, *Sherman's March Through the Carolinas*, preface.
    65. Collins, *Memoirs of the 149th Regiment N.Y. Volunteer Infantry*, p. 307.

Chapter XIII. "Cries of joyful recognition"

    1. Barrett, *Sherman's March Through the Carolinas*, pp. 190, 192.
    2. *OR*, ser. I, vol. 47, pt. 1, p. 730.
    3. Mindil to father, March 27, 1865, New Jersey Historical Society.
    4. Geary to Stanton, April 9, 1865, George Mindil papers, New Jersey Historical Society.
    5. Stryker, *Records of Officers and Men of New Jersey in the Civil War*, pp. 959–1003.
    6. Fouratt to Wood, March 29, 1865, Regimental Letter Book, National Archives.
    7. Mindil to state adjutant, April 4, 1865, New Jersey State Archives.
    8. Stryker, *Records of Officers and Men of New Jersey in the Civil War*, pp. 963, 971, 979, 993.

9. Georg Muller to parents, April 8, 1865, New Jersey Historical Society.
10. Sussex *Register*, March 24, 1865.
11. *OR*, ser. I, vol. 47, pt. 1, p. 28.
12. Barrett, *Sherman's March Through the Carolinas*, pp. 194–196.
13. Barrett, *Sherman's March Through the Carolinas*, pp. 197–198.
14. *OR*, ser. I, vol. 47, pt. 1, p. 30; Barrett, *Sherman's March Through the Carolinas*, p. 199.
15. Georg Muller to parents, April 8, 1865, New Jersey Historical Society.
16. George Mindil Diary, New Jersey Historical Society.
17. *OR*, ser. I, vol. 47, pt. 1, pp. 699, 736; Nathaniel Bray Diary, John W. Kuhl Collection; Stryker, *Records of Officers and Men of New Jersey in the Civil War*, p. 959.
18. Newark *Daily Advertiser*, April 10, 1865.
19. Newark *Daily Journal*, April 10, 1865.
20. Paterson *Daily Press*, April 10, 1865.
21. Sussex *Register*, April 14, 1865.
22. Barrett, *Sherman's March Through the Carolinas*, pp. 200–203.
23. *OR*, ser. I, vol. 47, pt. 1, p. 736.
24. Georg Muller to parents, April 29, 1865, New Jersey Historical Society.
25. *OR*, ser. I, vol. 47, pt. 1, p. 700, 736.
26. Barrett, *Sherman's March Through the Carolinas*, p. 207.
27. *OR*, ser. I, vol. 47, pt. 1, p. 700.
28. Boyle, *Soldiers True*, pp. 297–298.
29. Barrett, *Sherman's March Through the Carolinas*, pp. 209–210.
30. *OR*, ser. I, vol. 47, pt. 1, pp. 700, 736: Nathaniel Bray Diary, John W. Kuhl Collection.
31. Barrett, *Sherman's March Through the Carolinas*, p. 226.
32. John Toffey to parents, April 17, 1865; John Toffey to grandmother, April 20, 1865, Rutgers University Special Collections.
33. *OR*, ser. I, vol. 47, pt. 1, p. 700.
34. Boyle, *Soldiers True*, p. 302.
35. Barrett, *Sherman's March Through the Carolinas*, pp. 231–232, 235–236; Nathaniel Bray Diary, John W. Kuhl Collection.
36. Barrett, *Sherman's March Through the Carolinas*, pp. 233, 237–244.
37. Barrett, *Sherman's March Through the Carolinas*, pp. 252, 254–255.
38. William Lloyd to Mary Lloyd, April 21, 1865, Western Reserve Historical Society.
39. Mindil to Stockton, April 23, 1865, New Jersey State Archives.
40. Barrett, *Sherman's March Through the Carolinas*, pp. 267–268.
41. *OR*, ser. I, vol. 47, pt. 1, pp. 700, 736.
42. Barrett, *Sherman's March Through the Carolinas*, pp. 267–272.
43. *OR*, ser. I, vol. 47, pt. 1, p. 736.
44. Sussex *Register*, May 12, 1865.
45. Georg Muller to parents, April 29, 1865, New Jersey Historical Society.
46. William Lloyd to Mary Lloyd, April 29, 1865, Western Reserve Historical Society.
47. *OR*, ser. I, vol. 47, pt. 1, p. 700.
48. *OR*, ser. I, vol. 47, pt. 1, pp. 700–702, 736; Nathaniel Bray Diary, John W. Kuhl Collection.
49. Davis, *Sherman's March*, p. 280.
50. Collins, *Memoirs of the 149th Regiment N.Y. Volunteer Infantry*, p. 327.
51. *OR*, ser. I, vol. 47, pt. 1, p. 736.
52. *OR*, ser. I, vol. 47, pt. 1, p. 702.
53. Newark *Daily Advertiser*, May 19, 1865.
54. Newark *Daily Advertiser*, May 22, 1865.
55. Davis, *Sherman's March*, p. 289; Collins, *Memoirs of the 149th Regiment N.Y. Volunteer Infantry*, p. 329.
56. Newark *Daily Advertiser*, May 25, 1865.
57. Boyle, *Soldiers True*, p. 309.
58. Davis, *Sherman's March*, pp. 290–293.
59. Newark *Daily Advertiser*, May 25, 1865.
60. Davis, *Sherman's March*, p. 292; Newark *Daily Advertiser*, May 25, 1865, and June 3, 1865.
61. Mindil to Stockton, May 29, 1865, New Jersey State Archives.
62. Mindil to Thomas, May 29, 1865, Regimental Letter Book, National Archives.
63. William Lloyd to Mary Lloyd, June 10, 1865, Western Reserve Historical Society.
64. Newark *Daily Advertiser*, June 3, 1865.
65. Georg Muller to parents, June 8, 1865, New Jersey Historical Society.
66. William Lloyd to Mary Lloyd, June 13, 1865, Western Reserve Historical Society.
67. Stryker, *Records of Officers and Men of New Jersey in the Civil War*, pp. 959–1003.
68. Fouratt to Skipper, July 6, 1865, Regimental Letter Book, National Archives; Stryker, *Records of Officers and Men of New Jersey in the Civil War*, pp. 959–1003.
69. William Lloyd to Mary Lloyd, June 27, 1865, Western Reserve Historical Society.
70. Newark *Daily Advertiser*, June 6, 1865; Newark *Daily Journal*, June 26, 1865.
71. Sussex *Register*, July 7, 1865.
72. Stryker, *Records of Officers and Men of New Jersey in the Civil War*, pp. 967, 971, 975, 985 and 989.
73. Newark *Daily Journal*, July 14, 1865.
74. John Toffey to grandmother, July 11, 1865, Rutgers University Special Collections.
75. Newark *Daily Advertiser*, July 22, 1865; Newark *Daily Journal*, July 22, 1865.
76. Newark *Daily Advertiser*, July 22, 1865.
77. Newark *Daily Advertiser*, July 22, 1865; Newark *Daily Journal*, July 22, 1865.
78. Newark *Daily Journal*, July 24, 1865.
79. Hudson County *Democrat*, July 29, 1865.
80. Paterson *Daily Press*, August 2, 1865, August 7, 1865, and August 10, 1865.
81. Fox, *Regimental Losses in the Civil War*, pp. 482–483.
82. McPherson, *For Cause and Comrades*, pp. 18–19, 85–86, 104, 110–112, 116, 118.
83. Linderman, *Embattled Courage*, pp. 17–18, 23.

84. McPherson, *For Cause and Comrades*, pp. 77, 79.
85. Mitchell, *The Vacant Chair*, pp. 25–27.
86. Newark *Daily Advertiser*, September 28, 1863.
87. Paterson *Daily Press*, October 23, 1863; Paterson *Daily Register*, October 23, 1863; Newark *Daily Mercury*, October 17, 1863.
88. Hudson County *Democrat*, October 31, 1863.
89. Newark *Daily Advertiser*, January 7, 1864, and September 23, 1864.
90. Sussex *Register*, August 5, 1864, February 17, 1865, and May 12, 1865.
91. McPherson, *For Cause and Comrades*, p. 118.
92. Paterson *Daily Press*, June 4, 1864.
93. Georg Muller, February 28, 1864, April 17, 1864, July 29, 1864, and August 5, 1864, New Jersey Historical Society.
94. William Lloyd to Mary Lloyd, January 9, 1864, May 21, 1864, June 9 and June 21, 1864, Western Reserve Historical Society.
95. McPherson, *For Cause and Comrades*, p. 9.
96. Georg Muller to parents, June 9, 1864, July 29, 1864, and April 8, 1865, New Jersey Historical Society.
97. William Lloyd to Mary Lloyd, October 3 or 9, 1863, October 23, 1864, December 26 and 27, 1864, Western Reserve Historical Society.
98. James McPherson, *Drawn with the Sword*, (New York: Oxford University Press, 1996), pp. 63–65.
99. Davis, *Sherman's March*, p. 261.
100. Hitchcock, *Marching with Sherman*, p. 314.
101. Mitchell, *The Vacant Chair*, pp. 153, 159.

Bibliography

PERIODICALS

Hightstown *Gazette*
Hudson County *Democrat*
Jersey City *American Standard*
Newark *Daily Advertiser*
Newark *Daily Journal*
Newark *Daily Mercury*
Paterson *Daily Press*
Paterson *Daily Register*
Somerset *Messenger*
Sussex *Register*
Verona Cedar Grove *Times*

BOOKS

Adams, George Washington. *Doctors in Blue*. New York: Henry Schuman, Inc., 1952.
Ambrose, Stephen. *Citizen Soldiers*. New York: Simon and Schuster, 1997.
Anderson, William M. *They Died to Make Men Free: A History of the 19th Michigan Infantry*. Dayton, Ohio: Morningside Press, 1994.
Barrett, John G. *Sherman's March Through the Carolinas*. Chapel Hill: The University of North Carolina Press, 1956.
Baumgartner, Richard A., and Larry Strayer. *Echoes of Battle: The Atlanta Campaign*. Huntington, WV: Blue Acorn Press, 1991.
_____. *Echoes of Battle: The Struggle for Chattanooga*. Huntington, WV: Blue Acorn Press, 1996.
Bernstein, Iver. *The New York Draft Riots*. New York: Oxford University Press, 1990.
Bilby, Joseph G., and William C. Goble. *Remember You Are Jerseymen*. Hightstown, N.J.: Longstreet House, 1998.
Billings, John D. *Hardtack and Coffee: The Unwritten Story of Army Life*. Lincoln: University of Nebraska Press, 1983.
Blair, William Alan, ed. *A Politician Goes to War: The Civil War Letters of John White Geary*. University Park: Pennsylvania State Press, 1995.
Blue and Gray magazine. *History and Tour Book of the Atlanta Campaign*. 1976.
Bradley, G. S. *The Star Corps*. Milwaukee, Wisconsin: Jeremain and Brightman, 1865.
Boyle, John. *Soldiers True*. New York: Eaton and Mains, 1903.
Bull, Rice. *Soldiering: The Civil War Diary of Rice C. Bull*. Novato, California: Presidio Press, 1977.
Castel, Albert. *Decision in the West*. Lawrence: University of Kansas Press, 1992.
Collins, George K. *Memoirs of the 149th Regiment N.Y. Volunteer Infantry*. Hamilton, N.Y.: Edmonston Publishing, Inc., 1995.
Conyngham, Daniel P. *Sherman's March Through the South*. New York: Sheldon and Co., 1865.

Cox, Jacob. *Sherman's Battle for Atlanta.* New York: DaCapo Press, 1994.
_____. *Sherman's March to the Sea.* New York: DaCapo Press, 1994
Cozzens, Peter. *The Shipwreck of Their Hopes,* Urbana and Chicago: University of Illinois Press, 1994.
Cunningham, John T. *Newark.* 3rd Edition. Newark, N.J.: New Jersey Historical Society, 2002.
Davis, Burke. *Sherman's March.* New York: Random House, 1980.
Dunkelman, Mark H., and Michael J. Winey. *The Hardtack Regiment: An Illustrated History of the 154th New York State Volunteer Infantry.* East Brunswick, N.J.: Associated University Press, 1981.
Foote, Shelby. *The Civil War: A Narrative.* 3 vols. New York: Random House, 1974.
Foster, John Y. *New Jersey and the Rebellion: A History of the Services of the Troops and People of New Jersey in Aid of the Union Cause.* Newark, N.J.: Dennis and Company, 1868.
Fox, William F. *Regimental Losses in the American Civil War 1861–65.* Albany, N.Y.: Brandon Printing Company, 1898.
Futch, Ovid. *History of Andersonville Prison.* Gainesville: University of Florida Press, 1968.
Gillette, William. *Jersey Blue: Civil War Politics in New Jersey, 1854–1865.* New Brunswick, N.J.: Rutgers University Press, 1995.
Glatthaar, Joseph T. *The March to the Sea and Beyond.* New York: New York University Press, 1985.
Hess, Earl J. *The Union Soldier in Combat.* Lawrence: University of Kansas Press, 1997.
Hitchcock, Henry. *Marching with Sherman.* Lincoln: University of Nebraska Press, 1995.
Horowitz, Tony. *Confederates in the Attic: Dispatches from the Unfinished Civil War.* New York: Pantheon Books, 1998.
Kennett, Lee. *Marching Through Georgia.* New York: Harper Collins, 1995.
Linderman, Gerald F. *Embattled Courage: The Experience of Combat in the American Civil War.* New York: The Free Press, 1987.
Lonn, Ella. *Desertion During the Civil War.* New York: The Century Company, 1928.
McPherson, James. *Battle Cry of Freedom.* New York: Oxford University Press, 1988.
_____. *Drawn with the Sword.* New York: Oxford University Press, 1996.
_____. *For Cause and Comrades.* New York: Oxford University Press, 1997.
Mitchell, Reid. *The Vacant Chair.* New York: Oxford University Press, 1993.
Murdock, Eugene. *One Million Men: The Civil War Draft in the North.* Madison: The State Historical Society of Wisconsin, 1971.
Nichols, George. *The Story of the Great March from the Diary of a Staff Officer.* London: Samson Low, Son and Marston, 1865.
Pullen, John J. *A Shower of Stars.* Mechanicsburg, Pennsylvania: Stackpole Books, 1997.
_____. *The Twentieth Maine.* Dayton, Ohio. Morningside House, 1991.
Scaife, William A. *The March to the Sea.* Saline, Michigan: McNaughton and Gunn, Inc., 1993.
Siegel, Alan A. *For the Glory of the Union: Myth, Reality, and the Media in Civil War New Jersey.* Cranbury, N.J.: Fairleigh Dickinson University Press, 1984.
Stryker, William S. *Records of Officers and Men of New Jersey in the Civil War, 1861–1865, Compiled in the Office of the Adjutant General.* 2 vols. Trenton, N.J.: John L. Murphy, Steam Book and Job Printer, 1876.
Sword, Wiley. *Embrace an Angry Wind.* New York: Harper Collins, 1992.
_____. *Mountains Touched by Fire.* New York: St. Martin's Press, 1995.
United States Government. *The War of the Rebellion: A Compilation of the Official Records of the Union and Confederate Armies.* 128 vols. Washington, D.C., 1880–1901.

Articles and Manuscripts

David Peloubet Diary. John Toffey papers. Rutgers University Library Special Collections.
Department of State, New Jersey State Archives at Trenton, N.J. Record Group: Department of Defense, Subgroup: Adjutant General's Office (Civil War) Series, Regimental Records, Thirty-third New Jersey.
Fenner Family Papers, Manuscript #475. Camden County Historical Society.
Georg Muller Papers. New Jersey Historical Society.

George Metcalf Autobiography. GAC files. Harrisburg Civil War Roundtable Collection. United States Army Military History Institute.
George Rolfe Diary. Chickamauga and Chattanooga National Military Park Library.
George W. Mindil Papers. New Jersey Historical Society.
John J. Toffey papers. Rutgers University Library Special Collections.
Martin Bushnell Diary. Chickamauga and Chattanooga National Military Park Library.
Nathaniel Bray Diary. John W. Kuhl Collection.
Pierson, Stephen. "From Chattanooga to Atlanta in 1864 — A Personal Reminiscence." *Proceedings of the New Jersey Historical Society*. Vol. 16. 1931.
Stone, Henry. "Part 1: Opening of the Atlanta Campaign." In *The Atlanta Papers*, comp. Sidney C. Kerksis. Dayton, Ohio: Press of the Morningside Bookshop, 1980.
Thirty-third New Jersey File. Chickamauga and Chattanooga National Military Park Library.
Thirty-third New Jersey Records of Events, Record Group 94, Records of the Adjutant General's Office, 1780s–1917. National Archives.
Thirty-third New Jersey Regimental Letter Book, Record Group 94, Records of the Adjutant General's Office, 1780s–1917. National Archives.
William Lambert Memorial Service. United States Army Military History Institute.
William Lloyd Papers. Western Reserve Historical Society. William P. Palmer Collection of Civil War Manuscripts, Mss. 3947.

Index

Numbers in ***bold italics*** indicate illustrations.

Abbeville Railroad 199
Abernathy, John 130, 225
Acworth, Georgia 108, 110, 112–13
Adairsville, Georgia 99–100
Adams, James 185
"Adelphia" 226
Alabama Regiments: 27th 130, 225
Alexandria, Virginia 21, 221
Algood, Daniel ***162***
Allatoona, Georgia 101, 103, 108, 110, 154
Alston, South Carolina 196
Andersonville 55, 113, 131–35, 141, 154
Anys, Charles 67, 131, 134
Anys, John 67
Army of Georgia 215
Army of Tennessee (Confederate) 78, 154, 178, 188
Army of the Cumberland 25, 39, 41, 43, 68, 78, 79, 81, 103, 108, 113, 121, 124–25, 142
Army of the Ohio 39, 78, 81, 108, 110, 124, 142, 147, 215
Army of the Potomac 22–23, 26–27, 72, 76, 158, 215
Army of the Tennessee 39, 78, 81, 90, 124, 137, 140–41, 147, 215
Aspen, Nicholas ***18***
Athens, Tennessee 51, 54
Atkinson's Plantation, North Carolina 216
Atlanta 122–23, 148, 150, 153, 157–59
Atlanta, Battle of 139
Atlanta Campaign 76–79, 90–91, 99–2, 112–14, 121–25, 137, 142–43, 146, 148
Augur, Christopher 218
Augusta, Georgia 155, 160–61, 187–88
Aversboro, Battle of 209

Babcock, Hiram 66
Baker's Creek, Georgia 172
Baltimore and Ohio Railroad 26
Bark Camp Creek 172
Barnum, Henry 176
Barrett, Edward 223
Barry, William 66
Bartlett, Henry 25, 30, 45, ***82***, 88
Bartlett, Japhet 203
Battle Creek, Tennessee 30–34, 36
Beaufort, South Carolina 188
Beaver Creek, North Carolina 207
Beech Branch, South Carolina 192
Begbie, George 74
Bell, Alvan 18
Bellaire, Ohio 27
Bentonville, North Carolina 210–11
Bergen, Alfred ***23***
Beyer, George 88
Biegelow, Moses 9
Big Black Creek, South Carolina 204
Big Buffalo Creek, South Carolina 204
Big Cohera Creek, North Carolina 211

Big Horse Creek, Georgia 173
Big Salkehatchie Creek, South Carolina 193
Bimble, Herman 155
Black River, Georgia 180
Blacks (Negroes) 165
Blackville, South Carolina 193, ***194***
Bladensburg, Maryland 223
Bligh, James 57
Blue Spring, Georgia 164
Boggs, William 31, ***38***, 42–43, 58, 61
Booth, John Wilkes 218
Bounties 9, 11, 15–16
Boyd's Trail, Georgia 91
Boyle, John Richards 1
Braan, John 67, 155
Braan, Martin 67, 131
Bradley, Mark 88
Bragg, Braxton 26, 39, 41, 43, 49, 78, 210
Bray, Nathaniel 9, 72, 74, 96, 184, 191, 193, ***196***, 198–99, 204, 206–7, 209, 214, 216, 218–21, 227
Brehm, Charles 66
Bridgeport, Alabama 27, 29–31, 33, 69
Broad River, South Carolina 196, 198–99
Brogan, Charles 155
Brown, Walter 88
Brown's Ferry, Tennessee 33, 37, 39–41, 43
Brush Mountain, Georgia 113
Bryant's Farm, Georgia 99
Buck Head Church, Georgia 172

273

Buck Head Creek, Georgia 172
Buckhead, Georgia 125
Buckhead Station, Georgia 164
Buffalo Creek, Georgia 170, 172
Buffalo Creek, South Carolina 206
Buford's Bridge, South Carolina 193
Bull Run, Virginia 22
"Bummers" 172, 177
Bundy's Battery 130
Burke, John 72
Burkgard, Frederick 215
Burnside, Ambrose 39, 49–50, 53
Burnt Hickory, Georgia 103
Bushbeck, Adolphus 45–46, 72, 82
Butler, James 215
Butterfield, Daniel 92–93
Buzzard's Roost, Georgia 79

Cadmus, Theodore 134–35, 221
Caitlan 19
Caldwell, Thomas 185
Calhoun, Tennessee 51
Camden, New Jersey 11
Camp Frelinghuysen 12–13, 15–16, 19, 227
Candy, Charles 126, 130
Cape Fear River, North Carolina 187, 205, 207–9
Carolina Campaign 186–88, 196–97, 203, 205, 207–12
Cassville, Georgia 99–100, 102
Catawba River, South Carolina **200**–3
Catlett's Station, Virginia 24–26, 221
Centreville, Virginia 22
Chancellorsville Battle of 111, 221
Charleston, South Carolina 155, 160, 185, 187
Charleston, Tennessee 50, 54
Charleston & Augusta Railroad 188
Charlotte, North Carolina 225
Chattachoochee River, Georgia 101, 103, 113, 118, 121–24, 132, 143, 146, 148, 154
Chattanooga, Tennessee 19, 29–31, 37, 49–50, 54, 57, 61, 69, 76, 143, 146, 154–55, 159
Chattanooga & Cleveland Railroad 37
Chattanooga Campaign 26–27, 33, 37, 39–41, 43–46, 48–49
Chattanooga Valley, Tennessee 37
Cheraw, South Carolina 200, 204–5
Chesterfield Courthouse South Carolina 204
Chickamauga, Battle of 26, 37, 39, 79, 154

Chickamauga Creek 49
Chickamauga Station 43, 49
Childs, Francis **60**
Citico Creek 42, 45, 57, 61, 67–68
Civil War Combat 83–85, 93
Clark, Henry 110
Clark, John 19
Clerburne, Patrick 41, 43, 45, 48, 50
Cleveland, Tennessee 50, 54, 57
Clyburn's Store, South Carolina 203
Coburn, John 148
Cochrane, William 69, **114**, 116
Columbia, South Carolina 187–88, 194, 196–97
Columbus, Georgia 155
Confederacy, Final Surrender 215, 219–20
Congaree Creek, South Carolina 195
Congaree River, South Carolina 196
Conklin, Ezra 131
Conklin, George 89
Connasauga River, Georgia 99
Connecticut Regiments, 20th 91
Connor, Jeremiah 155
Coosawattee River, Georgia 99
Coosawhatchie Swamp, South Carolina 192
Corduroying 173, 189
Corput's Battery 46, 48, 94–98
Courtois, Charles 15, **24**, 30, 59, 116, 155, 219, 229
Couse, Joseph **28**, 72
Crock, Charles 227
Crooked Creek, Georgia 165
Crooked Run, Georgia 173
Cunningham, Bartholomew 131

Dahlgren, John 180–81
Daily, Patrick 74
Dallas, Georgia 101–4
Dalton, Georgia 78, 81
Dandelion 180
Daniels, Morgan **153**
Darby's Farm, Georgia 117
Davidson 208
Davis, Jefferson 39, 78, 124, 154
Davis, Jefferson C. 49
Davis Ford, Tennessee 51, 53–54
Davisborough, Georgia 170–71
Dawson, Elsi **44**
Dease, Dennis **163**
Decatur, Georgia 161
DeCosta, Henry 89
Deegan, James **85**
Delaney, Patrick 36
DeMolay 20–21
Denham's Tannery, Georgia 164–65
Dennis Mill, Georgia 165
Dennis Station, Georgia 165

Denniston, Martin 80, 84, 95–97, 230
Desertion 15–16, 22, 24, 27, 152–53
Deshler, C.D. 136–37
Disease 29, 66, 102, 118, 123, 133, 140, 169, 212–13
Dodge, Jeremiah 55, 134–35
Donald, James 144, 172
Donnelly, Patrick 96
Downs, Charles **61**, 74
Draft 7–9, 150–53
Drake, Britton 97
Drake, Theodore 36
Drowning Creek, North Carolina 206
Dry Creek, Georgia 172
Dudley Buck 20, 29
Dug Gap, Battle of **80**, 82–83, 86–88
Duncan's Bridge, South Carolina 193
Dutcher, Newton 117

Earl, Aaron 96
Eason, Alexander **63**, 74
East Point, Georgia 141–42, 156
East Tennessee & Georgia Railroad 49
Eaton, Thomas 134–35, 221
Eatonton, Georgia 164
Eaves, Thomas 116
Ebenezer Creek, Georgia 190
Edisto River, South Carolina 188, 195
Ehrnest, Frederick 131
Eleventh Corps 24, 26, 33, 39–40, 42, 49–51, 74, 78
Emancipation Proclamation 165
Ernst, Jacob 155
Etowah River, Georgia 99–102, 113
Everly, John 16
Ewing, Hugh 45
Ezra Church, Battle of 141

Fairfax, Virginia 22
Fairmount Cemetery, Newark 61, 63
Falling Creek, North Carolina 211–12
Farrell, Thomas 117
Faull, John 9, 53, **62**, 67, 89, 116, 120, 122–23, 144, 183, 191, 220, 225, 230
Fayetteville, North Carolina 205, 207–9
Felty, Joseph 110
Fenner, John 30, 57–58, 69–70, 89
Field, Charles 30, 42, **106**, 110–11, 113
Fifteenth Corps 110, 159, 196–97, 199, 211
Fite's Ferry, Georgia 99

Five Mile Post, Georgia 175
Folt, Andrew 66
Foraging 102, 162, 167, 176–78, 187
Ford, Henry 21
Ford, John 66
Ford's Theater 218
Forrest, Nathan 178
Fort Albany, Virginia 22
Fort McAllister, Georgia 180
Fort Rosecrans, Tennessee 178
Fort Wood, Tennessee 40–41
Fortune, James 131
Fouratt, Enos *14*, 15, 27, 69, 90–91, 93, 96, 107, 115, 127, 129–31, 140, 143, 188, 201, 206, 216–17, 220, 225, 227
Fourteenth Corps 122, 126, 159, 188, 198, 201, 203, 210
Fourth Corps 93, 108, 146
Franklin, Battle of 178
Frazer, Barent *64*, 72, 121, 145–46, 185, 219
Frazier's Run, Virginia 22
Freshly's Mill, South Carolina 198

Garrett Mountain, Paterson 29, 37
Gastlin, John 116
Gaylesville, Alabama 154
Geary, John 46, 74, 82–83, 86, 93, 97–98, 103, 105, 108, 114–15, 117–18, 120, 126–27, 131, 142–43, 146, 148, 156, 159, 161, 163–64, 172–74, 176, 180–81, 184, 191–95, 198–201, 205–7, 209–12, 214, 218–20
Georgia 155, 159–60, 166, 182
Georgia Central Railroad 170
Gettysburg, Battle of 7, 111, 178
Gibson, James *119*
Gilgal Church, Georgia 113
Glade's Crossroads, Georgia 164
Glass Farm, Tennessee 46
Goldsboro, North Carolina 187, 203, 211, 214, 216
Gott, John 19
Grand Review of the Western Armies 222–23
Granger, Gordon 49–50
Grant, U.S. 27, 33, 39, 45, 48–50, 53, 76, 78, 121, 155, 158, 186, 214–16, 218, 220
Grantham's Store, North Carolina 212
Graysville, Tennessee 49
Great Black Swamp, South Carolina 191
Great Pedee River, North Carolina 204
Gregson's Farm, Virginia 221
Green, William 131
Greensboro & Columbia Railroad 199

Greiner, Charles 66
Griswoldville, Battle of 166
Guerin, Orlando *129*
Gum Creek, Georgia 169
Gutherie, John 117

Halleck, Henry 20, 121, 143, 186
Hampton, Wade 199, 231
Hampton Township, New Jersey 215
Hand, James 191
Hanging Rock, North Carolina *202*
Hanging Rock Creek, North Carolina 203
Hanging Rock Post Office, North Carolina 201
Hardee, William 102, 120, 127, 139, 180, 209
Hardtack 101
Harker, William 116
Harpers Ferry 208
Harriot, Robert (Mickey Free) 12, 68, 197, 208
Harris, George *128*, 129–30, 134, 155
Harrison, Robert 131, 134
Harrison, William 31, *65*, 74
Harrison's Farm, Georgia 80
Hebron, Georgia 170
Heckinger, August 227
Heiss, Abraham 89
Hell Hole (New Hope Church) *105*, 111
Hemlee, Charles 74
Henderson, Thomas 66
Hennessy, Joseph 116
Herbert, William 12
Herman, John 144
Hessdorfer, Andrew 144
Hetherton, George 96
Hickerson, Tallmand 117
Higgins, John 134
Hildebrand, Andrew 57
Hilton Head, South Carolina 186, 221
Hitchcock, Henry 219–20, 231
Hiwassee River, Tennessee 50
Hoboken, NJ 11–12
Hoffat, Louis 225
Hood, John Bell 92, 98, 103, 105, 120, 124–26, 130, 137, 139, 141–43 , 146, 148, 153–57, 178
Hooker, Joseph 26, 33, 35, 37, 39, 49–50, 63, 74, 78, 93, 95, 99, 103, 107, 115, 118, 120, 126, 130–31, 141
Horton, Everett 117
Howard, Oliver 24, 39, 42–43, 45, 49–50, 53–54, 57, 63, 67, 93, 108, 141, 147, 159
Howell's Mill, Georgia 126, 139, 148
Hudson County *Democrat* 16, 227
Hughes, Joseph 110

Hull, Lucius 190
Hutchison's Island 176, 180, 186

Illinois Regiments 34th 31
Indianapolis 27
Iowa Regiments, 5th 40
Ireland, David 126

Jack's Creek, Georgia 189
Jackson, Allan 127, 129
Jackson, John W. 68–69, *71*
Jackson, William 191
Jasper, Tennessee 31, 34
Jeffcoat Bridge, South Carolina 194
Jefferson General Hospital 136
Jeffersonville, Indiana 27
Jersey City 11–12, 15, 151
Jersey City *American Standard* 136
Johns, Charles 12
Johnson, Theodore *135*
Johnston, Joseph 78, 81, 88, 92, 94, 98–102, 105, 112, 114, 117, 121–22, 124, 203, 210–11, 216–20
Jones, James 40
Jones, Joel 40
Jones, Patrick 116, 126–27, 130, 155, 159, 164
Jones Crossroads, North Carolina 220
Jonesboro, Battle of 146–48
Jonesboro, Georgia 161
Jordan, Lee 164

Kearny, Phillip 9, 13
Kelley's Ferry, Tennessee 35
Kelley's Ford, Tennessee 34–35
Kelly, Joseph 110
Kennesaw Mountain, Battle of 117–18, 120
Kiefer, Michael 144
Kilpatrick, Robert 98
Kingston, Georgia 99–100
Kingston, North Carolina 212
Kishpaugh, William 225
Kitchell, J. William *138*
Knight, Isaac 131
Knoxville Campaign 49–50, 53
Kolb's Farm, Battle of 118, 120
Krom, Martin 66

LaFayette, Georgia 154
Lambert, William 9, 13, 15, 20–23, 27, 29, 31–*32*, 36, 39–40, 42, 51, 53, 57, 61, 67–69, 72, 74, 85, 97–98, 107–11, 116–17, 131, 140, 148–49, 219, 227
Lathrop, James 131, 134
Lathrop, Oscar 36
Lawtonville, South Carolina 192
Lay's Ferry, Georgia 92, 98
Leaphardt's Mill, South Carolina 198

Leaver, Edmund 66
Lee, John 191
Lee, Robert E. 78, 121, 216
Lee, Steven 141
Lee, Thomas *140*, 189
Letts, Lemuel 116
Lexington, South Carolina 196
Lincoln, Abraham 12–13, 26, 53, 63, 76, 141, 148, 154, 158, 165, 182–83, 186, 215, 218, 226, 231
Lincoln Army Hospital 65
Linderman, Gerald 176
Little Horse Creek, Georgia 173
Little Lynch's Creek, North Carolina 203
Little Ogeechee Creek, Georgia 173
Little River, South Carolina 165, 199
Lloyd, William 12, 20, 22, 24, 29–31, 33, 35, 64, 68, 70, 72, 74, 96, 98–101, 110, 118, 121–23, 140, 144–46, 156–58, 166, 177, 183–86, 208, 219–20, 223, 225, 230
Locke, Charles 116
Lockman, John 116
Lockwood's Hotel, Newark 227
Logan, Joshua 110, 141
Long, John 131
Longstreet, James 39, 41, 49, 51, 53
Lookout Mountain, Tennessee 37, 39, 41, 45–46, 49, 74, 79
Lookout Valley, Tennessee 20, 33, 35–37, 39–40, 45, 54, 57, 63, 67–69, 79, 110
Loomis, John 46
Losey, James 131
Lost Mountain, Georgia 110
Loudon, Tennessee 51
Louisville, Georgia 171
Louisville, Kentucky 27, 135–36
Louisville, Tennessee 53
Lovejoy's Station, Georgia 148, 154
Lumber River, North Carolina 206
Lynch's Creek, North Carolina 204
Lyons, Cornelius 144

Macon, Georgia 137, 141, 143, 146–47, 157, 160–61
Macon & Savannah Railroad 171
Madden, Samuel 203
Madison, Georgia 161–63
Magee, William 178
Mailey, John 134
Manassas, First Battle 13, 15
Manassas, Second Battle 13, 131
Manassas Junction, Virginia 26
Mangold, Lewis 48, 58
Margeson, William 225
Market Street Depot, Newark 226

Mark's Creek, North Carolina 206
Marrietta, Georgia 43, 101–2, 108, 113, 118, 121–23
Marsh, Thomas 43
Martinsburg, Virginia 26
Massachussets Regiments: 33rd 156
Matonia, Charles 40
McArdle, John 116
McCallum, David 67
McClean, Patrick 223
McClellan, George 147, 154, 158
McClure's Ferry, Georgia 99
McCombs, James 131
McCormick, James 223
McCoy, William *145*, 219
McDonald's Gap, Tennessee 55, 57
McFarland's Bridge, North Carolina 206
McGill, Alexander 131
McGlynchy, Andrew 97
McPartland, Francis 89
McPherson, James 78, 86, 88, 90, 110, 120–21, 124, 126, 130, 139, 141, 176, 229–30
McSorley, James 97
Meade, George 24
Medal of Honor 13, 42, 178
Medical Care 48, 88–89, 135–37
Metcalf, George 43
Methodist Episcopal Church, Newark 61
Milam's Bridge, Georgia 102
Military Park, Newark 61, 226
Mill Creek, Georgia 82
Mill Creek Gap, Georgia 79, 81, 91
Mill Creek Valley, Georgia 82
Milledgeville, Georgia 161, 165–67
Millen, Georgia 144, 160, 167, 172–73
Miller, Elias 9
Miller, John *70*, 74
Miller, Joseph 30, 72, 84, 88
Miller, Louis 72
Miller, William 74
Milroy, Robert 178
Mindil, George Washington 5, *8*, 9, *10*, 11–13, 15, 22–27, 30–31, 36, 42, 49, 53, 63–64, 67–68, 74, 79–80, 84, 90, 143, 153, 155, 161, 164, 177, 188, 191, 211, 214, 215–16, 219–20, 222–23, 226–27
Missionary Ridge, Tennessee 37, 39, 41, 43, 45, 48–49, 57
Mitchell, Reid 231
Moakler, Francis 191
Mobile, Alabama 157
Moccasin Creek, North Carolina 216
Monteith, Georgia 174

Monteith Station, Georgia 174
Monteith Swamp, Georgia 174
Montgomery, Alabama 123
Moran, Patrick 215
Morris, David 225
Morris & Essex Railroad 216
Morristown, NJ 107, 123
Morton, Thomas *147*
Mower, Joseph 215
Mud Creek, Georgia 117
Mullen, John 89
Muller, Georg 29, 33–3*4*, 40, 68–69, 72, 74, 131, 140, 142, 145, 152, 155, 158, 185, 188, 211–13, 215–17, 220, 223, 225, 230
Mulvey, Francis 57
Murfreesboro, Tennessee 68, 155, 178
Murphy, James 134
Murray, Peter 116

Nancy's Creek, Georgia 124–25, 148
Nashville, Tennessee 26, 67, 70, 136–37, 143, 153, 178
Nelson, Thomas 16, 215
"Nemo" 68
Neuse River, North Carolina 205, 212, 216, 218
New Baltimore, Virginia 23
New Bern, North Carolina 187, 203, 214
New Brunswick, New Jersey 15
New Hope Church, Battle of 101–3, *104*–5, 105, 107–8, 110
Newark, New Jersey 5–6, 11–12, 16, 29, 137, 147–48, 151, 216, 226–27
Newark *Daily Advertiser* 11–12, 19, 21, 51, 61, 67–68, 91, 131, 135–36, 148, 197, 208, 216, 221–23
Newark *Daily Journal* 7, 9, 12, 15, 35–36, 43, 59, 147–48, 226–27
Newark *Daily Mercury* 7, 9, 11, 15, 25, 31
Newton, New Jersey 217, 225
Newton's Ferry, Georgia 99
New Jersey Regiments: 1st 15; 4th 15; 5th 12; 9th 225; 13th 16, 91, 191, 228; 26th 16; 27th 5, 9, 13, 59; 33rd New Jersey Formation of Regiment 5, 7, 9, 11–13; Battle Creek, Tennessee 30–33; Battle of Chattanooga 40–43, 45–46, 48–50; Battle of Dug Gap 82–86, 88–89; Battle of New Hope Church *104*, 105, 107–10; Battle of Peachtree Creek 126–27, 129–31; Battle of Pine Knob 115–17; Battle of Resaca 91–93, 95–98; Bladens-

burg Camp 223, 225; Bridgeport, Alabama 29–30; Carolina Campaign, Columbia to Fayetteville 198–208; Carolina Campaign, Fayetteville to Goldsboro 209–13; Carolina Campaign, Savannah to Columbia 186, 188–97; departure from Newark 16, 18–19; desertions 15–16; evaluation of Regiment's Service 91, 227–30; final phase of Atlanta Campaign 139–40, 143–44, 146, 148–50; final pursuit of Confederate Army 216–18, 220; Grand Review 222; Knoxville Campaign 50–51, 53–55, 57–58; life in Atlanta 155–58; life in Savannah 183–85; Lookout Valley 39–40; losses in Atlanta Campaign through New Hope Church 112; march from Acworth to Pine Knob 113–14; march to Lookout Valley 34–35; march to New Hope Church 99–100, 102–4; march to Rocky Face Ridge 79–81; march to Washington, D.C. 220–21; movement towards Peachtree Creek 122, 124–25; prisoners at Andersonville 134–35; return to Newark and discharge 226–27; river accident 35–36; Savannah campaign 161–65, 169–76, 180–81; travel to Virginia 20–24; trip West 26–27; Western hospitals 135–37; winter quarters 1863–64 63, 65–70, 72

New York Regiments: 60th 148; 119th 83, 95, 105, 116, 159, 189; 123rd 107; 134th 42, 82–84, 95, 105, 127, 130, 157, 159, 189; 136th 43, 67; 154th 82, 105, 130, 159, 189

Nicholson's Creek, North Carolina 207
Nix, John 89
Nolan, Charles 113, 134
North Carolina 203–5
North Edisto River, South Carolina 194–95
Nose Creek, Georgia 118

Oconee River, Georgia 164–66
O'Connor, Michael 191
O'Connor, Thomas 19, 23, 42, 93, 116, 124–25, 137, 140, 143, 150, 209
Ogeechee River, Georgia 167, 171–72, 180
Ohio Regiments: 5th 98
Ohio River 26–27
Oliver, William 215
Onderdonk, Leonard 110

Oostanaula River, Georgia 92, 98–99
Orange, New Jersey 155
Orchard Knob 41, 43
Orethle Charles 225
Ossabaw Sound, Georgia 180
Owen's Mill, Georgia 103

Pace's Ferry, Georgia 124, 146, 148
Palmetto Station, Georgia 154
Pardee, Ario 176, 199
Parker, Cortland 9
Parker, Joel 9, 63, 226
Park's Mill, Georgia 164
Paterson, NJ 11, 15, 29, 116, 131, 216–17
Paterson *Daily Guardian* 227
Paterson *Daily Press* 59, 155, 227
Paterson *Daily Register* 30, 161
Pea Vine Church, Georgia 81
Peachtree Creek, Battle of **124**, 126–27, 130
Peay's Ferry, South Carolina 200, 203
Peck, John 19
Pedee River, North Carolina 205
Pegue's Ferry 204
Pelobuet, David **8**, 15, 23, 25, 30, 41–42, 45, **47**, 49, 51, 53–54, 57, 59, 61, 67, 69, 229
Peninsula Campaign 13
Pennsylvania Troops: 23rd 13; 27th 25, 42, 45–46, 82; 73rd 40, 45–46, 82, 105, 159, 189; 109th 95, 97, 105, 159, 189; 111th 95, 148
Personett, John 117
Petersburg, Virginia 121, 216
Phalon, Michael 113
Philadelphia, Tennessee 51, 54
Philadelphia Church, Georgia 165
Pickett's Mill, Battle of 108, 110
Pierson, Stephen 9, 30, 67, 79, 84–85, **86**, 89, 93, 95, 104, 107, 109–10, 115–16, 120, 122, 127, 129–31, 143, 150
Pine Knob, Battle of 115–18, 150
Pine Mountain 113–14
Polk, Leonidas 100, 102, 114
Post, William 43, 58
Pumpkin Vine Creek, Georgia 103, 105
Puppy Creek, North Carolina 207

Raccoon Creek, Georgia 102
Raccoon Creek, North Carolina 216
Raccoon Mountain, Tennessee 33
Railroad Destruction 162, 167
Raleigh, North Carolina 216–20
Rations 101–2

Ravencroft's Mill, South Carolina 198
Ray, Peter 134–35, 221
Red Clay, Tennessee 49
Reiley, James 116, **207**
Resaca, Battle of 92–95, **94–96**, 98–99
Rheinheimer, Nicholas 66
Ribble, Joseph 29
Riceville, Tennessee 51
Richmond, Virginia 121, 216
Riker, Charles 191
Riley, John 12
Ringold, Georgia 49–50, 80–81
Ringold Gap, Georgia 50
Roain, William 40
Robertsville, South Carolina 188, 191
Rock Ridge, Georgia 162
Rockfish Creek, North Carolina 207
Rockingham, North Carolina 205
Rocky Face Ridge, Georgia 78–79, 81–82, 90–91
Rocky Mount, South Carolina 200
Rogers, Andrew 15
Rooly Creek, Georgia 165
Rosecrans, William 26, 33, 37
Roseland, New Jersey 88
Rossville, Georgia 80
Rossville Gap, Georgia 80
Rough & Ready, Georgia 147, 153
Rousseau, Lovell 178
Rubsam's Brass Band 61, 226
Runyon, M.C. 225
Runyon, Theodore 9, 216, 226
Russell, David 185
Rutledge's Station, Georgia 162
Ryan, Edwin 117

Salt Horse 101
Salt Port 101–2
Saluda River, South Carolina 196, 198
Sandersonville, Georgia 167, 170
Sandford, James **8**, 84, **87**–88, 89
Sandford, John 25, 30, 223
Sands, Thomas 117
Saunder's Plantation, North Carolina 218
Savannah, Georgia 155, 158, 160, 172, 175–76, 184–86, 188–89
Savannah Campaign 153–55, 158–60, 162, 166, 167–69, 178–82
Savannah River 172, 176, 186, 188–90
Schafer, Casper 88
Schawager, Oscar 16
Schnarr, Lorenzo 88
Schofield, John 78, 120, 124, 147, 178, 211–12, 215
Seering, Samuel 48, 58

Sequatchie River, Tennessee 31, 34
Seven Mile Creek, North Carolina 210
Seventeenth Corps 113, 159, 201, 211
"SH" 68, 72, 117, 161, 163, 174, 178, 189, 229
Shaw, William *73*
Shay, John 19
Sheffield, Georgia 162
Sherman, William Tecumsch 39–40, 45–46, 49–50, 53, 76, 78–79, 81, 86, 90–91, 93, 99, 101–2, 107–8, 110, 112–14, 117–18, 120–21, 123, 125, 139–43, 145, 147–48, 154–55, 158–59, 161, 165, 167–68, 172, 176–77, 180–83, 186–88, 196–97, 201, 205, 208–12, 214–20
Sherwood, Henry 19, *179*
Shields, Hugh 131
Sister's Ferry 188–91, *190*
Slattery, Patrick 68–69
Slavery 123, 165, 231
Slocum, Henry 141, 148, 159, 181, 193, 210–11, 215
Smith, John *156*
Smith, Sidney 84, 88–89
Smith, William 33, 39
Smithfield, North Carolina 209, 216–18
Snake Creek Gap 79, 81–82, 86–88, 90–91, 154
Sneedsborough, South Carolina 204
Snyder, Charles *157*
Social Circle, Georgia 162
Somerville, James 19, 35
Sortsman, John 66
South Carolina 170, 186–88
South River, North Carolina 210
Spotsylvania Courthouse, Battle of 221
Spring Creek, Georgia 172
Springfield, Georgia 174, 189–90
Stanley, Charles 137
Stanton, Edwin 26, 76, 214
Station 10½ 171
Station 11 170
Station 13 170
Steer, Henry 40
Stewart, Alexander 127
Stickney, Charles *169*
Stiger, J. Henry 9, *17*
Stockton, Richard 11, 63
Stoll, George 117
Stoll, James 57
Stone Mountain, Georgia 161–62
Struble, James 153–54, 158
Struble, John 185
Substitutes 7, 152–3
Sugar Creek, Georgia 164
Sugar Valley, Georgia 91
Sussex *Register* 191, 215, 220

Sutton, Charles *160*, 164
Sweeney, Terrence 180
Sweetwater, Tennessee 51, 54
Swift's Creek, North Carolina 218

Taylor, Franklin *171*
Taylor, John *175*
Taylor's Ridge, Georgia 81
Tennessee Campaign of 1864 178
Tennessee Regiments: 10th Rebel Infantry 134
Tennessee River, Tennessee 30, 31, 33, 39–41, 43, 45, 51, 178
Tennille, Georgia 170
Terry, Alfred 208, 212
Thomas, George 39, 41, 45, 49, 78–79, 81, 113–14, 117, 124–25, 139, 155, 178
Thompson, William 131
Titman, James 9, 35–36, *56*, 74
Toffey, John 27, 31, 39–43, *52*, 59, 64–65, 218, 226, 229
Totten General Hospital 135–36
Townley, William 66
Travers, Patrick 131
Trenton, New Jersey 226
Trinity Church, Newark 61
Troutvetter, Emile 225
Trowell's Farm, South Carolina 192
Tully, Francis 221
Tunnel Hill, Georgia 190
Tunnel Hill, Tennessee 45–46, 49, 57, 79
Turkey Creek, Georgia 174
Twelfth Corps 26, 33, 39, 74, 78
Twelve-Mile Creek, South Carolina 198
Twentieth Corps 74, 78, 80–81, 86, 91–93, 99–100, 102–3, 110, 118, 126–27, 137, 141, 146, 150, 154, 156, 158–59, 162, 165, 168, 170, 172, 174, 180, 187–88, 193, 195–96, 199, 201, 209–12, 215, 217, 222
Twenty-third Corps 103, 108

Ulcofauhachee River, Georgia 162
United States Infantry: 5th Regiment 134; 14th Regiment 15
Upton, Philip 145, 158
Utoy Creek, Georgia 142

Van Buren, Martin 185
Vanderhoff, Abraham 116
Van Nostrand, Lawrence 40
Vermont Regiments: 3rd 15–16, 18–19
Verona, NJ 144
Veteran Reserve Corps 19, 65, 226
Vining's Station, Georgia 122

Virginia 159, 187, 215
Volunteer Refreshment Saloon, Philadelphia 226
von Steinwehr, Adolph 25
Vorhees, John 131

Walden's Ridge, Tennessee 33
Waldron, Samuel (Miles Alienus) 25, 35–37, 42–43, *56*, 57–59, 61, 63
Walker, Thomas 148
Walker's Ferry, Georgia 165
Walsh, Livsey 116
Ward, Marcus 183, 222–23, 226–27
Ward Army Hospital 208
Warrenton, Virginia 22–23, 25
Warrenton Junction, Virginia 23
Wateree Church, South Carolina 200
Wateree Creek, South Carolina 198
Waters, Geroge 57
Watkin's Bridge, Georgia 171
Weigamonn, Frederick 116
Wenckler, Peter 131, 185
Western & Atlantic Railroad 37, 154
Wheeler, William 110
White, Sgt. 19
White Star Division 74
Widow Bird's Plantation, Georgia 189
Widow Hull's Plantation, Georgia 113
Williams, Alpheus 92–93, 120, 130, 141, 159, 215
Williams, Thomas 131
Williamsburg, Virginia 12–13
Williamson, Charles 134, 155
Williamson's Creek, Georgia 171
Willis, Amzi 134
Wilmington, North Carolina 18
Wilmington, Charlotte & Rutherford Railroad 205
Wilmington Railroad 212
Wilson, Benjamin 131
Wilson, William *205*
Winnsborough, South Carolina 196, 198–200
Wirz, Henry 133, 135
Witt, Frederick 88
Witte, Louis 36
Wolf, David 134
Wolf, William 225
Wood, Thomas 41
Wounds 86, 88–89

Yellow River, Georgia 162

Zion Church, Georgia 174
Zion Church, South Carolina 196
Zouave units 13, 30, 36, 64, 80

www.ingramcontent.com/pod-product-compliance
Lightning Source LLC
Chambersburg PA
CBHW081544300426
44116CB00015B/2752